THE FIRST THREE YEARS OF LIFE

THE FIRST THREE YEARS OF LIFE

New and Revised

Burton L. White

PRENTICE
HALL
PRESS

New York   London   Toronto   Sydney   Tokyo   Singapore

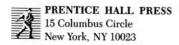 **PRENTICE HALL PRESS**
15 Columbus Circle
New York, NY 10023

Copyright © 1985, 1990 by Burton L. White Associates, Inc.

PRENTICE HALL PRESS and colophons are registered trademarks
of Simon & Schuster, Inc.

Library of Congress Cataloging-in-Publication Data

White, Burton L., 1929–
    The first three years of life / Burton L. White. — New and rev. ed.
        p.   cm.
    Includes bibliographical references.
    ISBN 0-13-317678-9
    1. Infant psychology.   I. Title.
  BF719.5.W45   1991
  649'.122—dc20   89-23107
                                CIP

Manufactured in the United States of America

10 9 8 7 6 5 4 3

Acknowledgments

Since this book covers virtually my entire career as a child development researcher, the number of people who have contributed to this work is very great. Perhaps a chronological organization is the only way to cope with the task.

The initial inspiration came from my father more than anyone else. Academically, Abraham Maslow's studies of "self-actualized" people, Lois Murphy's studies of healthy children, Piaget's work on the growth of the mind, and J. McVicker Hunt's analyses of the effects of experience on development were probably the most influential on my thinking.

Over the years, funding agencies and particular officials were of vital assistance. The list of agencies is long: The Foundations' Fund for Research in Psychiatry, the National Institute of Mental Health, the Federal Office of Education, the Carnegie Corporation of New York, the Federal Office of Economic Opportunity, the Federal Office of Child Development, and the Robert Wood Johnson Foundation. Dean Theodore Sizer and my close colleague Gerald Lesser provided administrative support at Harvard University, along with John Herzog. Edith Grotberg, then at OEO, has been a strong supporter of the research.

My greatest debt in the area of research support, and much more, is to Barbara Finberg of the Carnegie Corporation.

In the early years of my research, Peter Wolff provided valuable guidance and arranged for me to work at several hospitals including the State Hospital at Tewksbury, Massachusetts. There, among many personnel who were helpful, Helen Efstathiou and Frances Craig were unfailingly kind and cooperative.

In those early days, faithful and highly competent research assistance came from Peter Castle, Kitty Clark, Melvin Zolot, and Harold Haynes.

From 1965 on, at least thirty people worked with me at Harvard on the Preschool Project and another fifty in the early stages of the

Brookline Early Education Project. Of the former, I must single out Barbara Kaban, Mary Comita, and Bernice Shapiro, who have worked closely with me for many years.

The Preschool Project research is the major source of ideas for this book. That project was made possible not only by research personnel, the University, and the granting agencies, but also by the cooperation of many public and private schools and especially by several hundred families.

In 1981, working with Mrs. Mildred Winter and Commissioner Arthur Mallory, and Assistant Commissioner P. J. Newell of the Missouri State Department of Education, and with Mrs. Jane Paine of the Danforth Foundation, I have been very much involved in the creation and operations of the Missouri New Parents as Teachers project. Some of the findings of that exciting new program have contributed substantially to this revised edition.

It should by now be abundantly clear that anything of value in this book rests upon the efforts of a large number of people.

Finally, I am proud to thank my four children and loving wife for making my life so rich.

Contents

Preface to the New and Revised Edition

The mid-1960s saw the beginning of the Head Start Program and the initiation of the "Sesame Street" television series. These major events, along with an enormous amount of publicity and numerous related activities, resulted in a dramatic increase in awareness on the part of the American public of the importance of learning during the first years of life. By 1978 it was reported that on the average there had been some thirty new books on child rearing published each year between 1970 and 1976. Since 1976 many more books on child rearing have been published, although it appears to me that lately the rate of new publications has been declining. Interestingly, of the more than five hundred books on the subject published in this country during the last twenty-five years, fewer than fifteen of them (excluding medically oriented texts) have survived longer than a year. This is the third edition of this book. The first was published in 1975, the second in 1985. This book, fortunately, has survived the rigors of the marketplace.

It has now been some thirty years since I first began to study babies, and some of my earliest subjects are now well into their thirties. My professional focus remains today what it has been since the beginning: "How can you help any child become the best possible six-year-old she can be by providing the most beneficial learning opportunities from birth on?" For years I have bemoaned the failure of the government to attend to this very important subject. There was a brief period between 1965 and the early 1970s when the federal government, under pressure from civil rights groups, did indeed pay some attention to this issue, at least for children from poor families. These efforts, in the form of experimental educational programs like Head Start, Follow Through, Home Start, and Parent-Child Centers, were both extraordinary and valuable. Unfortunately, they have not led to high-quality early-education programs for all children. To some extent they have been taken over by state governments. I have written extensively on a remarkable experimental program I helped initiate in Missouri between 1981 and 1985 called New Parents as Teachers.[1] That program, performed with more than three hundred Missouri families *of all kinds*, was an attempt to apply the ideas presented in this book through the public education system. Its subsequent success (see pages 348–351 for details) has been followed by a dramatic expansion of such services across all 543 school districts in Missouri and to more than twenty-five other states. Yet these events have left a bittersweet taste in my mouth. On the one hand, to have a confirmation of the power of these ideas within a public education setting is enormously exciting. On the other hand, after the completion of the successful pilot program, Missouri, and other states, has been operating the newer version of the New Parents as Teachers Program with a much lower budget, with far less staff training, and, in general, at a substantially poorer level of quality. We seem to have reached the point where state governments, while aware of the desirability of helping *all* new parents, are not addressing the serious problem of quality control.

In 1975, and again in 1985, I cautioned readers about the incomplete nature of our knowledge about how to help a child develop well. That caution remains true today. We are far more knowledgeable about the subject than we were thirty or forty years ago, but much more work remains to be done before it can be said that we have a true science of early human development. Having said that, let me point out my solid conviction that the information you'll find in this book, while necessarily incomplete and certainly not 100 percent correct, is the best you'll find anywhere. *No other collection of ideas about how to raise babies has ever been tried out successfully with hundreds of ordinary families in ordinary public school systems.* Although this does not make it a guarantee that these ideas are all wonderful, I am certain it will give the reader confidence in their value.

This edition aims to bridge the period from 1984 (when the second edition was written) to 1990. In it you will find coverage of several new and important insights into the details of early development. You will also find discussions of new and ongoing trends that concern parents of babies, for example, the "superbaby" phenomenon and the child-care controversy. Evaluations of important new research, books and other writings, and toys are also provided.

[1] White, B. L. *Educating the Infant and Toddler*. Lexington, Mass.: D.C. Heath & Co., 1987.

Preface to
the Revised Edition

It has been approximately ten years since the writing of the original edition of *The First Three Years of Life*. Since that time I have remained professionally involved exclusively with the same subject: How to help each child get the best possible start in life during the first three years. My conviction that those first years are far more important than previously thought remains unshaken. Unfortunately, the fact that very few children get the best possible start in life also remains true. That is not to say that we haven't made progress. We estimate that some 10,000 programs in North America alone (established mostly during the last decade) now focus on learning in the first years of life. These programs, however, are generally modest in size and scope, and, as a result, it is still a rare young family that has the kind of comprehensive preparation and support for the parenting function that I believe are needed. A comparatively rare example of a full-fledged service of that sort is the Missouri New Parents as Teachers Program. The problem is that though there is a well-entrenched awareness in the minds of a large number of people (mostly middle-class parents and early childhood professionals) about the importance of learning in the first years, the federal government has turned away from support for such programs since the middle 1970s. It is not totally clear why, but it would appear that the poor economic circumstances in the United States during the 1970s, combined with a lack of interest on the part of government agencies, are the principle reasons.

In the first edition of *The First Three Years of Life*, I tried to present the best possible information then available on what parents could do to help their children to the best possible start in life. The central purpose of this new edition is the same. Because research in early human development has continued to move forward at a more rapid pace than was the case until the mid-1960s, and because of my own continued involvement, especially with the Missouri project, it is now possible, and in fact necessary, to produce a new, more extended and refined picture of early learning.

In the preface to the first edition I recommended several books on parenting to be purchased by new parents. I still feel comfortable recommending Dr. Spock's book on babies' physical well-being, as it has, in recent years, been revised and updated. You could also choose the excellent volume from the Children's Hospital, *The Encyclopedia of Modern Health Care.* In addition, there are several first-rate books on the emotional circumstances surrounding parenthood, featuring outstanding writings from parents in a variety of circumstances; there are also recent valuable works on the role of the father. Such books will be discussed in the recommended-reading section.

Earlier, I bemoaned the lack of easy access to authentic and useful information on the parenting role. Unfortunately, that condition still exists. Publishing on this topic is still largely a matter of private enterprise. One result of that situation is continued confusion as to which books make the most sense, especially when, as they often do, they conflict with each other.

As was the case ten years ago, I would like to remind the reader that we still have an incomplete science of early human development and, therefore, there are some questions for which even now, we don't have answers. Again, it is my claim that this book contains the most accurate information available on what babies are like as they change rapidly in their first years, and also on how to help them learn as well as possible.

To end this preface on an optimistic note, those of you who are embarking on the adventure of raising a child for the very first time are potentially far better off than earlier parents because of the advances in knowledge in the last twenty years. Interestingly, it was the onset of the civil rights movement in the late 1950s that led to the massive amounts of research and new services initiated in the mid-sixties to help young children. Whatever the causes of the activities since 1965 with the introduction of the Head Start Program, the end result is clear. We now really do have far more reliable and useful information than ever before. With a reasonable amount of luck, today's parents have a better chance of getting their children off to a fine start in life, maximizing pleasure and minimizing pain for both the child and themselves.

Preface to the First Edition

After seventeen years of research on how human beings acquire their abilities, I have become convinced that it is to the first three years of life that we should now turn most of our attention. My own studies, as well as the work of many others, have clearly indicated that the experiences of those first years are far more important than we had previously thought. In their simple everyday activities, infants and toddlers form the foundations of *all* later development.

I now believe that not more than one child in ten gets off to as good a start as he could. From close observations of children developing both well and poorly, I am convinced that most families, given a little help, are potentially capable of doing a good job of raising their children. Unfortunately, adequate preparation and assistance for parenthood are not currently available for most families. This book is intended to offer up-to-date information about how you can help your child to acquire a solid foundation for full development. I will try to explain what you can do during those very important first thirty-six months to ensure that your child will develop the full range of social and intellectual skills that now appear to be necessary for good subsequent development.

Although this book should prove useful to anyone responsible for the care of the very young child, it is meant primarily for parents. I am well aware that rearing children is far from being an easy task. Although it can be one of life's most exciting, pleasurable, and rewarding activities, for too many parents childrearing can also be accompanied by much stress and unhappiness. In most of the young families I have known, the very quality of everyday life seems to depend to a remarkable degree on how well the child-rearing process is proceeding. I am confident that if young couples were better informed about childrearing, they would find more pleasure in family life as a whole.

Thus I have several reasons for writing this book. In spite of the ready availability of such excellent books as Dr. Spock's *Baby and Child Care*, government publications such as *Infant Care*, and the literally hundreds of magazine articles and thousands of newspaper reports that appear each year, people seem to feel they do not have as much reliable and useful information as they would like about certain important aspects of child-rearing. I hope that my book may help to fill that information gap.

A note of caution. I believe the information in this book is the best currently available on how to educate a child during the first three years of life. On the other hand, it is surely neither perfectly accurate nor 100 percent complete. Sadly, detailed dependable knowledge about how to rear a young child is very difficult to acquire. Furthermore, for many reasons, far from enough has been acquired to date. I am confident that over the next several decades, that deficit will be substantially overcome. For now, this book contains my best judgments about the topic in the light of studies of child-rearing to date. With the information presented here, and a measure of good luck, I am confident that most families can do an excellent job of helping their new children make the most of their potential. I should like to think also that this book will not only help children to get a better start in life, but will help assure that childhood will be as rich and pleasurable an experience for both children and parents as it can and should be.

THE SPECIFIC ORIENTATION OF THIS BOOK

The First Three Years of Life, as the title implies, is restricted in focus. It will deal with the period from birth to three years of age. It will deal with the education of children during that time, and the educational goals dealt with are meant to be comprehensive. Although sensori-motor developments, such as eye-hand coordination and walking and climbing, will be discussed because they are prominent in every young child's behavior, they will not be treated as primary educational goals. Most children manage to achieve the sensorimotor abilities of the preschool years without difficulty. Such is not the case, for example, for several social skills.

This book will also concentrate on the normal, near normal, and well-developing child. It will have little to say about seriously handicapped or underdeveloped children.

When people look for advice on rearing young children, they are usually looking for either physical or mental health information, management assistance, or guidance in helping a child develop his abilities as fully as possible. For physical health issues, I recommend Dr. Spock and/or your family physician or pediatrician. For mental health issues, I cannot recommend anyone. As to the development of a baby's abilities, I honestly believe that anyone who wants to provide a good educational beginning for a baby during the first three years of life will find that topic well covered in this volume. And if this book provides any assistance to you in helping a child make the most of those formative years, I shall be delighted—and so, I hope, will you.

The Author

Since 1958, supported by several large private foundations and federal agencies, and assisted by several dozen talented people, I have studied the problem of how to educate babies. To my knowledge, no other individual researcher has studied the problem of influencing the development of abilities in the first three years of human life so extensively. That, in itself, is no guarantee that what I will tell you is either totally true or even more true than what you will read elsewhere. Only time will provide that answer. But what follows does come from a unique source: The most sustained (and expensive) scientific study of the role of experience in the development of human abilities in the first years of life conducted to date.

The research that has led to this book was carried out under the administration and with the support of Brandeis and Tufts Universities, the Massachusetts Institute of Technology, and Harvard University. It was also carried out at home. As my final credential, I am the father of four children, two boys and two girls, aged seven to thirteen years. I am happy to report that these children seem to be developing rather well. But I must also confess that when my wife and I were guiding them through their first years, we knew as little about the subject as most average parents.

Introduction

When I arrived at Brandeis University in 1958 as a graduate student in psychology, I was distressed to find that so little about human behavior was understood. There seemed to be very little agreement about how a healthy, vital person got to be that way; yet it was clear that to predict how a person would behave in a test situation, at leisure, or in a social situation, one invariably needed to know about that person's previous experiences. Although Freud's ideas were losing ground, most students in human behavior acknowledged in one way or another a basic shaping function in the experiences of the early years of life.

Some believed that a person was largely "born to be" what he or she would become, and that experience in general was of little importance. Others, while acknowledging limits determined by inheritance, believed that life's experiences were generally of prime importance. This latter group focused on the identification of types of important experience and on the times in life likely to be of particular significance in terms of overall development.

With the help of Peter Wolff, a research psychiatrist, I began to become acquainted with babies. With the help of another research psychologist, Richard Held, I became acquainted with issues in the development of eye-hand behavior (for example, reaching for seen objects). Guided by the writings of Piaget on the origins of intelligence, and Konrad Lorenz on ethology, I began to study the details of the day-to-day growth of abilities in babies.

In 1958 few psychologists were actively pursuing research with children less than three years of age. Nor was the public, although interested in a general way in infant care, generally aware of any special educational significance of the early years. It was not until the late 1960s that the idea that the first few years of life might have a special importance began really to take hold. Once it did, large grants of government and private money produced a great deal of interest in research on the first years. Unfortunately, early in the 1970s the country went into a period of economic decline. Money for research and innovative programs soon fell off markedly. From then on, government and foundation sponsorship of increased information and better practices declined in a corresponding manner. Interestingly, however, the private sector refused to lose interest in the idea that the first years of life were of lasting significance for the quality of human development. Year by year there has been a continued growth of privately sponsored educationally-focused programs to help parents of infants and toddlers. We estimate there are about 10,000 such programs in existence today. In addition to the sustained growth of interest on the part of informed lay people or parents and grandparents, there also has been a parallel growth in related activities in industry. There has been a veritable explosion of new products from the various toy companies. There has been a continued high rate of publication each year of how-to books on living with and raising the young child. While government and academic leadership has waned, clearly the notion that the experiences of the first years are important and that most parents would benefit from more reliable information and occasional professional assistance is today firmly established.

EXPERIENCE AND THE INFANT

From 1958 to 1965 I spent many hours watching infants in their cribs. I learned a good deal about what they could and could not do as they developed from near helplessness at birth to the comparatively rich talent of the average six month old. In a series of experiments I began to see how infants would respond with enthusiasm or, at times, annoyance to alterations in their ordinary routines and physical surroundings. Over a period of years my colleagues and I produced research that seemed to show that even during the first months of life babies responded with enthusiasm to circumstances that were specifically designed to meet their rapidly changing interests and abilities.[1] In addition, we found that how alert an infant was, how soon she began looking at her hands, and when she mastered the skill of reaching for objects were dependent in part on the design of her world.

I might have continued my work with very young infants indefinitely, but for the previously mentioned general surge of interest in early development in the 1960s, signaled by the creation of the Head Start Project in 1965. Under pressure from civil rights groups, and with support from new research findings, President Lyndon Johnson in

---

[1] My principal colleagues in this work were Kitty Riley Clark, Peter Castle, Harold Haynes, and Richard Held.

1965 announced that the federal government was going to do something about early educational failure. The purpose of Head Start was to see to it that no child entered the first grade seriously unprepared. Along with unprecedented expenditures of money and effort on preschoolers from low-income families, there came dramatically increased support for all manner of research and service programs for children less than six years of age. Educational research in particular began to flourish.

One of several new educational research programs was established at Harvard, which had promised to include the study of early educational development in the work of its new center. Since Harvard, like many graduate schools of education, had concentrated on studies of school-age children, it found itself without personnel for preschool studies. Research on compensatory education for three- and four-year-olds who were headed for educational difficulty was still favored by the majority. I did not take that direction for two reasons: first, I did not believe that we had enough basic knowledge about poorly developing preschool children to design programs well; and second, I believed that the more fundamental need was for research on how to help *every* child, not just the so-called disadvantaged child, get the most from early experiences. Harvard, with its power and rich resources, was one of a handful of institutions capable of acting on such a long-range outlook.

I was offered a chance to implement such a study. In September 1965 the Preschool Project was launched. I hired four young Ph.D.s and over a dozen research assistants, and we began to face the question of how to structure experiences during the first six years of life to help all children make the most of their potential. For the next thirteen years, averaging about ten people working under my supervision and with a typical budget of about $150,000 to $200,000 per year, we studied development during the first year of life. As our ideas evolved, so too was there a parallel evolution in thinking about early human development on the part of educational policy makers, federal research planners, and the public.

In 1965 the federal view of how to deal with educational underachievement focused on preventative programs for four-year-olds. A year or two later, preventative programs were extended down to three-year-olds and enriched programs were added as supplements to the elementary school experience. By then our research was teaching us that by the time a child reached three years of age, he had already undergone a great deal of "education." We had found that in any group of 20 or 30 three-year-olds, there was likely to be at least one remarkably able child. In their everyday behavior these children showed the same pattern of special abilities we found in outstanding six-year-olds. By 1968 we had become convinced that a long-term approach to understanding good development had to start with a focus on the first three years of life.

In our studies we were not only impressed by what some children could achieve in the first years, but also by the fact that a child's own family seemed so obviously central to the outcome. Indeed, we came to believe that the more informal education that families provide for their children "makes more of an impact on a child's total education than the formal educational system. If a family does its job well, the professional can then provide effective training."[2] If not, there may be little a professional can do to save a child from mediocrity. This grim assessment is the direct conclusion from the findings of thousands of programs for remedial education, such as the Head Start and Follow Through projects.

In 1970 Dr. Robert Sperber, Superintendent of Schools in Brookline, Massachusetts, and I began a project that we called the Brookline Early Education Project, or BEEP. Its purpose was to test the question whether the public educational system should provide professional guidance for the learning process from birth on, rather than from the conventional beginnings at kindergarten age. That project, which provided educational services to more than 300 families, was the first of two exciting field experiments I became involved with that, in my judgment, represent what will someday be a substantial revolution in public education. The second project, at this date in its third year of operation, is based in Missouri and is sponsored by the State Department of Education. It is called the New Parents as Teachers Program.

In 1978, having been for some twenty years continuously involved in research on how to help children get off to the best start, I decided that a considerable amount of valuable information was available but not being used broadly enough. I therefore left university life and established a nonprofit organization known as the Center for Parent Education. The Center has two purposes. First, to advocate better educational services for families starting to raise children; and second, to try to help professionals already doing that kind of work through special training programs and identification of the best new test procedures, program practices, toys, films, and so on. In 1981, with the help of the Danforth Foundation of St. Louis, Missouri, the Center entered into a venture with the State Department of Education

---

[2]As an aside I might comment that if a family provides a solid initial educational experience in the first year, the child will probably make the most out of any formal educational experience. In such cases a few years in a mediocre educational system will not seriously hinder the child.

in the State of Missouri to once again test the notion of whether public education should provide help to new parents.

Since I endorse the view of the family as the first and most fundamental educational delivery system, I must offer parents the following words of warning. From all that I have learned about the early education and development of young children, I have come to the conclusion that most American families get their children through the first six to eight months of life reasonably well in terms of education and development. Perhaps no more than 10 percent, however, manage to get their children through the ages of eight to thirty-five months as well educated and developed as they could and should be. Many studies indicate that the period that starts at eight months and ends at three years is of unique importance in the development of a human being. To begin to look at a child's educational development when he or she is two years of age is already much too late, particularly in the area of social skills and attitudes.

Given the importance of the parental role in early childhood development, it is ironic that so few parents are properly prepared for parenthood. Not only is there little information available, but, even if we did have sufficient research-based knowledge about effective child-rearing practices, it would not be routinely transmitted to parents. In spite of progress in the last twenty years, our society still does not educate its parents to assume the role of first teachers of their children.

I have tried over the years to accumulate dependable knowledge about what babies are like, what their interests are, and how to provide useful and beneficial experiences for them. In the course of my research, my strategy has been to single out—at all income levels—families that seem to be doing an outstanding job with their young children without the benefit of any special training. What I have learned from that and related research, as well as the extensive field studies that have followed, is the subject of this book.

The following phase-by-phase study of the child from birth to three years of age contains the distillation into practical terms of the findings of almost thirty years of research. I hope that it will provide for parents some of the guidance they need to help their children develop the full range of human abilities.

THE DETAILS OF DEVELOPMENT

CHAPTER ONE

Birth to Crawling: Guidelines for Phases I to IV

GENERAL REMARKS

The first eight months of a baby's life (what I shall later describe as Phases I to IV) have a special quality that sets them apart from all subsequent periods. During these early months a baby's general progress and development is largely assured by nature. If parents provide a baby with generous amounts of love, attention, and physical care, nature will pretty much take care of the learning process. I do not mean to imply that it is impossible to do a bad job of childrearing during this period; it is always possible, through stupidity or callousness, to do lasting harm to a child of any age, and especially during the first months of life. Nor do I mean to say that the "normal" pattern of development during the first eight months cannot be improved upon. But it appears that nature, almost as if it had anticipated the uncertainties that beset new parents, has done its best to make the first six to eight months as problem free as possible.

ESTABLISHING GOALS

No discussion of how to educate babies can make much sense unless one starts with the issue of goals. In a general sense, what most parents want out of the early years is a well-developed child, along with a good deal of simple pleasure for both the child and themselves. Also on every parent's mind is the avoidance of unhappiness, anxiety, and, of course, danger to the child. If infant education were incompatible with enjoyment, both parent's and baby's, it would be unfortunate. Happily, as far as I can tell, such is not the case. Every child-rearing activity I can recommend, especially in the first months of life, leads to both an involved and pleased baby and a generally contented parent. And when it comes to the later stages of infancy and toddlerhood, I have found that the well-developing baby is by far the most pleasant to live with.

General goals, however, are not enough. After you have decided you want a well-developed child, then what? How do you achieve that goal? Indeed, what does that goal mean? In thousands of situations around the world, rich or poor, most children do quite well education-ally during the first six to eight months of life. In our present society, neither the child who will achieve superbly nor the one who will be seriously behind by the first grade, seems to show any special qualities during the first year of life.[1] But in our studies we have concluded that rearing children well becomes much more difficult once they begin to crawl.

The goals we recommend parents work toward during the first eight months of life can be grouped under three headings:

1. Giving the infant a feeling of being loved and cared for.
2. Helping her to develop specific skills.
3. Encouraging her interest in the outside world.

As we follow the developing child from Phase I through Phase IV, we will refer repeatedly to these basic aims. Let us examine them more closely:

A FEELING OF BEING LOVED AND CARED FOR

During the first two years of life, all children appear to have a special need to establish a strong attachment to one or more older humans. In the process they begin to become sociable. By two years of age we have found that all children have acquired a first social style. By then a child can have become spoiled. Although the first signs of spoiling begin to surface in minor ways at about six months, when a child may begin to cry frequently for attention, the more serious problems of spoiling are far more common and well entrenched by two years of age.

As concerns the first seven to eight months of life, the story is

---

[1]There are exceptions to this statement. Somewhat under 15 percent of all children are either born with a significant handicap or acquire one during the first year of life. Such exceptional cases are beyond the scope of this book.

much simpler. Erik Erikson, the famous personality theorist, called the primary social goal of this period a sense of "trust." I believe this term is an appropriate one. The frequency and degree of discomfort a baby feels depends largely on the kind of treatment he receives. Some discomfort is inevitable. There is no way to prevent a fair amount of unhappiness from such factors as hunger, indigestion, teething, or a cold diaper. On the other hand, you can easily see how such unhappiness can be prolonged and allowed to escalate if the avoidable discomfort is not dealt with promptly.

Fortunately for most babies, especially those reared at home by their parents, loving care and attention are the rule. However, many people are confused about the issue of spoiling an infant. There are those who believe there is a benefit to be derived by letting a baby "cry it out." Although there will be occasions when nothing you can do seems to console an unhappy (but otherwise healthy) baby, it is clearly in the baby's best interest during the first several years of life to respond promptly and regularly to the baby's signs of discomfort. Recent research has demonstrated that babies whose crying is responded to in this manner during the first months of life are better off in the long run. Just about everyone who has studied the mental health of infants agrees on this topic.

There may be times when nothing you can do will comfort the baby. Such moments will be difficult to endure, but you must expect them from time to time. One of the best things you can do in such a situation is seek out the advice of an experienced and sensible mother. Age-old practices, such as holding and rocking an infant, work remarkably well regardless of the cause of the discomfort. Many parents, as a last resort, put an inconsolable infant into a car bed and take her for a long ride. The pacifier, a recent rediscovery, also seems to be a lifesaver. Although some infants have some difficulty mastering the art of holding it in the mouth, a pacifier works well for most; and dentists advise that there are no harmful later effects on the teeth. You should feel free to make use of the pacifier as soon as your baby will accept it.

On the subject of breastfeeding—if you can and want to breastfeed your child, I urge you to do so, both to give the child a sense of being cared for and because most mothers who breastfeed successfully find it a marvelous experience. Again, recent research underlines the desirability of breastfeeding, especially in the case of boys, since a clear link has been established between middle-ear infections and threats to good hearing and methods other than breastfeeding. The decision is a highly personal one, but breastfeeding is a fine way to promote closeness of mother and infant and, for the baby, it usually leads to a strong positive feeling of being cared for.

No requirement of good childrearing is more natural or more rewarding than the tending of your baby in a loving and attentive way. Although there is little reason to think that an infant of eight months has more than a simple awareness of his mother, most students of human development agree that the basic foundation of a child's personality is being formed in his earliest interchanges with nurturing adults.

HELPING THE INFANT DEVELOP SPECIFIC SKILLS

Few living creatures are as helpless as a newborn baby. At birth, an infant cannot think, use language, socialize with another human being, run, walk, or even deliberately move around. When on her back she cannot lift her head; on her stomach she can barely lift her nose off the surface she is lying on. The list of things she cannot do is almost as long as the complete list of adult human abilities. What *can* a newborn infant do?

A newborn infant has a small number of reflexlike sensorimotor abilities. When placed prone, he can usually lift his head high enough to avoid suffocation when left with his nose in the mattress. His hands and feet will grasp objects with some strength, but only, as a rule, if someone else elicits the behavior in the correct manner. If the target is large enough (more than a few inches), contrasts well with the background, is no closer than six to eight inches but no farther away than approximately twenty-four inches, and is moving through his line of sight at or near the speed of about one foot per second, he may glance at and follow it with his eyes for a few seconds. As soon as the target stops moving, he will lose interest in it. Moreover, he will perform such a visual act only when awake, alert, and inactive, a condition he is likely to be in for about two or three minutes an hour during the day. Otherwise, he is not yet much interested in looking at the world around him.

Newborns are also generally capable of finding a small object touching them near their mouth (rooting behavior) and of then sucking on the object. They cry when uncomfortable. They also possess a variety of simple motor reflexes, like blinking when an eyelid is touched or receives a puff of air, or the knee jerk (the patellar response) when a proper stimulus is applied. Of particular interest is the startle reflex, which can be a source of needless concern to parents. A newborn will often startle if he is lowered through space rapidly, hears a sharp noise nearby, or even if the light is turned on in a dim room. More unusual than this form of sensitivity to abrupt changes (which lasts for about two months) is the spontaneous startle. During deep sleep, particularly when movement has been infrequent, babies will startle in the absence of any external stimulations as frequently as every two minutes. During states when the infant is slightly more active, spontaneous startles occur, but less regularly and less frequently. In general, the more activity, the less frequent the startles. Spontaneous startles usually drop out of the child's behavior by the end of the third month of life.

From about six weeks of age, a baby begins to acquire increasing facility in dealing with the world. By the age of seven months, she has acquired a good deal of control over her body, can hold her head erect for lengthy periods, can turn over easily, can sit unaided, and may even be able to crawl a bit. She cannot, as yet, ordinarily pull herself to a standing posture, walk, or climb, but she is quite skillful at using her hands to reach for objects. Her sensory-motor abilities are extensive. She apparently sees as well as a young adult, (and better than her father if her father is over forty). She locates sounds with admirable accuracy. Socially, she recognizes her family, and may even begin to be choosy about who picks her up and holds her close. As for intelligence, while still some distance from abstract-thinking capacities, she begins to solve her first simple problems, which consist solely of pushing an object aside in order to reach another one.

This vigorous, semiskilled creature has, in other words, begun to accumulate a fair number of specific skills. *Good childrearing in the initial stages of a baby's life* includes knowing what the normal pattern of emerging skills is and facilitating their emergence. It should be pointed out, however, that most of these skills will evolve unaided under average circumstances. The more important reason for facilitating their development involves our third goal.

ENCOURAGING INTEREST IN THE OUTSIDE WORLD

Whether a child learns to reach for objects at three or four months rather than five or six is probably of no consequence. It has been my experience, however, that *the kinds of circumstances that facilitate the acquisition of the specific skills of the early months simultaneously seem to result in a more interested, cheerful, and alert child.* In other words, if a young infant's world meshes with his developing skills, he not only moves along a bit faster, but he seems to enjoy himself more and develop a fuller taste for exploration, learning, and enjoyment. *Good early childrearing includes seeing that your baby (especially after the first six to eight weeks) is regularly involved in activities that interest him.* After the first ten to twelve weeks he should be actively enjoying himself at least some of the time. This goal is relatively easy to achieve, as we shall see in later chapters.

In summary, during the first eight months of life, a baby should be reared in such a manner that she comes to feel that she is cared for, that she acquires all the specific skills within her capacity, and that her inborn tendency to learn more about and to enjoy the world around her is deepened and broadened. We will be referring to these three goals throughout the text.

CHAPTER TWO

Phase I:
Birth to Six Weeks

GENERAL REMARKS

"Helpless as a kitten" is a popular way of describing a newborn baby, but a kitten is considerably more able at birth than a human infant. If the human newborn, like a kitten, had to depend extensively on his own abilities to find nourishment, he would not last long. The human newborn seems to be only partially prepared for life outside of the womb, and the first four to six weeks of life seem more like a transitional period between very different modes of existence than a time of rapid development.

To begin with, life out of the womb depends upon the action of the lungs and several other systems that were not previously in use. In addition, for many infants the birth process itself is a physically difficult experience. It is, of course, not known how exhausting or stressful the typical vaginal delivery is for a baby. The conservative view holds, however—especially when labor is prolonged or complicated—that the process of birth is likely to be at least as tiring for the infant as it is for the mother. The extensive sleeping by the newborn in the first post-natal weeks lends additional support to this view.

GENERAL BEHAVIOR DURING THE POSTNATAL PERIOD

Sleepiness and Irritability

Perhaps the most obvious quality babies show in the first weeks of life, aside from total dependence, is sleepiness. In the first days you can expect a baby to average about three minutes an hour of alertness during the day, and less at night. Such periods of wakefulness will lengthen rather slowly over the next month to an average of six or seven minutes an hour.

When she is not asleep, do not be surprised to find a newborn easily irritated.[1] On the other hand a newborn, unlike an adult, can shift from what seems to be great distress to a state of apparent comfort very abruptly. These quick changes of mood persist for many months and are often dramatic reminders that infants very probably experience life quite differently from adults.

Fragmented Nature of Infant Behavior

Another rather unusual aspect of the newborn's behavior is its fragmented nature. Offer a six-month old a small rattle he has never seen before, and more often than not he will look at it, reach for it, and take it. He will then concentrate on examining it by staring at it, gumming it, or feeling it with his other hand.

Offer such an object to a newborn, and he will hardly look at it. If you try to put it into his hand, you will have some difficulty because his fists are usually clenched. However, once you have unfolded his fingers, the infant will grasp any small object placed high in the palm, especially if you are extending his arm and bending his hand back slightly as you make the attempt. Once he has the rattle, he may quickly drop it, or he may retain it for as long as several minutes. In either case, especially in the first weeks of life, that is all he is likely to do with it. If he has dropped the rattle, he will neither try to retrieve it nor show any awareness of its existence. If he retains it, he will neither look at it, gum it, nor explore it with his other hand.

From an adult point of view, such behavior is unexpected. It is convincingly explained, however, in Jean Piaget's brilliant *Origins of Intelligence*. According to Piaget, a baby's behavior at birth consists of a rather small number of somewhat clumsy, unfinished, and isolated reflexes. These simple bits of behavior (rooting and sucking, grasping, occasional glances at nearby objects) are the foundation elements of all

---

[1] Here and elsewhere it must be remembered that my remarks will not be perfectly accurate for all babies. Although in general infants behave remarkably alike in many situations and respects, one of the best-established principles of human development is the fact of individual differences. Especially in the area of irritability, there is great variability among babies. Often several children in the same family will differ remarkably in their characteristic moods from the first days of life. Over the last decade a fair amount of research has been done on these congenital differences in temperament among infants. It has been clearly established that some babies are far more difficult to live with from the very outset than others. For interesting work on this topic see the work of Birch, Chess, and Thomas (for example, *Your Child Is a Person*), and that of Brazelton (especially, *Infants and Toddlers*).

later intelligence. There is reason to believe that these behaviors constitute ancient fragments of what long ago made up useful, organized, instinctive patterns. In a stunning analysis, documented by detailed reports of the development of his own three children, Piaget described and explained the emergence of problem-solving and thinking ability in the first two years of life. But such effective action is far beyond the capacity of the baby in Phase I. Her reflexes are triggered by internal and external circumstances of which she has no awareness. They operate briefly and mechanically and, as far as anyone can tell, are in no way deliberately controlled by her.

During Phase I an infant's reflexes become more reliable and efficient through repeated triggering. In addition, the first signs of coordination among them begin as the baby's fist is increasingly brought to her mouth and gummed or sucked. In this manner, an object is grasped and occasionally brought to the mouth and gummed or sucked. But let that object be dropped and there will be no further sign that the baby knows it still exists. Out of hand (or mouth) is out of mind.

These early bits of behavior, the automatic grasping reflexes of the hand and foot, the rooting responses of the mouth, the coordinated arm and leg movements, are perhaps understood a bit more in the light of the behavior of other animals. In a recent movie absolutely incredible footage of a red kangeroo fetus is pictured: long before its actual birth, the kangeroo fetus is seen traveling from its mother's uterus through the cervix, out of the vaginal opening, up the abdominal wall to the opening of its mother's pouch, there to climb down into the pouch, seeking and finding a nipple and fastening on it for the balance of its fetal development. The kangaroo fetus gets absolutely no assistance or

The tonic neck reflex ("fencer's pose")

teaching from its mother to facilitate this necessary journey. Making this remarkable trip is a one-inch long, hairless and blind kangaroo fetus. It uses the same reflex elements present in the newborn human: that is, the grasp reflexes of all its limbs, the coordinated limb locomotive motions, and its capacity to root and, therefore, find its way using its sensitive snout area; finally, it uses its ability to fasten on and suck at a nipple to consummate this miraculous trip. These reflexes are orchestrated through genetic mechanisms that have developed over the evolution of the red kangaroo; these reflexes are not utilized by the human newborn, nor are they needed. In place of this marvelous coordinated instinctive pattern, the human newborn is ensured its survival by the behavior of a parent.

We learn at least two fascinating notions from this comparative research. First, we learn something about why the human comes equipped with isolated, apparently useless reflexes. Second, we learn something about the difference in the applicability of the concept of instinctive behavior in humans versus other animal species. In general, full-fledged instinctive patterns such as those seen in the kangaroo fetus—and also in the case of spiders spinning webs and birds building nests, etc.—simply do not exist in full-fledged form in human behavior at any stage of postnatal life. What does remain, however, are vestigial remains and other contributions, especially in connection with the early attachment process, wherein the young human forms its first social relationships to older people during the first two years of life.

Lack of Mobility

When on her back, a baby in Phase I cannot turn her torso so that she is lying on her side, or otherwise move her body about except under one condition. Some babies, when angry, manage to propel their bodies the entire length of the crib by repeatedly digging their heels into the mattress surface and thrusting out with their legs. A soft bumper placed around the interior walls of the entire crib or bassinet is therefore mandatory. It should also be noted that a baby as young as a month or two of age, when placed on a blanket on the floor or some other surface without confining walls, can, under similar circumstances, move quite a distance. Parents are well advised, because of the existence of this little-known capacity, to be careful.

By four weeks of age the characteristic posture of a baby, when on his back, is the tonic neck reflex, or "fencer's pose," with both hands fisted. About 85 percent of the time a baby's head is turned to the right, although all babies exhibit both right- and left-facing postures. At birth this posture is not yet predominant, and the baby may lie in a more symmetrical position.

Ordinarily, when a Phase I baby is on his stomach, he is only capable of barely clearing the mattress surface with his nose for a moment or two. Again, however, when angry he may do considerably better. In general, it will be several months before a baby can cope well with his disproportionately large head. Propped into a sitting position, his head will slump alarmingly. It is best *always to provide head support* for a Phase I baby, expecially when lifting or holding him.

Hypersensitivity

Along with sleepiness, frailty, and irritability, the Phase I infant is generally unusually sensitive. This sensitivity can make a jumpy parent even more apprehensive. It is perfectly normal for an infant to startle and cry at any abrupt change in stimulation during her first weeks of life. Such common reactions include a response to sharp nearby noises, or to jolts to the crib or bassinet, or to any rather sudden change in position, particularly when the baby has been inactive. A second, less dramatic indication of sensitivity at this age is the infant's avoidance of bright lights.

A Phase I infant will keep his eyes tightly shut in a brightly lit room or when outside in the sun. In fact, he is much more likely to open his eyes and keep them open in a dimly lit room than in one at an ordinary level of illumination. Another curiosity of behavior is that a Phase I infant's eyes will often open when he is lifted and held upright. This behavior is called the "doll's eye effect." This special sensitivity to bright light is markedly reduced by the end of Phase I.

Smiling

The smiling behavior of the Phase I infant is also worthy of note. It is quite common for new parents to report that their infant smiles at them frequently during the first six weeks of life. I must somewhat reluctantly insist that smiling is actually quite rare in this period. Furthermore, on the rare occasion that the infant seems to be wearing a smile, she is not likely to be looking at another person. Vision skills and social awareness are simply too primitive during the first six weeks of life to support significant examination of nearby visible details. All of us would like to think that our children feel an immediate and deep love for us, but I don't believe this is so. Toward the end of the infant's first months, however, you may begin to notice her looking at your face with increasing interest. This interest becomes possible because of rather dramatic acquisitions in focusing ability. The region of the human face between the hairline and the eyes seems to be particularly attractive to Phase I babies. This new interest represents a preliminary to true social smiling.

The Visual Discovery of the Hand

The six-week-old baby, when placed on his back, continues typically to lie in the tonic-neck-reflex position. Able to turn his cheek off the surface of the mattress with increasing ease, the baby still rarely looks directly overhead. His hands, although still usually held fisted, are now frequently held aloft. The hand on the side to which his head is turned is, from time to time, directly in front of his eyes; but whether the hand is still or moving through his line of sight, *the child does not seem to notice it.* The effect on an adult can be somewhat disconcerting because the baby appears to be blind. Such is very rarely the case. The Phase I baby is simply not yet able to see small nearby objects very well. One reason for this is that since his eyes do not yet converge or focus accurately on such objects, he is not yet ready for refined three-dimensional vision.

Sometime after five or six weeks, if you observe your infant closely, you will notice her give an occasional brief glance at her hand as it moves through the line of sight. Indeed, she may do a double-take slightly after her fist has moved through her line of sight. Each day the frequency and length of this activity will increase, changing gradually into sustained hand regard. *This pattern of staring at the hand is universal, and is a signal that the infant has entered into Phase II* (see page 32). Hand regard may begin as early as one month of age (in rare cases), but is normally first seen between two and three months. In the months that follow, it will lead to the gradual mastery of the use of the hand in deliberate reaching for objects. It is also a first step in the development of problem solving or intelligent behavior. Further, it seems to be a first step in the evolution of curiosity, for during the hours spent examining her hands an infant appears extremely involved and studious.

APPARENT INTERESTS OF THE PHASE I INFANT

Perhaps the toy most often bought for newborns is the rattle. Unfortunately, young infants have no interest at all in this toy. Even when they are four to six weeks old, babies show negligible enjoyment or even awareness of rattles. In referring back to earlier sections of this chapter, the major reasons for this lack of interest become clear. First of all, for the first few weeks of life the baby is not very interested in *any* aspect of the external environment. As we have seen, if a rattle is wedged into his clenched fist, he neither looks at it nor feels it with his other hand. Since he is not yet teething, even if he were to hold a sterling silver rattle to his mouth, he would not be rewarded by the relief from pain the coolness effect of the metal could bring. If a rattle is not a smart buy, what then *does* interest a newborn?

Simple Comfort

Any extensive study of newborns leads to the feeling that their major "concern" is comfort—or the absence of discomfort. The newborn infant is easily and regularly discomforted. This is, unfortunately, inevitable. She is very likely to be restless and in distress just before feeding. She may very well cry a good deal immediately after and between feedings. She will most likely cry if her diaper is not changed fairly promptly. (Interestingly, babies don't seem to object to a wet diaper so much as they do to a cold diaper.) Any sharp, loud noise or abrupt change in her position will often produce a startle and a series of piercing, "all-stops-out" squalls. It would appear that any of the several ways in which she can be disturbed from her predominant sleep state creates in the infant *an urge for relief, for peace.* In this respect, the newborn infant is unique, for beginning with Phase II, and increasingly from then on, the normal infant seeks out stimulation throughout the day, except for nap time.

Being Handled and Moved Gently Through Space

People have known for years that one way to soothe the easily disgruntled newborn baby is to pick him up, hold him close, and rock him or walk with him. As mentioned above, an automobile ride can work wonders for an infant when he seems inconsolable. Such experiences seem somehow to be so comforting or pleasurable to the Phase I infant that they can at least temporarily dispel discomfort from many sources.

Sucking

As the Phase I child develops, her capacity to get her fist to her mouth and keep it there increases. Whenever the fist or any similar object is at the mouth, if she is awake, the baby is likely to suck. If you are patient you can get your baby to suck on a pacifier, especially in times of moderate distress. (A raging baby seems less interested and less able to suck a pacifier). Since sucking her hand is a very common activity in an infant of this age, we must assume the activity is very satisfying.

LEARNING DEVELOPMENTS DURING PHASE I

During the first weeks of life, learning development consists primarily of a stabilization of the unsteady, somewhat fragile pieces of behavior present at birth. These pieces of behavior were cited earlier in this chapter. For example, you will find that during the first weeks of life the baby becomes more skillful at finding and sucking the nipple, bringing her fist to the mouth and holding it there, and locating and tracking a slowly moving nearby object. In essence, what seems to happen is that the modest collection of simple reflexlike acts present at birth undergoes a gradual finishing process during the next six weeks.

Though Phase I is not characterized by dramatic learning development, some discussion of the major areas of development may be useful, partly to indicate what a baby should *not* be expected to do.

Intelligence

Students of human development are in general agreement that babies neither begin life with any extensive intelligence, nor do they acquire any for several months at least. Definitions of intelligence vary widely, and judgments about when babies first reveal any such capacity will depend on the particular definition one chooses to use. One common definition of the earliest kind of intelligent behavior focuses on a simple problem-solving behavior. According to this view, well expressed by J. McVicker Hunt of the University of Illinois, the first signs of intelligence in babies are evidenced when they intentionally push aside obstacles in order to get at desired objects. Such behavior is not often seen before a baby is six months old.

Most adults think of intelligence as involving the perception and manipulation of ideas in the mind. As far as anyone can tell, such forms of intelligence do not make their appearance in any substantial form until late in the second year of life. There is little reason to think that Phase I babies do very much thinking, in the ordinary sense of the term. Throughout the first eighteen months of life, most of whatever intelligence a baby possesses is reflected in his actual behavior, especially those with his hands and eyes, which he will use most commonly in a trial-and-error style of problem solving. In other words, you can see problem solving in the actual actions of the baby between six and eighteen months of age.

The initial collection of reflexlike behavior that newborns show is not, however, irrelevant to intelligence. According to Piaget, it is from these simple isolated acts, like grasping and glancing, that mature intelligence develops.

Emotionality

The Phase I infant has few mood states. Her favorite condition, day and night, is sleep. When awake, she will present one of several emotional-behavior sets: groggy, sober, inactive, and quiet; or alert, sober, inactive, and quiet; or alert, sober, and active, with an occasional noise or two; or alert, active, and in mild distress, with occasional squalls; or obviously very unhappy (active and raging).

Through the first year of life, babies shift moods with surprising speed. As noted earlier, many kinds of distress can be relieved by gentle handling and rocking. A particularly useful item during this stage is a rocking chair and/or a rocking cradle. This old standby will not only soothe a cranky newborn, but can offer you many pleasant moments as well. In like manner, a very unhappy newborn can find comfort from sucking, even when that sucking is not followed by swallowing of milk or juice. It is as if the satisfaction from rocking or sucking were so all-satisfying that it simply shuts off any other sensations. This is seldom the case later in life. *When a toddler is badgering you for attention, do not expect him to be satisfied with a pacifier.*

Motor and Sensory Skills

During Phase I an infant's motor abilities increase noticeably. By four months of age he will be routinely holding his head in an upright position for many minutes at a time, and even at six weeks of age his head control will be noticeably better than at birth. He should now be able to hold his head just clear of the surface he is on for a few seconds at a time. It will be obvious, however, that lying on stomach or back is much preferred by the Phase I baby over any other position.

Similarly, the newborn's initial tendency to turn her head and grasp with her mouth an object touching her at or near her lips will be more regular and efficient by six weeks. Some progress, too, will be made in tracking slowly moving objects with the eyes. By six weeks of age, reasonably smooth, reliable tracking is often seen. To test for this ability, hold a large (more than five inches in diameter) brightly colored object about a foot over the baby's eyes, shake it to get her attention, and move it rather slowly to the side. You may have to recapture her attention after a few moments. The difference in average performance between the newborn and the six week old in this activity is ordinarily substantial.

Another easily observed improvement in motor ability is the increase in facility at getting the fist to the mouth and keeping it there. The newborn seems to be only partially in control of the movements of arms and hands. By six weeks of age he much more often manages to hold his fist at his mouth. His purpose, of course, is to have something to suck. This ability, by the way, may help mother in that it provides for occasional self-pacification.

The surprising strength of grasp of the newborn is well known. Especially when alert, the newborn usually has about two pounds of pulling power in each hand. This automatic "holding-on" persists throughout the first six weeks and gradually disappears shortly thereafter. Perhaps the earlier description of the usefulness of this behavior in fetal kangaroos helps to explain its presence. An accompaniment to the act of holding-on by the newborn is the typical fisted position of the fingers. It appears that the Phase I baby has no control over this situation, preventing extensive tactile exploration during the first six weeks of life. By three months of age this restriction disappears, as does the tendency to grasp with the toes as well as the fingers.

Sociability

Newborns are not sociable in any ordinary sense of the term. However, two simple signs of sociability do emerge routinely during the first six weeks of life. The first is a tendency, which may begin as early as the

Phase I babies will smile at this kind of pattern.

first week, for the baby to look toward the eyes of the person holding her. The second is the aforementioned appearance of the first modest "smiles" while doing so. These behaviors have a mechanical, almost impersonal, quality to them. You can often elicit similar behavior by presenting a young infant with a view of a pen-and-ink sketch of that section of the human face between the tip of the nose, and the top of the head. It seems that one of the universally inherited human behaviors is the tendency from six or seven weeks on to smile at human faces (or things that look like them), especially when such a face is between eight and twelve inches away.

Language

The Phase I infant is far too young to understand words. Such a capacity will not be had for at least six months. However, he is not deaf; although his hearing is not quite as acute as that of normal young adults, he can discriminate an impressive range of sounds, even during the first weeks of life. As noted, loud noises of all kinds—particularly when he is resting in light sleep—are likely to cause him to startle. This special sensitivity is most pronounced in the weeks after birth, and the startle may be followed by a good deal of crying. A baby who does not startle readily under those conditions may have a hearing loss, and is more likely to be a cause for concern than one who does.

Phase I babies do make noises. They not only cry and shriek but may produce simple sounds when not in distress. Although they show little interest in listening to these sounds in the first weeks of life, by three to four months of age babbling during play will become common.

RECOMMENDED CHILD-REARING PRACTICES: PHASE I

Childrearing practices in Phase I should reinforce the general goals laid down in Chapter 1, keeping in mind the infant's specific skills and interests. It is also important in this regard to remember what an infant *cannot* do and *is not* interested in.

Giving the Infant a Feeling of Being Loved and Cared for

As noted earlier, I recommend you handle your new infant frequently, *and that you respond promptly to his cries as often as you can.* You should also get into the habit of checking to see whether there is any obvious reason for the distress, but do not be surprised if you cannot always find one. Take care to look for underlying causes of distress routinely and to check with a professional if the symptoms are persistent or severe. This goal of giving the infant a *feeling of being loved and cared for* is, in my judgment, the single most important goal in getting a child off to a good start in life. I cannot overemphasize its importance.

Helping the Infant Develop Specific Skills

I do not believe there is much point in an extensive attempt at encouraging the development of abilities for the first few weeks of a baby's life. Placing a baby on her stomach several times each day (unless she won't tolerate the position) does, however, have the benefit of inducing head rearing. If the infant is always on her back, she cannot practice this behavior. (Parenthetically, it should be noted that some medical practitioners advise against routine placement of a baby on her back for the fear that spitting up may cause choking.)

Since the baby is mostly a sleepy individual, visual powers are limited and the field of visual interest covers a narrow part of space (from about eight to twenty-four inches from his eyes); therefore, providing interesting things to look at is probably of limited use at this time. When he is being held, various bodily responses to his changed positions are presumably being exercised; but beyond these simple fragmentary notions, there is not much point in being concerned with specific skill development in the first few weeks of life. Gradually, toward the end of the first month of life, babies begin to show more interest in the world around them. We have found that many three- and four-week-old babies will look at suitably designed mobiles. Since very few properly conceived mobiles are commercially available, you may prefer to make your own (see below).

How To Make a Mobile for a Three- to Nine-Week-Old Infant: A mobile should be placed where the infant tends to look. A baby of this age lying on her back will look to her far right 80 to 90 percent of the time, and to her far left for the remainder. (Whether or not this early preference is predictive of later handedness is not yet known.) A mobile for a baby this age should, therefore, *not* be placed directly over the baby's midline, but rather off to her far right or far left or, if you choose, to both sides.

A mobile should be placed at a distance the infant prefers. In the age in question (three to nine weeks) most babies avoid looking at objects closer than five inches or farther than eighteen inches from their eyes. I would recommend a distance of about twelve inches.

A mobile should be designed with a view toward what the baby sees while lying on his back in the crib. Most commercially available mobiles are designed to look attractive to an adult customer looking for a gift rather than to a baby lying in a crib. Since babies are especially interested in looking at that area of the human face that lies between the tip of the nose and the top of the head, the mobile should feature bold contrasting colors and crude features that contain configurations similar to those in the upper front portion of the human face. Furthermore, that target should face the supine baby rather than the adult standing over the crib.

With very little effort, good mobiles can be made at home, particularly since the Phase I infant for whom they are designed will only *look at them.* You need not worry about a strong support for a first mobile. Any method by which you can suspend facelike patterns into the proper locations will do just fine. You can even use simple sheet cardboard as the basic material on which to paint or paste patterns. By the way, though an infant of this age cannot really perceive fine detail, it will do no harm to incorporate some in your design. So feel free to express your artistic impulses.

Although I recommend the use of mobiles, I cannot say that any striking gains in specific skill development will result from the use of such devices. Nevertheless, the earliest interest in the outside world involves visual examination of parts of the near environment, to the extent that these features are easily viewed by the baby. Very few objects meet those requirements except the face of whoever feeds the baby and a suitably designed mobile. Another useful device for this purpose is a mirror fastened to the side of the crib at mattress level. Use a good-quality unbreakable mirror for this purpose.

Beyond the activities of trying to hold his head up off the surface he is lying on, and staring at face patterns, there are no other specific skills to be encouraged in Phase I. Some people will advocate other ideas, but I know of no substantial basis for any.

AN IMPORTANT NOTE ON LANGUAGE DEVELOPMENT

Although it may not seem entirely natural to you, it is unquestionably a good idea right at the start to begin "talking" with your baby. If you are the kind of person who spontaneously talks a lot to your baby right from the beginning, so much the better. We have found in our studies, however, that many parents are not inclined to talk to an infant, not only in the first weeks of life, but right on to about a year and a half of age, at which time most babies begin to communicate through talking with some facility. The best language teaching occurs when the "talking habit" is begun much earlier than the first intelligible speech from an infant. True language learning, that is, the understanding of the meaning of the first words, doesn't start much earlier for the baby than six months of age. At that point, the baby still is not going to be talking and expressing himself in meaningful language, but he will be quite capable of beginning to understand the meaning of his first words.

To assure good early language learning, one of the most important things for parents to do is to begin talking in a particular way to their babies right from the beginning. What is that particular way? It involves identifying, as well as you can, what the baby is attending to at the moment. For the first two years of life babies are predominantly oriented toward the here and now. They are simply not capable of understanding references to nonpresent objects. Talking about a trip you are going to take in a week or two, for example, is much less likely to register with an infant than will comments about your own face or the baby's hand, if that is what she is looking at. The most effective talking, then, consists of trying to identify what the baby is attending to at the moment and then talking directly, in simple, normal language to that focus. Diaper-changing, bath, and play times lend themselves nicely to this type of teaching.

Encouraging Interest in the Outside World

There is no point in working at encouraging curiosity until the next phase of development, when the baby's interest in exploration really blossoms. You can, of course, provide a good mobile, a mirror, and perhaps an occasional change of scenery (by changing the baby's location several times a day).

Also, as mentioned earlier, feel free to use the pacifier as soon as your baby will accept it. Although the Phase I infant will not be very skillful at retaining the pacifier, and certainly will not retrieve it when it falls out of her mouth, it may nevertheless come in very handy at times. Indeed, this simple and inexpensive item may save you and baby from much discomfort during the first months of life.

SOME CHILDREARING PRACTICES NOT RECOMMENDED

In addition to recommended childrearing practices, I believe some comment on inadvisable practices is necessary to counteract existing "misinformation" about childrearing.

Providing an Infant with an Elaborately "Enriched" Environment

If someone urges you to stimulate all your newborn infant's senses by purchasing and using a set of "educational" materials, be skeptical. The concept of an enriched environment (which has come into vogue in the last decade) has merit, but only when used with discretion. Some commercial firms and some child-development personnel have misused the concept.

The Phase I infant is a poor candidate for an enriched environment, especially during the first half of the period (the first three weeks of life), when he is rarely alert. It is not very likely that enrichment benefits a sleeping infant. When he is alert, his limited sensory capacities, combined with primitive intellectual status, severely restrict learning capacities. In short, *it is too soon* to be seriously concerned with extensive environment enrichment.

Letting a Baby "Cry it out"

Infants brought up in institutions cry less and less as their first year of life proceeds. They seem to learn (at some primitive level) that crying usually produces nothing but fatigue. Home-reared infants, whose cries are ordinarily responded to quickly, do continue to cry more than institutionally reared infants, but not as much as home-reared babies whose cries are responded to inconsistently. According to research by M. Ainsworth at Johns Hopkins University, regular, prompt response to an infant's crying leads to a better quality of attachment between caretaker and baby, and is to be preferred to either deliberate or inadvertent ignoring of crying. It is important to note that occasionally you will not be able to make a Phase I baby comfortable. Some "crying it out" will have to happen. But *it should not become a regular practice*.

Neglecting to Handle Your Infant for Fear of Harming or Overstimulating the Baby

There is a substantial amount of evidence indicating that newborns are beautifully designed to be handled, caressed, and moved gently through space. The parts of the nervous system that are activated by handling are much better developed at birth than those involving the mind, the eyes, or the ears. In addition, handling a baby is clearly one of the few effective ways of changing a baby's state from distress to comfort.

As for overstimulation from gentle handling, as far as we can tell, there need be little concern at this age that this can occur. If for some strange reason someone should insist on trying to keep a groggy infant from falling into a deep sleep, overstimulation might be an appropriate label, but such behavior seems unlikely.

BEHAVIORS THAT SIGNAL THE ONSET OF PHASE II

There are several rather dramatic changes to look for as an infant passes from Phase I to Phase II. Keep in mind, however, that these will not occur overnight, nor precisely at a specific age. Development is a gradual process, and babies vary tremendously, although less so in the first months of life than they will later.

The True Social Smile

There is no precise age when true social smiling can be expected. Nevertheless, most home-reared babies do begin to smile regularly at the sight of nearby faces during their third month, and you may begin to see signs of such behavior as early as six or seven weeks of age. (You may also see such babies smiling at their own hands and other familiar objects at about this time.)

Hand Regard

Though the fist is likely to be regularly in line of sight increasingly during the second month of life, you can expect an infant to stare right through it as it moves. He is not blind; he is just not yet very skillful at looking at nearby objects. By the third month of life, however, visual abilities will have developed to the point where the infant can see a fairly clear single image of his own hand, particularly if it is between five and eight inches away from his eyes. At that time he will begin to spend increasingly longer periods of time studying his hand and its movements. Signs of this activity may be present as early as seven or eight weeks of age, but often not until a few weeks later. The first instances of hand regard may be in the form of brief double takes. After the hand has passed by where he is looking, the baby may abruptly look after it. Gradually, in the weeks that follow, the looking will become more sustained and the baby will seem to make regular attempts to keep the hand within view.

A Substantial Increase in Wakefulness

Soon after the sixth week, and especially as hand regard becomes a common activity, you are likely to observe a rather sharp increase in the number of hours each day a baby spends awake and alert. From about five minutes an hour at one month of age, the average infant of two months of age will move to about fifteen to twenty minutes of wakefulness during the daylight hours. Again I must remind the reader that babies vary greatly in the pace of their development. Suffice it to say that most two- to three-month-old infants seem to be visually alert very often during the day, whereas Phase I infants are characteristically sleepy beings.

CHAPTER THREE

Phase II:

Six Weeks to Fourteen Weeks

GENERAL REMARKS

Unlike the newborn infant, the Phase II infant appears to have a genuine interest in what is going on around her. This interest is most strikingly apparent in longer and longer periods of wakefulness. This is also the stage when social responsiveness really begins to surface. Thank goodness it is also the stage when sleeping through the night usually begins.

One of the most dramatic landmarks of this second phase is the appearance of genuine, frequent, social smiling. Another highlight of Phase II is the infant's visual discovery of her own hand, which will be followed by many hours of staring at the hand and, as the weeks go by, at the fingers as they move overhead. These two dramatic events, social smiling and hand regard, appear against the background of increased wakefulness and seem together to represent the beginnings of true interest in exploration. Learning during Phase II, however, will be modest in total amount and type because we are still dealing with a baby of extremely limited skills, who by her sheer helplessness has to cope with all sorts of limitations upon her activities. After all, this baby still cannot move about in any real way, and for the most part has little control over her head, which is still disproportionately large. Indeed, even her visual capacities, which are so important for all kinds of learning, are only partly developed throughout the major part of this particular phase. Nevertheless, adaption to and mastery of the environment has begun.

GENERAL BEHAVIOR DURING PHASE II

Body and Head Control

Although the Phase II baby is a very limited being in many ways, this particular period of life is the scene for perhaps the most rapid rate of development that will ever be observed in a young child. The Phase II baby cannot yet turn over, reach for objects, or, indeed, even turn her torso very much from side to side, yet her behavior is much more coordinated than it was in Phase I, and very different in many ways. To start with, at about six weeks of age you should still expect to see the baby, when on her back, lying in the standard tonic-neck-reflex position. That means that her head will usually be turned to one side rather than centered, and the arm toward which her eyes are oriented will be extended while the other arm will be flexed with the first generally held up behind her head. By the end of Phase II, however, the baby will have acquired freedom from the influence of that reflex. If you look at a fourteen-week-old baby lying on her back, you will very often find her with her head in the midline position, with both arms and legs flexed, legs held slightly off the crib surface.

Interestingly, between six and fourteen weeks, the child's favorite resting posture shifts gradually from the asymmetrical side orientation (with his head resting on his cheek), through a position where his cheek may well be off the crib surface; first just a few degrees, then gradually more, and finally to the point where he is capable of holding his head at the midline for long periods of time. Unlike the child of six weeks, when the child of fourteen weeks comes to favor the midline symmetrical orientation, he is not restricted predominantly to this preferred position. Whereas the six-week-old has very little fine control over head movements, the fourteen-week-old can move his head

Midline position of a Phase II baby

freely throughout the full 180-degree range when lying on his back. Also, his head position no longer dictates the position of the arms. Most Phase I babies spend 80 to 90 percent of their time with their heads turned to the far right. When such a baby does turn his head more than a few degrees, it generally ends up facing far left (on the left cheek). A fourteen-week-old, on the other hand, has complete control of his head (when lying on his back).

In the six-week-old, the positions of the arms are dictated by head position. To demonstrate this, if you gently turn the baby's head from one cheek to the other you will find that her arms will shift their position accordingly. The baby has no control over this linkage during Phase I. In the fourteen-week-old, however, the head position no longer determines the position of the arms. Furthermore, each arm and hand seems to be able to act more or less independently of the other.

Sociability

Another rather dramatic change occurs in the area of sociability. The six-week-old baby is a pretty sober individual. Except for an occasional fleeting smile (very often not oriented toward a human face or voice), the baby generally does little smiling. Not so the fourteen-week-old— these babies usually smile an awful lot, and what a wonderful gift this is to parents. As is frequently the case, there will be exceptions to these general statements, and you need not be alarmed if your child is not regularly euphoric. By and large, however, this is the time when children seem to be chronically high. Easy and frequent social smiling seems to begin at between eight and ten weeks of age, along with a very strong interest in looking at the human face, particularly between the tip of the nose and the top of the head.

Motor Behavior

A more subtle but important change that the baby shows as he moves through Phase II is in the quality of motor behavior. The six-week-old baby is in many ways like a small machine. If you gently turn his head from one side to the other, his hands and legs will slavishly follow. If you touch his lip lightly with your finger, particularly when he is alert, you will find he turns his head abruptly toward the stimulating finger to grasp and suck it. This rooting behavior is as mechanical as the knee jerk elicited by your pediatrician. By fourteen weeks of age, however, a touch of the baby's lip will not be followed by an abrupt rooting response, but instead by a pause and then perhaps a cautious searching for the finger. The machinelike, automatic quality is gone. This change seems to reflect neurological maturation.

The rooting response is not the only mechanical behavior Phase 1 babies show. Earlier I remarked that certain kinds of objects—particularly if they are large and colored in intense, contrasting hues—when held over a resting baby could be effective in getting the child to look and to follow. Although getting a child to look at and follow a target in Phase I is usually a fairly difficult chore, babies in the six- to ten-week group follow that same kind of target with great skill and rather high reliability. Again, though, the performance has a machine-like quality. I have seen early Phase II babies follow a seven-inch bright red circle overhead back and forth several dozen times in a row. It is as if they really do not have any control over their own behavior. At six weeks of age a large target held anywhere from twelve to eighteen inches from the child, particularly slightly off to the side of line of sight, then shaken lightly, will elicit his attention. If the target is then moved slowly, the child will often track it. By the time he gets to be fourteen weeks of age, the baby will be perfectly capable of—and interested in—tracking small, irregularly shaped, and multicolored objects. At this age you will notice that his tracking behavior no longer seems as "obligatory," or automatic, as it was earlier. The reason for this shift in style of looking has to do with the dramatic improvements in vision skills of this particular phase.

Another area in which machinelike, automatic responding can be seen has been studied in research laboratories. A three-inch black felt disk, started at thirty-six inches away from the baby's eyes and then slowly brought closer, will attract a six- to eight-week-old baby's attention (under ideal conditions) as it reaches about eighteen inches from her eyes. The baby seems to be obliged to watch this target until it comes as close as eight to ten inches, at which point she stops looking. Gradually over the next few weeks, the range over which a baby will maintain focus on the same target extends to its maximum, which may be from twenty-four or thirty inches all the way down to four inches. As the baby approaches twelve or fourteen weeks, her behavior changes—instead of what looks like compulsory staring, now you will usually see a brief glance at the target when it is about two feet away, and then a total lack of interest. These and other behaviors convince the students of early human development that the two-month-old baby does not actively seek contact with the environment, but rather seems to be forced to respond to stimulation. In contrast, the baby of three and a half months (the end of Phase II) no longer seems "stimulus bound." *She seems to be much more in control of her own behavior.*

Increasing Strength

Another rather dramatic change in babies during Phase II is the shift from weakness to strength. Although the six-week-old baby is considerably stronger than the newborn, he is still a relatively weak creature. To prove it, all you have to do is put him on his stomach and note that he can usually only manage to lift his head a few inches off the surface on which he is lying. By fourteen weeks, however, that same baby can ordinarily lift and hold his head up so that it is vertical to the ground. Furthermore, he will be able to continue to hold it up and look around for long periods of time.

A baby's arms and legs are also considerably stronger at fourteen weeks than they were earlier. Indeed, you will find that at this stage babies take great delight in exercising their newfound muscles. Phase II muscle development is accompanied by a marked weight increase resulting in a rounder-looking, sturdier infant.

Visual Development

Still another dramatic area of change in Phase II involves vision, an area closely linked to the learning process. The Phase I infant has essentially no flexibility in his visual focusing system. Thus a target can be focused on clearly in only a very restricted range. For most Phase I babies, seven to nine inches from the eyes is the ideal focusing range. Clarity of vision is, however, limited even in that optimal focusing range by other immaturities in the vision system. By the end of Phase I, however, most babies are able to focus clearly at distances between six and twelve inches and to perceive fine details fairly well. During Phase II the full development of flexibility of the focusing system takes place in most babies. The fourteen-week-old baby can adjust the focus of his eyes for objects at *all* distances and, in fact, is slightly better at focusing on objects that are close (three to four inches away) than is the normal adult. This is because his eyes are set more closely together than those of an adult, making the task of turning both eyes in toward a very close target (convergence) easier than it is for a grownup.

Another major visual system is also undergoing very rapid development during Phase II. This is the system that allows us to see a single three-dimensional object when we are looking at targets less than one meter (39.37 inches) from the eyes. The capacity to turn both eyes in as a target approaches the face is not present in the newborn, and does not really manifest itself until the child approaches two months of age, at which time it seems to come into the baby's repertoire rather abruptly. A child under two months of age—when looking at an object five to seven inches away—not only has to contend with weak focusing ability, but also has trouble keeping both eyes on the target. *A baby of three and one-half months has near-mature visual capacities.* By observing the way your baby looks at small, detailed, nearby objects at different points in the first three and one-half months of age, you will find that if he does attend to such objects before he is seven or eight weeks of age, he is likely to give them no more than a brief stare. In contrast, in the following weeks he will not only be much more inclined to look at small, nearby objects, but as he looks at them you will find that he is glancing from point to point along their surfaces with skill and speed. He has become a sophisticated visual creature.

Hand Position and Hand Regard

Another development of consequence, and one that is easily observable, has to do with the baby's hands. As we have seen, the six-week-old baby generally rests with her hands in a fisted position, and the hand toward which her head is oriented is generally not actually looked at. Sometimes during Phase II, however, she will start to stare at her hand, at first as described earlier in a brief double-take fashion, and then for longer and longer periods. By three months of age she may be gazing at her hands for five to ten minutes at a time and repeatedly throughout the day. This new habit of prolonged hand and finger regard appears at about the same time as the developing visual maturity discussed above, since the child now has the visual capacity to focus clearly on and create a single image of a nearby object.

Accompanying the onset of hand regard is another interesting development. The apparently obligatory fisted position of the fingers undergoes a change at about the same time. You will find that somewhere during Phase II the fisted posture will gradually be replaced by hands held loosely clenched and even occasionally totally unflexed. What this does (most conveniently) is to provide the baby with an even more interesting visual spectacle, because the four fingers and thumb are capable of much more interesting variations in position than the fist. Therefore, during the third month of life you will see a good deal of finger movements accompanied by fascinated staring at them.

Another emerging universal behavior of normal infants at the end of Phase II is what we call "hands to the midline and clasped." Whereas the six-week-old baby lying in the tonic-neck-reflex position was unable to have his hands touching each other except on rare occasions, as the infant gets to be three months of age or so you should be on the watch for the tendency when lying on his back for the infant to bring both hands over his chest, where they will begin to explore each other.

This behavior will soon be followed by the visual study of what must be a fascinating set of mutual tactile sensations. In the weeks to follow, during the day, you can expect to see your child repeatedly bringing his hands to the midline where they touch, feel each other, are brought together to the mouth for gumming, and then moved away to be looked at intently as they simply clasp each other or touch each other in many varied ways.

Leg Position

Another in the long list of striking changes in Phase II involves leg position. Sometime during the fourth month (usually by the end of Phase II), the baby's legs will have reached such a degree of strength and musculature that they are very often held elevated an inch or two above the surface of the crib. Furthermore, they seem primed to thrust out; and, if any surface happens to be available that provides pressure to the soles of the feet, those flexed legs will push against it powerfully and repeatedly. Another evidence of increased strength in the legs and the tendency to extend them when pressure is applied to the soles of the feet can be seen in the surprising ability of the baby by the end of Phase II to support much of his own weight when held upright with his feet against a surface.

Curiosity

While you could characterize the younger Phase I baby as a seeker of peace and quiet and the older Phase I baby as a beginning "looker," the Phase II baby is a very different kind of person.

Increasingly, between six weeks and fourteen weeks of age, the baby's hands begin to play a prominent role in her explorations. This interest in her hands will be a central feature in the baby's daily life from about two months of age on through to at least eighteen months of age and should not be underestimated. We have found that if you present a small, attractive object such as a rattle five or six inches from a child's eyes and off to his right when he is about eight to ten weeks of age, he will not only look at the target, but, in addition, in many cases his right fist will abruptly rise, approach the target, and strike it. This so-called "batting" or "swiping" behavior is likely to first appear a week or two after the first episodes of sustained hand regard. From here on babies are no longer content to "just look." They want to get their hands as well as their eyes into the exploratory efforts. Bear in mind, however, that in spite of their curiosity, Phase II babies are extremely limited in their explorations by their physical immaturity. The world has to be brought to them in order for them to examine it. Imagine for a moment that you were unable to move about, yet were equipped with a lively curiosity, and you may to some extent capture the situation of a normal three-month-old baby.

The three-month-old baby shows her curiosity in many ways: by her interest in your face; by her interest in her own hand movements; and by her interest in feeling various objects around her, such as clothing and crib sheets. One consequence of this desire to get hands on anything within reach is that mobiles for the Phase II baby cannot be constructed with the same sort of flimsy support devices that were perfectly adequate for the child under six or seven weeks of age. In Phase II the baby is ready for a crib gym, to be put together with the expectation that it is not merely to be looked at, but that it is going to be interacted with manually as well. Indeed, if it is a really successful device, it will be subjected to extensive abuse.

Coordination of Behavior

As we have seen, the newborn baby comes equipped with a small number of reflexlike behaviors *that function independently of each other* resulting in fragmented behavior (that is, the automatic grasping of a rattle placed in the palm without indicating any mental awareness of its presence). The Phase II baby, on the other hand, is considerably more mature in this regard. As we have seen, a ten week old may take a swipe at an object placed within his reach. A slightly older child (twelve to fourteen weeks of age) is likely to show other hand and arm behaviors at the sight of a nearby object. When an object is placed in his hand, particularly after ten weeks of age, he is very likely to both look at it and bring it to his mouth to be gummed. According to Piaget, these combinations of activities that occur in response to the presence of small objects show that *several action systems (grasping, looking, and sucking) are to some extent now coordinated.*

Another new evidence of the coordination of behaviors can be seen when the baby is between twelve and fourteen weeks of age. A new action pattern is commonly seen—an action pattern we call "hands to the midline and clasped with mutual fingering." When shown a new, small, reachable object, the fourteen-week-old baby very commonly responds by bringing both hands over her lower chest and clasping them. (This must be a curious experience for an infant who up until now has not usually had the opportunity for one hand to contact the other.) Furthermore, an object "placed" in either of the baby's hands at this particular age will often be incorporated into the hands-to-midline pattern. The other hand will join the one holding the object and engage in some fingering of the target or the object. This fingering is a form of tactile exploration, and again illustrates how an object being grasped is now also examined by the other hand as well as the eyes.

THE APPARENT INTERESTS OF PHASE II

Exploration

If there is one label to characterize a baby's major interest in Phase II, it would have to be exploration. Unlike the sleepy Phase I baby, the Phase II baby, particularly from the middle of the period on, impresses the observer with the brightness of his eyes and with increasing alertness and responsiveness. He goes about his explorations in several interesting ways.

Looking

First of all he is a looker—he is all eyes. He is particularly interested in looking at faces or pictures of faces. He is very much intrigued by small detailed objects that are not far away, and he is attracted especially by slowly moving objects. He is still not very much interested in looking at anything that is very much farther away than two or three feet from his eyes, but interest in more distant objects is gradually evolving.

Feeling

As I mentioned earlier, while the Phase II baby is looking, her second exploratory means (the use of her hands) will be exercised whenever possible. Whether she is in your arms, looking up at your face, holding a small object, or looking at anything within reach, after two months of age she is likely to try to use her hands to explore the objects. She will finger surfaces once her fingers are free to do so. She will move objects back and forth, thereby getting a different view of them as well as a different feel for them.

Gumming

A third means of exploration at this age is the mouth. Gumming small objects is another favorite occupation. At first the most common small object he will gum will be his own fist. As the weeks go by, his fingers will be gummed and sucked; as a matter of fact, just about anything that can be brought to the mouth will be gummed. There are two apparent reasons for this. One is that the mouth is an exploring organ. The other is that in advance of the eruption of teeth, gums may be tender and somewhat painful. Such discomfort can occasionally be relieved to some extent by the pressure involved in gumming objects.

Listening

Another more subtle sign of exploration and interest toward the end of Phase II is that the baby now seems to begin to be interested in listening to the sounds he can make with the saliva in his mouth. This interest in sounds will become more prominent in later months.

Motor Exercise

Another emerging interest during Phase II is motor exercise. The baby is considerably more active now; and, in addition, her arms and legs and neck muscles are considerably more substantial and powerful than those in the Phase I baby. If you place a baby on her stomach at this age, she is likely to rear her head repeatedly up to a vertical position from the surface on which she is lying, and to look about from that position. You are likely to find the fourteen-week-old baby kicking at nothing when lying on her back, and you are likely to find active batting with the arms when anything battable is nearby.

EDUCATIONAL DEVELOPMENTS DURING PHASE II

General Remarks

Unlike the Phase I baby, who is predominantly getting used to living outside the womb, the Phase II baby is beginning to familiarize himself with the external environment. In a sense, his education can be properly said to have begun. As previously mentioned, the rate of development between six weeks and fourteen weeks of age is dramatic. Such milestones as the release from the effects of the tonic neck reflex and grasp reflex, the maturation of visual motor capacities, and the emergence of sociability all help free the Phase II baby for further learning.

Intelligence

As we have noted, Phase II marks the beginning of the coordination of various simple action systems. We have already examined the sequence of activities. The hand is much more often successfully brought to the mouth for sucking, and gradually that hand is also looked at as well as sucked. When the baby is three months of age he will not only have found his hand visually, but he will also be bringing his hand to his mouth to suck—often just after having spent some time staring at it. What happens in this sequence of activities is that one object—his own hand—begins to be involved in several previously separate action systems. The hand is now something to be seen, moved about, brought to the mouth, and sucked. Shortly after the appearance of steady staring at the hand, objects that are placed in the baby's hand and grasped will routinely be brought to the mouth for sucking. In this way, objects seen become objects to be sucked, and two major action systems become intertwined. Another coordination begins to be found in Phase II: a link between hearing and looking. Things heard begin to be things to look at as well as to listen to. In other words, while the newborn will on rare occasions turn to the source of sound, the Phase II baby will routinely do so. In Phase I most nearby sounds will regularly produce at most an alerting response or some other sign of listening in the very young baby, but will not link up with his looking tendencies. The baby in Phase II, on the other hand, will begin to both listen and turn his head to look.

From birth all babies undergo an absolutely vital and totally normal kind of learning sequence no matter how well they are attended to. No matter how healthy they are, they commonly experience distress many times every day. That distress is usually followed by the arrival of an older person who tries to make the baby feel better. Because of the way babies are designed, and because their needs are comparatively simple most of the time, that attempt is ordinarily successful. During the first months of life babies routinely undergo hundreds and hundreds of such sequences. By the time the baby is well into Phase II, she has learned at a very primitive level to associate distress with the arrival of a person who looks, feels, sounds, and smells in certain ways. That association is also linked to the experience of reduced stress. This type of automatic learning, which in fact takes place in innumerable ways throughout the lifetime of all of us, and for that matter in other creatures as well, is extremely important even though it doesn't involve any degree of conscious awareness or thinking on the part of the very young infant. Repeated experiences of this sort are vital to the establishment of a solid basis for all later development, and also help us to understand when and why babies begin to use crying intentionally in order to get attention during Phase III.

There are other evidences of modest amounts of learning that are taking place during this time. For example, you can expect to see a child begin to show signs that he has learned something about feeding. When the child of twelve to fourteen weeks of age, for example, stops thrashing about or sucking when his mother appears to feed him, it is often a fairly clear indicator that he has some sense of what is coming. Furthermore, if you watch the sucking movements of your child you will notice that at about the same age, in advance of feeding, a child may begin to suck actively at the sight of the bottle, or the breast, or when he is being prepared for nursing. In these modest ways a child is behaving differently from the way he did in the first weeks of life. Such changes seem to represent a step in the growth of the ability to deal with the world around him, albeit at a simple level.

Emotionality

The first signs of "positive" emotional expression are found with the onset of social smiling. By the end of Phase II regular smiling to another person should be a common experience in the child's daily life. What the smile means about sociability and about the baby's emotional state is less clear than the fact of regular smiling to a human face. As mentioned before, it has been shown in research that with a black and white sketch of that part of the human face between the tip of the nose and the top of the head, you can rather easily get most babies of about eight to ten weeks to smile repeatedly. In fact, if you are very clever at designing this target, you may get them to smile more reliably to that target than to their mother's face. That fact, coupled with another— most anybody is able to get an eight to ten-week-old baby to smile regardless of whether the baby has had any previous experience with them—suggests a rather interesting notion from the point of view of the survival of the species. It would appear that babies are designed to smile at just about any kind of sight that resembles a face in these very earliest stages. Upon reflection this behavior makes sense, because a defenseless baby has to have some guarantee of a positive response from another creature who can help assure its survival. The smile of the typical two-month-old baby is a very powerful force indeed in winning over an older human. Therefore the question of the relationship of the smiling to sociability is a bit more complicated than meets the eye.

As far as the relationship of the smile to the baby's true emotional state is concerned, again the picture is not as clear as it might seem on the surface. When adults smile, it is usually because they are feeling comfortable or happy. In the case of a two-month-old, however, the most we can conservatively conclude is that when she is wearing a smile she is at least very comfortable, and at the most, experiencing a feeling of physical well-being. You do not see either laughter or high hilarity in the Phase II infant (except during the end of the period).

Another complicating factor in respect to the early smiles comes once again from the work of Piaget. He has observed, and others have confirmed, the fact that the first smiles very often come when a baby is not looking at a person's face or even at any part of another person, but when looking at her own hand or a toy hanging from the crib or other parts of her environment. What could account for such strange behavior? The explanation ingeniously offered in Piaget's work is that the early smile is to some extent a first sign of familiarity. Smiling at her own hand, for example, is not seen when the child first discovers that hand visually, but only occurs after several hours of sustained regard. The same thing is true with respect to fringes of fabric or to a familiar toy hanging over the crib. Indeed, once researchers were tuned into this kind of behavior, it has been reported routinely. Although there is no doubt that smiling is very common to the human face in the Phase II baby, and certainly represents the beginning of expressions of contentment and sociability, it also in the very beginning seems to represent a primitive intellectual milestone.

The Phase II child reflects also the other apparent emotional states of Phase I; that is, she is still capable of showing rage. I don't believe such an infant's rage is more "personal" than are her first smiles. Such rage seems to be simply a response to significant physical discomfort at this stage of life. Toward the end of the first year, the child will begin occasionally to express rage that is clearly directed toward another person.

Concern

Phase II, therefore, is a time when only a limited number of emotional states are likely to be seen: the feeling of well-being (signified by the presence of a full smile); a feeling of neutral emotions (manifested by a sober and alert expression); feelings of gross discomfort (revealed by fussy or rage behavior); and finally, a very interesting emotional indicator that might best be labeled "intense concern," which seems to be present when the two- to three-month-old is staring steadily at his own hand or finger movements. You regularly see such behavior with children in Phase II. The concern expressed during this prolonged staring does not seem to reflect worry, but rather a serious, studious state.

Motor and Sensorimotor Skills

The Phase II infant accumulates an impressive collection of motor abilities in the period from six weeks to fourteen weeks of age. Motor abilities in this phase can be discussed under two headings: those the baby brought with him at birth and that are fading out, and those which are emerging.

Inborn Motor Abilities

Rooting: Included among inborn motor abilities is the rooting ability, the aforementioned skill that helps the baby to find the nipple in order to suck. This kind of behavior, which seems to be mechanical and increasingly efficient in the first six weeks of life, remains efficient and mechanical in the early stages of Phase II. By the time a baby is three months of age, however, searching with the mouth is accomplished in a more smooth, deliberate manner.

Visual Tracking: Another interesting behavior that bridges the first two phases of life is visual tracking. As we have seen, the Phase I baby has a built-in tendency to be alerted to rather large, highly contrasting objects that move slowly and slightly off his line of sight. When the very young baby looks toward such an object, he is essentially centering it in his visual field. He brings the target into the line of sight where human eyes are best suited to fine visual examination. Unfortunately, for the very young baby, his eyesight is not yet developed enough for fine visual inspection, so once the object is centered in his line of sight he cannot see it clearly and he therefore quickly loses interest in it. You can usually get a baby to track an object over a couple of feet, even though he is less than six weeks of age, by repeatedly recapturing and dragging along his attention (by his eyes) a few inches at a time. During Phase II, as with the rooting behavior, visual tracking or pursuit remains a dependable behavior; indeed, it reaches a peak of efficiency for a few weeks at about six to eight weeks, then gradually drops out, to be replaced by what looks like more voluntary, more adult function. The ten-week-old baby tracks objects very smoothly as they move slowly overhead. One reason for that smoothness is that she has acquired considerably more control over her head motions; the other has to do with the aforementioned shift from apparently involuntary tracking of targets to a more controlled type of activity.

Finger Position: Still another kind of motor development that spans Phase I and II has to do with the fingers. The grasp reflex and fisted hand, both characteristic of Phase I, gradually drop out as the child moves through Phase II. By the time she nears three months of age she can put a single finger in her mouth and suck it, whereas before she was largely limited to sucking some large surface of her fist.

Startles: The startle response common to the Phase I baby gradually drops out during Phase II. Both spontaneous startles most common during deep, inactive sleep and elicited startles recur less and less frequently as the child moves through Phase II.

EMERGING PHASE II SKILLS

With the decrease in influence of his inborn motor reflexes, we find a far more able Phase II baby. You can expect, for example, that the six- to eight-week-old baby can more or less hold his head about forty-five degrees off the horizontal for a few minutes at a time. Each week that passes will bring steady improvement, so that by fourteen weeks he should be able to hold his head so that its main axis is at about ninety degrees from the horizontal for several minutes at a time.

The other emerging motor skills of the Phase II baby were discussed in detail at the beginning of this chapter. Let me say in summary that at the end of this phase a child is a very competent visual motor creature, has good general hearing abilities (if he is lucky enough to avoid chronic respiratory distress or allergies and if he was born with basically normal hearing apparatus), and has greater hand and body control. He is on the road toward developing the arm and leg strength he will need in the months to follow in order to maintain an upright sitting posture, to achieve a pull-to-stand posture, and ultimately to walk.

Social Development

Just when the fatigue of tending to the Phase I baby may be getting the average parents down to their last ounces of reserve strength, two

Three and one-half months: head at 90° position

lifesavers are likely to arrive almost simultaneously on the scene. I refer to the tendency of late Phase II babies to sleep through the night, and to engage in genuine social smiling. (Additionally, many bouts of colic clear up rather abruptly toward the end of Phase II.) Social smiling is a well-documented phenomenon. It is very clear that you can expect most children reared in their own homes to begin reliable social smiling by about two months of age. Some people swear that babies are smiling regularly long before two months; but to be on the conservative side, two months, even as late as two and one-half months, is a perfectly reasonable time for you to expect such smiling to begin. Once a child engages in smiling very regularly there is no mistaking what social smiling is. It is total, unqualified engagement on the part of the baby. It has been so designed as to melt all but absolutely frozen hearts. You can easily see what an effective survival tactic it is for a young, totally dependent creature. Though early smiles are not reserved exclusively for a baby's family, they are there, they are glorious, and they are to be enjoyed.

We have already commented upon the euphoria of the late Phase II child. The fourth month of life is simply a marvelous time to be, and to be with, the baby. It is the time when photographers take pictures of young children for advertisements. The child is more chubby. She has usually lost any unattractiveness caused by the birth process. The result is that most fourteen-week-olds not only smile a great deal, but look quite handsome while doing so.

Special Relationships with Parents

Research shows that by fourteen weeks of age a child's parents, if they have been the principle caretakers, are more able to elicit a smile from a baby, and more able to continue to elicit it for long periods of time, than anyone else. Although conclusive evidence is not at hand, it appears very likely that this kind of special relationship can develop with people other than a baby's parents. The key seems to be the people who spend the greatest amount of time caring for the baby in those first months. They are the people the baby will single out by the fourth month of life for special responses. The baby seems to have begun a special relationship with those people. Their smiles, especially if accompanied by their voices, seem to be significantly more powerful in eliciting his smile reaction than just about anything else in his ordinary experience. Although his parents may be uniquely powerful as elicitors of such sociability, that is not to say that the child will not smile readily to other people as well. Indeed, he is extraordinarily gregarious at this point. Most anybody who comes by can still rather easily get the child to smile at him.

Language Development

The Phase II baby is still too young to understand words—indeed that capacity is still several months away. Earlier I mentioned that she very probably could hear well enough to discriminate words. We would expect her hearing skills to be approaching those of a normal adult by the time she is fourteen weeks old. She is no longer as oversensitive to loud and sharp noises as she was during Phase I. The startle response that we talked about in the first period of life is dropping out, although occasionally during deep sleep it may be triggered by abrupt stimulation. Interestingly, at about fourteen weeks babies do get to the point where they can be conditioned rather easily. By that I mean they can be trained to respond to sound in a manner that enables skilled audiometricians to determine with some precision just how well they hear. There has been a good deal of work in the Soviet Union and at Brown University showing that conditioning techniques (similar to the techniques routinely used to train animals) can be applied to the human infant of twelve weeks of age. The fourteen-week-old baby who hears well will turn rather quickly and accurately toward any nearby sound. This reflexive behavior allows us to screen for the surprisingly common mild to moderate hearing losses that plague young infants. This behavior, in turn, allows parents and professionals to identify a significant threat to optimal learning at a very early stage of the game. We shall return to this very important issue in a later section of this chapter.

The Phase II infant emits considerably more sound than the Phase I infant. You will find when he is very excited about either you, a toy, or what he sees in a mirror, for example, he will start to gurgle and make delightful baby sounds. You may even hear shrieks of delight emerging from him in the fourth month of life. As noted earlier, another new phenomenon he will engage in is playing with the sounds made possible by his own saliva. He can entertain himself in this way for long periods of time.

RECOMMENDED CHILDREARING PRACTICES: PHASE II

Giving the Infant the Feeling of Being Loved and Cared for

Childrearing practices in Phase II are again best thought of in the light of the three educational goals set down in Chapter 1. The recommendations for Phase I in regard to the first goal, assuring the baby that she is cared for, apply to Phase II as well. I would like, however, to reemphasize one point and make a comment. Your baby, through dozens of events each week when she experiences discomfort and cries out, accumulates a generalized expectation about her world. If her cries are routinely responded to promptly, she acquires a desirable expectation about the degree of caring from the world about her. If on the other hand she is routinely not responded to (allowed to "cry it out"), she acquires an importantly different expectation. I'm not talking about a developed intellectual awareness on the part of the baby. It is not possible to talk with precision about how a child acquires these expectations in the light of the primitive nature of the mental capacities of the infant. I do feel, however, that at some very basic and important level, these early experiences play a role in the cumulative growth of the sense of being cared for or loved. Giving a Phase II infant the feeling that you care is easier to do at this point than at many other points in the young child's life, because the Phase II child is generally such an exciting, endearing, and lovable creature.

HELPING THE INFANT DEVELOP SPECIFIC SKILLS

Let us consider the skills, in turn, that are developing during this period—with the knowledge that whether you do very much at all the child is going to acquire these skills during this particular stage of his life, although perhaps not so rapidly as he will with an appropriate set of experiences.

Head Control

One of the skills we expect to develop in this phase is head control. The child who lies on his back most of the time is less likely to achieve head control as early as the child who regularly has the experience of being placed on his stomach. To foster this development you can place the baby on his stomach for at least one-half hour a day, perhaps five or ten minutes at a time after meals. This will assure him of opportunities to practice headrearing and head control. Medical authorities also recommended prone placement to reduce the chance of an infant gagging on the fluids she may "spit up."

Visual Skills

As regards vision, the child when placed prone for the purpose of inducing headrearing is also going to be in a position to see things from different angles, and look at scenes he ordinarily would not have been able to see. He is therefore able to engage in an interesting set of visual experiences at the same time that he is practicing his headrearing. The more skilled his headrearing becomes, the farther he can look away from his body.

Babies from about six to ten weeks of age are still interested in properly designed mobiles. Thus any device you might have created for the Phase I baby can be used up to ten weeks of age. From the time the baby begins staring at her own hand, however, she will become less and less content to merely look at nearby targets. (More about that in a moment.) In addition to prone placement and the provision of mobiles, I would suggest two other procedures to provide interesting visual experiences for children. One is the use of a mirror, particularly from the time a child is eight or nine weeks of age. A mirror placed about seven inches away from her eyes will be looked at increasingly by a baby from that time on through the next month or so. In her mirror watching, you will find a rather interesting sequence of activities. Babies tend to engage in modest flirtations and then mild love affairs with their own mirror image during this particular time of life. It is all part of their growing sociability.

A final remark in this area concerns the desirability of using an infant seat to provide a change of scene and to increase interchanges between parent and child. If from time to time you have the child near you as you go about your daily work by placing her in an infant seat, you will ensure that she will have a wide variety of visual experiences. If you use an infant seat, however, remember that until the child is about fourteen weeks of age she will not be able to support her head or torso particularly well. You are therefore going to have to prop them up, perhaps using a small blanket on either side of the baby.

A general remark about these recommended visual experiences is that there is no evidence that any of them are especially necessary in regard to visual development. As far as we can tell, development of visual focusing, convergence, and pursuit skills will proceed quite well irrespective of any special arrangements of the world around the child.

Hand-Eye Activities

The third set of specific skills to be encouraged during Phase II involve hand-eye activity. Sometime toward the end of Phase II the baby will acquire the new skill we have called "swiping." It consists of a rather abrupt, fisted attack on any small, suitably located nearby object. I learned a good deal about this behavior in extensive research on the development of reaching abilities in young children. In the past I have designed experimental and commercial materials (not currently available) to exploit this natural tendency on the part of children. An object that could both be seen and touched by the Phase II baby was arranged so that it would be in range of his right or left hand. The result was that eight- to twelve-week-old babies spent a good deal of time watching their hands batting and feeling the surfaces of these objects. Such experiences are perfectly natural and appropriate for a baby who has been engaging in sustained hand regard for a few days or more.

Crib Toys for the Phase II Infant

The Phase I baby has no need for a mobile he can touch; when he begins to explore, it will be primarily with his eyes. Since the Phase II baby becomes interested in learning to use his hands as well as his eyes, by eight to ten weeks of age a baby ought to have objects appropriately placed so that he can easily get his hands to them—that means no more than six to eight inches away from his eyes.

Crib devices should be semirigidly supported. There is nothing more frustrating to an infant less than six or seven months of age than an attractive nearby object suspended by a long string. A baby is acquiring more and more skill each day, but coping with a ring or a ball that is suspended by a four- or five-inch string is generally very difficult for him. Anyone who has ever fumbled overhead in the dark for a long string to light an old-fashioned ceiling lamp realizes how frustrating such a device can be even to an adult. We have found that using semirigid plastic or taping suspended objects used in commercial toys—which guarantees that the object the child is interested in reaching for, batting, or feeling, is going to be pretty much in the same place each time he goes after it—is much more effective.

Crib toys should be strong enough to stand abuse. Toward the end of the period, the Phase II child is becoming a surprisingly strong and vigorous creature.

A properly designed crib toy will undergo a good deal of battering and general abuse. If it is a good one, that battering will continue either until the child breaks the toy or until she outgrows it. A crib toy for a child more than seven weeks of age should therefore be very solidly made. Unfortunately, most of the crib gyms that are available are poorly designed. There are a few exceptions, and currently available ones will be listed in the section on recommended toys. Briefly, however, I should reassure you that although some crib toys of this sort are offered for sale at well over a hundred dollars, others are available for less than five or six dollars, and are just as likely to be useful to the infant.

Crib toys should not produce sharp or very large sounds, or any abrupt changes in stimulation, such as bright flashing lights. We have noted that particularly during the first half of Phase II, children are still susceptible to startling as a consequence of abrupt changes in stimulation. Therefore, crib toys with the above features should be reserved for when your child gets to be a bit older.

Crib toys must be removed from the crib when the baby seems nearly able to pull herself to a sitting posture. *It is extremely important for reasons of safety to follow this advice;* there have been episodes in the last decade of children becoming seriously injured by entanglement with crib gyms used past the time the child was able to sit up.

Encouraging Interest in the Outside World (Curiosity)

If you encourage specific skill development using appropriate mobiles, small mirrors, an infant seat, and changes of scenery, you'll find that your child will show a great deal of curiosity. Even if you do none of these things, she will display increasing curiosity in her studious examinations of her own hands and fingers, and in her visual inspection of the mutual fingering done by one hand on the other, and so forth. In other words, it's hard to get in the way of the growth of curiosity. However, should you provide some of the additional experiences I've suggested, I'm confident you'll see even greater growth accompanied by many signs of enthusiasm and glee in your child.

MATERIALS YOU SHOULD NOT
WASTE YOUR MONEY ON
AT THIS STAGE: PHASE II

Rattles: A rattle is still not a good investment at the Phase II stage. Although a child will hold onto a rattle considerably longer in Phase II than she would in the first weeks of life, may spend some time looking at it, and may even bring it to her mouth and gum it a little bit, nevertheless, if she drops it (and she will—usually in less than a minute), she is not likely to either look for it nor to be able to retrieve it. All in all, it is still not much of a toy.

Most Crib Toys

There are large numbers of crib toys on the market today. Somewhat over a decade ago a flock of toy companies entered this field in response to increased demand from parents. Within the last few years their numbers have multiplied because of an even greater interest on the part of many parents in early learning. I have had extensive experience now with several of the major toy companies and have examined a large percentage of their offerings on the market. It is my opinion that the vast majority of them provide inadequate amounts of play value and have very little educational merit. There are several exceptions. An extensive treatment of toys and other materials for babies will be found later on in this book, and the best of crib toys will be recommended in that section.

CHILDREARING PRACTICES NOT RECOMMENDED

In the discussion of the Phase I child it was suggested that you beware of the abundant misinformation about childrearing that is available. I suggested that you need not feel guilty if you have not provided an expensive and elaborately "enriched" environment for your child. This still holds true. Although there is more that you can do in Phase II, if you still do little, in my opinion you have *not* done a *terrible disservice to your young child*. Indeed, most of the basic learning processes will proceed quite nicely.

The second point I made during the discussion was that the idea of spoiling your child during Phase I made no sense. This applies as well to the Phase II baby. I strongly urge you to respond naturally and promptly to any signs of distress in your baby; try to find out what is wrong, make certain there is no serious problem, and do the best you can to alleviate the discomfort. Only let a young infant "cry it out" as a last resort. This of course will be necessary at times. I've had quite a number of parents report attempting to prevent all episodes of crying, which totally wore them out. Let's hope you're lucky enough not to have to put up with too many of those uncomfortable episodes.

A third point I made was that babies are designed to be handled, caressed, and loved, and there is no reason at all why you should not indulge yourself in this regard.

Behaviors that Signal the Onset of Phase III

Head Control: When you feel confident that your baby, in an upright posture, whether she is being held or is in an infant seat, has good control of her head (such that you do not have the sense that it is going to tip or fall), you have one sign of a baby leaving Phase II and entering Phase III.

Torso Control: As we have seen, prior to about fourteen weeks few babies can do much with their torsos. Unlike the control they have acquired with respect to their head and eyes, hands, fingers, and legs, the torso remains too much for most babies to deal with until the end of Phase II. At around fourteen weeks you will notice they begin turning their body up onto one side or the other. This pattern will be followed by the capacity to turn over within a few weeks.

Kicking Out: Another emerging characteristic of motor maturity as Phase II begins is a tendency for a baby to hold her feet somewhat off the crib surface from time to time and thrust out vigorously, particularly if there is some pressure against the soles of her feet. This tendency to exercise the newfound leg strength leads ultimately to the ability to use them for support when standing and walking.

Special Response to a Familiar Person's Face and Voice: Though somewhat less obvious, it should become clear that along with the growth of sociability, the fourteen-week-old baby is now especially oriented toward the appearance of his primary caretaker's face and voice.

The Tickle, the Giggle, the Laugh, or the Emergence of Hilarity: I've already discussed briefly the emergence of the capacity to be tickled. This phenomenon is part of a rapidly growing tendency toward euphoria and enjoyment that characterizes the Phase III baby. Although I've mentioned that the Phase II baby moves into a period of high spirits, it is in Phase III that a baby is most impressive in this regard.

CHAPTER *FOUR*

Phase III:

Fourteen Weeks to Twenty-Three Weeks

GENERAL REMARKS

The period of fourteen to twenty-three weeks is a time when an interesting style of life and set of behaviors fade out. It is also a time when a remarkable quality of mood prevails. There are many cultures in the world where very young babies are carried and therefore held upright for large periods of the day, but in our society the first three and a half months of life are mostly spent with the infant lying either on his back or on his stomach. But starting from fourteen weeks and on, the child will spend his waking hours more commonly in a vertical orientation.

Another general comment about the end of Phase II has to do with the baby's special concern with getting to know various parts of his body. A good example of that early introductory period can be seen in an infant's discovery of his hand, first tactually and then visually. This discovery is followed by a kind of "courtship" with the hand, culminating in the dominance of mind over hand when the child gets to be about five and a half months of age. In lesser fashion, the child explores other parts of his body during Phase III. Sometime during this period, for example, she discovers her feet, which as far as her eyes are concerned did not exist until this time. In Phase IV and subsequently, she will move on to explorations that presuppose a fairly informed and intimate relationship with her arms and legs and other parts of her body.

This is also the last Phase when babies are predominantly oriented toward those things that are within a yard or so from them. Babies under three and a half months do not spend much time looking across rooms or at scenes out the window.

The final point worth remarking about is the tremendous geniality of the Phase III baby. The only things likely to disturb his marvelous mood are the appearance of teeth, occasional illness, or indigestion.

General Behavior During Phase III

The Phase III baby is likely to be awake at least half of the daytime hours. This is fortunate because he has a great deal to do. While he is doing the various things we will be talking about, he will seem very happy most of the time. He will show this happiness most dramatically in the presence of other people, especially his parents, but he will also exhibit it while playing with toys or simply exercising. For example, if you make use of mirrors and well-designed crib toys, you'll find the Phase III baby occasionally having a delightful time interacting with these devices even when alone.

This particular age range is a period of much physical activity. In fact, such activity becomes characteristic of all of infancy beyond this stage.

Large Muscle Activity

With respect to large muscle activity, you'll find vigorous activity of all the limbs to be a characteristic of Phase III. It is as if the baby is simply delighted to be alive and gets a great deal of pleasure out of sheer exercise of the large muscles (which have only recently been endowed with substantial strength). You'll find the baby practicing new motor skills as they appear. Once he begins to turn his torso from side to side, you'll find that behavior to be a regular feature of his daily waking life. As he first becomes capable of turning over you'll find him working very hard at this skill and enjoying practicing turning from back to stomach and from stomach to back. When he's on his stomach, you'll find him repeatedly lifting his head up and holding it there for increasingly longer periods of time when he scans the world around him.

Small Muscle Activity

With respect to the smaller muscles, physical activity is extraordinarily frequent and interesting in the area of hand-eye activities. Ordinarily Phase III will see the gradual emergence of the capacity to use the hands as reaching tools under the guidance of vision. The child will engage in many kinds of hand activities that lead to this important skill. While she is engaged in bringing her hands together over her midline, or in mutual fingering, or in exploring the clothing she is wearing, or the sheet, or the fabric in the bumper; you'll notice that her concentration of gaze is remarkable. She seems to be thoroughly examining the things she looks at, and there will be an impressive intensity in her gaze.

Interest in Exploration

Another general characteristic of Phase III is an interest in exploration. As an infant learns to use his hands to reach, he is of course exploring. He also explores visually when he is placed prone and rears his head to peer about, or when someone approaches him while he is lying supine, or when he is in an infant seat. In addition to visual explorations, you'll find evidence (as mentioned earlier) of a strong exploratory drive in his experimentation with his own sounds, especially when he has saliva in his mouth. (This behavior is best observed when a child is unaware that you are nearby.)

Another principal form of exploration involves the sense of touch. If you look closely you'll find babies spending a good deal of time exploring how things feel, sometimes while simultaneously watching their hands, other times while looking elsewhere. Exploring through feeling takes place both with the fingers and the mouth. It is very common for held objects to be brought to the mouth and gummed.

In summary, the child of this age spends a great deal of time exercising, practicing motor skills, responding to people to the extent that they are available, exploring the sounds that she herself can make, listening to any sounds that may happen to be nearby, and, in particular, actively exploring anything that is nearby, especially her own body and hands.

The Apparent Interests of the Phase III Baby

The Phase III baby can best be described as a doer, a socializer, and a bon vivant with an absolutely irresistible smile. She is a doer in the sense that she is far more active in all ways than she was earlier. She is a socializer in the sense that she is marvelously responsive. She is a a bon vivant in the sense of seeming to get more out of life than human beings do at just about any other age.

Visual Exploration

During Phase III the baby continues to show an intense interest in the nearby visual world. He will be very involved in looking at and actively exploring everything within reach of his hands and feet and also everything within view, especially if such objects are within a yard or so.

Mastery of New Skills

Another major category of interest is that of mastery of new skills. We've remarked about emerging gross motor skills in the area of torso control, head control, and turning over; the very important sensory motor ability of visually directed reaching is also a focal point for activities. The Phase III child not only is interested in exploring the nearby world, but the process of mastering the skill of reaching per se has a very special power for him.

Socializing

The third major area of obvious interest is in people and socializing in general. It is extraordinarily important for the human infant to firmly establish a relationship with a caring adult. The events of this period of life provide an almost certain guarantee that the baby will not only learn to like the nurturing adults, but also that the nurturing adults will come to feel an extremely powerful affection and responsibility for the baby.

Interest in Body Functions

The fourth area of interest is an apparent sheer delight in physical strength or simple body function. This is a time of life when an interest in gymnastics begins.

Educational Developments During Phase III

In the preceding chapter, I stressed the fact that parents and other childrearers should not be stamped into feeling guilty if they do not take elaborate (and expensive) steps to stimulate the educational development of a child in the first months of life. This remains true for Phase III. I believe that the average environment contains the majority of what children need in order to move ahead properly as learners. My remarks about educational practices should be taken in that light.

It is undoubtably true, however, that the more you know about the details of development, the better you can arrange for at least part of a child's day to be spent in circumstances that mesh with his emerging interests and abilities. My research experience has led me to believe that a child who has spent a fair amount of his second, third, fourth, and fifth months of life engaging in pleasurable and exciting experiences is more likely to be better off educationally than the child who passes the time lying in a crib or sitting in an infant seat and doing nothing more than occasionally looking here and there, listening, or being smiled at.

The Origins of Intelligent Behavior

A baby in Phase III is not yet intelligent according to the common definition of the word. She does not solve problems. She is, however, moving toward being able to solve problems and becoming an intelligent being. The steps she is taking have been outlined in a masterful fashion by Piaget, whose name continues to be mentioned throughout the text as the leading expert on the growth of intelligence.

In Chapter Three we saw how the isolated behaviors of early infancy begin to become coordinated during Phase II. This interrelating process continues during Phase III, and is highlighted by the gradual mastery of the use of the hand under the guidance of the eyes, a behavior focused on extensively by Piaget. This ability ordinarily emerges sometime during the sixth month of life, although recent research has demonstrated that a child who plays with suitably designed crib toys can learn to reach as early as three and a half months of age.

When the child is finally reaching for objects routinely (usually about five and a half to six months of age), he is demonstrating coordination of several systems of behavior. First of all, before he reaches he has to find the object with his eyes. Then he'll move his hand out rather quickly and accurately to where the object is; and in a mature reach, just before the child contacts the object, he will either open his fingers or close them slightly to grasp the object. He may do any number of things with it once he grasps it. Most commonly he will stare at it for awhile. He may also move it back and forth, and twist it about to get different views of it and to see what it feels like in different positions. Another typical behavior is to bring the object to his mouth and gum it.

An additional kind of behavior the child is likely to engage in after she has grasped an object is to bring it closer to her, where her other hand may join the scene and either take the object or feel the object while she holds it with her first hand. This tactile exploration is sometimes accompanied by transfers of the object back and forth from hand to hand.

In Phase III the child engages in more complicated and more focused hand-eye behavior than he did in the first two stages. While he is engaging in other behaviors he is beginning to show increasing interest in the object itself. Phase I and II babies are not terribly interested in the object world per se. From Phase III forward, however, exploration of objects (particularly small ones that can be grabbed, chewed, swung, and batted) becomes an increasingly important occupation for infants.

Emotionality

The four-month-old child is a delighted and delightful creature. The smiling that began at anywhere from two to three months of age is now fully established, and except for those cases where the child is either ill or uncomfortable, smiling lights up her and your time for many hours every day. This is an age that firmly solidifies the baby's hold on a parent's affections. Now, in addition to a broad and irresistable smile and a chronically good mood, babies show two other interesting emotional changes. For the first time you'll hear your baby laugh and giggle. Laughter is not terribly visible in most children until this stage. But sometime during the fourth or fifth month you'll find your baby regularly become excited and actually giggling.

Response to Tickling

Babies usually become ticklish for the first time during Phase III. The fact that you cannot elicit a tickle response from a child before she is about fourteen weeks of age has always intrigued this author. Perhaps it is related to the fact that adults cannot tickle themselves. (Try it if you have never attempted it before.) My guess is that an underlying interesting fact explains both situations. I believe that the effectiveness of the tickle is primarily dependent upon the "ticklee" perceiving that *another person* is producing the stimulation. Therefore, you cannot tickle yourself because you know that you are not another person applying the stimulation. The child younger than about fourteen weeks of age is probably not well enough developed socially to have reached whatever awareness of another is necessary to make the tickle functional.

MOTOR AND SENSORY MOTOR SKILLS

Developing Motor Skills

Sometime during the fourth month of life the child will usually acquire the ability to turn his body up onto his side. This capacity to turn the torso from side to side is followed fairly soon by a second significant motor achievement—the capacity to turn from the back to the stomach position, which appears toward the end of Phase III. Once this ability begins to surface, children practice it repeatedly. This of course is true throughout infancy when it comes to emerging fundamental skills.

Most children can turn from back to stomach by the time they are five- and a half months. Although they will become increasingly capable of turning their torsos over, it will be some weeks before they are capable of pulling themselves up to a sitting posture and sitting unaided. With occasional exceptions most children learn to turn from their stomachs to their backs a week or two after they learn to turn from their backs to their stomachs.

Kicking Behavior

The third motor development worth noting at this point is kicking behavior. By Phase III the leg muscles of the baby have become considerably more substantial than they were earlier; indeed, he'll begin to look more substantial in general. Now, for the first time, his feet are frequently held up off the crib's surface while he lies on his back, whereas in the first two phases his heels usually rested on the crib's surface. In addition, provided that there is pressure against the soles of the feet, the child will get huge enjoyment out of thrusting out powerfully with his legs. This can be demonstrated in either of two ways. You can attempt to get the child to support some of his weight by holding him erect with the soles of his feet touching a table surface or a rug, or your thighs, or you can provide pressure to the soles of his feet while he is lying in his crib. In the first situation you'll find that he can briefly support himself in the upright position. In the second situation you'll find he'll resist that pressure; and, if you hold your hands firmly against his feet, he may push his whole body away by extending his legs. The development of a powerful leg thrust makes good sense of the fact that by nine or ten months of age the child will be pulling himself to a standing posture and moving about while holding onto various supports; shortly thereafter, he'll be walking.

Arm Muscle Development

The Phase III baby's increasing interest in using the large muscles of his legs is paralleled by an interest in using the large muscles of his arms. You'll note that they too become considerably more substantial, and again, if you provide an opportunity for him to exercise them, he will do so and have a great deal of fun in the process.

Developing Sensorimotor Skills

The distinction between sensorimotor and motor skills, while somewhat technical, is worth noting. Sensorimotor skills involve the sensory
systems, such as vision, hearing, and touch, as well as associated mus-
cular activity. Typical motor skills are crawling, climbing, and walking.
Though they involve the senses, their principal component is muscle
control.

Visually Directed Reaching

One of the most vital achievements of Phase III is the mastery of the
use of the hand as a reaching tool under the guidance of the eyes. This
particular skill is very basic for the child. It is through this skill that
much of the familiarity with a child's environment is learned over the
next year or so. Visually directed reaching also plays an important role
in the development of intelligence. The remarkable levels to which
adult human beings develop their facility to use their hands under the
guidance of the eyes set humankind off from most other animals in the
same sense that language and culture do.

Eye-Ear Coordination

Another interesting and important sensory-motor change in the third
phase is the considerable improvement in eye-ear coordination. Right
from birth babies have some very limited skill in localization of sounds,
but during Phase III they routinely become very accurate and reliable
in turning their eyes and body toward the source of a nearby sound.
Like most of the earlier skills they have shown, this is a reflexlike
behavior. You can expect a child in Phase III, unless preoccupied or
very sleepy, to turn quickly and accurately to the source of any nearby
sound, even those that aren't terribly loud. The importance of this new
behavior is surprisingly great, because it enables us to easily screen for
mild to moderate hearing losses beginning at about age fourteen to
sixteen weeks. Being able to identify this very common threat to good
hearing (from routine respiratory ailments and allergic reactions) has
turned out to be a development of extraordinary significance. More
about this subject will be discussed in the section recommending
childrearing practices.

Touch

A third major area of sensory-motor skill involves touch. Remember,
during most of Phases I and II, that the child's hands were mostly

fisted. Fisted hands prevent exploration of the surfaces of objects. Once the child gets into Phase III he acquires the use of his fingers for such explorations, and from then on he will use his fingers as well as his mouth and eyes to explore the different textures, hardnesses, and shapes of materials and objects within reach.

Sociability

We've already emphasized the marvelous mood state of the Phase III infant. This mood state cannot help but make life very pleasant for parents, particularly parents of firstborn children. As noted earlier, a child's spectacular smile plays a large role in cementing the close affectional tie with her primary caretaker. If her cries of discomfort, or delight, are responded to often and promptly, she will get used to that consequence of her own vocalization. If on the other hand she is left to cry in discomfort repeatedly and for long periods of time, she will get used to that state of affairs as well. Babies are remarkably adaptable in this regard. Infants I worked with in a state institution began to cry less and less during Phase III to the point where, by the time they were six or seven months of age, they cried rarely. On the surface that situation would seem a desirable state of affairs. In fact, however, those children had learned that the payoff for crying was only fatigue; for me there are few sadder stories that can be told.

CAPTURING ADULT ATTENTION: THE EMERGENCE OF INTENTIONAL CRYING

One set of fundamental social skills that we've found to be a sign of very good development in three- to six-year-old children is a collection of socially acceptable behaviors for getting and holding the attention of another person, particularly an adult. A fascinating development becomes observable during Phase III in respect to the emergence of the capacity to get attention and, perhaps more importantly, in respect to the early signs of spoiling in young children. Earlier we described an inevitable cycle of experience that all infants undergo. That cycle started with feelings of distress from any of several causes. That distress is followed routinely by the baby's cry. That cry, given a typical or an average environment, is heard by an older person who more often than not will respond by attempting to make the baby more comfortable. Since such episodes of distress are very numerous during the first months of life, and since babies for some reason not fully understood are usually comforted by being picked up and handled and moved gently through space—even when the cause of the distress has not been identified or removed—infants gradually build up large quantities of experience that begin with distress and fairly soon thereafter are followed by the reduction of that distress. Although clearly not able yet to truly understand what is happening, babies do learn (at some primitive level) from these experiences. They learn to associate the sight, the smell, the sound, and the feel of people who regularly comfort them with the experience of feeling better. A remarkable and very important shift takes place in respect to crying during Phase III. Whereas initially and throughout Phases I and II babies have cried solely as a response to discomfort, toward the end of Phase III a second important reason for crying will surface. That second reason is to bring an adult into their company and hopefully be picked up and cuddled by that adult. That second use of the cry constitutes the emergence of *intentionality* in behavior. Put another way, children under three to four months of age cry primarily when undergoing physical distress. Children in Phase III begin also to cry for attention.

Another relevant consideration in this regard is that the Phase III child, while increasingly able to be comfortable when upright and full of curiosity about the world, is unable to move out on her own and find interesting things to do. The cry is one of few tools they have that can be used to bring an older person to them for either holding or socializing.

Regarding the roots of spoiling, some twenty-three-week-old children cry out—in order to be picked up and held—at a rate that is not only mildly inconvenient but is much higher than other children. On balance, however, most professionals would rather see a Phase III infant cry too much for attention than cry too little and risk inadequate attention during the first few months of life. Understanding this early process helps parents to deal with and indeed minimize sleep problems, which very commonly surface during the second half of the first year of life.

Language

Very often parents of babies in Phase III become delighted to learn that their child apparently understands her own name. Sometime during the fourth month of life parents, in their routine interchanges with their child, may call her by her name and, unlike earlier stages, the baby rather promptly turns, looks toward them, and smiles. Once a parent experiences this kind of delightful response from the child, it is easy to see why they begin to indulge in this activity fairly frequently: it's great fun. The fact is, however, that the baby is not showing name recognition, but rather that she has good hearing and ordinary eye-ear reflex behavior. Remember earlier we pointed out that during Phase III infants will turn routinely and promptly under most circumstances to any sound in their nearby world. That's what is happening when a four- or four-and-a-half-month-old baby turns toward her parents when her name is called. To prove this, you can call the baby by any name you choose and the child will respond in exactly the same manner. Understanding the meaning of the first words will surface fairly soon, usually at about eight to ten months of age. These understandings are routinely tested in babies of that age by offering them a variety of familiar objects and then asking them to orient toward one or another, thereby giving them the chance to make a mistake.

There is therefore no appreciable understanding of language in the mind of a Phase III baby as yet. There is progress, however, in related areas. During the fourth month of life a baby will begin to play with sound, especially in connection with the sounds he makes with saliva. You may notice when passing his crib that he is repeating small sounds to himself in what seems like experimental fashion. These delightful episodes are common in the fourth month of life and will persist. A more subtle development that is likely to be taking place in the area of language has to do with the regular association of the voice of the primary caretaker with his or her presence. Ordinarily when a mother interacts with her baby, whether it is to feed, comfort him, change his diapers, or bathe him, she is likely to both smile and speak to him. Such behavior along with the aforementioned response to discomfort leads to a strong association between the parent's physical appearance, the sound of the parent's voice, and the feeling of being comforted. The child at the same time is learning to identify the parents' voices, regardless of the words they use, through their particular sound qualities. Research has shown that by four to five months of age a parent's voice can be identified from among other voices by most babies and is a very powerful evoker of smiles and attention from the baby.

RECOMMENDED CHILDREARING PRACTICES

Giving the Infant a Feeling of Being Loved and Cared for

As in Phases I and II, I suggest you only let a child cry for a long period of time if you simply cannot avoid it. If crying persists, try to determine what is wrong and remedy the situation, comforting the baby as well as you can. By all means use a pacifier if it helps. In addition to routine prompt attention to your child's distress, I would strongly urge you to play with your child regularly and enjoy her. Provide as many experiences with your child in which you are simply having a good time. While you are doing so be demonstrative, be affectionate, and talk a lot, especially about what the baby is paying attention to at the moment. It may seem unnecessary to advise parents to be demonstrative with their own baby, but some people have ambiguous feelings along these lines. We must also reinforce the notion of acting naturally and warmly with your child.

Helping the Infant to Develop Specific Skills

To reiterate an often-stressed conviction, even if a parent pays little or no attention to specific skill development in the first six months of life, most of these skills of early infancy will appear anyway, and pretty much on time. Nevertheless, I do feel that the most suitable early experiences for a child are those that are relevant to his naturally emerging skills. If you learn what those are, and can provide opportunities for them to function, on balance, a child's educational development will proceed better and his zest for life will increase. Bear in mind, however, that if visually directed reaching (a major specific skill) does not manifest itself exactly on schedule, for example, there is no reason to become concerned. Furthermore, if the child begins to reach two or three months before most children, no great significance should be attached to that event either. The story of early learning is more complex than that.

Intelligence

The development of the foundations of intelligence may be encouraged during Phase III by giving a child a variety of things to look at and to handle. You can accomplish this first goal by supplying your infant with good crib toys, moving him about the house in an infant seat as you work, and taking him for outings. This does not mean that he needs repeated changes of scenery, but you should avoid leaving him in a playpen or in a crib for six or seven hours a day.

Perhaps more important to the development of the child's mind in Phase III is having appropriate nearby objects that she can examine and handle. Not only is she likely to acquire hand-eye abilities a bit sooner, but more important, she'll be feeding her curiosity in a natural and unquestionably beneficial manner.

An important warning on infant seats: Many different types of infant seats are commercially available; some considerably better than others. Infants are perfectly capable of limited control over their torsos during Phase III. But you must make sure of two things in connection with an infant seat. First, make sure the one you use is well-made, that is, has a low center of gravity, is sturdy, and unlikely to tip over easily. Second, never leave a Phase III baby in an infant seat that is any higher than a few inches above the floor without constant supervision. More information about materials for this age will be presented in the section on recommended materials.

Emotionality

You can enlarge the plesasure your child has in life, and his tendency to laugh and enjoy himself, through natural and affectionate play. It is also wonderful for you. Do it!

Motor and Sensorimotor Skills

The caretaker's main job here is to avoid impeding development. Swaddling a child, for example, or insisting that he stay on his back, if done consistently, may get in the way of his practicing headrearing, torso movements, leg and arm thrusts, turning over, and visually directed reaching. Crib toys that promote skill development will be discussed in the recommended-material section.

Social Skills

When your baby cries I urge you to respond often and as quickly as you can in the manner described earlier. In fact, you should make it a habit to respond to your child's coos and gurgles as well. She will gradually learn to associate making noise with your arrival and your presence, and with pleasure—or at least with reduction of discomfort.

Language

It is important to get into the habit of talking to the baby, particularly about what he is oriented to at the moment. This behavior on the part of the parent intensifies the naturally growing interest in any kind of sound, including language, and is a very desirable practice for parents to acquire, increasing the likelihood that when true language learning begins, the parent's role will be as effective as possible.

ENCOURAGING INTEREST IN THE OUTSIDE WORLD (CURIOSITY)

If you focus on specific skill developments, and if you get into the habit of talking a lot to your child about what he seems to be attending to at the moment, you'll find that the child's natural curiosity will be subtly enhanced and enlarged.

Warning: The Special Importance of Monitoring Hearing Ability

Only within the last decade has it become clear that a surprisingly large number of otherwise normal infants suffer significant delays in development because of repeated episodes of mild to moderate hearing loss during infancy. The problem seems to stem primarily from two sources: the infant's limited capacity to resist infections, and the susceptibility of many infants to allergies. It has been reliably estimated that repeated episodes of otitis media with associated fluid in the middle ear are suffered by anywhere from a quarter to a third of all infants in the United States. That percentage can be markedly higher in areas where pollen counts are very high at certain times of the year. Sadly, such repeated minor threats to the baby's physical health often constitute substantial threats to the child's learning process. From the third month of life on children begin to exhibit substantial interest in sounds, which of course gradually leads to their ability to acquire language. That ability underlies not only learning success later in life but also early developments in language and, interestingly, in social skills. We do, after all, teach our babies about relating to other people largely through our spoken words.

Unfortunately, the problem of temporary hearing losses due to infections and fluids in the hearing system is not always dealt with well by the medical profession. If a child is born with a profound impairment, that situation is rather quickly noticed, if not by the physician then certainly by lay people who spend any time with such a baby. Children with losses above 50 to 60 decibels (sound units) are considered seriously impaired, and the impairment very rarely goes unnoticed for more than a few weeks. Early identification and treatment takes place even with families with minimally adequate health care. Unfortunately, however, children with mild to moderate losses are far more numerous and are much less likely to be identified and treated during the first years of life. Many parents have told me with anguish about their children who were not diagnosed as hearing impaired until they were six or seven years of age, in spite of regular medical attention from birth. Most commonly one or both parents had suspected a hearing problem and had brought their suspicions to the attention of their pediatrician or general practitioner, who advised them not to worry about it, usually with an explanation like this: "Infants behave rather strangely in a wide variety of ways, and in most cases the behavior means nothing at all. There's no need to be unduly alarmed. Pay no attention to it, the child will grow out of it." Such situations are anathema to pediatric speech and hearing specialists, but they are not rare. Do not be surprised if you run into the same sort of response yourself; it happens every day. Even in our current model program in Missouri, which has the support of the head of the state pediatric association, we still have trouble getting full cooperation from some of the pediatricians our families deal with.

With the innate tendency of the normal-hearing child—from about fourteen weeks and on—to turn accurately toward any source of nearby sound, we have a valuable tool for early screening. Just about anyone can apply these screening procedures.

How to Screen for Mild
to Moderate Hearing Loss
in Children from Fourteen Weeks and up

When the child is in a comfortable state, awake and not intensely engaged in an activity, call to her in a normal voice, from out of sight, six to ten feet away. The baby should, in less than a minute, pause and turn accurately toward the source of sound. A few moments later reinitiate the activity from a different position, again from six to ten feet away and out of sight. Once again the baby should respond in the same fashion. If you call to the baby four times in this manner from different positions and the baby responds reliably those four times, you will have then set up a simple game orientation in the baby's mind. Next, repeat the entire procedure, but this time whispering the baby's name rather than using normal voice tones. Once again, the infant over fourteen weeks old should respond in the same manner. If she doesn't, you should not run off to a hearing specialist or get alarmed. The behavior of babies is variable enough that, on any given occasion, they may not perform the way you expect them to. Repeat the procedure later in the day and on the following day. If on three or four occasions the baby doesn't react appropriately, refer the whole situation to your medical practitioner. If your medical practitioner refers you to a pediatric audiologist for an audiometric examination, you're in good shape. All major hospitals either have such a person on staff or can refer you to one. Your medical practitioner may, however, not act this way. He may try to reassure you that there is nothing worth being concerned about. He's very likely to tell you that middle-ear problems are very common during infancy, that they are not life-threatening and, especially, if not accompanied by a high fever, likely to disappear in a matter of days. One reason why medical practitioners respond this way is because much that a healthy baby does in the first months of life is very disconcerting, especially to first-time parents. After all, our society does not routinely prepare or support first-time parents for this vital responsibility of caring for a new child, and so anxiety about the numerous and worrisome but routine behaviors of babies is a normal state of mind. If medical practitioners did not calm and reassure parents, especially first-timers, the consequences would often be chronically anxious and somewhat debilitated parents. In addition, it is true that fluid in the middle ear, especially if not accompanied by infections, is rarely an indicator of a damaging illness. Indeed there is ongoing disagreement among medical practitioners on whether to actively attack such conditions, using antibiotics and the familiar small pressure-equalizer tubes surgically inserted into the ear drum. That controversy remains unresolved, but the fact of the matter is that repeated middle-ear problems very often are accompanied by a diminished capacity to hear well. A child who has repeated middle-ear infections or allergic reactions and associated congestion is living with a learning obstacle of a potentially serious nature. We strongly urge all parents to insist on treating this sort of condition the same way that a medical practitioner would treat a fever: medical practitioners don't tell anxious parents that babies will outgrow fevers. From an educational standpoint, we don't think medical practitioners should be telling parents not to be concerned about repeated middle-ear problems.

If you do not have a cooperative medical practitioner in this kind of a situation, we suggest that you ask your practitioner if he would mind if you got a second opinion. If he doesn't, you should then seek out the services of a specialist, in this case a pediatric audiologist available through any sizable hospital. *Few things a parent can do are more important to assure that a new child gets off to a very good start in life than to watch carefully for repeated middle-ear problems; they must seek medical treatment for the infant promptly.*

RECOMMENDED MATERIALS FOR PHASE III BABIES

Mirrors

As noted earlier, babies first come to be interested in mirrors at about six to seven weeks of age. From earlier remarks you know that babies are most intrigued by that portion of the face between the tip of the nose and the top of the head. In addition, their own face has a special quality of attractiveness for them because, unlike the face of someone else, the image of their own face reflected in a mirror will move in a manner determined by their own movements. For these reasons a properly placed mirror is very appealing to the Phase III baby.

A reasonably good stainless steel mirror, a minimum of four inches in diameter and a maximum of six, is ideal. Most of all, remember that the mirror should be placed approximately seven inches from the baby's eyes. A mirror placed much more than seven inches away will be less effective because the target the baby sees in a mirror is twice as far away from his eyes as the distance to the mirror. In other words, if you place the mirror seven inches from the baby's eyes, he will see the reflection of his face apparently fourteen inches from his eyes.

Objects more than a foot and a half away from a young baby are less likely to attract and hold her interest during Phase III. A mirror positioned over a crib gives a baby something interesting to look at from time to time. It may be easier to fasten if you place it to the far right or the far left of the baby, because you can use the side of the crib as an anchor. Suitably placed, a mirror can also be a useful device at diaper time.

Infant Seats

A second kind of device suitable for use at this time is an infant seat. We have already described the major safety factors to be concerned with when selecting an infant seat. (See p. 50.) Again, a reminder that babies in Phase III can occasionally fall from infant seats, so care must be exercised. Note also that the delightful social interchanges characteristic of Phase III—because of the baby's tremendous reponsiveness and chronically happy mood—are facilitated by placing the baby in a nearby infant seat.

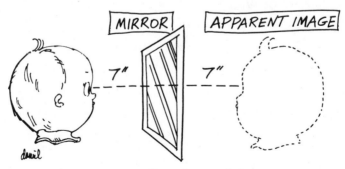

Locating a mirror for a Phase III baby

Crib Toys

Phase III infants will continue to enjoy batting and feeling the firmly mounted, sturdy objects they interacted with in Phase II. Older Phase III infants, who have learned to reach, enjoy moving onto the next stage of hand-eye activity, which is making simple things happen by using their hands as tools. In some of the experimental materials that we created, we used a simple windmill device that would spin when the baby pulled on the handle, and this device was very popular with new reachers. Unfortunately, no currently available toys for this age include features quite like this.

There are many crib toys currently on the market, but only a few are recommendable. The Fisher-Price Play Gym at about ten dollars is basically a good product, but it has one weakness—the objects that the child is supposed to reach for and bat, swing away from the baby too easily. You must figure out a safe way to prevent them from rotating so that they remain in place. Masking tape, strategically placed, works fine. I would even recommend using some epoxy cement or some other adhesive to fasten the swinging arms.

Shelcore, a fairly new company to the infant toy business, makes a good gym, as does Johnson & Johnson. For years there has been available a simple cradle gym, selling for under five dollars, that is as good as any of the ten- to twelve-dollar items just mentioned. It does have one weakness, however, in that several of the items are attached with short lengths of string. String is not advisable for such toys because it is frustrating to the child newly acquiring skills in the use of his hands.

Another point to make about crib gyms is in reference to the Semper Line from Sweden. Semper is to Sweden what Mattel is to the United States—a giant company that makes good-quality materials. It has had a line of crib toys on the market for about a decade; very expensive, they come embellished with accessories and rhetoric. The rhetoric will have you believe they are well worth the $150 or so that you can end up spending for all the various attachments. That simply is

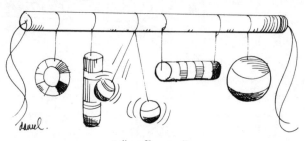

A "cradle gym"

not true. Basically, they do no more in the way of providing pleasure for a baby than the $10 Fisher-Price or the $9 Johnson & Johnson "Piglet" toy. One of their attachments is a reasonably good mirror, but that can be obtained for less money elsewhere as well.

One last comment about crib gyms. The Ambi Toy Company of Holland makes a crib gym they call the "Baby Trainer." This toy is a bit more expensive than the others, selling generally for about twenty dollars, but it is definitely a good investment and is especially well made.

Toys that Involve Leg Action

There are basically two kinds of toys involving leg action available for children in Phase III. One is a kick toy, a toy that can be positioned in the crib so that a baby can practice leg extensions on it in safety. You'll find that your Phase III baby will enjoy this very much. Several years ago there were one or two such toys available; I have not seen many recently, but this is a fast-moving field and they may surface at any time.

The second toy worth consideration is a walker. Over the last year or so there have been several warnings issued about walkers. They have tended to give the toy an undeservedly bad name. There have been accidents attributed to walkers, and some specialists in orthopedics are inclined to think that they interfere with normal learning-to-walk patterns. In every instance these warnings have applied to children over seven months of age. I believe that walkers can serve a very useful function for children from about four months on up to about seven months, and that thereafter they should not be used. Let me explain why.

The Phase III baby has powerful leg muscles and very much enjoys using them. She has an enormous amount of curiosity and can see and hear across the room. Unfortunately, she cannot move around on her own yet. Nor will she be able to for several months. The average age of the onset of crawling is approximately seven to seven and a half months. The result is that from about four months on the baby, when in an upright orientation, spends a lot of time interested in first-hand explorations but is unable to engage in them unless somebody keeps changing the child's immediate surroundings. A well-designed walker changes all that. By well-designed, I mean one that has a low center of gravity and an adjustable distance between the floor and the child's body, and has no features that might pinch small fingers. Babies, when placed in such a device, will soon feel the pressure on the soles of their feet and extend their legs. For the first week or two you'll find the four-to five-month-old baby pushing herself backwards. Sooner or later she will learn to lean forward before she extends her legs and the result will be forward motion.

Babies very much enjoy both the exercise such a walker provides for their leg muscles and the opportunity to move around to different parts of the room, bringing themselves close to the front of the dishwasher, the leg of a table, and the innumerable places that they have only been able to see from a distance.

To be sure, a baby in a walker can more easily get into danger than the baby who does not have access to such a piece of equipment. Ordinarily we talk about danger and childhood accidents from the time a baby is about seven months old, because that's the point from which they can start to move about on their own. The younger baby in a walker is immediately subject to the same danger because of the mobility she gains. Babies can, for example, move over to a door and start to examine the hinges. Someone else may come along and swing that door, with bruised or crushed fingers as a consequence. And, indeed, they can get into many other sorts of trouble. One should not underestimate the number and seriousness of potential accidents from the use of a walker with four- to seven-month-old children. Neverthe-

A kick toy

less, if you are willing to provide these experiences *always under constant, and I mean constant, supervision*, they will make sense developmentally for the baby, and the baby will certainly have an enjoyable time.

MATERIALS NOT RECOMMENDED FOR PHASE III BABIES

I advise parents to be extremely suspicious of many of the so-called "educational" infant toys currently in vogue. This warning applies even to playthings endorsed by major manufacturers and leading authorities in child development. One symptom of the lack of genuine professionalism in the toy industry is the marketing of a toy for one age group when it is really appropriate for another. Manufacturers are often unaware of the play value of their various toys. There are direct-mail campaigns that offer an "education toy of the month" for infants. There are automated and illuminated "instructional" cribs for sale for several hundred dollars. There even used to be ridiculous crib gyms that featured live fish (in a sealed plastic pouch) for the baby to explore with her eyes.

It is fair to say, however, that over the last five or six years the quality of toys available for very young infants has improved substantially. Fisher-Price Company, for example, has been upgrading its materials, which have always been sturdy but are now more accurately designed from an educational perspective. Johnson & Johnson toys are considerably better than most of what has been available up until recently. I cannot, however, give them a blanket endorsement, because quite a number of their toys are inferior.

My principal point is simply to warn you about the hard sell and oversell. They are natural byproducts of the increased interest in early learning, especially among literate parents, and are a continuing problem in the field.

BEHAVIORS THAT SIGNAL THE ONSET OF PHASE IV

Visually Directed Reaching

One of the more obvious landmarks signaling the emergence of Phase IV is the mastery of the use of the hand to reach for seen objects. This fundamental skill typically appears at approximately twenty-three weeks, give or take a few weeks. In our research on this topic we found that reaching ability can emerge as early as age fourteen weeks, given experience with certain kinds of crib materials. There is, however, no reason to be concerned (educationally or for any other reason) if reaching does not appear before six months.

Turning Over

The second landmark ability to look for is facility in turning the body from supine (on the back) to prone (on the stomach) and vice versa. As mentioned earlier, turning from the back to the stomach usually occurs first, followed by turning from the stomach to the back a few weeks later. It is also true that babies will occasionally manage to turn over much earlier in the game, especially when they are very angry. The powerful leg thrustings that accompany rage in the very young infant will sometimes inadvertently result in a flip from back to stomach.

CHAPTER FIVE

Phase IV:

Twenty-Three Weeks to Eight Months

GENERAL REMARKS

Phase IV is the final prelocomotive period of life. The baby is, in many ways, much abler than at birth. He has greater command of his body, and his eyes and ears function on a par with those of a typical young adult. In addition, most babies at this stage can turn their bodies from back to stomach and vice versa at will.

Although the baby now has significant control over his head movements, can use his hands to reach for objects under the guidance of his eyes, can localize sounds, and can turn his body back and forth, he still cannot do one very important thing: he cannot move about on his own. If left on a rug in the middle of a room, for example, he is not able to propel his body any distance through space. (There are exceptions to this statement. Some babies acquire a precocious ability to get from place to place by rolling over and over; and of course when extremely angry some Phase IV babies are able on occasion to propel themselves when supine by digging their heels into the surface they are lying on and thrusting powerfully with their legs.) The eyes, which for the first few months of life were only oriented toward objects within a few feet, are now more inclined to attend to objects several feet away. Particularly if the baby spends more and more time in an upright position (in an infant seat or some substitute), the field of view is now considerably more extensive than it was.

In a sense, the Phase IV baby is faced with a situation parallel to that of the three-month-old baby who has a mobile over his crib that can be looked at but cannot be reached. He can see and is attracted to many things, but he cannot do as much as he would like to. The result seems to be a naturally frustrating situation. Often, toward the end of Phase IV he will overcome one major handicap. On his own, he will be able to assume and maintain an upright position. He will also overcome his other major handicap: He will acquire the ability to move about through crawling or some similar motor ability (scooting or dragging himself forward with his arms). As we have studied children over the last several years and have seen the remarkable behavior of most of them from the point they started to crawl, it has become more interesting to speculate on how much a child's curiosity is being primed in the weeks just prior to the onset of crawling. Although there is no firm evidence on the topic, I suspect that there is an interesting and important relationship between the building up of curiosity during Phase III and IV and the opportunity to satisfy it as the child first begins to move about and explore more distant objects.

The result of this state of affairs is that Phase IV is a rather unusual period of infancy in several important ways. The normal baby at this age has a very deep and powerful desire to learn about the world around her. With her newly expanded capacity to see and hear things at a distance, she would love to get up close to the many places around her, but she can't do it on her own. Occupying a baby during this time is therefore a rather difficult task for parents unless a walker is utilized (and remember the warnings about important dangers). Toys, for example, all have to be brought to the baby. Since to date there are no toys or other materials that can keep such a baby occupied for long stretches of time, the result is that for most Phase IV babies, time hangs heavy on their hands. Because the Phase IV baby is now quite skillful at calling for attention and very much enjoys that attention—especially when picked up and held—many parents find themselves carrying their now fairly heavy infant quite a bit during the day.

My colleagues and I have characterized this particular phase as "the lull before the storm." We regularly remind parents we work with that life will change dramatically as soon as the baby acquires the ability to move about on his own. Phase IV then is an excellent time for parents to pause in their childrearing and consider what is coming in the balance of the very important first three years, to prepare themselves for the exciting events that will happen soon. Also worthy of note, some normal children will not begin to move about on their own at the most common age of seven to eight months, but will only do so several months later. Should you be in that situation, you'll find living with your child more of a strain than if the baby does start to move about at the more typical time. To avoid overattachment by a baby who does not begin to crawl by seven or eight months, the walker is especially valuable.

GENERAL BEHAVIOR DURING PHASE IV

Phase IV, like Phase III, is usually a comparatively easy time for parents. There is a general continuation of chronic good humor in most children throughout the age of five-and-a-half to eight months. My advice to you is to enjoy it while you can, because when the child acquires the ability to move about, the situation is going to change! You will find considerably more stress associated with rearing a baby in the months to follow, indeed, in the year that follows this particular stage.

Small Object Play

What kind of a baby do we have at this time aside from her chronically good mood state? Hands and eyes are still the center of the child's behavior. Bear in mind that the child is still physically handicapped in the sense that she cannot move about. Yet she does have a good deal of interest in exploring her world.

If you watch a Phase IV child closely, you'll observe all sorts of things going on in connection with her hands and eyes. The child will be spending more and more time in an upright position. Occasionally, while she waits for you (as you prepare food, for example), you may provide her with small toys or other objects to play with. This is the age when children start showing a great deal of interest in dropping and/or throwing small objects to the floor as soon as they are placed within reach. It is also the age when infants begin to study the consequences of banging objects against different surfaces. We will talk more about this particular collection of behaviors in the section on intellectual development. Suffice it to say that small object play is a key activity at this stage.

Fascination with Small Particles

A related kind of activity, which is characteristic of this age range, is a special interest in very small particles. Sometime around six months of age you should start looking for special staring behavior, directed at little crumbs and other very small objects on the surface before an upright child. It is a rather strange-appearing behavior, probably related to the development of the fine, detailed vision that children normally acquire in its final form at this stage of life. This very strong visual interest in small particles has been explored in some very interesting research studies. In one test, ball bearings of various sizes, ranging from as little as one-sixteenth of an inch in diameter up to one-quarter inch, were used to attract the attention of seven- and eight-month-old babies in the following ingenious way. Since the objects could easily be swallowed by the infants, the experimenter placed some of them in a box with a clear glass top. He held a powerful magnet beneath the box so that he could move a metal ball by moving the magnet around beneath the box. If the ball was a quarter of an inch in size, most babies were perfectly capable of seeing it and, because of their special interest in small particles, tended to follow it with their eyes as it was moved about. As the size of the ball used was reduced, the point was eventually reached at which the baby would not follow the target visually or attempt to reach for it with his fingers; and at that point the examiner concluded that the limits of the child's visual discrimination had been reached.

Concern with Motor Activity

Another general characteristic of the Phase IV child is interest in physical exercise. Devotion to motor activity, and especially activity that uses newly emerging motor skills, remains typical of the entire early childhood period right on through the preschool years. We will examine the educational implications of this interest in later chapters. It is, of course, this deep, universal, natural tendency that underlies the success of the newly created infant exercise programs that have become so popular around the country. Many such programs promise a great deal to parents, indeed, overpromise in our judgment. Nevertheless, those operated by reasonable, caring people can indeed provide hours of genuine and appropriate pleasure to parents and infants.

Arm and Leg Exercise

During Phase IV the infant's pleasure in exercising her leg muscles continues. It is this behavior that of course underlies the effectiveness of a properly designed walker. It is also this same natural behavior that underlies the enjoyment infants find in jumping devices; but we do not recommend them. The kind of device we refer to consists ordinarily of a canvas seat suspended by a support that includes a spring and is hung from an overhead support fastened to a sturdy timber or a door jamb. Although it is unquestionably true that babies at this age get a great deal of pleasure out of jumping with vigor in such equipment, our associates in pediatric orthopedics have warned us that it is far too easy for various degrees of injury to growing bone joints to result from such activity. We would urge you to consult your family physician before you consider using such a device. These objections do not apply to the kind of jumping equipment that sits on the floor, but only to the previously·described devices.

In addition to leg thrusts, you will find a tendency of the Phase IV baby to use her newly developed arm muscles for hard physical activity to the extent that the opportunities present themselves. In our experimental materials we devised a trapeze arrangement that hung over the supine baby, which she could use to pull on with great force whenever she was so inclined. We unfortunately do not know of any such equipment currently available.

Turning Over

As noted earlier, another emerging motor ability in Phase IV is the capacity to turn from back to stomach and back again. We have found children practicing this skill repeatedly during this ten-week period. Also, a reminder that an occasional infant in Phase IV will use this newfound torso control to move quite some distance by rolling his body over and over in one direction.

Sitting Unaided

The next motor skill to emerge during this period is the achievement and maintenance of the sitting posture without assistance. You can expect children to begin practicing this particular skill sometime after they reach six months of age. By the time they are seven months, most children should be able to sit unaided, although others do not achieve this ability until many weeks later.[1]

Preoccupation with Sound

Another characteristic of children of this age is a growing interest in the world of sound. The same interest shown by the Phase III baby in the sounds he produces, especially the ones using his own saliva, continues to grow in Phase IV. This involvement with sound is a prelude to the beginnings of true language learning, a characteristic of the Phase V child.

---

[1] Although generally we expect children to begin to crawl sometime from seven-and-a-half to eight months of age, it is quite possible that you will find your Phase IV baby starting to move about on the floor even sooner. Indeed, it is not unheard of for babies to be moving about by six months, and walking shortly after eight months of age.

THE APPARENT INTERESTS OF
THE PHASE IV CHILD

New Motor Skills:
Testing Their Effect on Objects

There seems to be a four-step process with respect to the amount of interest a child has in small objects. The first step is characterized by no interest whatsoever in such objects; this is the condition of the new-born child. As we have seen, if you place a rattle in her hand, the newborn may clasp it (if you are skillful at prying open fingers). Also, she will look briefly at certain targets that are shown to her. By and large, however, that interest is short-lived.

The second step of the process begins when the infant is about eight to ten weeks old and is revealed in more sustained visual examinations. These examinations are made possible by the dramatic improvements in visions skills toward the end of the second month of life. The Phase II baby will look at his own fist or a mobile, even though his interest is confined to staring behavior.

The third step of the process is a transitional phase, during which the child's newly acquired motor skills are being tried out on objects. Now the focus of the child shifts from the motor act itself (for example, reaching for objects and batting them) to the "effect" of that motor act on objects. A good example of this particular kind of divided interest between the motor act and the object in question is what occurs when a six-month-old baby repeatedly drops things over the edge of a high-chair tray and watches what happens to these objects as they fall.

The fourth step of the process, starting at about eight months and continuing for several months, is one in which the motor act (reaching, batting, banging, releasing, etc.) is now well within the ability of the child, and therefore is accomplished rather quickly and indeed taken for granted. Now the concentration is on the "characteristics" of the object. More about this fourth step in our discussion of Phase V.

The Phase IV baby is in step three. He is especially interested in the effects of his newly acquired motor skills—hence the various dropping, throwing, and banging actions that he displays with objects. Also at this time you'll find that on occasion the child will become interested in the effect he can create by using his feet under visual control, although opportunities for coordinated eye-foot play, of course, are much less common than eye-hand control. During the early stages of this transitional interest in objects, the child's interest in the patterns of movement of objects will be limited to the beginnings of the movements. That is, if the child begins to drop an object off the highchair tray, she is not likely to look over the edge and follow the movement of the object all the way to the floor and through a bounce. She is much more likely to simply study the releasing act and the beginnings of the fall of the object. As the weeks go by, looking closely you will notice her direction of gaze moves to watch the complete path of fall of the object.

People and Affectionate Interchanges

Babies are very special at this point in life, and especially in the first two-thirds of this phase seem to be pleasantly oriented to just about anyone. All members of the nuclear family will be especially favored with frequent and easy smiling. During the first half of Phase IV you can expect your baby to be a "hale fellow well met." It appears that anyone who spends a lot of time with a Phase IV baby will be inclined to fall in love with him. From a biological standpoint, this reality makes very good sense. After Phase IV, babies become far more troublesome and difficult (at times) to live with. It is of fundamental importance that some older person fall *intensely* in love with that baby before the baby becomes a crawler. Toward the end of Phase IV, however, very often a dramatic change takes place. That previously incredibly agreeable, smily, ticklish, giggly, and beautiful creature may very well abruptly reject nonnuclear family members who try to get close to him. (More about that a bit later.)

Over and above the simple responsiveness when somebody tries to elicit a smile from the early Phase IV child is the genuine pleasure she seems to get in prolonging play with adults. Children of this age are inclined to giggle a lot and really enjoy exchanging smiles and sounds with their parents. This is the time when you can begin to play social games with children, and, unless they are terribly hungry or uncomfortable for some other reason, they will be very responsive. As noted earlier, tickling around the chest and under the arms will very often produce gales of laughter. Again, I think this phenomenon is symptomatic of the tremendous importance of a solid relationship with an adult figure in the first years of life.

Stranger Anxiety

It is very possible that as early as six months of age you will see a dramatic shift in a baby's social behavior. This change, called "stranger anxiety," has been noted for many years in the research literature. In stranger anxiety, people other than members of the immediate family are suddenly reacted to with hesitation and then fear, no longer with the great big smile of only a few weeks or even days earlier. Recent research, however, has tended to cast some doubt on the universality of this kind of behavior. Indeed, it turns out that some normal children will move right through the balance of the first years of life, never showing fear and displeasure reactions to close contact by nonnuclear family members. This kind of behavior, however, is clearly not typical. Probably no more than one baby in four or five fails to demonstrate through dramatic rejections of everybody but immediate family that he or she has chosen who they will attach to in this once-in-a-lifetime process during the first two years of life.

Sounds

Phase IV is a time when children are increasingly interested in sounds, both those made by the people with whom they interact and those they produce themselves. This is a good period to activate a tape recorder near the baby's crib early in the morning, or any other time of the day when the child is likely to be awake and content. There is a delightful quality to the baby's first explorations with sound.[2]

At the beginning of Phase IV the baby will respond to sounds, but will not understand the meaning of any words. Toward the end of Phase IV, however, she will truly begin to respond selectively to a few simple words. The first words in a baby's vocabulary are almost always the same for babies who have English as a first language. Those first words predictably feature *Mother* (or some variation), *Daddy, bye-bye,* and *baby.* In the first half of this phase, however, there is no significant evidence of interest in the words per se, but there is a good deal of activity on the part of the baby in regard to her own gurgling and the simple sounds that you can make in interplay with her. You will notice in particular that when the baby has saliva in her mouth she can make sounds that are somewhat different than her ordinary sounds. She seems to enjoy playing with the sounds (making them and varying their characteristics), either alone or with another person. One of the most pleasant experiences new parents have with their first child is listening in on their child playing by herself with these sounds.

---

[2] If the child sees you he will forget his solitary play; there is nothing more interesting to him than to look at and exchange pleasantries with you. The human face, particularly that of the parents, is at this point an extremely powerful attraction for most babies.

PRACTICING MOTOR SKILLS

Reaching

As we have seen, most babies have mastered the use of the hand for reaching by the beginning of Phase IV. Once that skill comes in, and at least for the first half of Phase IV, you can expect the average baby to reach repeatedly for anything within reach. Babies of this age do not reach out for objects that are five feet away, even if they are large and attractive, nor do they reach for objects that are one inch from the eyeball. But offer a baby who is lying on his back or sitting in an infant seat anything graspable, and if that object is from three to eight inches away, and easily seen, you will find that in most instances he will reach for it. Reaching is important to a child for many reasons. Not only is the use of the hand as a reaching tool better developed in humans than it is in almost any other animal, but in Piaget's theory of the development of intelligence, reaching is seen as one of the major ways most children begin to explore the object world and build the foundations of intelligence.

When the Phase IV child reaches for an object, he is likely to either gum it or hold it at a comfortable distance from the eyes (usually about 6–8 inches), and simply look at it, or transfer it from hand to hand, or move it about while watching it.

Another common activity related to reaching involves bringing the hands into play. At least four out of five children of this age favor the right hand, and if an object is offered on the left side, the child may reach over with his right hand to grasp it. If he should take it with his left hand, or if you place it in his left hand, his right hand is likely to begin either to explore the object while it is being held by his left hand, or to take the object. This pattern of both hands involved in tactile exploration through visual guidance is very common at this stage, and even at times includes repeated transfer of the object from one hand to the other. Interestingly, when the object is dropped at this point the child will react as if he knows that he has lost something, whereas such was not the case with the two-month-old baby. Nevertheless, early in Phase IV he is not yet adept at following the path of the dropped object or of retrieving it.

Turning Over and Sitting Up

In addition to practicing reaching, babies of this age are very much into the business of practicing turning their bodies from stomach to back, and from back to stomach. By now they should be reasonably skillful at this behavior. Toward the middle of Phase IV, you will begin to see them working on the problem of bringing themselves to a sitting posture. By the end of this phase they will usually acquire this ability. Each new skill will be practiced over many hours.

Crawling

The culminating motor skill of this phase is crawling. When babies start to crawl they sometimes do it in classical fashion, getting up on their hands and knees and moving in a coordinated manner using all four limbs. There are some babies, however, whose first locomotive efforts are accomplished either by scooting—by using their elbows to pull themselves forward, their legs dragging passively behind them. Some babies manage to move about by rolling over and over. The most important point is not the style of locomotion chosen, but the fact that most children attempt to move from place to place at the first available opportunity. Why they want to move has partly to do with their desire to exercise new motor skills; but it is due even more to the burning curiosity to conduct first-hand investigations of the many things they have been able to see from a distance for several months.

LEARNING DURING PHASE IV

Intelligence

Experiences of this age play a basic role in the formation of the roots of intelligence in the same sense that they have since birth. Again, the main source of this information is Piaget's work on the development of the mind.

Interest in Objects

In Phase IV the child seems to be gradually shifting the focus of her interest from her own motor skills to the objects she interacts with. As noted, the dropping, banging, and throwing behavior of Phase IV are good examples of activities that reveal a beginning of a serious interest in the movements of the objects involved. The classic example of this interest occurs when a seven-month-old drops a spoon from a highchair and then looks carefully to see where it went. This interest in the effects of hand-eye interactions on objects is part of a surprisingly intense and long-lasting interest in such effects. This pattern that began with sustained hand regard at about two months of age will continue to be a primary focus for all healthy children right on through to the second half of the second year. Understanding how vital this kind of activity is to a young child is an important basis for selecting toys for children during the first two years of life.

Interest in Cause and Effect

A second aspect of the development of intelligence in Phase IV is the child's beginning interest in causality (cause-and-effect relationships). Crib gym toys that offer an immediate effect to the child's eye-hand activity stimulate a child's growing interest in making things happen. Crib gym toys that feature sound-producing devices or simple mechanical connections such that pulling on one part of them produces an effect on another—especially when that effect is accompanied by a moderate noise—are typical of early signs in this regard. This interest in making simple things happen is yet another developmental theme that begins to gather momentum during Phase IV and grows throughout the balance of the first three years of life. From Phase IV on through the second year of life the child will spend much time getting to know what happens as a result of the many kinds of actions that he becomes able to perform. In a few months he begins to explore what happens when he pushes a large ball or full-sized door. He will also play the "researcher" in repeatedly flipping a light switch and looking up to see the consequences, and also in his fascination with simple jack-in-the-box toys.

Another closely related theme (one which Piaget talks about) is the appreciation of time and of sequence of events. Every cause-and-effect relationship involves some sort of temporal order or sequence of events in time. The baby pushes on a part of a crib gym and another part makes a noise or continues to move about. The baby drops an object from his highchair and then watches the consequences. There is no reason to assume that a newborn child has any understanding of either cause-or-effect relations or the time relationships between events. Yet it is clear that later on during infancy he learns the fundamentals of such relationships in the course of innumerable simple activities that all babies experience, especially with small objects, during this period.

Memory

Another topic of special interest in examining the growth of intelligence is memory. The most common approach to studying human memory involves asking subjects to tell you about events they have experienced in the past. This procedure obviously cannot be used with infants. But in some of the films of Professor J. McVicker Hunt illustrating Piaget's theory of the early growth of intelligence, the topic of memory is ingeniously explored. Hunt and Uzgiris[3] have produced a film called *Object Permanence,* in which the task of the baby is to find a small toy that has been hidden under a scarf or some other piece of fabric or a pillow. The year-old baby usually has no trouble whipping the scarf off the toy and finding it; but if there are three scarves on top of the toy, the year-old baby very often pulls off the first scarf and then seems confused and gives up. The two-year-old baby, on the other hand, will continue to pull scarves off until she finds the toy. Although one cannot be certain, it is reasonable to assume that the persistence of the image of the missing toy in the baby's mind is greater in the two-year-old than it is in the case of the one-year-old or younger child.

One of the most dramatic examples of how limited are a baby's notions about small objects is what happens when you hide a toy in front of an eight-month-old child in the Piagetian test. By hiding a toy under a pillow or a scarf on the baby's right side, you'll find that most eight-month-old babies will be able to find the object quite quickly. If you hide such an object in that manner four or five times in a row, you will find that she routinely succeeds in finding it. If you immediately afterwards hide the same toy directly in front of the child but on her left side, while retaining the pillow or scarf on her right side as well, typically the baby will, after a slight delay, reach for the object on her right, *where she had previously found it, rather than on her left side where she had just seen it.* This behavior can be mildly startling when first viewed, but it is used by Piaget to illustrate the fact that at first the existence of a small object is tied to the activities that the child has been involved in with that object, rather than to any general set of rules about the existence of objects.

Recently there has been some fascinating research performed at Rockefeller University wherein the gradual development of short-term memory has been studied in the period between six months and two years of age. That research has shown that short-term memory begins to stretch at seven or eight months of age. It does so steadily in the months that follow, such that by the time a child is a year-and-a-half old it will last for at least twenty-four hours. Desirable objects hidden one day will immediately be located when a child is given an opportunity a day later to seek such objects.

This information, combined with what we know about the insatiable and all-encompassing curiosity of the infant, has great practical

[3] With I. Uzgiris of Clark University, Worcester, Massachusetts.

value when it comes to the important issue of setting limits for children when they are involved with objects that we would rather they not have. Then, too, to be able to look beneath the surface of the baby's activity and understand something about the wonderful world of the development of the mind makes raising a child even more exciting than it might be otherwise.

Emotionality

As previously mentioned, the usual emotional tone of most babies, especially during the first half of Phase IV, is one of contentment or delight. This is especially true in terms of interpersonal relationships. This is also a time when children exhibit rather abrupt mood changes. A baby who is crying can often easily be induced to stop crying and to start smiling, even laughing, quite abruptly. This capacity to move quickly from one mood state to another is remarkable, and it is probably somewhat related to the baby's lack of memory.

Motor and Sensory Skills

Motor devleopment plays a very instrumental role in early education. As a child acquires each new ability, he gains additional freedom to learn, because he is gradually shedding limitations he was saddled with at birth. The activities of dropping and throwing objects, and what these activities teach about object qualities and the physics of objects, are much easier and better entered into, for example, once the child can sit unaided (at about seven months of age). After all, lying on his back or even his stomach does not allow him to drop objects very far, or to throw them very well, or to monitor their movements. Also, once the child starts crawling the opportunities for learning become considerably greater than they were until that point in time.

Sociability

We have already remarked that it is during times when the child is interacting with others that she most often reveals her capacity for hilarity and pleasure at this stage. We have also noticed that as Phase IV draws to a close, the child will begin to stop showing affection for "all" people. She will start to focus on the nuclear family as preferred people and is likely to become shy or apprehensive with others. Her disposition may also be marred at times by the pending eruption of teeth.

TIPS ON SPOILING

As we proceed with this book it will become clear that raising a bright three-year-old is much easier than raising a pleasant unspoiled three-year-old. We have learned over the years the general shape of the process by which some children turn into delightful three-year-old human beings whereas others don't. Interestingly, the roots of over-indulgence and later selfish behavior lie in the first months of life, and Phase IV is a very special time to begin influencing the process. Phase IV children have learned that crying very often will bring someone to them and pleasant times will follow. It is vital that the Phase IV child have that state of mind about the arrival of older people. Under ordinary circumstances this indeed is the case. The child's inevitable distress from the first day of life will have been routinely responded to promptly on thousands of occasions, and that response will most of the time have led to decrease in discomfort and to learning about that connection. The wonderful, pleasant moments initiated by the smiles and general joy of babies in happy interchanges will have reinforced the feeling in the baby that good results can be expected when the older person arrives. Parallel to these inevitable experiences of the first three phases is the increasing tendency of a child to act intentionally. During the first few stages babies are responders to stimulation. Contrary to some popular views we are inclined to think that there is good evidence to say that they don't intentionally initiate interaction with adults. Put another way, in the first four to five months of life babies cry because they feel pain or discomfort. From five months on they cry sometimes because they are uncomfortable and at other times in order to get somebody to come to them. They have begun to deliberately use the cry as an effective method of getting attention and company. The result of this normal learning is that the six- and seven-month-old child who has had a lot of loving from birth is inclined to call increasingly to be picked up.

Now, what has all this got to do with the spoiling process? Well, it turns out that by two years of age, unpleasant, selfish children are rather common. At thirteen and fourteen months of age, children reveal routinely that they are able to skillfully control adults by using a whine or some other vocal expression to overcome resistance, and they will just make more noise when they want something badly. Moving back further in the process, the emergence of problems late at night with children who insist on company and won't sleep seems to surface commonly between eight and ten months of age. Finally, coming down to Phase IV, we believe we see the beginnings of this process in the increased tendencies of babies to cry in order to get company. Over several years we have become increasingly convinced of the validity of this pattern of development and we have also learned something about how to cope with it. As with most of these early formative processes, the later you get into the process, the more difficulty you will have in shaping it the way you would like. What we suggest as the easiest way of avoiding an overly self-centered three-year-old is to begin in Phase IV to be sensitive to the increased rate at which babies call to be picked up and held and to not overindulge that kind of request. Now we realize that that is a fairly difficult chore for parents, especially first-time parents. Surely, few things are more pleasant than to be called for by your baby and then to pick that child up and to wallow in the warmth that follows. We certainly don't want to encourage you to ignore your baby's calls for attention. What we suggest is that you monitor how often this is happening and try to prevent it from being the predominant activity of your day. If you find that you are picking up your child and playing with her seven or eight times an hour for six or seven hours a day, you are probably moving into a pattern that will cause you some grief fairly soon. This is one of the reasons why the use of a carefully selected walker *under constant supervision* is more appealing to this author than it otherwise might be. After all, the Phase IV child before the onset of mobility is a child who is inclined to be bored. It is very difficult to keep such a child interested by herself. A walker on the other hand can provide wonderfully exciting things for such a baby to do for a couple of hours every day. Furthermore, as soon as the baby can crawl, if you follow the rest of the guidance offered in this book, this problem of undue emphasis on crying to be held and so forth will rather easily subside. (More about this later.)

This then is one of the very special situations that surface in the first years. What researchers have learned over the last twenty-five years can be of very important practical benefit to parents, and we urge you to give these ideas serious consideration.

Language

Somewhere toward the end of Phase IV the baby's first words will begin to have true meaning for him. By this I mean that the word "bottle" may begin to signify a bottle, or something that looks like a bottle, and nothing else. Also the baby's own name means "him" rather than anything or anyone else; and "Mommy" or some reasonable facsimile, even "Dada," means only mother rather than mother or father. By referring back to page 84, you can see just what these first words are likely to be.

The Phase IV baby is not likely to understand even the simplest instructions, but very soon he will. Once he starts to learn language, you will witness a remarkably interesting process. The rate at which he will acquire ability in this area is slow at first and then accelerates dramatically from the middle of the second year. However, one caution: Although he probably will acquire substantial language skill over the next year, he may very well not say anything at all during that time. It is not unusual for children not to utter words until they are eighteen months to two years old. What you should watch for is how rapidly the child is learning to "understand" words, phrases, and grammatical structures.

RECOMMENDED CHILDREARING PRACTICES AT PHASE IV

General Remarks

I have characterised Phase IV as the last period of infancy during which you will be living with an essentially stationary creature. It should, therefore, be enjoyed as the lull before the storm.

Prior to eight months of age there are, of course, difficulties of one sort or another. Some infants go through problem periods during their first months that are lumped under the title of "colic." Other infants may not sleep through the night, especially during their first six weeks. Some infants experience discomfort associated with precocious teething. But from eight months on, the difficulties one experiences in childrearing are of a somewhat different order. Once the baby starts to crawl about the home, you are going to have much more to cope with, both in terms of the very real dangers she exposes herself to and in terms of the possibilities of missing the boat on one or another important educational process.

Giving the Baby a Feeling of Being Loved and Cared for

Assuring the Phase IV child that he is cared for can be pursued in ways similar to those that I have recommended for the preceding three phases. Perhaps the only difference of consequence in this particular phase is that affectionate interplay with the baby is now even more rewarding than it was before, thanks to the Phase IV baby's greater responsive and positive mood. Furthermore, you can use interplay to focus the child's interest on various events. If, for example, while changing the child's diaper you talk about the process, referring to the diaper pins, powder, and the diapers or whatever, you will on the one hand begin to help him form linkages between words and objects, and on the other hand begin to focus his attention on sequences of activities. Along the way you will be reinforcing the very important habit of speech about the here and now, which is so essential to good language teaching. If you are engaged in a peek a boo game or point out something about his own feet (which he has, after all, had relatively little experience hearing labeled), you may help to reinforce his basic curiosity.

HELPING THE BABY DEVELOP SPECIFIC SKILLS

Language

As we have seen, language development begins in earnest during this phase for most children. I would suggest two kinds of activities on the part of childrearers to encourage early language development.

Talking to your child. During Phase IV you should continue to talk a lot to your child, doing so in a manner that is functionally effective with someone with such limited skills. The talk should be concrete, not abstract. You should emphasize events that are taking place at the time rather than those that will take place in the future or have taken place in the past. Abstract concepts especially won't register with a child this age. There is nothing "bad" about any kind of talk, but unless it is of the kind described, most of it will go over the baby's head. You and the baby are much better off if you will concentrate on tying your language to the here and now, talking about the sock that you are putting on, or the toy that you are holding before the baby, or some feature of your face, or the baby's fingers.

Motor Skills

Motor development is dramatic in Phase IV and will proceed pretty much on its own. You can, however, facilitate progress somewhat, and you should at least know what is happening so that you do not inadvertently impede it. Once again, the central skills that are emerging are torso control (turning over), the ability to sit unaided, some form of crawling or mobility, and continued leg and arm development in the form of increasingly frequent and powerful extensions and contractions.

There is little you can to do encourage the development of torso control or the ability to assume a sitting position. In the last few years a fair number of programs have surfaced to encourage you to provide exercises for your young child. Indeed, in addition to programs that involve parent and child, there are several books about this subject. The existence of these books and programs would seem to perhaps contradict our statements about motor skills and their development, because some of them clearly imply and others even state that you can encourage or enhance development by following certain procedures. I believe the bulk of evidence does not support such claims, but that does not mean that I'm opposed to infant exercise classes. There is no question at all that babies get great pleasure from mastering their bodies and exercising in appropriate ways. Furthermore, anything that they enjoy a good deal and that brings them into delightful activities with other people, especially their parents, obviously is recommendable. It is not true, however, that anyone has established that any collection of exercises makes a substantial difference in the acquisition of these early motor skills.

From an educational point of view, the most important motor ability that surfaces during this phase is the ability to move about on one's own. This capacity will usher in a time of tremendous importance for early learning and is central to the process, provided that you allow maximum access to the living area for your baby.

In order for babies to be safely turned loose to roam, it is essential that the home be modified for two principal purposes. The first is to make it a safe place for a baby to be, and to explore; the second is to make it safe *from* the baby.

COPING WITH SIMPLE PROBLEMS

In watching situations where children develop beautifully—through Phases V and VI in particular—we have observed that parents have taken precautions as soon as the child begins to crawl to make the home as safe a place as they can for the child.

Accident Proofing the Kitchen and Living Area

Making a home safe for a Phase V child starts with making the kitchen safe, because that is where she will ordinarily spend more of her waking time than any other place in the home. The first order of business is to accident proof all the low areas of the home. By "low" we mean areas less than three feet above the floor. Kitchens contain cleaning materials, sharp utensils, and breakable objects that must be treated so they are not likely to cause the child any grief. All substances that might be hazardous to the baby if she managed to put any into her mouth must be moved out of reach. Fragile glass or other breakable kitchen material should be stored in out-of-reach places. Objects that can cut, such as knives and sharpening utensils, must be moved away.

Electrical cords and outlets must be attended to. Wherever there is an outlet not in use, you should purchase at your local hardware store the kind of plastic cover that fits into the outlet. It is advisable to move all appliance cords out of reach of the baby. It is particularly important to see that all electric insulation is intact.

A less obvious but important problem to cope with is that of unstable physical objects. If you have an ironing board that folds down from the wall, for example, you should see that it is very difficult for the child to release it. If you have a chair that is easy to tip over, remove it. In addition, you should check any wood furniture for potential splinters. You'll also want to make certain that all paints within reach of the child are lead free. Plants can be a double source of difficulty. If they are within reach, they and the sometimes heavy pots in which they are contained can be pulled down onto a baby. Furthermore, a goodly number of common houseplants are actually poisonous to children. The best source of information about accidental poisons is your local poison control center. They exist all over the country.

You should be assured that any television or stereo controls in reach of the child constitute no shock hazard, and that knobs that might be removable do not come off easily and cannot be easily swallowed (that is, they are larger than an inch and a half in breadth).

Stairs

Not only are accidental poisonings very common between eight and twenty months of age, but accidental falls are another principal source of danger to the infant. All healthy and newly crawling infants love to climb stairs. Furthermore, they'll climb as many as there are. They will climb one or two; and they'll climb a hundred if given the chance. Why this urge to move up in space no one knows, but the urge is there. What to do? You can, as some advocate, put a gate at the bottom and top of all staircases. We don't think this is best, however. Instead, we suggest a gate about three steps up. With only three steps to climb, babies usually can't hurt themselves, and therefore don't require a great deal of supervision. More importantly, and in the spirit of this book, is the notion that babies normally very much want to climb and to learn how to do it well. The gymnastic interest of the healthy Phase V child is perfectly natural and probably very important. Putting a gate on the third step allows the child to practice safely what comes naturally and clearly gives her a great deal of pleasure.

Interestingly, we've learned something else about stairs that did not seem to be obvious to us at first: That babies apparently are fascinated by the "essence" of the step itself. The typical step is about six or seven inches high and seven or eight inches deep. We find, however, that children derive just as much pleasure in climbing a one-inch step that's deeper than seven or eight inches as they do in climbing a conventional step. For those so inclined, you might consider building a special set of steps for your Phase V child. Arrange or construct a three-step toy where each step is an inch-and-a-half high and perhaps two feet wide and ten inches deep, with a broad platform at the top and then three similar steps coming down from the other side. Build guard rails on both sides. You'll find your newly crawling or walking baby enjoying the apparatus hugely.

The Bathroom

The third important area to concern yourself with is the bathroom. Phase V children have a universal interest in playing with water. But they have a tendency to pull themselves over the edge of the tub and, unfortunately, will occasionally fall in. It is our judgment that the only

Hide-and-seek

way to cope with the danger of accidental drowning and the damage that can come from banging a head against a hard surface is to declare the bathroom off limits. The door should be kept latched with an out-of-reach latch until the child gets old enough so that he is trustworthy and can understand instructions. This won't happen until the child is at least eighteen months old. Of special importance is seeing to it that *all medicines are kept out of reach of the child.* For just a few dollars you can buy a small strongbox that can be kept locked, in which to store all medicines. It is well worth the inconvenience and the modest expense.

Outdoors

You would be well advised not to leave a child of this age outdoors unsupervised for any length of time. Even if she is in the company of a slightly older child, you should keep an eye on your Phase V child whenever she is outdoors. You should of course be certain that there are no sharp objects around on which she can cut herself, and you should be especially careful of backyard pools. A child can drown in as little as an inch or two of water. In general, common sense should get you through the business of accident proofing an outdoor area. The cardinal rule is that it is unwise to expect the baby between eight and fourteen months of age to use good sense when it comes to safety. *You* are going to have to be his good sense.

Protecting the Home from the Baby

It is not only important to protect the baby from the typical adult-oriented home, it is also important to remember that a baby can be hazardous to your home. Any fragile, desirable possessions that you treasure should be placed beyond the reach of the baby at this stage of development. So get your breakable and precious belongings out of his way. Even possessions that you simply like having around, such as a plant that you may have spent three years growing from seed, is clearly in jeopardy. Be forewarned. I remember a time when a Phase V baby found a five-pound paper sack of flour in a cabinet. He then proceeded to decorate several rooms of his home with flour. The typical crawling child means extra work. There is no question that newly crawling children create far more housework than those who have not yet learned how to move about on their own.

There are several new pamphlets available on the subject of safety proofing homes. See the section of this book on recommended readings.

Intelligence

There are several ways in which you can encourage your child's intellectual growth at this stage, but don't expect any major impact yet.

Providing suitable small objects. This is a period when children enjoy dropping, banging, and throwing small objects for the very first time. In order to pursue these perfectly natural processes, children need access to many droppable, throwable, bangable things. Bear in mind that these objects should not be too small. Anything that is less than one-and-a-half inches in any of its dimensions might very well get stuck in the child's throat. Beware as well of very small parts of larger objects that could break off.

Exposure to simple mechanisms. Another area in which the Phase IV child shows a special interest is in how things work, or cause-and-effect mechanisms. You probably will begin to see some interest in the working of light switches at this point. If you operate a light switch, directing the baby's attention to what happens to the lights in the room, you will begin to see a dawning of interest. He will also show interest in jack-in-the-box toys during Phase IV. Some of the abrupt changes in stimulation like the jack-in-the-box toy may startle your Phase IV child. If your child has such a sensitivity, it is nothing to worry about, but you might wait a bit before you introduce situations of this sort.

Setting up simple problems. The Phase IV child also shows increasing interest in solving simple problems. The first problem that he is likely to be able to cope with will involve moving something out of his way when he is trying to procure an object. The baby, on his stomach, at six or seven months of age, is usually capable of reaching out with one hand while supporting his upper torso with the other arm or elbow. If objects are in the way, he will become increasingly sophisticated about moving them aside in order to get at what he is after. Although during Phase IV "out of sight" is still "out of mind," you can begin to play hide-and-seek with him, using your own face or any small object in which he may show any interest.

In summary, then, by providing a goodly number of small objects and allowing your child to indulge himself in dropping, banging, and throwing, as well as performing other simple actions with him, you will be feeding one dimension of mental growth. By giving him some exposure to the way simple mechanisms work, you will be nourishing another one. And by setting up very simple problems for him—those that involve an occasional easy-to-surmount obstacle in the way of his procuring some desirable object, or in hide-and-seek games, you will be providing a third kind of input to mental growth.

Encouraging Interest in the Outside World—Curiosity

In your use of language during your friendly give-and-take with the baby, in the provision of small objects and related materials for the child, and most especially in providing access to the home, you will be simultaneously encouraging and broadening the growth of her curiosity. By far the most effective way to encourage both intellectual growth and curiosity at this stage of development is to use a walker for several hours each day. *Remember, however, always supervise a baby in a walker.*

RECOMMENDED MATERIALS FOR PHASE IV

Crib Devices

Already mentioned was the kind of crib-kicking device that is enjoyable to children of this age range. The baby's interest in simple mechanisms can be fed by directing her attention to various items you routinely use, such as water faucets or stoppers in a tub or sink. In addition, there are a few toys on the market that can be suspended above a supine baby and will give her a chance to activate simple cause-and-effect mechanisms.

   Warning: Once a baby can sit up on his own, crib gyms must be removed. There is a danger that the baby may get caught in the materials used to suspend crib gyms.

   In selecting crib toys for the Phase IV baby you should look for devices that are relatively easy for the child to operate. Toys that provide the child with a large and relatively stationary object to pull on will give him pleasure. (Avoid toys that use objects suspended by string.)

Mirrors, Stuffed Toys, and Balls

The Phase IV child shows a declining interest in his own mirror image, but the use of mirrors above the changing table or the crib is still advisable. There are quite a number of stuffed toys available for a child of this age. I do not see anything wrong with them, but you should not expect the baby of this age to spend much time with a stuffed toy. He may occasionally look at it or gum it, but it is not likely to occupy his attention for long. Toward the end of Phase IV it is wise to start providing your child with balls of various sizes. The child who can move about is the child who becomes particularly interested in balls, partly because they can be made to travel so far with such little effort on his part, and partly because they are things to be retrieved and as such fit into his growing capacities to move about and to handle objects.

Objects to Collect

Many materials that will keep your child interested for a relatively long time at this age can be procured for free. If you allow a child from the time he is five or six months of age to spend a good deal of time on a blanket on the floor, with a variety of small objects and a few containers to put them in, you will find she will spend a good deal of time exploring those objects and practicing simple skills with them. They should be about two to five inches in size. Some should have fine details to be fingered and looked at because of the particular interest of children of this age in fine details. They should be of many sizes, shapes, and textures. Also provide the baby with a very large container or two, preferably plastic, into which she can put these objects and out of which she can pour them. This interest in exploring small objects and practicing simple skills is at the center of the educational process at this age and will stay there for a good year. You might just as well begin to encourage it at this point.

Infant Seats

I recommend the infant seat until the baby crawls because it gives you an opportunity to have the child near you during the day, facilitating affectionate interchanges. Bear in mind, however, that as the child nears the end of Phase IV the infant seat will become less and less appropriate because he will become impatient sitting in it for long and because he will get to be too big so that it becomes somewhat unstable and possibly dangerous. (*Warning: From the beginning of Phase IV on it would be highly advisable not to place the infant seat more than a few inches from the floor and to be mindful of the possibilities of a child tipping it over.*)

Walkers

Be sure to choose a walker that is well made and stable and will not pinch your child's fingers or legs. Also remember, use *constant supervision,* and put the walker away once your child begins to crawl about on her own.

MATERIALS NOT RECOMMENDED FOR PHASE IV

Busy Boxes

There is an interesting story about the now legendary busy box that I like to tell. Busy boxes have been available commercially for some time, and they have enjoyed a good deal of popularity. But busy boxes are not very interesting to infants. By this I mean that if you watch a fair number of infants repeatedly, you will find that beyond the initial exploratory interest they show in any new object, they rarely spend much time with the toy in the weeks that follow its introduction. Busy boxes do have a few cause-and-effect mechanisms. There is usually a small squeaky horn; there are spring-loaded devices that make sharp sounds when an object is pushed along a track; there are colored balls or wheels that show alternating colors when they are turned; and there is the ever-present telephone dial. But the fact is that none of these objects is very appealing to an infant at any stage of his development. An inexpensive, eighteen-inch in diameter, plastic beach ball will provide twenty times more enjoyment than any current commercially made busy box. By the way, it will cost about a dollar in contrast to the twelve- to fifteen-dollar price tags on busy boxes. Infants seem to demand more variety in terms of feedback than they get as a result of the actions of busy-box items. One of the reasons a mirror is so interesting to a young child is that he never sees exactly the same scene twice. Another example of variation that is enticing to infants is play with water. When an infant pushes a little button that produces a horn squeak, all he ever gets is the same old horn squeak. It just is not enough variation. The reason such toys have sold so well in the past is because they *look* like they should be interesting, they look like you are getting a lot for the money, and they have not had much competition until very recently.

Over the last decade as more and more interest in infant learning and development has grown, a large number of toy companies have moved into the field of infant toys. Very often one of the first toys they develop is yet another form of busy box. We have nicer looking, more smoothly working busy boxes than the original; we have Walt Disney busy boxes, we have Smurf busy boxes, we have Sesame Street busy boxes, we even have Snoopy busy boxes. None of them has very much play value. None of them is worth the money.

Overhead Suspended Jumping Devices

Jumpers that feature a canvas seat or a swing suspended by a springy support hung from the top of a doorway are controversial today. People in pediatric orthopedics believe there is a danger to the growing bones of an infant from exuberant bouncing in such devices. Since I am not a physician, I cannot comment on such claims directly. From a play value viewpoint I would say that a properly designed toy of this sort would be enjoyed by most children in this age range. But I would certainly recommend that you check it out with your pediatrician before you use such a device.

Playpens or "Playyards"

Finally, we turn to the topic of playpens. Playpens have been sold in huge quantities in this country for some time now. They certainly play a valuable role as a way of preventing accidents, but you are strongly urged to consider other ways of dealing with danger during infancy. The main reason is that children are usually put into playpens when they first begin to move about on their own. The very word "playpen" means that you are penning your child to play in a restricted area. You pen him in either to stop him from moving about or to protect him from other children or hazards in the home. We have watched hundreds of babies in playpens for hours at a time and we have come to the conclusion that *there is no way of keeping most children from being bored in a playpen for longer than a very brief period of time, perhaps ten to twenty minutes.*

It is my view that to bore a child on a daily basis by the regular use of a playpen for extended periods is a very poor childrearing practice. The same principle applies to the use of cribs, jumpseats, highchairs, and other restrictive devices to the extent that any one of these devices is used for the purpose of limiting a child's movement about the house for long periods every day. I will discuss this situation in greater detail in the next chapter, when we move fully into the phenomenon of exploration of the home by the crawling baby. Basically, I believe that caging your child as a way of saving work and aggravation, as well as preventing accidents, though effective, is the wrong way to solve such problems.

BEHAVIORS THAT SIGNAL THE ONSET OF PHASE V

Locomobility

The ability to move the entire body through space, usually through crawling, is one of the most dramatic and consequential emerging mobilities of infancy. It surfaces at about eight months of age (it can happen several weeks earlier or later), and it plays a large role in the story of how to educate an infant. Mobility and its repercussions will be discussed in detail in the next chapter. If you leave a Phase IV child, especially in the early stages of that period, on a blanket in the center of the floor, he will very probably be in the same place, give or take a few inches, when you return five minutes later. The Phase V baby, who can crawl or scoot about, definitely will not be in the same place after five minutes. There is no mistaking this new behavior. When the baby can crawl or move about in any manner beyond a few inches or so, you will know it. Some babies do not begin to move any distance of consequence immediately. For others there is a period of a few days when they may begin to move back and forth a few inches, perhaps even a foot or two, before they enter into that period when they can move across the room. At any rate, once locomobility has begun, you have entered Phase V, so brace yourself.

Understanding of First Words

As babies enter Phase V words begin to have meaning to them. We have noted that the first words likely to cause unmistakable signs of recognition on the part of the baby are such words as "mommy," "daddy," "bye-bye," and "baby." You can tell if the word "mommy" means "mother" by having someone else, usually the father, ask the baby where Mommy is. If you ask, "Where's Mommy?" when she is nearby, and when there are one or two other people to choose from, and if the baby turns toward mother and smiles when she does so, you begin to get a reasonably reliable indication that the word might be linked to mother. Although it may not be exclusively linked to her, it might be used for any creature that generally resembles her. Soon thereafter, children begin to understand simple instructions. One of the first is commonly, for obvious reasons, the instruction to wave "bye-bye." Waving bye-bye is generally an easily identified activity; when children begin to do it with some regularity, it is reasonable to assume that they have linked those words to a particular behavior pattern. Other typical simple instructions that are part of the early repertoire of a child are: "stop," "give me a kiss," "sit down," "get up," and "come here."

A Potential Change in Behavior Toward Nonfamily Members

Eight months has traditionally been considered to be the age at which babies exhibit rather dramatic fear reactions to nonfamily members for the first time. Closer inspection of the phenomenon, however, suggests that this so-called "stranger anxiety" is not universal, nor always intense. Nevertheless, from this point on, the child's social sophistication increases steadily and is fascinating to observe. During the second year, for example, the child's entire world will revolve around his primary caretaker (usually mother). He will then gradually move off during the third year toward the beginning interest in true socializing with children of his own age.

The first eight months of life can be characterized as a period when the baby is maximally attracted to all people, and for very good reason—survival. Somewhere in the vicinity of eight months of age the process comes to an end. The baby usually starts to become more selective as he begins to really form a unique attachment relationship. At about this time you will probably begin to notice a slight wariness in the baby's behavior when someone not of the nuclear family comes close to his face; do not be surprised if that wariness changes to outright screaming. This change of behavior, starting at about eight months of age, is another sign that signals the emergence of Phase V.

CHAPTER SIX

Phase V:

From Eight to Fourteen Months of Age

GENERAL REMARKS

The Special Importance of the Phase V Stage

With the onset of Phase V, raising a child becomes a dramatically different proposition than it has been before. Whereas most families in this country today get their children through the first six to eight months of life reasonably well developed, I have come to the conclusion that *relatively few families—perhaps no more than one in ten—manage to get their children through the age period from eight to thirty-six months as well educated and developed as they can and should be.*

Not all professionals agree with this author. There are child psychiatrists, for example, who think that the first weeks of life are the most important and that prospective parents must be educated in the best way to establish a healthy parent-child relationship. My response is that I am just as much an advocate of love and of close emotional relationships as anyone, but I do not believe that there are really very many parents who do not establish a solid relationship with their children in the first months of life. The minority who do not probably won't be reading books of this kind anyway.

There are, of course, exceptions. Tragically, everyday of the year some small fraction of American families are doing an apparently abominable job with young children. There are children who are abused physically, children in family situations so burdened with problems that neglect takes a heavy toll, and of course there are special cases of children afflicted with disease or physical anomalies. But my remarks are not addressed to these extreme cases. They are addressed to the majority of families who do not have to cope with such extraordinary difficulties.

There is a good deal of information that suggests that sometime during the middle of the second year of life, children begin to reveal the direction in which they are headed developmentally. Most children of this age begin to produce performances on achievement measures—especially in respect to language and thinking ability—that increasingly represent the levels of achievement they will be reaching and maintaining in the years that follow, including in school. Put another way, in the earlier phases—I through IV, and at the beginning of Phase V as well—what a child scores on a test of intelligence, motor skills, language, and social skills does not seem to bear any meaningful relationship to what he will score on similar tests when he is two or three years of age. The only exception to this concerns those 15 percent of children who look seriously weak from birth, or who, in tests during the first year of life, consistently score very much below most of the population.

The fact that test scores in the first year of life generally have no predictive power is very well established. It is a finding that people who emphasize development in the first months of life have great difficulty explaining away. To be sure, there is always the possibility that problems created in the first months of life may not reveal themselves until considerably later in the child's life. Nevertheless, there is also the real possibility that what people are claiming as problems in the first months are not indeed so very important. This author's own feeling is that the reason we do not see dramatic evidence of poor development in the first year of the lives of most children *who will do poorly later* is simply that they have not yet developed the deficits. Groups of children who go on to underachieve in the elementary grades almost never look particularly weak in terms of achievement at one year of age, but only begin to lag behind sometime toward the end of the second year of life. On standardized language and intelligence tests, for example, such children will pretty clearly reveal where they are headed educationally by the time they are three years of age. In report after report—whether from low-income urban American children or from children in low-income homes in Africa, India, or other parts of the world—the pattern of findings is pretty much the same. Such disadvantaged children make a fairly good showing during the first year of life on standard baby tests like the Bayley mental scales, even if they have not had the best of nutrition, and even if their parents have had little or no education. It is not until they reach the middle of the second year of life, at the earliest, that their scores begin to slide. Subsequently, it is all downhill. That is, it is all downhill for such *groups* of children, not necessarily for every individual child within those groups.

It is very important to point out that many low-income family children are not underachievers. Large numbers of such children, both in this and other countries, develop as well as any children, from the first two years on through to graduate school. To be born into a poor family is far from being a guarantee of academic underachievement.

This subject is complicated and emotionally charged, and confusing. Perhaps it is best to summarize the situation with a graph (page 108).

Curve A represents development for most children. In this figure, we refer to overall ability (excluding motor and sensory skills)—not just to performance on an IQ test, but to all the other major abilities of the young human, including social and language skills. This curve (A) refers to the average child from birth through five-and-a-half years. You will note that there is a second curve (B) that starts and stays lower than curve A. That curve represents the 15 percent of the population that for one reason or another is in substantial trouble from birth or shortly thereafter. That group stays in trouble. Note that starting about eight months of age two additional curves are sketched in (C and D). One moves up more rapidly than the average; the other falls back as compared with the average. Note that at about eight months of age, the divergences of curves A, C, and D begin.

THE EFFECT OF REARING CONDITIONS ON DEVELOPMENT

Let us move on to a subsidiary point which must be kept separate to avoid confusion. During the ten years spent studying the role of experience in the development of children during their first six months, we learned many interesting things concerning the rate of development as a function of different kinds of experiences in those early months. Through experiments with physically normal children, we became convinced that the rate at which children acquire abilities in the first six months of life, at least in regard to visual motor skills and to foundations of intelligence, can be modified rather dramatically by the manipulation of rearing circumstances.

It has long been known that you can easily prevent a child from reaching any significant level of development in the first six months of life. What we have also learned in our ten years of research is that if you provide certain circumstances for the young child in those first months of life, she can achieve some kinds of skills considerably earlier

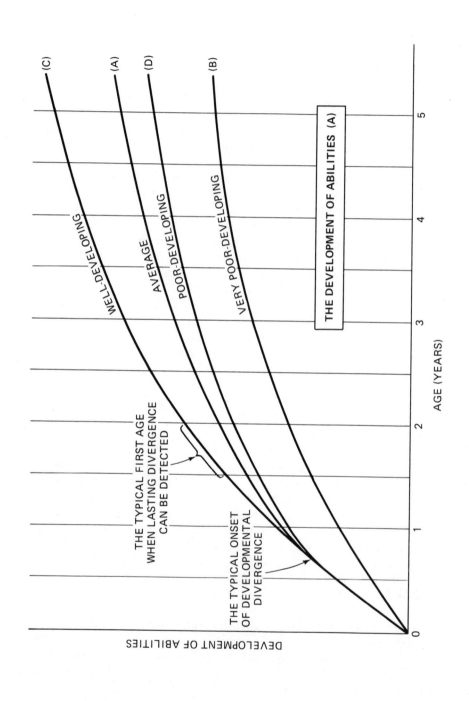

THE DEVELOPMENT OF ABILITIES (A)

(C)
(A)
(D)
(B)

WELL-DEVELOPING
AVERAGE
POOR-DEVELOPING
VERY POOR-DEVELOPING

THE TYPICAL FIRST AGE
WHEN LASTING DIVERGENCE
CAN BE DETECTED

THE TYPICAL ONSET
OF DEVELOPMENTAL
DIVERGENCE

DEVELOPMENT OF ABILITIES

AGE (YEARS)

0   1   2   3   4   5

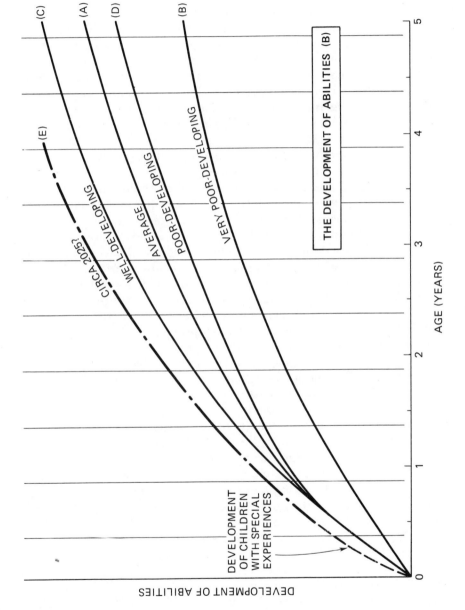

THE DEVELOPMENT OF ABILITIES (B)

than the average child—indeed, in some cases even earlier than the precocious child.

Take the skill of visually directed reaching that, as we have seen, is normally acquired at about five to five-and-a-half months of age by children in this society, as well in most others, that have been tested. Our studies—in which we provided objects for children to look at, bat, feel, and play with—starting from three or four weeks of age, resulted in the acquisition of mature reaching at a bit more than three months. Not only is this a considerable acceleration of the acquisition process, but, perhaps more importantly, the children involved had a marvelous time engaging in these activities. During the fourth month they were full of enthusiasm, giggled excitedly, played with the objects around them, looked happily into a mirror that we had placed overhead, and did a good deal of vocalizing. You can see how this kind of pleasurable and occasionally exciting play fits into the aforementioned goals of supporting the development of specific skills while nurturing the zest for life and curiosity of the child. The children who went through those studies seem to be spirited and very interested children at six and seven months of age, much more so than children who were like them at the onset but who had not gone through those particular experiences. From these research studies, we were able to design a rather nice collection of commercial toys. What this all adds up to is that we now have information at hand that could enable us to provide future children, at least in principle, with circumstances that are more suited to their earlier needs and interests than those to which they are normally exposed. It also means, very probably, that what we now call a normal rate of development will be considered—thirty or forty years from now—to be a slow pace. As you look at the following figure (page 109) you will see that in addition to the same curves that appear in the preceding figure, there is an additional curve that describes a course of accelerated development of children in our research studies in the first six months of life. This curve is labeled Curve E.

In the research of the intervening years we arrived at another telling conclusion. In addition to the notion that somewhere between the first and third birthdays children are beginning to reveal where they are headed in later years, we have come to the conclusion that *to begin to look at a child's educational development when he is two years of age is already much too late, particularly in the area of social skills and attitudes.* We have found that the two-year-old is a rather complicated, firmly established, social being. We have found that it is not uncommon that a two-year-old is already badly spoiled and very difficult to live with, or in more tragic situations, somewhat alienated from people, including his own family. We have seen these phenomena repeatedly. On the other hand, we have rarely seen an eight-, nine-, or ten-month-old child who in any important way seems to be spoiled or particularly well differentiated socially. Up through Phase IV, the first eight months of life, a child is, comparatively speaking, a very simple social creature.

You can trace your child's evolution as she goes from eight to twenty-four months of age by keeping a journal and taking movies or videotapes of her, preferably with sound. This will confirm the fact that the twenty-four-month-old child is as different from the eight-month-old as the eight-month-old is from the newborn.

From the above discussion you can see that the period that starts at eight months and ends at three years is a period of primary importance in the development of a human being. The period from eight to fourteen months of age is the first major phase of that exciting time span.

Educational Goals

Over the years three useful ways of describing educational goals for the period from eight months through three years have emerged. First, we have found that all healthy eight-month-old children seem motivated by three major interests aside from the physiological needs such as hunger, thirst, freedom from pain, and so forth. These three major interests are: getting to know the primary caretaker; the satisfaction of curiosity; and the mastering of newly emerging motor abilities. These interests have obvious survival value. They start out vigorous and in balance in all healthy eight-month-old babies. When development goes well, they each grow steadily and the balance is maintained. Too often, however, they develop unevenly between eight and twenty-four months of age, and the results are mildly or severely debilitating. Guiding the balanced, enriched growth of these primary interests will be discussed in later sections.

A second way of discussing educational goals is to talk of emerging competencies of special importance. These competencies are by no means guaranteed to develop well. We refer to the pattern of intellectual, linguistic, perceptual, and social competencies our research has found typical of beautifully developed three- to six-year-old children. These processes sometimes overlap with those to be discussed under other ways of dealing with educational goals. They will be dealt with repeatedly throughout later sections of this book. At this point, we should single out three social competencies that emerge in Phase V for special mention: (1) Toward the end of the first year, children begin to realize older people can be helpful; they begin to deliberately seek assistance from them. (2) Also at roughly the same time, seeking approval for simple achievement, cute behavior, seems to indicate the first feelings of pride and accomplishment. (3) Finally, shortly after the first birthday, children begin to manifest simple make-believe or fantasy behavior—common examples are "talking" on a toy telephone or pretending to be driving a toy truck, car, or airplane. Each of these emergences seems to play a special role in educational development. More on this topic will follow.

The third way we characterize educational goals of this special period in life is to describe four fundamental processes that undergo very special development at this time. These processes are language, curiosity, intelligence, and social development.

Language Development

We have seen that although children may respond to words in a very simple fashion during the first six or seven months of life, there is no reason to believe that they understand the meaning of these words. Early responses such as turning when their names are called are better understood as simple reflexive responses to any nearby sound than as indications of true language processing. It is true that a four-month-old will respond when her name is called. It is, however, also true that you can call her by virtually any name and, provided that she can hear you, she will respond in exactly the same way. From seven or eight months of age on, however, babies clearly reveal that they have begun to understand the meaning of particular words.

By three years of age, experts estimate that most children *understand* most of the language that they will use for the rest of their lives in ordinary conversation. There is an important difference between the growth of *understanding* and the growth of *producing* language. Children begin to understand language earlier and at a more stable and rapid rate than they begin to use it orally. The first five or six words should be fairly well understood by the time a child is a year of age. He may not, however, say five or six words until he is two years of age, or even older. Nevertheless, in both cases he is likely to be a normal child.

Language, like so many of the issues we will talk about, is interrelated during the first year of life with other major developments. There is no way that a young child can do well on an intelligence test at three or four years of age, for example, unless his language development is good. Indeed, you can usually predict a child's IQ once he gets to be three or four years of age with reasonable accuracy from any reliable assessment of his language skills.

Over and above language's fundamental role in the development of intelligence, it plays an equally important part in the development of social skills. So much of what transpires between any two people involves either listening to or expressing language. So, in a very significant way, good language development underlies good social development.

Development of Curiosity

Just about everyone knows that kittens go through a stage during which they are incredibly curious. We also know that monkeys and puppies are similar in this regard. Indeed, it appears that many young mammals go through an early period when they are consumed by the need to explore. (This is even true with young horses.) We have never really pinpointed such a stage with human beings before, perhaps simply because people charged with the responsibility of researching early human development have left much of that research undone even to this date. We believe, however, that research over the last two decades—especially our own research in the homes of many kinds of children—has helped to fill this gap in our knowledge.

We have never come across an eight-month-old child who is not incredibly curious. We have never known an eight-month-old child who needed to be reinforced to explore the home once she could crawl. Bear in mind that to have a very strong exploratory drive is of central importance for humans in that, unlike most other animals, humans go through a very long developmental period and come equipped with fewer instincts than other animals have to cope with the world. *Nothing is more fundamental to solid educational development than pure, uncontaminated curiosity.*

Development of Intelligence

According to Piaget, a child at eight months of age has turned a developmental corner, leaving behind his early introduction to the world and to his own basic motor skills, and starts to focus on the world of small objects. The year or so that follows is a period that features active exploration of simple cause-and-effect mechanisms; of the movement patterns of objects and of their textures, shapes, and forms. This is an incredibly rich time during which the child's mind is undergoing basic development with respect to the prerequisites of higher forms of thinking; the child is acquiring the foundations of higher mental abilities. Surely as far as education is concerned, few things are more central than the substructure of sensorimotor explorations upon which higher levels of intelligence are built. It is perhaps worth pointing out that the bulk of these acquisitions that underlie later thinking ability come about through thousands of simple explorations of small objects and without the benefit of any special input by other people.

Social Development

The two-year-old child is an extremely complicated and sophisticated social creature. His social world, for the most part, revolves around his primary caretaker (usually his mother, although not always in this day and age); and ordinarily he has worked out with her an extraordinary contract full of "ifs," "ands," and "buts" that describe a great deal about the various possible relationships for him within the home. He has learned whether or not she is a gentle, friendly person. He has learned all the subtle cues that help him to identify her mood state at any given moment. He has usually learned a whole other set of information about his father and about siblings, particularly those close in age to him. He may have, at age two, developed into a delightful human being who is a pleasure to live with, a minicompanion good for all sorts of extraordinarily delightful experiences; or, more sadly, he may have developed into an overindulged child who constantly badgers his mother, particularly if there is a younger child in the home. He may become, in other words, extraordinarily difficult to live with and unpleasant. Even sadder is the case of the child who at two has been consistently rejected by people, who has learned to be an isolate, one who has never had the pleasure of a free and easy, rewarding relationship with another human being.

Yet another pattern is that of the child who has learned a good deal about fear during the period between eight and twenty-four months of age. It is not at all uncommon for a young child to learn to stay away from his own mother unless she gives clear signals that an approach is desired. Far more common is the two-year-old whose slightly older sibling has made it clear through hundreds of small encounters that he doesn't care for her very much.

In my opinion, *everyone of the four educational foundations— development of language, curiosity, intelligence, and socialness—is at risk during the period from eight months to two years.* What do I mean by "at risk"? I mean that unlike the achievements of the first six or seven months of life, which I propose are more or less assured by virtue of their simple requirements and the characteristics of the average environment, the achievement of the educational goals of the eight- to twenty-four-month period is by no means assured. It is not at all inevitable that the child will learn language as well as he might. It is not at all inevitable that he will have his curiosity deepened and broadened as well as he might. It is not at all inevitable that his social development will take place in a solid and fruitful manner. Finally, although it would appear that the substructures for intelligence, that is, the sensorimotor foundations, are not particularly sensitive to common environmental variations, the higher mental abilities that begin to surface toward the end of the second year share with the other three foundation processes a similar susceptibility toward less than optimal development. Indeed, I must repeat that no more than one child in ten achieves the levels of ability in these four fundamental areas that she could achieve.

OBSTACLES TO OPTIMAL ACHIEVEMENT IN THE FOUR FUNDAMENTAL EDUCATIONAL PROCESSES

There are three common and significant obstacles to successful educational development in the period from eight to thirty-six months of age. They are ignorance, stress, and lack of assistance.

Ignorance

Typical young parents are quite unprepared for the responsibility of educating their first child. As noted earlier, we do nothing in this country, in a systematic way, to educate couples for the responsibility of raising young children. Up until recently, in fact, there has been yet another fundamental problem, the fact that we simply have not had enough useful information to teach.

We have known for some time, of course, when the typical baby starts to walk, to sit unaided, to wave bye-bye, and so forth. But sophisticated, extensive, and detailed information about the growth of the young human, and especially about the causes of good or poor growth, has been in remarkably short supply until very recently, in spite of all the opinions and all the words that have been written on it. The problem is simply that psychological and educational research people, while recognizing the importance of the processes developing in the first three years of life, have not, until very recently, for one reason or another, developed the necessary knowledge. Because of longstanding styles of raising children, until the late 1970s to do research on a child less than two-and-a-half years of age meant going to his home or making an appointment for him to come to your office or your laboratory. Going out to the home is a relatively inconvenient affair. It is also an extremely inefficient way to do research. Studying a child in his own environment not only requires transportation to and from the home, but, more important, does not provide ideal conditions for this kind of research. How much easier it is to have a group of college sophomores come to your laboratory, where they can be studied for thirty minutes at a time. The college sophomore coming into a psychology laboratory to be a subject doesn't bring his parents along. He is not overly apprehensive about what might happen to him, and he has been conditioned for years to do what he is told, particularly when he is told to do something by someone with high prestige or someone who is going to give him a grade in a course.

To complicate matters, there are so many different kinds of children. It is scientifically improper to make general statements about children on the basis of one middle-class Protestant child. Samples must be drawn from all major categories, depending upon the particular topic under study. Moreover, on one day a child of two years of age may do one thing in a test situation or in his spontaneous behavior; the next day, or even an hour later, he may do something else. Even if you have gone to a home five times, you cannot assume that you have acquired a fair sampling of a very young child's behavior.

All in all, it is not surprising that the actual basic building of the science of early human development made so little progress until the late 1970s in spite of hundreds of millions of dollars poured into the enterprise by the federal government and private foundations.

All sorts of misinformation has been offered to the public on child development, and, indeed, you can find many programs and books that purport to help parents in this regard. Scratch the surface of these materials, however, looking for the basis on which the recommendations about childrearing are made, and you'll generally find that the basis is very shallow. With few exceptions, if you wanted legitimate information about raising a very young child, you would probably have been better off asking an intelligent mother of several children.

During the last decade, as awareness of the special importance of learning during the first few years of life has grown, there have been serious attempts to make up for the lack of solid information. We have in our files at the Center for Parent Education,[1] for example, information on more than 800 programs that are designed to help people raise their young children effectively. The sponsorship of these programs is extremely diverse. Some of them are based in public school systems, others in preventive mental health programs, still others out of church groups, and so on. This diversity reflects the immaturity of this new field. Many of these programs do wonderful work. Most of them, however, suffer from the history of the field and its neglect of the informational needs of society. Many of the people operating the programs for young parents have received weak training in their own right, and whatever weaknesses there are in their backgrounds will

[1] In 1978, I established the Center for Parent Education as a non-profit resource agency. Its two goals are to advocate more services to new parents, and to help professionals who focus on learning during the first three years of life.

naturally be passed on to parents. It's unfortunately true that the subject of early learning is a complicated one. Thus it is especially difficult to identify reliable information and to translate it into a realistic program for both professional staff and families.

Stress

Not only are families less aware than they ought to be of the details of early learning, in addition they have to do their job under a fair degree of stress. I am referring here for the most part to the young mother, because she is the one most likely to have the major responsibility for baby's upbringing. This stress occurs routinely from pregnancy right on through the first years of life. During the first two months of the infant's life, the common practice of infants to awake repeatedly during the night very often leads to fatigue and related problems. In addition to these troublesome sleep difficulties, there is also the reality of the baby's initial digestive problems, loosely labeled colic, which add to the natural anxiety of new parents. And if that weren't enough, the fact that babies in the first two months of life are neither as good looking nor as responsive as our mythology leads parents to believe doesn't help matters.

There is a decided increase in the stress level associated with full-time parenting when babies start to crawl about the home at seven to eight months of age. If it's a first child, the principle sources of stress will come from fears of physical danger to the child (and to the home, for that matter), along with the extra work that is a consequence. Newly crawling babies are incredibly curious about everything they can see and reach; they use their mouths to explore, they don't know very much about the characteristics of objects, and they are inadequate masters of their own bodies. Certainly they don't know either how fragile or how valuable objects might be. The life span of the newly sprouted avocado seed in the hands of a typical ten-month-old is about ten seconds.

All this adds up to a worried parent, and rightly so. The period from ten to twenty months of age is, for example, the time when the vast majority of accidental poisonings take place. Remember that the child, when crawling about the kitchen, the living room, or the bedroom, finds everything new. She has seen some of these things from a distance, but she has never before been able to come up close to such intriguing objects as the bits of beautiful, shiny glass from a broken jar that happened to fall in an out-of-the-way place, or interestingly frayed sections of lamp cord.

There is nothing of more universal appeal to a ten-month-old than a set of stairs. Put her at the bottom and you can bet with confidence that she will attempt to climb. Some ten-month-olds are pretty good at climbing stairs. At times they will pause after climbing three or four, and in the moments that follow, may be distracted, perhaps by a mark on the bannister that captures their attention, or by a small toy left there by another child. This distraction may cause them to forget where they are, and they may simply turn around, the result of which could be a fall. No wonder anybody who's reasonable and loving worries about the safety and well-being of a child who is crawling about the home for the first time.

In addition to the stress from the worry about the dangers to the child, there is also the stress from the extra work that a child of this age produces. If you give a baby a chance to roam about the home, you'll find yourself spending more time in the course of the day straightening up the house, particularly if either parent happens to insist on keeping the household neat. Babies create clutter; it is natural as breathing. And a cluttered house with a ten-month-old baby is, all other things being equal, a good sign. In fact, an immaculately picked-up house and a ten-month-old baby who is developing well are, in my opinion, usually incompatible. If more adults were aware of this contradiction, it probably would save a lot of grief.

By far the greatest stress that is generated once a baby can crawl occurs if there is a slightly older sibling in the home, particularly if that sibling is a first child. You have to expect that there will be deeply rooted feelings of anger based in jealousy on the part of the slightly older sibling. The reality of sibling rivalry is reasonably well known but it is usually not fully understood by typical young parents. People are inclined to think that any such problem will begin as soon as the new child is brought home from the hospital. But sibling rivalry is rarely a major problem at that stage of the game. After all, the new baby is likely to weigh about six pounds, have a relatively soft cry, and live mostly in a box in another room, showing up only occasionally during the day. Thus the newborn makes a comparatively small dent in the life of the one-and-a-half-year-old. But the problems begin to surface with a vengeance when the new child becomes mobile. For all the reasons just listed, such a child has to have more attention by whoever is caring for her, and that attention, from the point of view of a two-year-old, is very difficult to deal with.

Because of the importance of this subject, we will discuss it in detail in later sections. For now it is sufficient to note that among studies of average families of various kinds, the biggest single source of stress encountered is generally the stress that comes from having closely spaced siblings.

The final form of stress worth noting in this brief summary is the negativistic behavior that emerges with most children in the second half of the second year. Although the eight- to fourteen-month-old baby creates a good deal of stress because of the aforementioned reasons, there seems to be nothing personal in those behaviors: The child is simply acting in accordance with his nature. For example, after he has destroyed a cherished plant, he will move on to the next interesting situation. His mother, coming upon the remains, may very naturally make a loud noise in expressing her displeasure. The typical response of a normal ten-month-old is to pause in his new exploration and to turn reflexively and promptly toward the noise made by his mother, and upon seeing her face regardless of its expression, smile.

That same child at fifteen or sixteen months of age is an altogether different person. From the time he has begun to crawl, he has been collecting experiences in which he has been forbidden to do A or B or to play with objects C or D. From about fifteen or sixteen months on, as his awareness of self begins to be more substantial, something in his nature we don't fully understand will lead him to deliberately try each of these forbidden activities, specifically to see what will be allowed and what won't. In other words, he will begin systematically to test the authority of the adult he lives with. Resistance to simple requests becomes very common at this time, and if there is more than one child around, this can be a low point in the parenting experience. Dealing with both a fifteen- and a thirty-month-old child day in and day out is usually an extremely stressful way of life. We will go into more detail on this topic in the next chapter.

Lack of Assistance

The last major obstacle to optimal educational development during this period relates to the fact that by and large young parents must go through these processes alone. Indeed, often the mother lacks the benefit of a sympathetic husband and has to cope with his dissatisfactions during this period on top of everything else. This constitutes cruel and inhuman punishment in our judgment. Pediatricians vary in the degree to which they provide support; the ones that *do* provide help are often revered. Very often, however, pediatricians have no extensive background in these topics and are ill-equipped to cope effectively with this part of their practice. There are in fact quite a number of "parent support" programs in existence today, but while they do wonderful work it is usually nowhere near sufficient to meet the need. There are even occasions when a young mother is on good terms with her mother or mother-in-law, in which case she can profit from the wisdom of experience and good sense often present in the minds of practiced mothers. But by and large, however, the typical young family—particularly the mother—has to go it alone.

GENERAL BEHAVIOR DURING PHASE V

The Remarkable Curiosity of Phase V Children

As noted earlier, at about eight months of age babies enter into a period that closely parallels the peak period of curiosity in the young of other mammals. One cannot help but be impressed by this curiosity, which shows itself in the baby's dedication to physical exploration as soon as he can move his body through space. Except in children who are ill or seriously damaged, this behavior is highly predictable.

It seems logical that in the course of the hundreds of hours prelocomotive children spend looking about at distant, unreachable objects, they will build up great anticipation with respect to exploring their environment. Remember that from the time the child was approximately four months of age the child has been comfortable sitting up, has had enough back and neck muscle strength to do so comfortably, and has also had the capacity to see and hear clear across the room.

"Why? Because it's there"

These new abilities are combined with an intense need to explore the world. As a result you can expect the crawling infant to explore if given the chance. If you have an eight-month-old-child who can move about on her own but who shows no interest in exploring her environment, I urge you to see your pediatrician or other health specialist promptly to see whether she is ill or has a handicap of some kind.

Situations that most adults would find uninteresting often fascinate a baby. Do not be surprised if you find your child swinging a kitchen cabinet door several dozen times a day for several consecutive days. Do not be surprised if small pieces of dust that have been picked up from the floor intrigue him. Do not be surprised if he is fascinated by the cellophane wrapper from a package of cigarettes. This means, of course, that razor blades will interest him, too, along with anything else that he can inspect closely, particularly if he can handle the object and bring it to his mouth. You can therefore see the dual nature of curiosity. It is the motivational force underlying most learning and achievement while at the same time it is a source of many childhood accidents, and certainly causes a great deal of normal anxiety for parents.

Motor Skills

The incredible curiosity of Phase V is accompanied by an equally intense interest on the part of all healthy babies in mastering the use of their bodies. From eight to fourteen months of age especially, new motor skills of a very important kind develop. It is the nature of the baby to practice each of those skills repeatedly until he gets them right. In addition and more subtly, in the practicing of these skills, children begin to learn a good deal about people, about their usefulness and about their emotional reactions to their efforts and their achievements. Although the acquisition of motor abilities is reasonably assured under a wide variety of childrearing circumstances, the social consequences are more likely to be at risk, especially today, and warrant extensive comment by us.

Crawling and Climbing

The first motor skill of Phase V is some form of crawling. This initial crawling is followed by the ability to get higher in space, a skill that takes two forms: (1) the initial ability to climb, and (2) the ability to pull oneself up to a standing posture.

The ability to climb is an extraordinarily interesting and momentous affair to infants. It also appears in two stages. The first stage emerges at somewhere between eight and twelve months, when children begin to climb relatively modest heights limited to about six inches. (This height is coincidentally just right for typical stair climbing.) You may find a child managing to ascend a low footstool when he is eight to ten months of age. He finds this capacity to get up off the floor very exciting and will practice it again and again. This practice is slightly dangerous to him in that his ability to maintain his balance is only marginal and his judgment as to where his behind will land if he turns to sit is not particularly good. In addition, his memory leaves something to be desired. Thus there is a strong likelihood of a daily fall or two as a result of this newfound climbing skill.

Sometime around eleven or twelve months of age babies acquire a second climbing skill, the ability to climb as much as a foot or so at a time. This improved ability allows the baby to get up on the living room sofa—and from there she will generally be able to climb onto the arms of the sofa, and then onto the top of the sofa, and so forth. Likewise, she can climb onto a kitchen chair, from the chair onto the top of a table, from the table onto the top of a counter, and so on. This two-step process seems to be universal with all infants; you can see immediately its important safety consequences—as well as its payoffs in the excitement of new places that she can now reach and explore. Obviously, with a baby capable of climbing twelve-inch rises you have to take special precautions with poisons and other hazardous substances and objects.

Standing and Cruising

Another early motor skill achieved during this period is the baby's pulling himself to stand. He will pull himself to stand against a piece of furniture or perhaps against your leg using your slacks, skirt, or any other article of clothing that is handy for support. This new skill is followed fairly soon by an activity called "cruising," which consists of moving about on two legs while holding on to supporting objects. Usually at about one year of age, but sometimes several months sooner, this cruising is followed by unaided walking. Walking is followed by running, and at about thirteen or fourteen months of age, by the capacity to straddle small four-wheeled objects and drag them about. These are the primary motor acquisitions having to do with the large muscles of the body. The new freedom of these skills means a great deal to a child, and he will spend a great deal of time practicing them if given the opportunity.

Staring Behavior

During our extensive observations of many kinds of Phase V children, we have been struck by the surprising frequency of a behavior we call "staring," or gaining information through vision. In observations of hundreds of children the single most frequent activity found in this age, other than sleeping, was simply looking at one or another object or scene. If you observe your child (when you cannot be seen) for any length of time, you can see for yourself that your Phase V baby is a "looker." She stares a lot. My colleagues who study other primates, the great apes and monkeys of various kinds, tell me that the young of those species also spend a good deal of time staring at objects, at other monkeys, and so forth. All human babies spend a substantial amount of time looking at their mothers or other primary caretakers. They'll stare at objects before a more active exploration of them, or just after. They also like to look out the window, and will watch other children playing at a distance. We have found that about 20 percent of all waking time during this phase is spent staring at one thing or another.

The First Responses to Words

The Phase V baby week by week will reveal greater and greater interest in and understanding of words and phrases. Now, the development of the understanding of language is slowly beginning. You will begin to find you have a companion as your young child becomes more of a person, more the kind you've been used to in your ordinary dealings with other humans. This first understanding of words will reveal itself in the compliant behavior of this period. Increasingly, children will tend to respond when you call their names, will look toward other family members whom you are addressing, and will go along with simple requests—to throw a kiss, wave bye-bye, or retrieve an object. But don't expect a great deal of talking by your child yet. A few children do indeed begin to talk before their first birthday, but not many. The picture will change by the time the child is about a year-and-a-half.

Increasing Interest in Mother

In addition to satisfying curiosity and trying new motor skills, the third principal interest of Phase V children is their interest in the person around whom the day revolves. From eight to fourteen months of age you will notice the steadily increasing orientation toward the primary caretaker, featuring at about ten or eleven months the first clear request for assistance from that person and the first expressions of anger directed at that person, hopefully on rare occasions. The first requests for assistance are most often for things like more milk or cookies, or sometimes for help when the child can't do something for herself.

Interest in Small Objects

The eight-month-old child very often will show a striking interest in tiny particles. While sitting playing at her highchair, or on the floor, you may notice her scrunching up her forehead and staring intensely at small objects, some which you cannot even see from a distance. Looking closer you may find the child concentrating on cracker crumbs or perhaps a small bug. You are seeing the result of two processes reaching maturation: the capacity to see very fine detail, and the capacity to explore that fine detail in new ways because of the newfound abilities of sitting up and locomotion. This interest is linked to the more general but equally deep interest in the exploration of the qualities of small objects. From eight months until two years or so, and increasingly during Phase V, children universally spend roughly 25 percent of all waking time in active exploration of small objects. That interest takes three principal forms. One is simply staring at the object. The second is what we call *exploratory behavior:* the child explores all the attributes of any new object he comes across. That exploration includes bringing the object to the mouth for gumming, banging it, striking it, throwing it, turning it around and then staring at it from different angles, rubbing it against things, and so forth. He will try out a wide variety of actions on the subject. The third type of small-object exploration is what we call *mastery experiences,* or the practicing of simple skills on objects. If the object has a base so that it can be stood up and then knocked down again, you may find the child engaged in doing this. If it is a crayon, you may find him rolling it back and forth and watching the motion. Phase V children also have a peculiar fascination with collections of items, particularly if they are irregularly shaped and have fine detail. One of the simple skills they practice at this time is the emptying of objects out of containers one at a time. Once those objects are all emptied out they may very well be systematically returned, one at a time, with the child pausing to examine each as he does.

Mouthing Objects and Other Materials

At this stage of life, the mouth continues to be a prominent tool for exploration. You can also expect with most children that new teeth will be erupting or about to erupt. Because of both factors, most objects will be brought to the mouth at this age, at times with unfortunate consequences for the child's safety.

Clumsiness

In spite of the fact that motor abilities are emerging rapidly, you must not forget that children of this age are not terribly skillful. You'll notice that by and large they are surprisingly careful about themselves. It is our estimate that at least four out of five children of this age are careful climbers. Nevertheless, there is that one child in five or six who seems to be bent on self-destruction. I've seen them too often not to warn you to watch closely.

Friendliness

The eight- to fourteen-month-old baby, particularly during the early stages of this phase, is a very friendly child when it comes to familiar people. By familiar we mean those with whom he interacts everyday. He may be causing you all sorts of grief, extra work, and anxiety, but he is not doing this in order to upset you. The difficulties he creates are simply natural accompaniments of this particular stage of his development. Furthermore, you'll be rewarded over and over again with gestures of affection and wide, totally irresistible smiles. If you are lucky, you may be spontaneously hugged and kissed—often—as well as on request. Enjoy this friendliness while it lasts; with the onset of Phase VI, things take a turn for the worse.

Anxiety and Shyness with Strangers

This friendliness is chiefly reserved for the primary caretaker and other people whom the baby sees every day. Normally during this phase the child becomes less and less gregarious with all other people. Two trends account for this decrease in general sociability. The first is a growing intensity of interest on the child's part in learning precisely what she can and cannot do in the home. The second is her interest in beginning the process of learning who she is. This double interest is absolutely central to her development and it can best be pursued with her primary caretaker. At the same time, the "hale fellow, well met" quality of the child during Phase IV is gradually receding, as if the child has made his social choices. Though not consciously, he has usually concluded by eight months of age that his security lies with his parents or other principal caretakers. He remains relatively friendly with other members of the nuclear family, but outsiders—even those as close as grandparents living elsewhere—are likely to be treated during Phase V with growing apprehension and shyness. These qualities will likely be more pronounced when the child is in a strange environment. Put him in his grandparent's home and, more often than not, he will seek his mother for security and stay close to her. This kind of behavior, normal at this age, may persist until the child reaches two years.

Behavior with Siblings

Two different situations with siblings are involved here, and each requires separate discussion. In the first, the child has a sibling who is three or more years older; in the second, the child has a sibling less than three years older, and therefore not much more than an infant also. Indeed, the second situation *is unquestionably the most common source of protracted stress that average families experience in raising young children.* For this reason a good deal of time will be spent discussing the consequences of such close spacing in the balance of this book.

Interaction with a Sibling Three or more Years Older

We have seen repeatedly that the older sibling in such arrangements tends to treat the Phase V baby with affection and interest on those occasions when she has a chance to interact. Somewhat surprisingly under most circumstances, siblings more than three years older than an infant do not spend a great deal of time with the baby. They have entered into a period of life where they are much more oriented to children their own age than was the case in infancy, and they are much more inclined to play with peers than with an infant brother or sister. A baby's most common experience with such older siblings therefore involves watching them either alone or playing with their friends.

Interaction with a Sibling less than Three Years Older

In the case of a baby with a sibling not much older than the baby himself, the situation is different in very important ways. The older child, especially if a first child, and especially if somewhat indulged— all of which happen together rather commonly—can be expected to gradually come to feel and to show genuine resentment and dislike toward the baby. This behavior, while very unpleasant to witness and to live with is so common that it must be considered normal. It also should be anticipated and has to be coped with by parents as well as the infant.

Due to the normal resentment and occasional anger felt by the older sibling toward the younger child, from time to time the older sibling will act aggressively and selfishly toward the baby. Notice that this topic of sibling rivalry was not introduced until we started to deal with the eight-month-old child. A newly crawling child is much more likely to get hurt than a much younger infant, and she is also more likely to break things and create extra work in the home as a result of her explorations. Both factors inevitably require that parents pay more attention to a child once she has started crawling. Attention—in the mind of an older sibling only eighteen to thirty months of age—means love. A five-day-old sibling newly arrived from the hospital doesn't trouble a toddler very much. After all, newborns sleep most of the day and tend therefore not to be a constant object of attention. Even when they get to be four or five months of age and are awake much of the time, they still do not intrude a great deal on the moment-to-moment experiences of the slightly older sibling. The picture changes dramatically, however, from the moment they begin to crawl about, especially if parents allow them to explore the home rather than confine them to playpens for most of the day.

Because of these realities it is totally natural for slightly older children to begin to act aggressively and selfishly toward the baby. The older child may hit the baby now and again, may knock the baby down, or take toys away from him. At first the younger child is likely to be bewildered by these behaviors, but sooner or later some of them will cause pain. That pain in turn will be followed by a cry, bringing a parent who is likely to size up the situation and conclude that the older child was the cause of the pain that the baby is experiencing. A harsh word or a slight spank on the bottom of the older child is natural under such circumstances, but it certainly doesn't ease the tension in the mind of the older child. As Phase V continues, this emotionally loaded process will evolve. We expect to see an escalation of jealousy, hard feelings, and aggression on the part of the older child, and a learning on the part of the younger child to cry sooner and sooner and louder and louder. The result very often is that by the eleventh to twelfth month, the younger child may flinch and cry even before being abused by the slightly older child. The older child, having gone through dozens of learning experiences in respect to the effectiveness of the baby's cry, enters gradually into a period of frustration. He has clearly learned that aggression toward the baby, or more properly speaking, the cry of the baby, is likely to lead to punishment by the central person in his life. As a result, by about a year of age, or midway through Phase V, a standoff often develops. This temporary armistice is likely to persist through the balance of Phase V and to take a surprising turn once the younger child enters Phase VI (to be discussed later).

The severity of this problem seems to be very directly related to the age gap between children. The closer they are in age, the more frequent and intense the hostile behavior from the older child to the younger one during Phase V. This hostile behavior, by the way, as you can imagine, comes as quite a shock to many young parents. After all, they've had approximately a year and a half during which that first child brought them an incredible amount of pleasure and pride, and now, try as they might, they cannot avoid concluding that their older child is capable of active dislike of their equally precious baby. Coping with this kind of unhappy situation is something that parents have been ill prepared for. One of the benefits of the new knowledge in child development is that we now understand the origins of this kind of behavior. We have found that when parents are informed before the fact, things can go much better.

Younger babies in this situation do learn during Phase V about how to cope with older siblings, how to defend themselves, how to avoid getting into difficulty, and, sadly but truly, how to behave in a manner similar to the aggressor.

We will talk more about interreactions between siblings in later sections. Suffice it to say that spacing children at least three years apart is an extremely good idea. To be sure, there will be times when the older child will treat the younger with genuine affection, but don't be surprised if such events become fewer and fewer in number during Phase V.[2]

The Apparent Interests of Phase V

We have found it useful to characterize the central interests of the Phase V age in the following manner: (1) intense social interest in the primary caretaker, (2) interest in exploration of the world in the service

[2] In addition to the important day-to-day increases in stress caused by close spacing of siblings, there is reason to believe that the long-term intellectual consequences of very close spacing should be of some concern to parents. In a 1976 *Science* article, P.B. Zajonc of the University of Michigan reported on a study of the IQ test scores of 1,379,000 children from four Western countries. He found that the closer in age the children were spaced, and the more children in the family, the lower the test scores. There was one interesting exception to this find: last children, especially those widely spaced from the preceding siblings, tended to do considerably better than all but the first-borns.

of satisfying curiosity, and (3) interest in practicing new motor skills. These three areas are most relevant to educational achievement.

Interest in the Primary Caretaker

How children progress from eight months to about two years of age in respect to their interest in their primary caretaker is very exciting. The topic of attachment to another person has been a popular one in child development research in recent times and, by other labels, has been popular for many years. Popularity does not always produce wisdom, but I think in this case we have learned a great deal about the details of the attachment process in the early years of life.

We know for certain that the newborn baby simply cannot survive without a relationship with a more mature and capable human. A newborn baby is helpless; physical survival is impossible unless someone provides for him. We talked earlier about the various assets babies have during the early months of life that seem to heighten the probability that someone from the species will come to love them dearly, to care for them, to nurture them, and to protect them. A new phase of that ongoing development begins in earnest at about eight months of age.

Between eight and twenty-four months a good deal of the child's waking activities will revolve around her primary caretaker (usually mother). She will watch mother's actions for substantial portions of each day. She will use mother as a haven whenever she is feeling threatened. She will use mother for assistance whenever she can, increasingly from about ten or eleven months of age. She will learn from mother. She will learn, for example, whether she can pull on the curtains, climb on furniture, climb on her own or mother's bed, touch the plants in the living room, or go out to the porch. She will learn thousands of specific answers to questions that will arise as she goes about her explorations. She will learn something about mother's disciplinary style and, by the time she is thirteen or fourteen months of age, she will become rather sophisticated in all these areas. If the parent is a talker rather than a doer, she will learn that threats are only words and will not be followed by actions. She will learn how to determine whether or not a parent means business. She will learn, albeit imperfectly, whether a parent is the kind of person who gives baby her undivided attention or is often distracted. She will learn whether an instruction or an admonition requires immediate compliance or can safely be disregarded after a brief pause.

By the time a child is two years of age, and often much earlier, she will have established an elaborate and detailed social contract with her primary caretaker. That contract is relatively hard to alter or modify subsequently. What children acquire in those first two years is the first set of social skills and attitudes they will begin to use with other family members, and with other children as they enter into peer relations.

As noted earlier, you probably can't spoil a child in the first eight months of life beyond some overcrying to be picked up; but surely between eight and twenty-four months you can turn a child into a self-centered and annoying person to live with. I believe one of the greatest opportunities parents have to influence their children for a lifetime is through the quality of their interactions during the period between eight and twenty-four months of age.

You can observe a decline of interest in parents at this point if certain conditions prevail. If a child of this age is prevented from having a free and easy exchange with his parents or some other primary caretaker in these months, and if, for example, he is provided with all sorts of toys and areas to explore, you may find him showing less and less interest in people and more interest in objects. (Given most circumstances, however, the interest in people will not only remain strong throughout this period, but may very well overpower the interest in objects. More about that later.)

Interest in Exploration of the World

The child at eight months of age is an explorer. He wants to see everything, touch everything, and bring everything that he can to his mouth. This interest is shown in his active exploration of any area to which he is allowed access. You'll find there is absolutely no need to induce him to explore and to learn. He'll do it for the sheer joy of it. Any small, portable object will be explored for its novelty or whenever it can be used to practice simple hand-eye skills. The child will show interest in the controls on the TV, the radio, the stereo. He's interested in door knobs. He's interested in the contents of kitchen cabinets and pantries. He's interested in particles of dust, leaves—just about anything he can make contact with.

The Phase V child's deep natural interest in the object world has several important ramifications. One is the role that interest plays in deepening and broadening his curiosity, and in promoting the development of the foundations of intelligence. Another is the role it plays as a "balancing agent" against the interest in social relations with the primary caretaker. (The Phase V child appears to start out with his three main interests in balance, but there is no guarantee they will remain that way in the year or so that follow. Furthermore, when that balance is distorted, it appears that the educational progress of the child tends to become less than ideal. And one common way balance is thrown off is if the normal focus on the mother tends to expand at the expense of the other two interests.)

The final point to be made concerning the Phase V child's interests in exploration is the apparently universal appeal of water play—which includes playing in the toilet bowl. Phase V children will pull themselves up to stand near the bowl and play with the contents therein. This seems to be a common development in the lives of many children we have studied. Needless to say there are many other, more hygienically suitable ways to encourage water play.

Interest in Practicing New Motor Skills

In an earlier section we described the sequence of emerging motor skills, from crawling to standing to climbing. Phase V children spend many hours practicing their new ability to move through space in all directions, provided of course they are given the opportunity. Again, one of the most common interests in this stage is in climbing stairs. It is amazing what a hypnotic power steps have on the very young child.

LEARNING DEVELOPMENTS DURING PHASE V

Let's preface the following discussion by reemphasizing some points made earlier. First, it is my belief that the educational developments that take place roughly from age eight to twenty months are *the most important and most in need of attention of any that occur in human life*. Absolutely basic educational foundations begin to develop in very important and fundamental ways as soon as a child starts to crawl about the home and simultaneously begins to master language. The four basic educational foundations discussed earlier in this chapter are now central in determining what a human being will become.

Again, I would like to emphasize my belief that solid development of those educational foundations *is by no means assured*. The responsibility for the quality of the educational outcome for most children rests with their own families and, more specifically, with whoever is the primary caretaker. As we have seen, parents are not routinely prepared for their job, nor are they given very much assistance. Once more, my view is that not more than two-thirds of our children currently get adequate development in the areas dealt with here, and no more than 10 percent do as well as they could during the first three years of their lives. This state of affairs may be a tragedy, but it is by no means a twentieth-century tragedy. *In the history of Western education there has never been a society that recognized the educational*

importance of the earliest years or sponsored any systematic prepara-
tion and assistance to families or any other institution in guiding the
early development of children.

Language Development

Language development was dealt with extensively on pages 112 and 113. Let me stress again that language is absolutely central to the development of intelligence and social skills, and that a child doing well linguistically has a solid asset in his attempts at becoming a well-rounded human being.

The Development of Curiosity

The importance of curiosity for the Phase V child was discussed on pages 120 and 121. Here I should only like to reemphasize my belief that curiosity can be broadened and deepened by intelligent childrearing during this period, but that relatively few families do the job as well as they would like to and could.

Social Development

Children two years of age can evolve into delightful companions who have free and easy social relationships and who, at the same time, maintain a profound curiosity about the world at large. Unfortunately, they can also develop into human beings whose world revolves excessively around an older adult, usually the mother. Often the mother is badgered from morning to night by a consuming desire on the part of the two-year-old to monopolize her time and attention. This type of child very often loses intrinsic interest in exploring objects or motor skills and now sees a new toy primarily as a tool for manipulating mother.

It is even sadder to see a child who by two has learned that his mother is not generally an approachable human being unless she shows several obvious signs: that she is in a good mood, and that she would like him to approach. We have seen children systematically turned off from their primary caretakers by repeated rejections during Phases V and VI. This particular pattern is tragic to see, and when it is accompanied by a lack of interesting physical materials and opportunities to explore the home, you get the saddest situation of all—a child who seems to be somewhat empty at two years of age. I believe that poor social development can be avoided fairly easily. More about how to achieve the desired patterns will follow.

Earlier we listed three important emerging social competencies of special importance. These are (1) using an adult as a resource, (2) showing pride in achievement, and (3) engaging in make-believe or role-play behavior. From our research, these new behaviors seem to be very important for the best educational progress. A discussion of how to encourage such optimal development will follow.

NURTURING THE ROOTS OF INTELLIGENCE

I have described a powerful and near universal urge in healthy eight-month-old children to explore the world. This urge is the principal motivating power underlying the acquisition of intelligence. That force can be deepened and broadened, or it can be made more shallow or more narrow by childrearing practices.

The Growth of Learning to Learn Skills

The underlying motivation to learn is as important as any other factor in regard to a child's educational well-being. In addition to developing that urge, children are collecting learning skills, learning how to learn, during Phases V and VI. Piaget has described the exciting and fundamental events of this age. Our own research on many children as we have watched them develop during this period adds many details to the story.

"Learning to learn" skills come easily to the child who is given the chance to explore the world, as well as a healthy dose of encouragement and assistance by adults. Children do not produce products of any consequence in this particular phase, nor will they until they are at least two years of age; but they are learning prerequisite skills. You won't find Phase V children drawing pictures, for example, but you will find them learning to handle small devices like those they will use later to write and draw with. You will begin to see signs of an interest in scribbling toward the end of Phase V. The innumerable efforts directed at getting to know the characteristics of objects, whether they bounce or roll, plop or slide, will later be used in the construction of products such as towers, ships, trucks, and scenes that feature dolls, animals, and buildings.

The retrieval skills that children are learning when they roll or throw a ball and then seek and reclaim it are also in and of themselves prerequisite elements in the more complicated and elaborate activities that come a year or two later. At this time they are also learning their first lessons in how to put things together and take them apart. You'll find that Phase V and VI children are very much interested in putting objects into each other. For example, putting lids on containers is a common interest seen at this point; sliding one gadget into and out of another is another activity of particular interest at this stage. These simple motor skills are interesting to a child in and of themselves, but they are also preparing the child for later, more complicated experiences.

Hinges and Hinged Objects

A curious related interest of Phase V are hinges and hinged objects. Early in our observations of Phase V children we noticed their fascination with the activity of swinging doors back and forth. The most common door we have seen used in this manner is a kitchen cabinet door.

Interest in hinged objects is also revealed in the Phase V child's fascination with Jack-in-the-box toys—or other small boxlike devices with covers that can swing open and be closed—in spite of the fact that the typical Jack-in-the-box toy cannot be operated properly by most children under two years of age. This difficulty is because they usually require the young child to perform two somewhat difficult acts at once: the child must press a cover down on the figure inside the box with one hand while he rotates a handle to lock the cover in place with the other. Such complicated motor coordinations are considerably beyond the capacities of the Phase V child.

An exception is the Disney Busy Poppin' Pals, formerly known as the Busy Surprise Box, which has five small Jack-in-the-boxes lined up next to each other in a single plastic box. In order to get the lid to swing up, revealing a small animal figure, the child has to perform one of five simple motor activities including pushing a lever one way or the other, or rotating a telephone dial or pushing a button. Of the five activities, the only one a child of this age can manage is pushing the lever one way or the other. We have found that most Phase V babies enjoy this particular toy. By "enjoy" we mean they will play with it for as much as five to ten minutes at a time. This relatively prolonged use of a commercial toy is most unusual at this stage.

An even more subtle manifestation of the apparently universal interest in hinged objects is the Phase V baby's interest in books. She is particularly intrigued by those that have stiff cardboard pages. Her interest is based not so much on what is printed on the pages, but in what is required in hand-eye skills to turn those pages to open the book, turn it upside down, and so forth. In other words, the small book with cardboard pages is an object on which she can practice simple motor skills. One of the skills she is particularly interested in involves treating any single page like one-half of a hinge and swinging it back and forth.

It is relatively easy to see how some of the simple skills that are practiced by babies in Phase V will play a role later in more complicated activities. It is not quite that easy to see how an interest in swinging kitchen cabinet doors fits into the larger scheme of things but, whether or not we can understand the reason for this interest, it is indeed there.

Along with their value as materials to feed the interest in perfecting hand-eye skills of Phase V babies, books can begin to be of some use at this stage in connection with language acquisition. The rate of language acquisition during Phase V is quite slow in comparison with what will come in the balance of the first three years; nevertheless, language learning is taking place. Books without stories, ones which simply illustrate objects that are likely to be familiar to a Phase V baby, are the most suitable for language teaching at this stage of the game. The language teaching should be principally in terms of labeling. If you can manage to get the Phase V baby to sit still long enough to actually attend to what's on the page once in a while, naming the particular picture can sometimes be a pleasurable and profitable activity. You shouldn't be discouraged if you have a particularly active Phase V baby who simply refuses to sit still for simple activities with books, let alone story telling. If on the other hand you have the kind of child who will listen to very simple stories, especially at bedtime, so much the better. Bear in mind, however, the typical fourteen-month-old child can only understand approximately three dozen words and a few simple expressions, and as a result stories of any complication are not likely to make much of an impression on him. Labeling of course shouldn't be restricted to books. It's the most natural thing in the world for parents to put names on anything a baby of this age is interacting with, and this makes good sense. Indeed, the more you do this, the better.

The Growth of Short-term Memory

Phase V is a remarkable time for the growth of memory. Before Phase V a baby doesn't seem to have much memory of any kind. For example, at five months of age a baby who drops a rattle doesn't pause to look around for where it might have gone or in any way indicate any sign of interrupted activity. Sometime around the beginning of Phase V, however, a change in behavior occurs. In his now classic studies of the growth of what he called *object permanence*, or the independent existence of objects, Piaget demonstrated the beginnings of memory. He hid from one of his young children (age eight months) a small interesting object under a pillow. The child removed the pillow and easily found the object. After a moment or two, he took the object away and hid it again under the pillow. Once again, the child after a brief hesitation removed the pillow from the hidden object, found it, and grabbed it. Piaget repeated this process several times, and then hid the same object immediately afterwards with a second pillow near the child. The child's response was to look at where the object was now hidden and then *seek to find it, not where he had just seen it hidden, but where he had previously found it.* This finding has been repeated many times. Piaget uses it as one of dozens of experiments to illustrate the child's growing but incomplete sophistication about the world of objects. The eight-month-old child still conceives of objects only in terms of the activities with which he has been engaged with them. That is, the existence of the desired object was linked in the child's mind to the act of finding it. In contrast, an older child (or an adult) is fully aware of the fact that the object, like all objects, has its own independent existence. This is what Piaget meant by *object permanence.*

In the period that begins at eight months of age, the capacity of an infant to retain some sort of mental image of objects stretches from a matter of a second or two to longer and longer periods. Using more and more obstacles between a baby and a desired object, making it take longer and longer to get to the hidden object, has allowed students of child development to plot with some precision the actual limits of Phase V object permanence. The child of about one year of age, for example, will easily find an object hidden under one pillow, but if you place three or four coverings on top of an object, requiring that the child persist for ten to fifteen seconds in his search, he is very likely to abandon the search before he succeeds in getting the object. Even by the end of Phase V the child's capacity to remember an object is nowhere near full development.

There are valuable practical consequences of this new knowledge. When you combine the limited memory of a Phase V child with his intense curiosity about everything new, you have the basis for distracting a child once he gets involved with something you'd rather he did not have. If, for example, the nine-month-old child has found a cigarette butt, offering a set of plastic spoons to the child will usually result in the child's turning his attention away from the cigarette butt toward the spoons. After four or five seconds of play with the spoons, the child is not at all likely to seek the cigarette butt again; he has forgotten about it. Once the child reaches twelve to fourteen months, however, given the same circumstances, the child will turn back and seek the first item he played with. But move the child to another room and provide him with *three* new objects, and his preoccupation with them for twenty to thirty seconds is usually long enough so that he forgets the object at the beginning of the episode.

RECOMMENDED CHILDREARING PRACTICES AT PHASE V

The primary caretaker has three major functions during Phase V, and indeed these roles persist throughout the balance of the first three years. These are: (1) "architect" or "designer" of the child's world and daily experiences; (2) "consultant," someone to provide assistance and encouragement to the child; and (3) authority, the source of discipline and limit-setting. Let us examine each of these in turn.

THE PRIMARY CARETAKER'S ROLE AS DESIGNER

Providing Access in the Home

Once the home has been made safe *for* and *from* the baby, the next basic step in designing a young child's world is to *give her maximum access to that living area.* Even the smallest, simplest home is an extremely rich environment for the Phase V baby. At this age everything is new and fascinating. Simply providing the Phase V child with maximum access in the home will nourish her *curiosity* in a natural and powerful way. You give her, at the same time, the opportunity to encounter and work on *physical* challenges. Finally, you give her innumerable opportunities to confront *social* circumstances that ultimately teach her about people and their reactions.

By providing maximum access to a safe home you have also gone a long way toward preserving the balance of the child's three major interests. Just think for a moment of the contrasting situation in which, to avoid danger, extra work, stress, and so forth, you routinely confine your child to a playpen, a small gated room, or crib. You may in the short run have an easier time of it, but in the long run the negative effects of such confinement on a child's curiosity, and on the growth of his capacity to play alone, far outweigh the short-term returns.

Supplying Playthings

I recommend you have available certain toys and other materials for special times. Occasionally even children who are allowed maximum access to the home appear bored during Phase V, although boredom is not nearly as common then as it is later in life. More about this topic in the section on recommended materials.

The Primary Caretaker's Role as Consultant

You can be sure that if you've provided your Phase V child with a safe home and a few stimulating materials he will explore and find things that interest and occasionally excite him. In addition he'll sometimes find himself in situations that are frustrating or that cause him modest pain. In all of these occasions you can be sure that the child sometimes will turn to you for assistance, shared enthusiasm, or comforting. When your child approaches you, you have another primary opportunity to really be effective as your child's educator.

A baby's interests during this stage of life are relatively easy to identify most of the time. If you have a child who comes to you excited by something pleasurable or aroused by something difficult, you have a motivated child. If you know what he is focusing on, you have ideal learning circumstances. What effective parents do in this regard is, first of all, to be available for such experiences. In the course of a typical day, you can expect that there will be about ten such overtures an hour. Second, effective parents usually respond promptly to most of these overtures. (Interestingly, however—and very importantly—when appropriate, instead of stopping their own activities to tend to the child's needs or requests, such parents often say to the child, "I hear you now and I'll be with you in a moment, but you'll have to wait because I'm busy right now." This is important. From a very early stage, children can begin quite painlessly to learn a vital lesson in interpersonal relations: they cannot always have what they want immediately, and the needs of other people will sometimes come before theirs.) Third, good parents take a moment to see what is on the child's mind. This is most always very easy to do with a Phase V child. Now the child is motivated and attending to a topic that you're aware of. What you do in the next thirty seconds or so is therefore very likely to get through to the baby.

Why is this approach more effective than others? Consider someone who has been told that language learning is vital at this stage and routinely tries to get a child to pay attention to a book or to flash cards. Here, the parent begins with a need to direct the attention of the child to something the *adult* is attending to. But when the *child* comes to you, all one has to do is to identify the object of attention and deal directly with it.

The next step, of course, is to provide what's needed, whether it be a kiss on a hurt finger, or the separation of two stuck objects, or some enthusiasm about a discarded box. Respond with ordinary language. Use full phrases or sentences rather than single words and include a related idea or two. It really makes no difference what that idea is as long as it is linked to the subject at hand. Once the baby seems satisfied with the interchange and shows an interest in moving on, the baby is then allowed to do so. This entire process takes on the average of about twenty-five seconds, and this kind of parent-child interchange is seen with just about every developing exceptional child.

In this response pattern we have a beautiful mechanism for the effective education of a young child. First of all, the child is learning to use another person as a resource in situations that she cannot handle herself. This is a vital social skill, one which will serve her well in the years to come. Second, she is beginning to learn a bit more about the nature of other people, which will stand her in good stead when she begins to interact with people other than those of the nuclear family. Third, she is learning that someone values her excitement and the satisfaction of her curiosity. Fourth, she gets language instruction, because someone is providing language that is relevant. Fifth, her intellectual world is being broadened by the content of the information. Sixth, in cases where she asks for assistance, she is learning about completing simple tasks. Seventh, on those occasions where she is attempting something that will not work, she is being taught realistic task limitations as well. Finally, in those instances when she is made briefly to wait, she is beginning to learn a fundamental lesson: she is very important and precious, but her needs are no more important than anyone else's. We believe the wisest attitude for parents to take with their eight to thirty-six-month-old children is what we call *healthy selfishness*. As one mother puts it, "I love my child's curiosity, but she doesn't have to play with my makeup." Few parenting behaviors are more important. As you can see, the issue of how to respond to overtures from the Phase V child is a topic of paramount importance.

In the role of consultant you'll find it both natural and very enjoyable to nourish the emerging social competencies. Some of the Phase V child's overtures will be requests for assistance. Your natural inclination will be to help. By all means do so. But be careful, as the child passes his first birthday, not to let yourself start to become the child's all-purpose tool. Watch for the subtle differences between the use of you when (A) the child has determined he can't handle the task himself, versus (B) you are just the easiest way to achieve a goal, or (C) the use of you simply to monopolize your attention. A is fine, but B and C lead to an overindulged child.

Some of the child's overtures toward you as he turns fourteen or fifteen months of age will be attempts to gain praise or exclamations of delight for remarkable achievements like climbing down a single step safely. Encouraging healthy growth in this area is a real pleasure.

Another pleasure involves the child's first make-believe play. Often the behavior is hugely entertaining, especially when the child seems very serious and grown up in his involvement, for example, in nurturing dolls. Increasingly during the second year you'll be called upon to participate in such episodes. Lucky you.

The Primary Caretaker's Role as Authority

In the homes where children are developing well, in contrast to homes where children are developing poorly, we've always seen parents run the home with a loving but firm hand. The babies in these situations clearly don't have any question about who is the final authority. In homes where children don't do very well, however, there is often ambiguity with respect to the setting of limits and the determination of who is going to have the final say on disagreements. You need not fear that if you are firm with your infant, if you deny him things from time to time on a realistic basis, or even occasionally on an irrational basis, that he will love you less than if you were lenient. Children in the first two years of life do not become detached from their primary caretakers very easily. Even if you were to spank them regularly (which I do not recommend), you would find their attachment remains constant.

Be firm. You do your child no favor by yielding to her routinely in situations where your good judgment suggests that you shouldn't. This can be a special problem if it is a first child. In our work with many delightful families trying their best to produce a wonderful child, probably the biggest source of difficulty they have is overindulgence. It's not hard to see how overindulgence develops. After all, the first child is very often an absolutely unique blessing, a source of love, pride, excitement, unlike anything ever experienced previously. To deny such a child anything is often very difficult for parents. Babies learn the rules of interpersonal relationships primarily through interactions with the primary caregiver. A parent who routinely lets the child impose upon him or her, to the point where the baby learns again and again that his needs are more important than anyone else's, does the child no long-term favor. The guiding principle we recommend for our parents is to teach the child during Phase V that his needs are very special and that he is a very special person, but his needs are no *more* special than those of anyone else.

Discipline

It is important to begin to establish a pattern of solid and effective discipline during Phase V in order to prepare for more difficult challenges when the child is a bit older. We have very rarely seen effective parents repeat themselves more than once in attempting to control Phase V babies. If a child does not respond in the desired way after the message is repeated once, the parents act, either moving the child to another situation, or removing a forbidden object, and so forth. Distraction is a perfectly adequate technique throughout most of Phase V. The main thing, however, is to avoid ambiguous kinds of discipline, as, for example, when you insist that the child stop doing something and do not follow up when he doesn't stop. Such behavior, extraordinarily common, only lays the foundation for later problems.

Parents often wonder whether this author advocates physical means of punishment, such as spanking. Let me begin to deal with that subject here, with the Phase V child. There is no need to use physical punishment with a child under fourteen or fifteen months. Indeed, many parents do a wonderful job with their children in spite of never having used spankings or other aggressive disciplinary actions through the first three years of life. Fortunately, because of the relatively short attention span and the generally compliant nature of the Phase V child, spanking a child is not even an issue during this stage of life. The key to good limit setting is a clear understanding that *the child has to learn limits at this stage of the game*, not later, and that proper follow-through when there is a limit set is a day-by-day responsibility. These, plus the other principles described in this section, constitute the basic guidelines for functioning as an authority with a child during Phase V.

Sleep Problems

Phase V unfortunately is often the time when parents begin to have difficulty with children who will awaken long after they have been put to sleep for the evening and then insist on staying awake. In working with parents as we have over fifteen years or so, certain issues recur so commonly that they become classical. A common example is the ten-month-old baby who keeps parents awake at one or two in the morning. Such sleep problems can be very bothersome to young parents. In a sense, however, they are especially interesting to those of us who study the development of the young child. They seem to grow quite logically out of the typical history of loved children. We believe that the emergence of such problems grows directly out of the cry of the newborn human and the natural consequences of that expression of discomfort. In an interesting sense sleep problems are actually a good sign. Children reared in institutions, for example, who have very limited caring from overtaxed staff, rarely have the same sort of sleep problems in Phase V. In fact, during their waking hours they don't cry nearly as often as do home babies. Unfortunately for them, they have learned that the cry is rarely worth the investment.

The home-reared baby cries from birth. In the first couple of months the home-reared baby experiences hundreds of episodes in which parents respond to the cry and comfort the baby, teaching that baby that the arrival of older people usually means imminent comfort. Toward the end of Phase III the cry of a child becomes an intentional tool. The late Phase III baby cries not only because she feels discomfort, but also because she has learned that the cry will bring the adult and good times. From that time forth, parents ought to be on the alert to the increasing use of the cry for company; if they are not, they may find themselves carrying a six-month-old baby for many hours every day. It is a lot easier to reduce excessive crying for attention once a child gets to be a Phase V baby and starts to crawl about the home. This is because the newly crawling baby can occupy himself for many hours each day, satisfying curiosity and coping with motor challenges.

You can see how this discussion relates to the balance of the child's three major interests. If the child's mobility is restricted once he gets to Phase V, opportunities for exploration and motor practice will be correspondingly lessened and there will be more of an inclination to pursue the third major interest, the primary caretaker. Children who can crawl but who are kept in playpens for long periods of time tend to cry for attention much more than those who are given access to the home. The Phase V baby who begins to wake up at eleven or twelve at night, or unhappily even later, and cries for attention and insists on company for long periods is a baby who is often simply insisting on the pleasure of his parent's company rather than sleep. In the light of the child's learning history, this makes very good sense for him. Unfortunately, it's by no means convenient for most parents.

Our recommendations therefore are as follows: If the Phase V child—or for that matter even one slightly younger—begins to awaken well after bedtime and starts to cry, parents should respond (as always) promptly. There is after all the possibility that something is significantly wrong, and in any event the cry of any infant should not be ignored when it first occurs. The parent should go to the infant promptly, comfort the infant, check to see if there is anything that needs attention—a cold diaper, or an incipient ailment, or any of the routine discomforts that could be the source of the cry. If it appears that there is nothing wrong with the child, our next suggestion is that you kiss the child goodnight and, with just a couple of words, make it plain that it is bedtime. You should then put the child down gently and leave. The child may very well cry again or whimper. As hard as it may be, the best practice at that point is not to return to the room. The chances are pretty good that if this sort of behavior has only just surfaced, the child will simply go to sleep. The longer it has been in existence and reinforced by parents staying with the child for extended periods of time late at night, the more difficult it will be to extinguish. At its very worst we have found that it takes seven to ten days for parents to shift their child out of the habit of insisting on their company late at night. Happily we can report, however, that these procedures work.

In our view, when you are dealing with a healthy child in Phase V who shows this kind of problem, the origins of the behavior lie in the pattern that we've described, starting with the cry of the newborn. The behavior itself is both understandable and normal. But it is also a clear sign of where the child's minor needs are beginning to impose upon a more important need of the parents: to get a good night's sleep. Dealing effectively with this pattern from the beginning, therefore, is consistent with our suggestion of beginning to set reasonable limits on a child's inclinations during Phase V. You'll turn out a two-year-old child whom you will not only admire but will enjoy living with as well.

You should know that there are child development specialists who do not endorse this advice. Some authorities believe that a child should never be allowed to cry herself to sleep under any circumstances; they would have you take the child into your own bed, perhaps, and certainly would not allow the child to undergo the kind of discomfort that will inevitably take place for a short time if you follow our advice. We cannot responsibly claim that our method is the only way to deal with sleep problems. No child development professional has absolute proof on this subject. But we do base our approach on the consistency with which our analysis fits into the larger story of early development, and on the fact that in working with hundreds of families these procedures have not led to any observable disturbances in the child's emotional well-being. The choice of what you do is, as always, yours.

Sibling Rivalry

Earlier in this section we explained that problems with sibling rivalry are likely to become very substantial when the space between children is less than three years, and that such problems will begin to develop from the point when the younger child begins to move about the home, that is, from the beginning of Phase V. We suggested that jealousy and aggression are to be expected from the slightly older child. The younger child now becomes much more a part of daily activities and tends to receive attention in much greater quantities than before, often at the expense of the older sibling. If you understand what's going on in the mind of the slightly older child, you've taken the first step toward dealing with the situation. But of course, there is more to be done than merely understanding why your previously angelic older child has started to behave in a most reprehensible manner. Is there anything you can do, or are you locked into two years of civil war?

There *are* steps you can take. The first is to *protect the baby from aggression.* It makes no sense to try to make the older child feel guilty—after all, his dislike of his sibling is natural. But it must be made clear to him that aggression of any sort, while understandable, must not be permitted.

The second task is *to make life more bearable for the older child.* The happier he is, the easier will be life for the new baby and parents. Many parents have asked me if there is a way to prepare a two-year-old for the arrival of a new sister or brother. Unfortunately, rational explanations of complicated future situations are useless when the listener is less than three years old. Once the baby is home, however, you can reduce the upset in a variety of ways. First of all, avoid lavish praise of the younger child in the presence of the older one. Second, as soon as possible, provide out-of-home experiences for the older child. These help relieve the pressure in the family situation. If the older child, for example, is age two-and-a-half or more, a regular play group would be an excellent idea. In any event, the use of a baby sitter to take the older child on trips to the park, the zoo, and the like would help.

Although out-of-home experiences can help to reduce the older sibling's exposure to the new jealousy-producing situation in the family, they must never be allowed to make the older child feel he's being shunted aside. In our judgment it is terribly important that the older child have undivided attention from at least one parent every day, to reassure the older child in the only language he can fully understand that he is loved just as much as ever. Unfortunately, instead of trying to help the older sibling, many parents place extra demands on him. The older child, who is developing rapidly and is obviously much more mature than the baby, is expected to act with restraint and wisdom. Far from getting sympathy for the unhappy predicament he faces, he's asked to be extra grown up, not be a bother, and so on. Most often parents don't mean to be unfair to the older child, they simply overestimate his abilities.

Hard as it is on parents, the fact is that when there are two very young children in the home, *both* need special attention, and the parent's job is therefore going to be more than twice as demanding as it was before. Let me once again repeat my caveat: there is simply no way of making life with two closely spaced children as easy as dealing with a first child only or with widely spaced children. It is very important that both parents understand that fact.

RECOMMENDED MATERIALS FOR PHASE V CHILDREN

Toys: The Phase V baby may appear bored from time to time. Effective parents occasionally provide babies in this age group with a new toy or a new set of materials to rekindle their activity. Although not foolproof, this approach often works. The number of important developments in a child's life during Phases V and VI are so great, and their significance is so fundamental, that commercial toys rarely can compete successfully for the child's attention. There are no more than a small number of commercial toys for this age range that are really worth buying.

In an earlier section I described the three basic interests of Phase V children—curiosity, motor-skill challenges, and the primary caregiver. This information should be useful in helping you select toys for this age group. The situation today is far better than it has ever been before in respect to commercial toys. The dramatically increased awareness of the significance of learning in the first years of life, which surfaced in the late 1960s, has led to much greater activity by the toy companies. Although the vast majority of the newer toys that are being marketed continue to have little actual play value, there are a fair number of new toys that are indeed of substantial interest to children. Anything that provokes a young child's curiosity is very likely to be of some help in learning. For example, we have described how, from age two months through the second birthday, hand-eye activities are surprisingly interesting, in fact compelling, to the typical child. A Phase V child is of course right in the middle of that development, and it turns out that some of the commercial toys available are eminently suitable for practice in this area.

One example is Disney Poppin' Pals, formerly known as the Surprise Busy Box and described in an earlier section. The one part of the toy that the Phase V baby begins to master is the part that resembles a standard light switch and requires only that the child move a lever in order for the cover to rise abruptly, revealing a Disney character inside. Closely related to this kind of device are the simple plastic key sets that sell for under two dollars. Why should a simple set of plastic keys be appealing to a very young baby? It probably has something to do with the fact that there is just enough challenge in attempting to handle these forms to make it intriguing; also, there are numerous interesting configurations around the keys that are appropriate for this age child.

Similarly, there is the whole category of bath toys that feature interesting mechanisms. Quite a number of the major companies have produced toys that can be attached in one way or another to the side of the tub and can be used by the Phase V baby for water play. Containers that allow a child to pour water back and forth will be very interesting. But if added to that there are features like a water wheel that spins once water is poured into the top, or a squirting device, the level of interest on the part of the child will be substantially greater. Almost any of the water toys available are highly recommendable.

In the general area of manipulable toys, one has to include nesting toys of various kinds. Basically inexpensive, these are of near universal appeal. There are plastic cylinders (under seven or eight dollars) that children very much enjoy fitting together. In addition to hand-eye challenges, a second category of toys that begins to be extremely appealing for the Phase V child is balls. In our research, the most popular single toy throughout the second year of life is a ball of one sort or another. But even before the first birthday children can enjoy and play with balls. Probably the best single toy for a baby under two years of age and over seven or eight months would be a common plastic inflatable beach ball, still likely to be available for about one dollar. These balls come in several sizes, ranging from twelve to fourteen inches on up to at least twenty-four inches. Once the baby has started to walk toward the end of the first year, carrying such a ball becomes a source of enormous pleasure. Carrying it, throwing it, watching its motions and then trying to retrieve it are all favorite activities. There are a variety of other kinds of balls available that have some play value. One popular toy is the clutch ball with many indentations around the surface. Although this kind of ball is easy to grasp and may even be gummed occasionally, it doesn't have quite the appeal of the smooth-surface balls. A note of caution: Some balls made of a spongelike substance are not recommended for this age range. Once babies have teeth, they are capable of biting off pieces of this spongelike material and swallowing or, worse, gagging on them.

Books, of course, are desirable for this age range. They should have stiff pages rather than cloth or paper. Books with spiral bindings and pages that turn easily are best for this age range.

Telephones and dolls are recommended to encourage the fantasy play emerging shortly after the first birthday. Toy telephones with a dial or wheels and a pull cord do not have any special appeal. Pull toys are never particularly popular with babies, and the dial feature is also uninteresting, along with any squeeze-type squeakers. It is the opportunity to imitate the parent making a telephone call that makes telephones appealing for the Phase V child. The same thing can be said about dolls, doll carriages, and toy-like items such as brooms and vacuum cleaners: It is the fantasy applications that are interesting, not elaborate extra features.

Toys that are best for Phase V children are toys that challenge hand-eye skills, toys that give a child a chance to produce a dramatic physical impact, toys that feed a child's interest in movement, and variations in materials and toys that support imaginative play. In this section we have been trying to combine our understanding of developments at this stage with our observations of which toys children actually spend time with and are well-made. If you understand where a child is developmentally, you will be better able to choose wisely from the occasionally bewildering displays and claims found in any sizable toy store.

USEFUL ITEMS YOU DON'T HAVE TO BUY

Phase V children love collections of small, portable objects. Save large rigid plastic containers and accumulate several dozen small safe objects that can be used to fill that container. Plastic measuring spoons, empty spools from thread, containers from hosiery—just about anything is useable if it's not so small it's hazardous (at least an inch and a half in every dimension), nor coated with potentially hazardous substances, nor featuring small parts that could become disengaged. It's perfectly all right to mix in parts from various toys for that matter. Safety, diversity, and quantity are what count. Offer this container of objects to your Phase V child when she seems bored. You'll be pleasantly surprised by how much time she spends with this activity, taking each item out one by one, examining it, gumming it, setting it aside and reaching for another, or perhaps even pouring the whole batch out all at once. Then, too, this is the age when pots and pans are very appealing to the young child. My only reservation about pots and pans is that the resulting racket can be unpleasant.

MATERIALS TO AVOID

For a variety of interesting reasons, some toys have become popular when they don't deserve it. Other materials have been marketed very heavily when they aren't worth very much. Toy companies furthermore routinely put recommended age ranges on toy boxes that are inaccurate and generally overstate the period of time when they are appropriate for the child. Perhaps the most blatant example are the various forms of busy boxes or activity boards that you'll find in any toy store. These usually feature some eight to twelve "activities" that are supposed to fascinate infants from roughly six months to the second birthday. They have no more appeal than any small toy or object that is handed to an infant for the first time: Usually about ten minutes' worth. The toy may be explored later in the day for another few minutes and perhaps on one or two further occasions, but compared to a beach ball, a water toy, or the surprise busy box, there is negligible toy value.

Other traditional offerings with little appeal to the Phase V baby are the xylophone pull toy, form-sorting toys, and—believe it or not—stuffed animals and handpuppets.

CHILDREARING PRACTICES NOT RECOMMENDED

Forced Teaching

There has been a trend over the last four or five years toward "forced teaching," or attempts to help children acquire specialized skills much earlier than they ordinarily would. National magazines such as *Time* and *Newsweek* have featured stories on the so-called "super baby." There isn't any question but that young children even in Phase V are capable of learning some things that would otherwise come later in their lives. Programs to teach so-called prereading skills have been in existence for some time now. More recently people have claimed to be able to help parents teach premathematical knowledge, gymnastic skills, swimming, and even musical skills. Indeed, there is a booming business in connection with such activities, especially in major urban centers. I'll discuss this issue more extensively in later chapters, but for the time being I'd like to comment in an abbreviated fashion on the general trend.

All healthy Phase V children learn naturally. They are incredibly curious. They have an intense desire to master their bodies and an equally intense interest in learning about the people around whom their day revolves. Indeed, they have a full natural agenda. There is much basic learning of lifelong importance taking place during these first years of life. To add to the natural learning needs of the child a pattern of forced teaching is, in my opinion, inadvisable. We do not recommend the commercially available reading kits that claim to get children on the road to reading at nine months of age. Strong statements to the effect that you *must* read stories to your child or that you *must* buy educational toys only exploit the insecurities of American families and prey upon parents' widespread feelings of guilt and anxiety about whether they are doing well by their children. Such statements also reflect an overemphasis on the value of the bright child at the expense of whether or not he is a decent, likeable, secure child.

When someone advocates an educational program for a baby, the only sensible way to evaluate it is to think in terms of all the major processes that are developing in young children. Earlier we listed four educational foundations undergoing development during the age period of eight to twenty-four months. You should examine the consequences of any proposed educational program on each of those processes. It is very possible, for example, that in attempting to teach a child reading at one or two years, you may use procedures that are costly in time, energy, and money, or that bore or oppress your child. The result may be a negative impact on her basic curiosity and natural interest in learning. We certainly do not have a great deal of general knowledge about these issues. Therefore we advise you to be conservative in beginning any sort of infant-teaching program. An unfortunate by-product of some of this overemphasis on precocious development is a tendency to judge a child in terms of her achievement of artificially set goals rather than in her own right.

Restrictive Devices

Another childrearing practice we discourage is the use of restrictive devices like playpens, jump seats, and gates for lengthy periods every day. It is clear that such devices cut down on work, on hostilities between siblings, on breakage in the home, and on danger to the baby. These are four very good reasons to tempt a parent to prevent the child from moving freely about the home. Nevertheless, we have found in families where children are developing very well such restrictive practices are rarely used. In families where children are developing relatively poorly, restrictive practices play a prominent role.

Very rarely do you see a nine- or ten-month-old in a playpen for more than a few minutes without lapsing into what looks like boredom. When children get to be two-and-a-half or three years of age and go to nursery schools, they spend a lot of time waiting for group activities to begin. This waiting is an inevitable consequence of being forced to live in a group. Waiting is a common experience in elementary schools, too, where the reward for being obedient and prompt is to sit while other children slowly get into their seats and begin to pay attention to the teacher. We call this sort of experience *passing time*. There need be very little passing time in the life of a child in Phase V. Somehow children seem to find a wide variety of interesting things to do at this point, given the chance. If they are placed in a playpen, however, or a jump seat in front of the television set for long periods of time, or if they are given long "naps" morning and afternoon, they will end up passing a good deal of time.

Boring the Baby

Ways of putting a one-year-old child into a psychologically boring condition include trying to read a story to him when he is not interested, or trying to teach him something or otherwise force his attention when he is obviously not in a responsive frame of mind. Effective parents we have observed do not bore their children or force activities on them.

Substitute Childcare

Another point of likely importance at this stage of development, and sometimes even earlier, is whether or not the child should be placed in full-time substitute care. We have examined in some detail how children at this age enter into the vital social learnings that are critical to the basic social blueprint of the human being. During Phase V all of the major social skills that are involved in effective relationships with older people are being learned, including (1) refining the innate ability to get and hold the attention of another, (2) using an adult as a resource when a child can't do a job herself, (3) beginning to express emotions directly toward another person, (4) showing pride in achievement, and (5) beginning to engage in role play or make-believe activity. In addition, there are several related acquisitions in the social realm having to do with the child's first perception of herself—the budding awareness of parental discipline, and the learning of the rules of living in her home. All of these are ordinarily guided by the child's parents.

If both parents are working full-time during Phase V of the child's life, they obviously have much less to do with these early learning processes. If they leave someone in the home whose primary job is to take care of the house, then the child is going to be short-changed. If on the other hand, they leave someone whose job is defined so as to emphasize interreaction with the child, the child has a better chance.

But in my opinion a baby is not likely to profit as much from this type of early experience as he would from spending most of these special waking hours with members of his nuclear family, people who are the most likely to be in love with him. Parents who are aware of the importance of a child's development at this point will be more likely to try to retain their role as principal childrearers, at least for the better part of the day. Since most children of this age nap in the morning, I see relatively little loss to the child from some substitute care for up to four hours a day, even for seven days a week. Indeed, if one of the parents is a full-time parent, a few hours away from the child on a regular basis seems to be conducive to a better parenting experience. The stress caused by twenty-four-hour, seven-day-a-week responsibility for a precious baby is something very few parents handle with ease. Note we use the term *parents*. It seems clear that men can do this job as well as women in every respect except one. Recent research clearly indicates that breastfeeding for six months or longer is highly recommendable during the first year or so of life. In all other ways, however, fathers can and, in my opinion, should participate equally in this very special responsibility.

Overindulgence

Parents very frequently feel that the deepest love for a child is shown when they do everything they can for him. A corollary of this principle is the notion that giving in to a child's demands when he is being stubborn about something, even though it is against your better judgment, is advisable. Both for the child and the younger siblings and for other children he may deal with later, parents do their child no favor if they overindulge him or give in routinely to his occasionally unreasonable demands. The child is, after all, going to have to live in a world with other people, and he might as well start getting used to the idea fairly early. At the very least, if you are firm in these regards, he will not have as much of an adjustment to make when he gets to be two or three years as he otherwise would. *The effective parents we have studied have always been loving but firm with their children from early infancy on.* The principal problem that average families run into in this area is allowing the child to infringe on their own rights too much. The reasons why this is a general problem are obvious, but we liked very much the words of one of the mothers we worked with a few years back when she said, "I love my baby's curiosity, but she doesn't *have* to play in my makeup." Such healthy selfishness is a very important parenting quality.

Overfeeding

The Phase V baby rarely expresses herself clearly with words. Although her needs of the moment are usually obvious, from time to time they are not. Furthermore, if you have not provided suitable conditions to keep the baby interested, she can get bored. In many homes we have studied, parents have taken to offering the child snacks of juice, milk, cookies, and so forth throughout the day. Offering a small treat shows that you care, especially in certain of our subcultures. It also seems to be effective in subduing a child's minor discomforts or her occasional badgering efforts. And of course supplying treats is easy. But please don't do it very often. In our studies, Phase V children developing very well do nearly all of their eating and drinking at mealtimes. Frequent between-meal snacks more often than not accompany comparatively poor development. Furthermore, there are some indications that some cases of lifelong obesity have their roots in this rather common childrearing practice.

BEHAVIOR THAT SIGNALS THE ONSET OF PHASE VI

Negativism

Far and away the most significant behavior that signals the onset of Phase VI—or roughly from fourteen to twenty-four months—is what we call *negativism*. Negativism is a perfectly normal stage in the second half of the second year of life. In this negativistic behavior of the second year, the child seems to be providing parents with a preview of the coming attractions of adolescence. For the first time children begin to be aware of the fact that they are separate beings. Babies will start to use their own name, start to be possessive about their own toys and clothes, and will start resisting simple commands from their parents. They'll start testing their will against their parents. And they'll start finding that the word or concept "no" has a fascination for them. Negativism is the first and most compelling sign of the onset of Phase VI.

Hostility Toward Older Siblings

A second sign of the onset of Phase VI is present only when the infant has a slightly older sibling. But it deserves special attention as it is regularly associated with the onset of negativism and, furthermore, is routinely a source of substantial discomfort to parents in homes where there is a slightly older sibling, especially when the spacing is less than three years. In Phase VI the "worm turns" with respect to sibling rivalry. Earlier, in the first stage of relations with the slightly older child, we saw the older child expressing with increasing intensity his jealousy and hostility toward the baby and the younger child taking some abuse. During the intermediate stage between eleven and thirteen to fourteen months, the baby adapts to the situation, learns how to complain—that is, to cry more and more quickly—and begins to use a parent as a defense. Starting at fourteen or fifteen months of age, however, the baby will usually begin to initiate hostile activities with the older child as part of his new individualism and personal power.

Onset of Expressive Language

A third sign of the new phase is the onset of expressive language in quantity. Talking is, of course, not as reliable a sign as some of the others we have spoken about. Although some children cannot speak much before their second birthday, they generally begin to speak their first words between twelve and fourteen months of age. This particular phenomenon has a powerful effect on adults in that it is often the stimulus for adults to start talking to their babies much more than they had in previous months. Even though it can easily be shown that babies understand some language when they are one year old, the fact that most do not speak much seems to keep even knowledgeable and perceptive parents from using language extensively with them. There are exceptions, of course—for example, parents who talk a great deal regardless of whether anybody is listening. But by and large it is a common characteristic of parents to begin to talk considerably more to their children once their children enter Phase VI and themselves become more talkative. A very special bonus that accompanies this development is the very exciting opportunity to begin to understand the mind of a child in a way that simply was not possible before. Indeed, parents who are professionals in child development report regularly that the dramatic impact on them of the onset of speech by their children took them by surprise. No amount of reading in books prepared these parents for the delightful experiences that came with this newfound skill.

CHAPTER SEVEN

Phase VI:

From Fourteen to Twenty-Four Months of Age

GENERAL REMARKS

The Importance of the Phase VI Period

The fourteen- to twenty-four-month period, Phase VI, is, in my opinion, the second half of the most important period for educating the baby. It is also perhaps the most interesting, difficult, and exciting phase during the first three years of life. By the end of Phase VI the fundamental learning processes have developed so far that we researchers feel we have missed much if we see a child for the first time at two years of age.

Let us refer for the moment to the four learning processes that we feel are useful in understanding early development: language, curiosity, social skills, and intelligence. First of all, the two-year-old is a child whose language development varies greatly: It can be rather remarkable and extensive, including the capacity to understand and express hundreds of words and all the major grammatical forms; or language skills can be quite limited. Second, with respect to curiosity, the child arrives at age two either with a well-nourished, broad, and extremely healthy inquisitiveness, or she can have lost quite a bit of that spontaneous motivating force. In some cases her curiosity may have been constricted and channeled into a specialized area; some two-year-olds are extraordinarily interested in physical materials and not much interested in people; others are deeply involved with their primary caretaker and show surprisingly little interest in the physical world, in contrast to their behavior only one year earlier.

Third, a child's social style seems to have become very well established by the time she is two years of age. Almost every two-year-old we have seen has been a complicated social creature in the sense that her behaviors are far more sensitive to the particulars of a situation than they were when she was eight months of age. Along with the many nuances of emotional moods that she exhibits in interactions with people, the two-year-old is far less abrupt than the younger child in her shifts of mood state, from euphoria to darkest gloom or anger. She has a variety of social abilities and patterns; indeed, under the best of circumstances she has by now acquired most of the social skills that she will exhibit at six years of age. These skills include getting and holding the attention of adults, sometimes in very subtle ways. They also include using an adult as a resource to help deal with problems, expressing affection and moderate annoyance toward adults in a variety of ways, a budding capacity to direct the adult in various activities, and exhibiting fantasy behavior on an interpersonal level. We will examine these abilities in greater detail later in this chapter. All in all, socially the child is a complicated creature at age two. She has spent much of the preceding sixteen months working out an unspoken "social contract" with the people with whom she interacts regularly. You may recall that we spoke of the creation of a social contract during the period from eight to twenty-four months. This largely unspoken agreement is quite long and highly detailed. In it is contained what the child has learned through hundreds of interchanges with her caretakers. To the extent that another sibling has been regularly involved in her life, a whole set of behaviors has been assimilated with respect to interaction with other young people as well. Finally, in the realm of social development, there is the emergence of individuality and personal power—a development that is very exciting to experience.

The fourth major educational goal, nurturing the roots of intelligence, or the "learning to learn" skills, is another area where a child may have made tremendous progress by twenty-four months of age. He may have learned much more about the physical world, about the permanence of objects, and so forth. Indeed, during the months that immediately precede his second birthday, the child will have entered into a qualitatively new and vitally important style of intellectual functioning that features the use of ideas and images in the mind when solving problems rather than overt physical actions. This growth of thinking ability (including memory) interacts with his behaviors in the social realm.

It is apparent, then, that Phases V and VI cover a period when the basic shaping of a young human can be influenced in powerful ways by whoever is responsible for the child. Again, it is not possible to over-emphasize the importance of the sixteen months of life that comprise Phases V and VI.

Difficult Features of Phase VI

Not only is this period extraordinarily important, but it can also be very trying for parents. This is the time when children usually begin to oppose the will of their primary caretakers. All children we have observed go through this process, even those that are developing very well. During Phase VI, children begin to be aware of themselves as separate entities with interpersonal power. Coupled with this dawning awareness are the repeated episodes of testing that power with the people around them, especially primary caretakers. Living with a child who is not yet fully reasonable and yet is chronically self-assertive is often a rather stressful existence. Some families do better than others at coping with negativism. In general, families with well-developing children get through this period more easily than those with poorly developing children. Nevertheless, all parents should be prepared for a fair amount of friction during this phase.

Why a child has to become ornery and stay that way for a mini-

Negativism

mum of six or seven months is one of the mysteries that makes the study of early human development so rich and fascinating. Suffice it to say that the young human must somehow go from a position of total dependence and lack of self-awareness to one from which he can face reality on his own (adulthood). The second half of the second year represents a stage at which a major step in this process takes place. The next comparable step seems to occur at puberty and takes the form of adolescent rebellion. We leave it to other researchers to delve further into this fascinating problem.

Redeeming Features of Phase VI

As difficult and as serious as child development is at this age, it does have its redeeming features. The new achievements of this particular period are especially rewarding to parents. This is the time when children begin holding real conversations with family members. This activity is usually extremely enjoyable for parents and, of course, for grandparents. Children are now moving from babyhood into the first forms of personhood. Their personalities are becoming clearer, more reliable, and more individualistic. Furthermore, they are very much interested in you if you are the primary caretaker. Indeed, as this phase progresses, the intensity of interest in the adults around whom the child's day revolves reaches a peak that will begin to subside during the third year of life, ordinarily never again to be such a constant preoccupation. These developments—along with the ease with which children can now walk about—contribute to a general feeling that you are living with a very interesting young person rather than with a baby. Don't, however, be fooled by the impressive intellectual accomplishments of this phase. Lurking just beneath the veneer of maturity is an as yet not fully civilized or rational person.

Involvement with the Primary Caretaker

A special interest in the primary caretaker is another dominant quality of this particular age range. More than at any other time in life, most children will focus on their parents for substantial portions of the day during the second year. As in Phase V, the three general interests of this age range are the primary caretaker's actions, exploration of the world, and practicing new motor skills. In the best of circumstances these three interests are pursued and developed throughout later infancy and none interferes with the others. In situations where children are developing nicely, much of the child's interest will focus on his parents, in their roles as people to run to for assistance, counseling, nurturing, encouragement, and simple pleasantries. During the second year of life the child will seldom spend long periods of time without checking on the whereabouts of his primary caretaker. This orientation leads to the establishment of the social contract and the first reflected identity of the baby.

GENERAL BEHAVIOR DURING PHASE VI

Predominance of Nonsocial Activities

In spite of the child's intense interest in her parents during Phase VI, if you actually watch a fourteen-month-old baby as she goes about her ordinary activities during the day, you will find that she spends no more than 10 to 15 percent of her time interacting with her parents, or with any other person for that matter. The remainder of her time is spent in nonsocial activities.

Staring Behavior

The most common nonsocial behavior during Phase VI is simply staring—at objects, at people, or at events. As we have seen, between ages twelve and fifteen months some 20 percent of all waking time is spent in staring.

Exploratory and Mastery Experiences

Two other major kinds of nonsocial activity, which should be discussed jointly, have to do with a more active exploration of physical objects, usually small portable ones. As noted earlier, we call these two types of experience *exploratory* and *mastery activities*. In the case of exploratory activities, more common at fourteen months than are mastery experiences, the child spends a good deal of time examining the various qualities of as many objects as he can in the course of the day. These objects can be anything that is small, can be manipulated with one's hands, or can be brought to the mouth for gumming; they can range from toys to the cellophane wrapping from a cigarette pack. Children routinely try out a pattern of standard actions on these objects, apparently trying to get to know as much about them as they can. They will strike them against various surfaces, throw them, drop them, and look at and feel each of their surfaces. They will use objects to load and unload containers. They will mouth objects and chew on them, some-

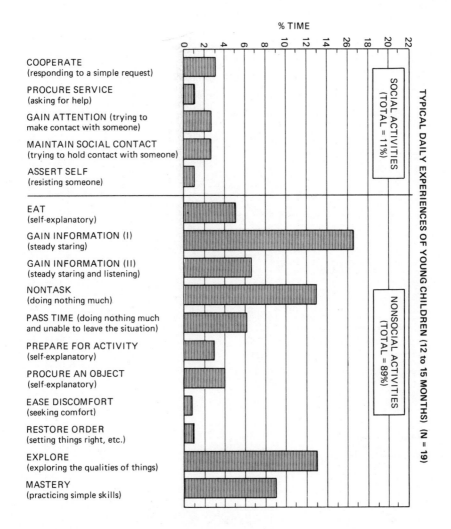

times to relieve tenderness in the gums. They will do many sorts of things with them, all of which amount to exploring their various qualities.

The second category—interaction with small physical objects to practice simple skills on them—involves mastery activity. Some of these skills are: dropping and throwing objects; swinging hinged objects back and forth; opening and closing doors and drawers, and placing relatively unstable objects into an upright position or knocking them down and replacing them; putting pieces of objects together and taking them apart; putting objects through openings; pouring materials

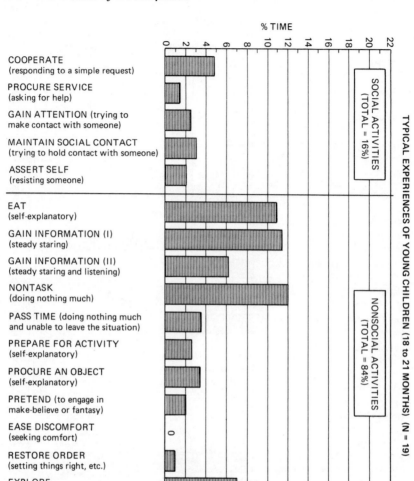

into and out of containers; manipulating simple locking devices and activating switches that produce light or darkness, or other kinds of interesting consequences like sounds or changing visual patterns.

As noted, together exploratory and mastery activities take up about 20 percent of the child's waking time early in Phase VI. All sorts of simple eye-hand skills are extremely popular at this stage, reflecting the continued fascination with hands and what they can do. A particularly interesting activity is the spinning of various sorts of wheels. Many times we have seen young children spinning wheels and watching the consequences. They can be the wheels of very small toy cars and trucks or of a cart or a tipped-over bicycle. The pedals on a tricycle are another object that children seem to be peculiarly interested in rotating. As mentioned before, the pages of books and magazines, especially books with stiff pages, are objects on which children like to practice finger skills.

Redundancy, repetition of the same developing skills, is the defining quality of these mastery experiences. If you have a piece of furniture that is relatively low and slightly difficult to climb, it is not uncommon for the toddler to climb the object, then carefully come down and start all over again. Toward the end of the fourteen- to twenty-four-month period, you will see more and more interest in gymnastics; for example, climbing and descending small slides. You will also notice that most children are quite a bit more careful than you might expect in performing most of these activities.

By two years of age there has ordinarily been a reversal in the way children play with small objects, a steady decrease in time spent in exploratory behavior and a corresponding increase in mastery or practice activities. We have also noted that children developing rather well have a steeper rate of increase of mastery experiences versus exploratory ones in regard to small objects.

Nontask Behavior

Another area of the Phase VI child's experience is what we call *nontask behavior*. By nontask behavior we mean activity that is apparently without purpose, in which the child seems to be just "hanging around" or idle. Such behavior is surprisingly common in the lives of young children. Phase VI children may spend up to 30 percent of their time in such a state on any given day, but most spend from 5 to 10 percent.

The amount of nontask behavior grows rather rapidly during Phase VI. We have seen two-year-old children who spend a great deal of time doing nothing, just standing in place. They may be thinking great thoughts; but frequent nontask behavior in two-year-olds has been so routinely associated with poor development in our studies that we are more inclined to think that they are indicative of blank states. If we see a two-year-old who spends 5 to 10 percent of her time in this fashion, we conclude that she is clearly within the normal range. Variations up or down of a modest kind are common, but when a child begins to approach the 15- to 20-percent range in this activity, we are dealing with a child who, at least for the cultures we have studied, may very well be showing signs of a considerably poorer pattern of development than we would like to see.

Passing Time

A related form of experience common in the lives of all young children is what we call *passing time*. In passing time the child is not doing much of anything; however, in contrast to nontask behavior, he is not free to get out of the situation and find something to do. A good example of passing time is when a mother says to a two-year-old, "Wait here please, while I get you a fresh diaper," or "Wait while I get a car seat; we're going for a ride." If the child does wait and cannot find anything to occupy himself with for more than a few seconds, we label that kind of experience passing time. Probably the most common type of passing time in the life of a fourteen-month-old is when he is placed in a restrictive device such as playpen, crib, jump seat, or highchair for long periods of time. Another common activity that usually produces the passing-time experience is the automobile ride in a car seat. If the child, restricted psychologically or physically, can find something to become engaged with, then we don't call it passing time. If for example a child in a playpen has a fascinating toy or a small object and plays with it for more than 15 continuous seconds, we consider the experience a form of active play.

We have found that it is extremely difficult to keep a child engaged in any form of active play when he is a psychological or physical captive in a playpen, highchair, crib, small gated room, or a car seat. You might expect that a Phase VI child in a car seat would spend a great deal of time drinking in the scenery on driving trips, but that isn't the case. We can't say why; but from our observations children under three in such restrictive situations simply find themselves with nothing interesting to do for most of the time.

Looking and Listening

Another category of special learning significance and one which takes up a substantial portion of a Phase VI child's day is what we call looking and listening to language. A typical example of such an experience is when a child is looking at his mother and older sibling who are talking at a level that is within his capacity to understand. The major classes of looking and listening experiences in Phase VI are (1) looking and listening to live language and (2) looking and listening to mechanical language. By *live language* we mean spoken language that the child may overhear or spoken language directed toward the child by another person. *Mechanical language* is usually delivered by a television set, but of course sources can also be a record or radio. We have found that how much experience children have in these categories varies quite a bit in Phase VI. As you might expect, the more live language directed to the child—especially about what he seems to be attending to at the moment—the better off he is in comparison to watching and listening to television.

Life without a Slightly Older Sibling

Let's examine now in a more general way what life can be like when dealing with a Phase VI child. First of all let us consider the case where there is no slightly older sibling in the home.

Exploration

When there is no slightly older sibling in the home, you will find that a Phase VI child will spend the bulk of the day, if allowed to, exploring her living area. This means that while parents are working in the home, most commonly in the kitchen, she'll be moving in and out of various parts of the home, returning frequently to the kitchen or wherever the adult is, to visit, to consult, or, at times, to seek comforting. If you have made the kitchen an attractive place for her, she will spend time exploring there as well. It is already most interesting to her because of your presence; but it can be even more interesting if, for example, you have accident-proofed the area and made one or two of the lower kitchen cabinets and some section of the pantry (if there is one) available to the child for exploration. You will find as she moves through the other rooms that she occasionally will, if she can manage it, climb on a small chair in order to spend time looking out a window. This is a very common practice with children in Phase VI. At fourteen months, if there are ungated stairs in your living room, she will spend a fair amount of time getting to them and practicing climbing. Stair climbing is of universal appeal to fourteen-month-old children.

Another focus of universal appeal is the toilet bowl. Unless you prevent her, she will make regular visits to the bathroom, stand next to the bowl, and splash the water around. If available, she will use small utensils to pour water and occasionally even drink it.

One place where she will ordinarily spend little time is in her own room with her own toys, at least during the beginning of Phase VI. She has too much else to see and do.

Television Viewing

There exists a good deal of mythology with respect to the television-viewing habits of young children. It was reported in print a short time ago, for example, that by the time children reach five years of age they will have spent 5000 hours watching television. The article claimed that children watched television from birth for several hours a day, seven days a week, and twelve months of the year. This, of course, makes no sense. Newborns don't watch television at all, and we have learned from extensive first-hand observations that television viewing isn't popular for extended periods for very many children throughout the first two years. There is only one reliable way to know just how much television very young children watch. That way is expensive and laborious. It involves a professional observer spending many hours in the homes of large numbers of children, recording where they are looking and what they are apparently listening to. As far as we know, nobody has done this research except our preschool project at Harvard.

After watching several hundred children in Eastern Massachusetts in their homes during the day, we have found that they watch very little television before they are two years of age and not very much during the third year of life. A rare child, one who is relatively well-developed and whose intelligence level is precociously high, may, toward the end of the second year of life, begin to spend a remarkable amount of time watching "Sesame Street." Indeed, one out of four precocious children during our observations had at times spent a full hour staring at "Sesame Street." However, our data shows that the average time spent by children in television viewing is approximately two minutes an hour for the waking hours. During the second year of life, television viewing is only momentary and sporadic. Indeed, the activity seems to consist of pretty much the same sort of behavior that is first seen in children during the fourth month of life. All children who are healthy and hear well will respond to any reasonably loud sound near them by turning promptly to locate the source of that sound. Such reflex behavior persists at least until the second birthday and could be considered television viewing, but in almost all cases the child, after turning toward the set, doesn't linger for more than a few seconds. Until at least a year-and-a-half of age, the child's language and intellectual abilities are too limited to support prolonged interest in what can be seen on the screen. The reason television commercials attract children is that they generally feature rather abrupt changes in sound (by design). In fact, "Sesame Street" uses this style in order to regularly reattract the attention of young children. Sustained viewing of television ordinarily doesn't begin much before the second year of life, and then it begins only slowly. There will be times during Phase VI when a child will seat herself next to an older sibling who is watching television and will occasionally look at the set. But here the child's purpose is primarily social rather than an interest in viewing television.

Outdoor Activities

Weather permitting, children usually spend a fair amount of time outdoors during Phase VI and ordinarily enjoy such activities very much. Given the opportunity, they will show the same profound curiosity in exploring a grassy yard, plants, dirt, picnic tables, and so on that they show indoors.

Occasionally, you'll find rather unusual and hard to understand behaviors being shown by children of this age in their first encounters with the outdoors. For example, occasionally a child will resist being put down on grass and will neither want to crawl on or walk on it; others tend to avoid asphalt surfaces. These are passing quirks and nothing to worry about. A favorite activity of children of this age is swinging through the air. A safe infant seat arranged on an outdoor gym set will be hugely enjoyed by your child. Another favorite outdoor activity is water play, and miniature pools are inexpensive and readily available. Be careful, of course, not to let a child play unattended in such a situation; serious accidents can occur in relatively small quantities of water. Sand boxes have always been a source of great pleasure to children in this age range. They particularly like the texture of the sand and pouring it from one container to another. Of course sand is also appreciated by neighborhood cats, and you are strongly advised to keep the sandbox covered when not in use and to check it from time to time for unwanted elements.

Life with a Slightly Older Sibling

A Phase VI baby's life is significantly different when there is a slightly older sibling in the house. So too are there important differences in the life of a full-time parent when there are closely spaced siblings at home. The major differences of consequence will be in the everyday social experiences of the baby. From eight months on through the second year of life, the baby will be involved in thousands of interchanges with the slightly older human with whom he shares the home and its adults.

In the period from eight to about twelve months the slightly younger sibling is on the receiving end of increasing manifestations of jealousy. From about twelve to fourteen months, a stalemate often develops because of the younger child's increased ability to use defensive tactics, especially the cry, more promptly to avoid getting hurt. During that period the older child will be increasingly frustrated since his jealousy continues to grow but his ability to act on it has been severely curtailed. For the older child the situation gets substantially worse once the younger child enters Phase VI, especially after fifteen or sixteen months or so. This is because the younger child, now beginning to sense his own interpersonal power for the first time, very often will become aggressive toward the older child. It is very common for Phase VI children to begin to employ biting, hitting, and pulling hair as offensive weapons. Since the older child has had considerably more experience in life, including the experiences of pain and parental punishment, it is not uncommon to find the younger one becoming dominant during this time of life. The impact on the older child is generally not a happy one, as you can imagine. The impact on a full-time parent is also not likely to be joyous. During Phase V, when a parent heard crying from another room, the cause of the commotion was very likely to be hostility vented on the baby by the slightly older sibling. Now it gradually dawns upon the parent that the older child is often innocent. As the weeks go by, a new emotion ordinarily creeps into the parent's repertoire—a sense of impotence. Now the parent doesn't know who started the trouble. This condition doesn't go away quickly, usually lasting for a minimum of six or eight months and sometimes for a year or more. *This condition is the single most common source of stress that parents have reported to us in study after study.* It is one of the major reasons for our strong suggestion that parents space their children at least three years apart if at all possible.

No one has yet studied the long-term consequences of chronic hostilities between closely spaced siblings. It is quite possible that once such siblings reach their teens they end up being close companions with no long-term price paid for these early experiences. It is also equally possible that deeply rooted, lifelong negative elements are created that prevent some closely spaced siblings from ever feeling fully comfortable with each other. Although there really is no substantial evidence of long-term impact of close spacing on the emotional ties between siblings, there is some with respect to intellectual development, and there is a good deal from our own research and other studies as to the immediate impacts.

The long-term evidence is based largely on a study of 1,379,000 children from four Western countries performed by R. Zajonc of the University of Michigan. He compared IQ achievement scores during the teen years of children who were closely spaced versus those who were only children or children with wide spacing in the family. He also examined the impact of numbers of children on test scores. His general conclusion: The closer in age children were, and the more children in the family, the lower the test scores. (The only exception was the last child in families with many children; the last child sometimes achieved rather well, but only when there was a gap of several years between the last and earlier children. The author suggested that last children tended to benefit from the teaching of the older siblings.)

Such studies cannot tell us what is going to happen in any specific family situation. There are many closely spaced siblings who grow up to be very bright indeed. But as a matter of general policy, Zajonc's major conclusion seems to warrant consideration when planning a family.

In the short run the effects are quite clear. The day-to-day existence of closely spaced children and anybody who lives with them all day long is going to be markedly affected. We feel most concerned for the older sibling in this situation, because she has to move over to make room for a younger competitor under conditions that change her pleasure in day-to-day existence rather substantially. The following anecdote drives home the older sibling's situation powerfully. Consider the case of a twenty-five-year-old woman, married for a year or so and very happy about that state of affairs. Her husband treats her like a princess; she gets every consideration, especially huge amounts of attention and love. One day her husband comes to her in a high state of excitement and says: "I have wonderful news for you; next week I'm going to bring someone else home to live with us. She's a full-grown woman, she is a little bit younger than you, and somewhat better looking than you; she's going to be our second wife. Now since she's going to be new to the family I'm naturally going to spend more time with her than with you, but I want you to love her as I will. And here's a box of candy to commemorate this happy occasion." It's easy to see how this would be a difficult situation for any woman. The dynamics involved fairly describe what's going on in the mind of the normal thirty-month-old child trying to cope with a Phase VI baby. Later in this book we'll talk about how to cope with this difficult state of affairs.

Within the Phase VI baby's social experiences the effect of the slightly older sibling will be seen in two situations. Most commonly, there will be many more child-to-child encounters than would otherwise be the case. Furthermore, as noted earlier, these encounters, in marked contrast to most of the child's other social experiences, will feature jealousy and, at times, outright abuse. This is not to say that a kind word will never pass from the older sibling to the baby, but the baby will almost certainly get a good dose of unpleasant social interaction over a period that may last for several years.

THE APPARENT INTERESTS OF PHASE VI

Interest in the Primary Caretaker

The three dominating interests of the Phase V child carry over into Phase VI. The Phase VI baby's interest in her primary caretaker takes the form of a general orientation toward the parent's location and regular overtures to that person. These overtures can be for several basic purposes: to simply socialize or to reestablish contact; to ask for help of some sort; or less commonly, to express affection or to seek approval for something she is proud of. When children are out of sorts because of fatigue or minor illness, they are likely to be even more clinging, more oriented toward their primary caretaker, than under ordinary circumstances.

It is relatively easy for a mother to indulge a child's interest in the parent to the disadvantage of the Phase VI child's other two dominating interests. After all, babies of this age are extremely attractive creatures and holding them close is very rewarding. Sometimes a parent finds it easier to indulge a child's self-interest rather than finding the child something to do or suggesting that she play by herself—especially if the latter suggestion leads to displeasure and hurt feelings. It should be stressed again that the young child's interest in relating to the primary caretaker is both important and healthy, but it can be overdeveloped in ways that are not in the child's best interests. (More about this topic in the section on recommended childrearing practices.)

Interest in Age-Mates

Along with the recent rise in substitute care for infant toddlers has come occasional claims for the importance of play with age-mates during the first two years of life. My position is that this statement is not founded on any substantial study of the young child. On the contrary the principal social interest of children during the first two years of life seems to revolve around the adults who care for them. Indeed, on occasions when children seventeen and eighteen months of age have an opportunity to interact, more often than not you will find episodes of surprisingly harsh treatment taking place. In loosely supervised situations of that sort we have routinely observed the stronger or more aggressive of the two using intimidation and physical force, especially in the early stages of their experiences together, in an attempt to establish dominance. In retrospect this is not terribly surprising. It is exactly what we see when infrahuman primates, various monkey species, are forced to live together in captivity. They seek to establish a dominant-submissive hierarchy. Phase VI children often behave the same way. They show no social niceties in their interactions with each other; consideration for the feelings of others is simply not usually observable. The situation with children who are younger than Phase VI is quite different. They show nothing in the way of true social interest, but rather treat each other more like interesting objects than like people. It is conceivable that group experience under close supervision during Phase VI may produce some social benefits. However, at this stage of research there is no evidence to support that claim. My advice to parents is don't buy anybody's claim that social play for Phase VI babies is a necessity. And if there is occasion to have your child with others of the same age during this time of life, supervise the situation carefully. Treat such a situation as you did the use of the walker with the Phase IV child—*as a situation that requires constant supervision.* True social interest in age-mates should be expected as the child moves into the third year of life.

INTEREST IN EXPLORATION OF THE WORLD

Interest in Objects

The second dominating interest for a Phase VI child is in exploring the world. Phase VI children show a continuing interest in small objects, marked by a gradual shift in emphasis from exploring their qualities to practicing simple skills on them. Toward the end of Phase VI and especially as the third year of life begins, children begin to synthesize what they have learned in the first two phases of small-object play and start to use objects for imaginative play, constructing scenes with dolls and animal figures and using objects to build towers, fortresses, ranches, and so forth.

New directions for curiosity: Beyond physical objects, which of course will include toys and many common household objects, the physical surroundings continue to intrigue the child, but less and less so as he approaches his second birthday. It is as if he is gradually becoming so knowledgable about what the living area looks like, feels like, and contains that the newness is wearing off. He now is becoming interested in new events that transpire within and outside the walls of the home. He will spend more and more time looking out the window at the new events of each day, a little more time watching people's interactions in the home, and will begin to spend a little more time looking at images on the television screen. His explorations are shifting into directions that are more changeable, likely to be different from day to day, than the more static qualities of the living areas that had occupied him during his first explorations of the home.

Water Play

Water play continues to be great fun for the Phase VI child, seeming to have more lasting appeal than many other kinds of play. Unlike most commercial toys, whose actions are restricted by their design and physical limitations, water can be used in an infinite number of ways.

Balls

In repeated observations of the use of toys and other physical materials, we have found the ball at the top of the list in terms of frequency of use. This is especially true in the first half of Phase VI. One of the best ways in which to engage the attention of a fourteen- or fifteen-month-old child is with a ping-pong ball, particularly when used on a hardwood floor. First of all, by just dropping a ping-pong ball, a child creates a lot of movement that lasts for quite some time. The movement has a kind of antic quality to it, a bouncing that is crisp and orderly, in contrast, for example, to a dead tennis ball or a piece of silly putty. Second, the bouncing is accompanied by interesting sound patterns. Third, the ping-pong ball is small enough so that the child can manage it much better than a ball five or six inches more in diameter. Fourth, it is light enough so that it can be thrown some distance by the child. Fifth, although of less significance from the child's point of view, throwing a ping-pong ball is not likely to incur any scolding from the parent in the way that throwing a baseball might. In addition, playing with a ping-pong ball can feed a child's growing ability to chase and retrieve thrown items. This latter interest feeds into the child's third dominating interest, the mastery of newly found motor skills.

A precautionary note: ping-pong balls are going to be put into the mouth. Although they are a bit too large for swallowing, you might be inclined to wait until the child is at least fourteen months of age and can at least understand simple instructions before you make them available. Also check once in a while to see that the ball is still intact, because the hard edges of a crushed ping-pong ball can constitute a hazard.

Probably the most appropriate ball for use during Phase VI is the inexpensive plastic inflatable beach ball, available just about everywhere. The bigger the ball, the better. Phase VI children, at least in the beginning, have usually only been walking for a few months. They seem to delight in trying to carry large light objects. The eighteen- to twenty-four inch beach ball is perfect for this game. Carrying it is a delicious challenge. Dropping it and watching it move, like the ping-pong ball, feeds their deep interest in the movement patterns of objects. Finally, in attempting to retrieve such a ball, the young Phase VI child is very likely to kick it away with her foot as she bends down to pick it up. This experience is apparently just frustrating enough to give the child an extra charge when playing with such a toy. All and all, especially considering that these items usually cost less than a dollar, you really can't find a better toy for the child during the second year of life.

Oral Exploration

Throughout Phase VI the mouth continues to be used as an exploratory organ. In recent studies that this author performed for a major U.S. manufacturer, we found that the Phase VI child is very likely to put any material to his mouth, whether it be solid or liquid. His next act is to gum the substance in question and then swallow some if possible. It is not surprising that this is the time of life when accidental poisonings reach a peak. You are advised to be doubly cautious about such matters in Phase VI. Our research underlined the impulsivity of children of this age: the subject children would put substance in their mouths without pausing to test the odor or the taste, or for any other reason; if they were thirsty, they ingested a little bit of just about anything. The poison control centers of this country report that Phase VI children swallow all sorts of foul-tasting substances, such as gasoline and cleaning fluid. Indeed, our research found that there is absolutely no effect of odor on the tendency of a child to swallow a fluid. We used odors ranging from pleasant foodlike smells, such as chocolate, to extraordinarily unpleasant, noxious odors like rotten eggs; the amount of swallowing was totally independent of the odor. Here is one place where the powerful curiosity of the child can have harsh consequences.

Interest in Practicing New Motor Skills

The third major area of interest in Phase VI is in motor development. The fourteen-month-old generally is a fairly good walker, although still slightly unstable and inhibited by a good deal of body fat. She is also at this point reasonably skillful at climbing and, as noted earlier, loves to do so. I would encourage you to let her climb, but always under close supervision until you are thoroughly assured that she can handle a situation well.

Beyond walking and climbing, the emerging activities of Phase VI include skillful running, a typical activity of the age, and playing with four-wheeled carts and wagons by straddling them and walking them along. Although the Phase VI child will enjoy practicing her new ability to move four-wheeled objects, she is not yet likely to be able to do much with even the smallest tricycle. In order to avoid frustration and minor accidents, we recommend that you hold off on the purchase of a tricycle until after the child's second birthday.

EDUCATIONAL DEVELOPMENT DURING PHASE VI

Language, curiosity, intelligence, and social development—the educational foundations that undergo important development between eight and thirty-six months—are still undergoing vital structuring during Phase VI.

Importance of Keeping Dominant Interests in Balance

We have already alluded to an additional way of evaluating educational development: the desirability of *maintaining a balance* among the growing major interests of the child (interest in the primary caretaker, interest in exploration of the world, and interest in practicing new motor skills). Imbalance, which can cause the child's learning progress to suffer, is most commonly caused by an overconcentration on the primary caretaker. Less frequently the child's interest in exploration and motor mastery are adequately supported by the environment but the normal growth of the interest in parents is interfered with, usually inadvertently by parental behaviors. (The saddest of all situations is when none of the three dominant interests are nurtured by a child's environment. This is most unlikely, however, except in rather unusual circumstances.)

Emphasis on Selected Abilities

The third way we deal with what is going on educationally in Phase VI stems directly from our research on well-developing young children. In that research, an early goal was to come to know in some detail what qualities identified a well-developing three- to six-year-old child as special. We came to our understanding of good development in three- to six-year-old children through extensive observations of such children in their homes, at nursery schools, and in daycare centers. The list of characteristics (or dimensions of competence) that follows shows the distinguishing behaviors of very well-developed three- to six-year-old children. The well-developed three-year-old child already shows the following abilities in greater and more impressive ways than the average or below-average three-year-old:

Social Abilities
- Getting and holding the attention of adults
- Using adults as resources after first determining that a job is too difficult
- Expressing affection and mild annoyance (when appropriate) to adults

- Leading and following peers
- Expressing affection and mild annoyance (when appropriate) to peers
- Competing with peers
- Showing pride in personal accomplishments
- Engaging in role play or make-believe activities

Nonsocial Abilities

- Good language development
- The ability to notice small details or discrepancies
- The ability to anticipate consequences
- The ability to deal with abstractions
- The ability to take the perspective of another person
- The ability to make interesting associations
- The ability to plan and carry out complicated activities
- The ability to use resources effectively
- The ability to maintain concentration on a task while simultaneously keeping track of what is going on around one in a fairly busy situation (dual focusing)

This list of abilities can serve as a guideline to childrearers in their activities with a child during the second year of life. Although some of the behaviors will not be observable until the child's third year, namely those social abilities used in relations with age-mates, it may be useful to be aware of them in advance of their emergence. Later in this chapter we will examine them more closely and see how some of them can be reinforced during Phase VI by proper childrearing practices.

RECOMMENDED CHILDREARING PRACTICES: PHASE VI

Coping with Negativism

We have already examined the intensification of negative behavior that ushers in Phase VI. This behavior takes several forms, none of which are terribly pleasant to live with. The child may or may not say the word "no," but he certainly will express the concept in his behavior.

The emergence of negativism is inevitable. It may appear as early as thirteen or as late as seventeen or eighteen months. Once negativism begins to take hold, it—along with other factors in the child's life, such as continued tendencies to explore and to bring things to the mouth—results in more pressure on the primary caretaker. With this increase in pressure, the issue of discipline becomes more salient. As we have seen, distraction is usually very effective in dealing with a Phase V baby. If the baby has begun to play with a trash container, a skillful caretaker may easily guide the child into other more acceptable kinds of play by offering a new toy or access to a previously unexplored household item or area. Distraction unfortunately does not work so well with a baby in Phase VI. It is at this point that sustained stubbornness rears its head for the first time with most children. They want their own way, especially if they see it is something that their parent disapproves of. This quality of interpersonally directed orneriness can be hard to live with, but there are two consolations for you. First, this happens with just about every child, so it is not because you are an inadequate parent or a disagreeable person that the baby is behaving this way. Second, the negativism will probably (though not certainly) go away.

Under optimum conditions, by the time the baby reaches twenty-one or twenty-two months of age, the pressures toward this kind of behavior subside. The clouds break, the sun comes out, and living with the child becomes delightful again. However, do not expect the perfect outcome, especially with a first child. It is more realistic to expect continued contentious behavior, at least until the second birthday. Children who are dealt with ineffectively in terms of limit setting during Phases V and VI routinely continue into the third year of life (Phase VII) with unresolved conflicts in connection with discipline and control. These are the children who during the third year exhibit temper tantrums. Given their increased strength, intelligence, and determination, they become considerably more difficult to live with than they might be. *I want to emphasize that we have learned that temper tantrums in the third year, while common, are not inevitable.* One of the more important benefits of setting firm and reasonable limits, from the beginning of Phase V onward, is that you won't have any temper tantrums of consequence during your child's third year.

Firm discipline is strongly advised during Phase VI. However, because it is clear that there are very great pressures on the Phase VI child (especially during the fourteen to twenty-one-month period) to contest and to win in this struggle with authority, wise parents are well advised to yield occasionally with a child in areas where the stakes are not very high from the parent's point of view. This does imply a general permissiveness or a general abdication of responsibility for controlling the home. The parents we have watched doing an effective job with their children *never* abdicate their control in this regard; but they are wise enough and personally secure enough to occasionally let the child win a minor struggle at this stage of life when it seems especially important for the child to flex her muscles a bit.

Language Development

In the preceding chapter we considered the most probable ways by which children learn language effectively during the first years of life. I pointed out that at about ten months of age children begin to make frequent overtures to the primary caretaker. When they make overtures, it is usually for one of a very small number of purposes. Usually that need is easy to identify, and if an adult responds according to the ways apparently effective parents respond, we believe that good language learning will almost always result. How we react to a child's overtures, plus understanding the particular level a child is at in language development, underlie effective language teaching. A list of first words can be found on page 84. In later sections you will find a chart describing in detail the total picture of language acquisition throughout the first three years of life. Talking to a young child is most effective if it is at or slightly beyond his apparent level of understanding. Also we have found that parents usually underestimate what a child can understand during these phases.

Language development, like any learning, occurs best when a child is paying attention. That's why I emphasize the desirability of doing a good deal of language teaching when the child comes to you with a particular interest in mind. If you correctly identify that interest, speak to it, and act on it, you will be assured of the child's attention. Trying to redirect the child's attention to your topic of interest is considerably more difficult—although as the child moves through Phase VI the combination of greater ability and the intense interest in the process of attachment will facilitate language teaching through the use of social situations, especially storytelling.

Reading Aloud

Reading simple, entertaining stories to your child, particularly at night before she goes to bed, is a very good idea. On the other hand, if you insist on story reading during the day, when the child wants to be doing something else, out of some notion that it is absolutely essential or very desirable, I don't think the results will be as good. Bear in mind that during Phase VI language acquisition is accelerating dramatically. That means that as each month goes by both the interest and the capacity for learning grow rapidly, making the teaching task easier and easier.

The Role of Television

Toward the end of Phase VI you can expect your child to pay more and more attention to television. Exposure to programs like "Sesame Street" probably will, in a modest way, have an impact on the child's level of language development, but rest assured that if he never sees a single television program he can still learn language through *you* in an absolutely magnificent manner.

Grammar and Comprehension

Even though the child under eighteen months still is not likely to speak much, the rate at which he is learning to understand new words and new grammatical arrangements like prepositions, negatives, and plurals is remarkable. The receptive vocabulary of a child in the second year of life, for example, is likely to increase from perhaps five to ten words at his first birthday up to about three hundred. Moreover, by the time he is two years old he will be able to cope with a substantial percentage of the grammatical structures that are the basis of communication and simple language. The fourteen- to fifteen-month-old child can understand a fair number of simple instructions, such as "throw me a kiss" or "wave bye-bye." This means that if the child's mother is feeling harried and wants very much to leave him alone for awhile, she is now for the first time able to say, "I do not want you to do A, B, or C," and have some confidence that he will understand the message. Toward the end of Phase VI, far more complicated instructions are comprehended by the typical child. You can, for example, ask the child to take a shoe to his room and then bring back a particular toy, having some confidence that the average two-year-old can not only understand but *continue* to keep such a sequence of instructions in mind as he completes the task.

In spite of the fact that the Phase VI baby has come a long way linguistically, it is clear that he still has far to go. For example, you should not use instructions and admonitions that involve consequences that might come several hours or a day or two later. If you tell a fourteen-month-old baby she'll be punished when Daddy comes home unless she does X or Y, you'll be misreading her capacities. Babies throughout most of the first three years of life live in the here and now. They are still responsive primarily to things they can see in front of them, rather than things that might happen sometime in the future. Therefore, while you should take advantage of the new levels of ability, you also run the risk of expecting too much from a child. Expecting too much from an infant, especially when a new baby arrives, is a relatively common phenomenon.

First Attempts at Speech

During the time from fourteen to twenty-four months most babies begin to speak. This is of course a gradual process. It is a rather unusual child who says nothing for several months and then begins to talk with full sentences and complicated phrases. What is more likely is that your baby will use a few words singly or in compressed fashion, like the word "some" intended to mean "I want some" or the word "more" meaning "I want more." Soon after the onset of these brief expressions the child will begin to expand into the use of phrases, and it is quite possible that shortly before her second birthday she will be speaking in fairly complete sentences. Another phenomenon that is interesting and fun is when the Phase VI child uses long collections of sounds arranged in sentencelike form, complete with inflections and emphasis, but with no recognizable word meaning. I have no notion as to the significance of this gibberish.

The Importance of Conversation

Once the child begins to speak fairly regularly, the potential for conversation comes into existence. This potential has many dividends. First of all, it is another sign of increasing personhood. Adults are not very used to creatures who cannot speak; the only nonverbal creatures typically in the home are pets. Obviously an infant is considerably more complicated and important than a goldfish; but at the same time, until he can speak he is different from older children and adults in very important ways. This picture starts to change during the second year of life, and perhaps the most conspicuous sign of change is the use of language.

One of the characteristics of the well-developed three-year-old is the tendency to hold conversations with adults as if they were peers. This peerlike quality to the conversations of three-year-olds has its in the earliest conversations of the Phase VI baby. In a good childrearing situation, the baby naturally interacts conversationally, sometimes for very serious purposes, at other times for fun, and at other times primarily to maintain social contact. Comfortable, effective parents move naturally into responding to such language and into carrying on modest conversations. Once this phenomenon surfaces, experiences with children become richer and the possibilities of encouraging growth in several dimensions of competence become greater. For example, the talking child is easier to encourage in his role play or fantasy experiences than a child who does not talk. Furthermore, it is very exciting to get a better look at a child's mind through his expanded capacity to communicate.

The Emergence of Thinking Ability

In Piaget's system the first signs of intelligence (defined as problem-solving behavior) are seen in connection with the reaching behavior of a six- or seven-month-old child. When the child pushes an obstacle aside in order to grasp an object, solving his first simple problem, he is showing practical or sensorimotor intelligence. Piaget does not describe the act of reaching as an act of intelligence. But when a child does action A, pushing an obstacle aside, in a manner intended to make action B, grasping an object, possible, there is a means-end relationship between the two behaviors. Piaget considers the use of a behavior to overcome difficulty in blocking a goal as a form of problem-solving and, therefore, of intelligence. A second less clearly understood form of early intentional behavior occurs slightly earlier. At around five months of age children will begin to use the cry intentionally in order to gain the company of an adult. In the weeks that follow it becomes increasingly clear that the child is at times crying not from pain, but rather to be picked up and held. This particular form of elementary intentional behavior was not described by Piaget, but it seems a legitimate example of early problem-solving.

In Piaget's system children begin to use manipulation of ideas to solve problems toward the end of their second year. In other words, children change from trial-and-error problem solving, dominated by eyes and hands especially, to insightful, thoughtful solutions to problems as they approach their second birthday.

Initial Indicators of Thoughtfulness

Children under eighteen months of age do not reflect upon ideas in any obvious way. In Piaget's system at least, it is not fair to call the child under eighteen months a thoughtful creature, although mental events may at times be happening. Beyond approximately eighteen months it is increasingly appropriate to talk about a degree of thoughtfulness in the behavior of children. You can actually begin to see the mind working, the wheels turning, in the behavior of the child toward the end of Phase VI. There are interesting and pregnant delays in a child's behavior, and you can often predict her next act on the basis of circumstances and her facial expression. Her next behaviors often confirm that she had actually been thinking about alternatives and options, or at least had been dwelling on a particular move that she was going to make. In the filming of our television series, *The First Three Years*, we captured in one scene a dynamic twenty-three-month-old who was showing off at the kitchen table for her mother and father. In asserting herself, she playfully refused to give her father some spoons that he wanted to put into the sink. As she attempted to move them away from his reach, she spilled a cup of milk and then looked down somewhat guiltily at the consequences. Her father then said, "Good show, kid, you're all right," and began cleaning the mess. While wiping the milk up he said in a mock-stern fashion, "Who did that, did you do that?" The child listened and then remained motionless with her head down for about ten seconds. She finally replied, "No, I didn't do it, Lisa [her older sister] did it." This piece of behavior beautifully illustrates what we mean by elementary thinking ability. There is no doubt that the child in those few moments was *thinking*—and as rapidly and skillfully as she could—of a way to avoid punishment. On the other hand, she seriously thought that her answer would work. The reason she thought it would work was not because she was dull (on the contrary she was quite bright), but rather because her early thinking was what Piaget called *egocentric*, that is, she was unable to take into account the point of view of other people. She couldn't, at that stage of development, factor into her answer the reality that both parents were actually watching what had happened and obviously would know that her older sister had not been involved. This limited understanding of other people's point of view besides their own will be overcome by well-developing children toward the end of the third year of life.

Children under eighteen months of age are much more impulsive than two-year-olds. They try possible solutions in the open rather than in their heads. In Piaget's original writings on the development of intelligence in his own three children, he described in detail how each of his children, at twelve and thirteen months, would experiment in similar situations by trying out different ways of getting something that was out of reach, for example, when they were confined to a crib. However, when the same sort of problem was provided for the children as each approached their second birthday, there would be a pause as they apparently thought about alternatives, and then the first act to follow the pause would be a correct or a near-correct solution to the problem.

More elaborate descriptions of the changes in the quality of intelligent behavior are beyond the scope of this book. The best, and indeed virtually only, place to find such materials are in the works of Piaget himself, which you will find listed in the recommended reading section at the end of the book. Suffice it to say that the possibilities in dealing with a child expand directly with the growth of their mental abilities. During Phase VI the child's capacity to understand explanations is growing, and the capacity to deal with phenomena that expand in time is growing because of her increased grasp of reality. During Phase VI her capacity for short-term memory develops to its completion. In contrast to the eight- or nine-month-old who can retain an image of an object in her mind only for a few seconds, the two-year-old can remember where a desirable object is from day to day. In spite of these remarkable developments, the Phase VI child, however, still exhibits clear signs of being far from mentally mature.

Phase VI and the Random Event

Another interesting example of the mental immaturity of the Phase VI child is the absence in the mind of a child of the possibility of a random event. One of the most common evidences of this is in misunderstandings between siblings: your two-year-old child who is accidentally hurt by his older sibling is apparently totally unable to understand the concept of an accident. He assumes that if he was hurt, someone "intended" to hurt him. It is as simple as that. You can argue the point with him, or explain it until you are quite fatigued. It is not going to make a bit of difference. In the work of Piaget there are some fascinating explanations of why children develop this way.

The Development of Curiosity

With respect to curiosity, the same general guidelines set down for Phase V continue to apply. Make certain that the child has maximum access to the living areas. Try to make the kitchen as interesting, as accessible, and as safe as possible. Get the child outdoors as much as you can. Have available a supply of materials, not ones that she has access to regularly, to stimulate her with when she seems bored or at a loss for something to do. Avoid creating boredom for her by misguided attempts at insisting she attend to something. Try instead to build upon her natural enthusiasm for learning by responding as warmly and as supportively as you can when she does make an overture to you and wants to share an enthusiasm. Try to build on her interest by introducing related information and ideas when she makes an overture. If, for example, she brings you a piece of playdough and mumbles something about what a wonderful car she has made, you can suggest that she try to make a boat like Daddy's or like her own toy. Or you can suggest that if she made a truck or another car, she would have several cars. It is not terribly important that you come up with a brilliant observation; the major requirement is that you support and broaden her curiosity. Implicitly, such behavior on your part makes it clear to the child that to be curious, to be learning, to be exploring is something that you strongly approve of, and what you approve of means a great deal to your child, especially at this particular phase of her life.

Social Development

The topics of curiosity and language are important, not merely because of intrinsic value, but also because when the child does not develop well in those areas it becomes nearly impossible to evolve good social development. A particularly poignant example exists in the case of hearing-impaired toddlers. In addition to delayed language and intellectual development, one common consequence of protracted poor hearing during the first years of life is poor social development.

Once again, the key to good results is to maintain a solid and balanced course of development. If you are insensitive to the need for balanced development during this period, you may encourage a child's natural tendencies to gravitate around you too much. It is very difficult to live with a thirty-month-old clinging vine. We have seen a fair number of parents get themselves into this situation and sorely regret it. In addition, such a situation can lay the groundwork for further grief if you are dealing with a first child and are soon to produce a second. A child who is excessively wrapped up in his primary caretaker and is relatively poorly developed in terms of his interests in the rest of the world is a child who is less likely to succeed in overcoming the difficulties brought about by the introduction of a second child into the family. He is also the child who is likely to have difficulty moving into the world of the nursery school.

You really should not, at this time, prolong unrealistically the child's initial conception that the world was made exclusively for and revolves solely around him. This prolongation is relatively easy to do, especially in the case of a first child. But you are doing the child a disservice to fall into such a pattern. Look upon Phase VI as a transitional period between early infancy and that time when the child is going to begin to move out of the home to play with age-mates or to attend nursery school, and so on. One way we speak to this issue in dealing with parents in our training programs (for example, Missouri's New Parents as Teachers) is to have them try to teach the child that he is terribly important: his needs and interests are special, but *he is no more important than any other person in the world, especially his parents*. This apparently contradictory message turns out to be very effective. Your goal, after all, is to turn out a delightful three-year-old as well as one whose skills you can admire.

Independence training is particularly important in the case of a first child. You may very well have come across programs or lectures or books that promise to help you prepare an older sibling for the arrival of a new child. These programs almost invariably advocate a good deal of talking to the older child, reading particular kinds of stories and so forth. *In my judgment, if the older child is under roughly two-and-a-half years the best preparation for the arrival of a younger sibling is to teach the older child during his first few years to respect the rights of his parents.*

The child of fourteen months of age with a slightly older sibling can find the combination of stresses too much to handle at times: he deals simultaneously with the onset of negativism and self-awareness, plus the consequences of having been repeatedly subjected to episodes of aggression by his older brother or sister, plus his own limited control of his emotions and ideas. Remember, too, if the older child is still less than three years of age, he is mentally and emotionally quite immature also. Given such circumstances, you as the parent may find yourself in one of the more painful kinds of childrearing situations.

If you find yourself in the above bind: continue to be firm but loving with the older child; reassure him that you still love him, not by telling him so, but by spending a small amount of time (perhaps an hour) alone with him daily. Also encourage his out-of-the-home interests, so that if he has an unhappy experience at home from time to time it will not be so crushing.

As we have discussed sibling rivalry in Phase V and VI, we have been taking the perspective of the child in that age range, while making occasional remarks about the point of view of the older child. A second important orientation that has to be understood is the point of view of the Phase VI child who now has to cope with the younger sibling. The same dynamics apply: we know how emotionally powerful Phase VI is as the child finishes up the early attachment process, and it's easy to understand how difficult it is for the late Phase VI child (particularly a first child) to move over and make room for a newly crawling baby.

At this stage of the game a third scenario of relevance is possible. A Phase VI child can have both a slightly older sibling and a slightly younger sibling. To understand social development in the first years of life, consideration of these constellations is essential. One saving factor for the child in the middle is that she never has known the exclusive attention of parents that a first-born child has. The displacement suffered therefore will not be anywhere near as great. Do not, however, assume that a middle child will not show any of the difficult behaviors we talked of earlier. They will be there. Although no one really fully understands the best ways to cope with these various constellations, especially this last one, we are confident that understanding the underlying dynamics will help.

Nurturing the Roots of Intelligence

The emergence of thinking ability during Phase VI is a remarkable phenomenon. One of the mysteries of the ages, it is one of the most dramatic and exciting experiences parents can have, particularly with their first children. This author cannot count the number of times that young parents have reported how bowled over they were by the new mental capacities of their eighteen- to twenty-four-month-old children. You can only understand this point thoroughly, in my opinion, if you have gone through it on a personal level. No amount of reading will have quite the impact that first-hand experience provides.

It does not require great resources for families to do a good job of fostering a child's thinking ability at this stage.[1] In the second year of life many facts and ideas about the world are beyond the child's comprehension. The core level of intelligence that any normal adult possesses is sufficient to promote learning. That's all it takes to facilitate intellectual development during the first two-and-a-half years of life.

This brings us to the interesting question of whether a parent should attempt to develop a child's intelligence in special ways. To respond to this question, we must remind parents that a child is much more than a possessor of intelligence. He is also a person who has his own pattern of social skills and his own set of attitudes about people and life. He is, in short, a complicated creature who is at least as much heart as he is mind. I describe *in part* what a child is in more technical detail in the list of abilities characterizing well-developed children, which we will examine in the next section. But note that in that list some abilities are not mentioned, such as a child's sense of humor or his motor skills. These important attributes are not listed because we have not found that well-developed children were unique in regard to these

---

[1] Once a child gets to be two-and-a-half years, people with good educational backgrounds may have some advantage over other parents in nurturing intelligence. Specific information and ideas become increasingly important to mental growth, and generally the more extensive your education, the richer the reservoir of ideas and information you have available to pass on to the child. Prior to two-and-a-half years, the child's language and intellectual capacities are limited so that most adults, even those with modest educations, are fully capable of providing the kind of input that children need to move ahead well.

qualities. It does not follow, however, that parents should neglect the development of humor or motor abilities in young children. I think any educator of a young child, especially his parents, should keep in mind the full array of developmental goals: the social, intellectual and linguistic skills referred to throughout the text, plus the general goals of a sound body and a humanistic value system. I believe each suggested set of childrearing activities should be evaluated in the light of its likely consequences for the entire array of desirable outcomes.

If teaching a child to recognize letters and numbers two years before most children do can be accomplished without in any way jeopardizing any other developmental goals, then I would consider doing it. If on the other hand such teaching runs the risk of unbalancing the child's development by, for example, focusing so much of his time on intellectual and verbal tasks that he tends to have little time left over for motor exercise or for interaction with other children, then I believe that it would be a disservice to the child. At the same time one could overemphasize motor skill development or social development to the point where some of the other developmental outcomes are in jeopardy. In addition, when excessive emphasis is put on intellectual achievement, parents run the risk of judging a child's value in terms of success or failure on the target goals; it is difficult to avoid disappointment if for one reason or another your baby doesn't reach them. Furthermore, there is the question of the child's natural pleasure in learning and natural curiosity about the world. Although there is no substantial research on this subject, it would appear that when children choose most of their own activities, within an environment that relates well to their developmental level, they are better off than when someone else sets the agenda. In sum, then, one should consider the possibility of special early education, but always in the light of the likely effects on the full range of developmental processes.

FOSTERING THE DIMENSIONS
OF COMPETENCE DURING PHASE VI

Social Ability

Getting and holding the attention of adults in socially acceptable ways: Gaining attention is the earliest social skill of babies. Because of their ability to cry, babies begin to get used to capturing the attention of adults very early in life. The Phase VI child is still very much involved in getting attention in pursuit of her fundamental social needs, which are especially powerful during the second year. Having lived for fourteen or more months, however, she now has a fairly wide variety of methods for gaining attention beyond simply crying. We believe some parents do a disservice to their children by hovering over them too much at this stage. If a parent routinely anticipates a baby's needs, a child is less likely to learn very much about different ways of getting someone else's attention. Second and third children are probably better off in this respect because parents don't usually spend as much time anticipating their needs.

Using adults as resources after first determining that a task is too difficult: During Phase VI the handling of a child's appeals for help becomes somewhat delicate. This natural tendency, on the whole very healthy, is intertwined with the child's intense desire for the attention of the adult as a part of the resolution of the early attachment process. The Phase VI child of course should understand that, when needed, you'll be there to help; on the other hand, you should be watchful for the child's tendency to ask for help not so much because he cannot do something successfully on his own, but simply to monopolize a parent's time. Especially with the first child, this latter tendency is often strong and can lead to overattachment by the second birthday.

Expressing affection and mild annoyance to adults: The capacity to express both affection and annoyance reflects a feeling of comfort and confidence in interpersonal relations. It is extremely relevant to the day-to-day life of the Phase VI child, whose tendencies toward expressing modest annoyance increase as she flowers as an individual and as she becomes self-assertive. A balance needs to be maintained at this age between overindulging a child's tendencies toward testiness and suppressing such tendencies in a way that stifles her capacity to relate naturally to people.

A parent's own deeply rooted feelings about the expression of positive and negative emotions will probably influence a young child's capacities in this area. I suggest you try to help the child acquire as much spontaneity of emotional expression as your own behavior patterns will allow.

Leading and following peers: The behaviors of giving and accepting peer leadership do not become visible until the third year since social behavior with peers is not much seen before the second birthday. Presumably, however, the behavior of a parent or other sibling is an influence on the later behavior of the child in this regard. Your child should be given the chance to direct some of your shared activities in first years of life. There will (of course) be many occasions during this early period when he will be asked to do what you say.

Expressing affection and mild annoyance to peers: The easy expression of feelings with peers parallels similar abilities with adults or older siblings. Expression of feelings with peers begins to undergo rapid development during the third year of life, as true social interest in peers emerges and grows.

Competing with peers: Some parents would rather not encourage competitiveness in their children. It is nevertheless found regularly in the behavior of the well-developed three- to six-year-old children we have studied. Since the value of competitiveness is viewed differently by different families, I would not try to argue anyone into encouraging this behavior in his child. Whether or not you wish to, however, during Phase VI you should be on the alert for the first signs of this behavior. It is most likely to occur in connection with rivalry with an older sibling.

Showing pride in personal accomplishment: Pride in self-accomplishment, which can be so rewarding for parents, begins to develop substantially during the second year as the child begins to achieve skills that she can crow about. Phase VI achievements are mostly manifested in new behaviors rather than in the creation of products such as drawings or block towers. The child very often shows a delight in her first successes at walking and is delighted with praise. Likewise, when she manages to move a four-wheeled toy about with some success she may often look to you with a light in her eyes that suggests she is quite proud of what she has done. I strongly urge you to support these feelings of pride and achievement.

Engaging in role play or make-believe activities: It is desirable to enter into a child's natural tendencies to fantasize and to pretend, particularly as he looks forward to being grown up. Do not, however, expect to see much elaborate behavior of this type during Phase VI.

Nonsocial Abilities

Good language development: We have already discussed a particularly effective style of response to a baby's overtures in our treatment of Phase V. This response style, emphasizing the identification of the baby's interest at the moment, is probably the single most important means by which parents can assist language development during a child's first years. Another useful activity was described in connection with the child's first interest in books. The first picture books to become interesting to children, at about one year of age, are primarily useful to facilitate practice of hand-eye skills. Nevertheless, labeling of simple, familiar pictures in such books is a useful language-teaching tactic. As the child moves through Phase VI, however, what with the increase in the rate of growth of receptive language (the understanding of language), as well as the growth of mental power, a third principal way of teaching language becomes much more appropriate. That way is the use of stories.

Provide as much story-listening experience as possible. In this regard we recommend very highly a book called *Babies Need Books*, by Dorothy Butler (Penguin Books, 1980). I have never found another book that expresses the importance of books to young children and describes specific developmentally appropriate material anywhere near as well as Ms. Butler's book.

The ability to notice small details and discrepancies: We have found that very well-developed three- and four-year-olds are very accurate observers. They notice small differences and anomalies faster than most children. This talent is not only apparent when somebody makes an error in a drawing or sets the wrong things on the table, but is also present in respect to temporal sequences and, interestingly, in areas of logic. Talented three- to six-year-old children quickly notice when somebody telling a story or explaining something makes an error in logic. They are also more able than most to keep track of the sequence of events in a story or a playtime activity, and then quickly notice when someone, for example, goes out of turn in a game. Keep these kinds of behaviors in mind in interchanges with Phase VI children, and try to bring similarities and differences in small details and interesting peculiarities to their attention routinely.

The ability to anticipate consequences: The baby as young as nine or ten months, when noticing his parents heading toward the front door with coats on, may begin to complain. Such behavior is a typical form of being able to anticipate consequences, an ability that in later life is reflected in such areas as effective driving. Perhaps the earliest signs of such behavior occur in connection with nursing, when the three- or four-month-old child may very well begin to suck in anticipation of being fed. By three years of age, stable differences among children in this ability are quite visible. This ability can be encouraged in the ordinary course of a day's activities. Again, it is easier to do so when the child brings a topic to your attention than when her attention is directed elsewhere.

The ability to deal with abstractions: Probably the two most common kinds of abstraction that children learn to deal with in Phase VI are words and numbers. This does not mean that they can count, nor does it mean that they can write words or even use them particularly well. But Phase VI children *are* learning that certain words apply to classes of objects rather than merely to individual items. To an eight-month-old child the word "bottle" may mean only *his* bottle, but "bottle" to the two-year-old usually means any number of objects that have bottle characteristics. In that sense the two-year-old has learned an abstraction. Toward the end of the phase, when children learn that "two cookies" means one cookie and one more cookie, they have learned an abstraction that they can apply to other things as well.

Always remember that a Phase VI child is a concrete thinker. He can communicate in a limited way about objects that he can see, feel, and touch, but he is not yet particularly adept at thinking or talking about other objects. Stay with the here and now. If you want to talk about a particular object or event that is not on the immediate scene, try to relate it to something in the current situation.

The ability to put oneself in the place of another person: Understanding viewpoints other than the child's own is a particularly interesting dimension of competence and one that is difficult to foster in a young child. As Piaget points out, the capacity to put oneself in someone else's place and see things from his viewpoint is generally not seen much before the seventh or eighth year of a child's life.[2]

In our research we have found that children who are developing very well during the preschool years exhibit the ability to put themselves in the place of another person—that is, well before seven or eight years of age. Indeed, primitive forms of this behavior have been seen in our work as early as age three.

The ability to make interesting associations: We have often seen clever association-making in talented three- to six-year-olds. If your natural style with the child features interrelated ideas and if you occasionally develop these ideas in story telling, you'll be providing a model for your child in a desirable area.

---

[2] Piaget's research on this topic was done with Swiss children during the 1920s. In general his discoveries have been shown to be true, but the modern American child has often been found to reach new mental stages earlier than Piaget's subjects did.

The ability to plan and carry out complicated activities: In nursery school only a few out of a group of 15 to 20 children can bring several others together and manage to organize proceedings. This function can be taught by example. You can also assist the Phase VI child in taking on and executing tasks that are a little more complex than the one- or two-step tasks common to the first year of life.

The ability to use resources effectively: Closely tied to managerial ability, effective resource use can be taught in a natural style if you show imagination in the way objects are used. For example, if, in order to reach something on a high shelf, you use a chair to stand on one time, and a step ladder another—or if you use several different utensils to stir food—you may teach the child a bit about the multiple uses of materials. If, without overdoing it, you show a capacity to use resources effectively and occasionally point out how you are doing it to the child, it will probably affect the child beneficially.

Dual Focusing: The capacity to maintain concentration on a task and simultaneously monitor or be aware of what is going on around you in a busy place is a fascinating behavior to observe. If you visit a nursery school or a daycare center where a group of children are engaged in such activities as doing puzzles or drawing pictures, you will note that a few of the children will be better at resisting distractions than the others. You will see this select group frequently looking around, as if to keep track of what is happening. This ability is something that we really don't know how to teach. Theoretically you could encourage a child's involvement in more than one task at a time, but if you attempt it too soon, you'll only interfere with her developing capacity to concentrate.

RECOMMENDED MATERIALS FOR PHASE VI

The following chart is a summary of selected recommended materials for the Phase VI child. It has been compiled on the basis of his special interests in exploring appropriate objects and practicing motor skills, especially climbing. No commercial toys are necessary to the child's educational development. Phase VI children are too involved in interactions with their parents, in practicing skills that help them master their own bodies, and in exploration of the living area and all its elements to spend much time with toys. Besides, toy companies rarely know very much about what really interests a child at this particular age.

LARGE TOYS

Especially Recommended	Of Moderate Use
Small wagons and other stable, four-wheeled devices on which the child can sit and move himself about (Fisher-Price makes one or two good ones) Doll carriages Swings (make sure they are safe) Small slides and related junior-sized gym equipment	Pull toys

SMALL TOYS

Especially Recommended	Of Moderate Use
Kohner's Surprise Box Busy Bath (or Sears version) Books with stiff pages Balls of all sizes and shapes, especially large, light, plastic balls, Ping-Pong balls, and footballs Dolls and toys that feature relatively small human and animal figures such as toy buses and airplanes Pails suitable for pouring Carriages	Toy cars and trucks, *but* no small cars with thin metal axles such as Matchbox cars or Hot Wheels Crayons and scrap paper Stuffed animals The simplest puzzles Plastic pop beads Three-dimensional puzzles, like the standard mailbox with triangular, circular, and rectangular openings and pieces Stacking toys like the Fisher-Price doughnuts with base Toy telephones

LARGER MATERIALS
Especially Recommended

Empty boxes of all sizes and shapes
Small children's chairs
Full-length door mirrors
Adult furniture such as ottomans
Low cocktail tables
Small cushions
Living room furniture in general
Stairs (with caution)

SMALL PORTABLE ITEMS
Especially Recommended

Pots and pans of all sizes and shapes
Plastic refrigerator containers of all sizes and shapes, with lids if possible
Canned goods (you must monitor play with these)
Plastic jars with covers and other expendable, safe household items

OTHER ITEMS
Especially Recommended

Water (a cheap medium with endless fascination)
Paper (a cheap medium with endless fascination)

CHILDREARING PRACTICES NOT RECOMMENDED

Permitting Tantrums

Do not allow tantrums. A child banging her head against the floor, throwing objects, and so on, has never, in the history of our observations of children, been associated with good development. When children first engage in such activities, they are usually seeking a limit, asking you to stop them. Tantrums can become common during the second year of life. I strongly advise you not to let them develop. Over the years since the first edition of this book appeared, quite a number of parents and professionals have asked for more specifics on tantrum control. Here they are.

Since it is a very rare Phase VI child who is anywhere nearly as strong as his parents, it is clear that physical restraint is always feasible when it comes to dealing with tantrums at this stage. Probably the most effective method is to pick up the child who is obviously losing control of himself, take him to another room and, holding him gently but firmly, tell him in simple language that he must not do what he is doing. You must be *very specific*. If he has been banging his head, or throwing things, these have to be referred to in simple terms, repeatedly. After a suitable cooling off period of about five to ten minutes, the child can be brought back to the original location; but if the tantrum behavior resurfaces, *follow-up must be prompt*. The follow-up should take the same form. This takes *persistence*, an underrated but absolutely necessary quality in effective parenting during Phase VI. *Persistence is absolutely essential to the effective socialization of this still-young child.*

Phase VI is often the time when parents consider the topic of spanking. Although I don't favor spanking as a method of discipline at this stage, it is certainly something that parents can consider using, in my judgment. I say that knowing full well that some people will object strenuously, but the reality is that about two-thirds of the effective families we have ever worked with or observed have, from to time, "spanked" their Phase VI children. Now, the spanking was never done with fury, it was never done to injure the child, it was never done harshly—but a quick, medium-speed pat on the behind to a child who is obviously out of control can be an effective means of bringing the child back to some degree of self-control. Clearly, if any parent reading this book finds such ideas unacceptable, there is absolutely no need for them to be used. On the other hand, people who do use such practices need not feel that they are doing any significant damage to their children. Nor in my judgment are they teaching violence, although others in child development might dispute that claim.

The notion of ignoring tantrums is something I can assure you will not work with a Phase VI child. This notion is based upon the assumption that the attention of a parent is the most powerful factor in shaping the behavior of a child. If attention is not given to bad behavior (the theory maintains), it will go away. There is, no doubt, some validity to the theory. It does not apply, however, during episodes of negativism. If you try to ignore such behavior, the normal response of the child will be to escalate the undesirable actions.

Contests of Will

As mentioned before, during the second year your baby will very likely start testing wills with you. Do not try to totally suppress these impulses; do not try to win all of the disputes you have with your child. Small victories seem to have a special importance to a child in Phase VI, a significance that will not likely occur again until the adolescent years.

Premature Toilet Training

It does not make any sense to try to force toilet training during this time in a child's development. Once the child gets to be about two years of age, he will train himself in a relatively short space of time under nearly any rearing conditions. Trying to toilet train a child much before two years of age is generally very difficult. If you attempt the training between fourteen and twenty-four months of age, you will be running headlong into negativism. Thus that period is the worst possible time to try. In passing, we might remark that the natural tendencies of the Phase VI child to imitate other members of the family usually leads to earlier toilet training with second and subsequent siblings as compared with the first child. If parents have a reasonably casual attitude about toilet habits, so that their Phase VI child can see how they handle the situation, children, in the absence of undue pressure from parents, will usually begin to initiate toilet training themselves during Stage VII.

Overfeeding

The book's comments about between-meal snacks in Phase V continue to apply to Phase VI. Whereas in Phase V the primary apparent causes of this practice are a desire to show that you care and inadequate knowledge of how to keep the child happily engaged, in Phase VI the normal negativistic behavior of the child may be the root cause. The Phase VI child can become chronically stressful, and almost anything that can give you some peace is likely to be considered. By following the suggestions of this book, you may be in less trouble on this score. If for any reason, however, you find yourself feeding snacks or drinks to the Phase VI child several times a day, pause and review the situation. Something has gone wrong. It is worth noting also that a goodly number of medical research studies indicate that the origins of long-term obesity seem to be in the first years of life.

MATERIALS NOT RECOMMENDED FOR PHASE VI

Wind-up Toys

At this point in a child's life I would advise you to stay away from a fair number of commercial toys, despite their popularity in stores. These include all Jack-in-the-box toys with the exception of the Disney Poppin' Pals and of some newly designed versions of the old Jack-in-the-box that do not require complete revolutions of a handle for activation. The manual skills necessary to make most Jack-in-the-box toys function are beyond most children under two years of age.

The same principle applies to wind-up toys. These toys, as mentioned earlier, require that a child turn a small knob 360 degrees several times while pushing a doll under a cover. This task is simply too great for most Phase VI children. We have learned, however, that some children can manage these rotational movements during the second half of the second year, so this is not an ironclad fact by any means. We have had many people write in to say that their child turns on faucets or unscrews the tops from toothpaste tubes; nevertheless, this ability is not to be expected during Phase VI. If you are willing to do all the winding with music-box toys, and if you and the child enjoy the activity, go right ahead. You should be warned, however, that Phase VI children tire rather quickly of the simple sounds of music toys. The common plastic nut-and-bolt toy is also inappropriate for Phase VI. Infants don't do terribly well screwing or unscrewing the nuts on the bolts.

Tricycles and Xylophones

Tricycles are often introduced into a child's life before her second birthday. Occasionally, you will find a precocious child and a wonderfully designed small tricycle; but it is preferable to reserve this toy for Phase VII. Another much-purchased toy for infants is the xylophone, especially in pull-toy form. Very few children that we have seen have ever seemed to get any enjoyment out of such a toy beyond the 15 minutes that every child in this age range devotes to any new item introduced by her parents.

Potentially Dangerous Items

You must be on guard against items that are small enough to be swallowed, sharp enough to cut, or small and heavy enough to be used as dangerous missiles. Examples of the first category would be marbles, checkers, or anything else under an inch-and-a-half in any of its major dimensions. It has recently been reported that choking on food is very common within this age range. The types of food most commonly involved are round, fairly hard chunks of food, such as a piece of hot dog. You should be especially careful of food items or toy parts that could cause suffocation.

An example of items potentially sharp enough to cut would be Match Box or Hot Wheels cars, because once the wheels are pulled off (which is not too difficult to do), the pointed axle that is left exposed is capable of inflicting significant damage to many young children.

An example of a potentially dangerous missile is a toy soldier. Toy soldiers, often made of metal, are small enough to be thrown by children of this age yet heavy enough to inflict damage on people and things.

BEHAVIORS THAT SIGNAL THE ONSET OF PHASE VII

Phase VII, the third year of life, is the final stage to be covered in this book. Several fascinating processes appear during this stage in a child's development.

The Emergence of Rationality

If all has gone well, you will find a general decline in negativism sometime around the second birthday. Not only will the child become less contentious, but you can expect an increase in general sociability and a delightful improvement in the quality of experiences with the child. Congratulations!

Emergence of True Social Interest in Peers

From the second birthday on, interest in play with other children— often outside of the home—will gradually and consistently increase, and the exclusive intense concentration on the nuclear family and the home will decline.

Increasing Mental Power and Emotional Control

With the emergence of Phase VII you will begin to notice a dramatic increase in your child's sheer mental powers and in his ability to control his emotions. You will find that you are living with a much more mature human being than you were six months ago. This rather impressive maturity is not, of course, going to appear suddenly, but you will be struck by the rate with which the child substitutes reasoning and impulse control for subrationally motivated actions.

An Increase in Conversation

Closely associated with the preceding phenomena is a general rise in talking and especially in conversational language. Phase VII children can usually deal with sentences and with streams of thought to an extent that makes it possible for them to carry on simple, pleasant conversations. This is one of the most rewarding experiences that parents will undergo in the first years.

CHAPTER EIGHT

Phase VII:

From Twenty-Four to Thirty-Six Months of Age

GENERAL REMARKS

The two-year-old is a fairly stabilized personality. She has constructed with great effort and persistence, over long periods of time and through many interchanges, an elaborate social contract with her primary caretaker. She has become truly familiar with and involved with the object world. She has achieved substantial control over her own body. She is in a condition that can perhaps still be characterized as "baby-hood," but to call her a "baby" by her third birthday would be misleading.

Some two-year-olds are not terribly pleasant to live with. There is no question that spoiling can be a well-entrenched reality by a child's second birthday. Furthermore, a two-year-old who has learned that his needs are more important than anyone else's and is also given to tantrums and related unpleasant behaviors is likely to persist in such behaviors for some time to come. Another less than ideal outcome in the area of personality by the time a child is two years of age is excessive fearfulness. In our research we have seen many a child who by two has simply had too much experience with hostility and fear in the period between eight months and two years. Most commonly, such experiences have come at the hands of closely spaced older siblings. Less commonly, but even more painful to watch, is that fear has been generated by a child's own parents. It is easy to ignore the fact that many children go through their first two years in conditions very much less desirable than we would like. Setting aside for the moment children of underdeveloped nations being reared in extraordinary poverty, there are unfortunately many children who enter family situations where there are perhaps too many other children, or parents with severe emotional problems. In such unhappy circumstances, children by two years of age often have learned that the world is occasionally a hostile place and that approaches to their parents have to be made selectively. Happily, in most situations such is not the case. Under the best of circumstances, a two-year-old can be an absolute delight, full of humor, originality, and self-confidence, and a remarkable source of pleasure for parents.

Another interesting shift that takes place at around the second birthday is the movement away from what one might call "subrational behavior" to reasonableness. The civil behavior that is often seen toward the end of the second year of the child's life—as she becomes more sophisticated, more aware, and more practiced with people—is, in actuality, only a thin veneer. Lurking just beneath the surface is a person who rather easily loses control of her own emotions and may under such circumstances show all kinds of unpleasant behavior. Under good circumstances babies tend to leave such behavior behind as they move into the third year of life. This is most obvious, of course, in the much greater capacity to communicate verbally that most children show during their third year, but it is more general than just language facility. The thinking ability of the child in Phase VII reinforces the notion of growing maturity and early childhood rather than babyhood.

In the third year we also see a substantial and steady rise in interest in other children and true social interactions with them. We usually see a steady rise in activities outside of the home, along with a lessening of the intense, exclusive forcus on the nuclear family and parents. We find a substantial increase in the child's mental powers, which are growing at a really remarkable rate; he seems more aware of things, particularly in the social realm. Whereas the one-and-a-half-year-old can be overwhelmed rather easily by feelings of anger or hurt, the three-year-old is far more in control of his emotions.

Along with these dramatic developments comes the flowering of speech and the resultant inclination toward conversation. In addition, the newly developed ability to use the body with skill for climbing and running adds to the feeling that we are now dealing with a relatively complete junior human being. Babyhood is over. The distance traveled by a three-year-old in terms of human development is staggering.

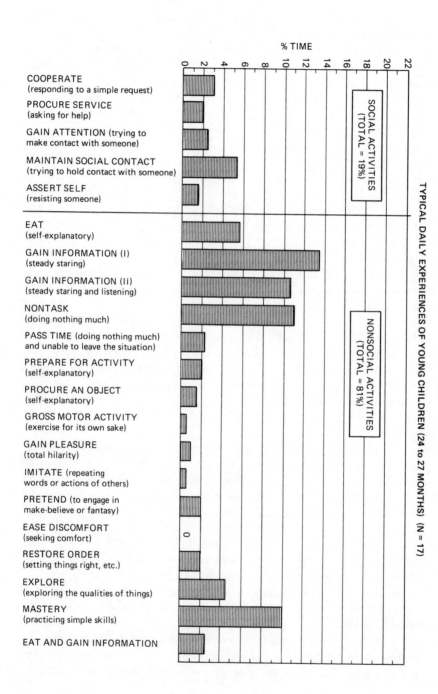

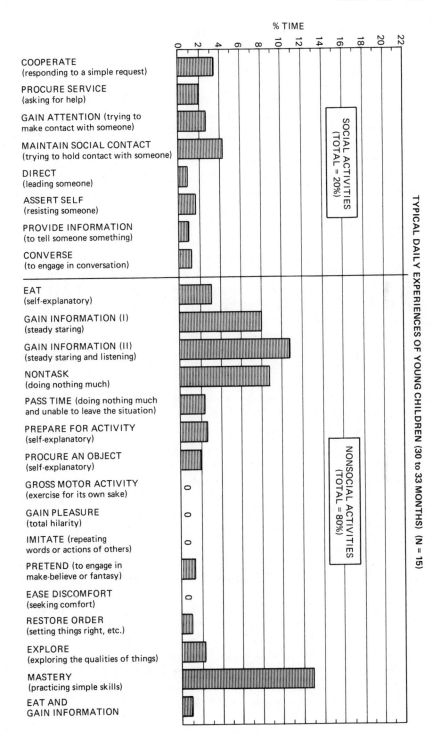

GENERAL BEHAVIOR DURING PHASE VII

The Decline of Nonsocial Experience

Starting with a child's first birthday, experiences oriented toward people begin to increase at the expense of experiences not oriented toward people. Near the first birthday about 10 percent of all activity is people-oriented. For some 6 minutes out of the average hour the child will try to create an effect in other people, trying to get their attention or trying to get them to perform a certain action. By about two years, the balance is about 20 percent social experience to about 80 percent nonsocial. But by the time the child reaches three years of age the figure is closer to 30 percent for social experiences, and nonsocial experiences have dropped correspondingly.

The major nonsocial experiences of the Phase VII child are similar to those she engaged in during Phase VI. Exploration of object qualities and practicing simple skills on objects remain a prominent part of the child's waking life, but their relative importance is lessening. Whereas at eighteen to twenty-one months our research indicates that children engage in those two major small-object activities about 18 percent of their waking time, by two and a half years such activities have decreased to about 14 percent. As the years go by the child will move beyond these simple kinds of interactions with small objects to more complicated ones, often involving social interaction with other children. Active play with small objects, however, still occupies a substantial amount of time in Phase VII.

The third year of life is also marked by a sharp decrease in staring behavior. As we have seen, at one year of age we routinely find such behavior accounting for slightly under 20 percent of all waking time; at two years staring has dropped to about 14 percent of waking time, and at three years it has dropped to 6 or 7 percent. As simple, steady staring decreases, a related kind of activity increases. That activity is gaining information by both looking at a source and listening to relevant language. It occupies a little over 6 percent of the child's waking time at one year of age, and about 11 percent of that time at two-and-a-half years.

Since Phase VII is a time of tremendous growth in language ability, it is no surprise that children in this age group are very much interested in attending to language of one sort or another. We know there are several sources of language that children can attend to at this point in time. Language can come from a human being speaking in their presence (live), or from a television set, radio, or record player. Live language can be language a child listens to as his mother talks with an older brother or sister, or language directed to the child himself. We believe the latter is the most important with respect to learning.

The next nonsocial experience of consequence is what we call a "nontask experience," or empty time. Such behavior generally declines during the third year of life, dropping from 10 to 12 percent of waking time during the second year to 7 or 8 percent during the third year. Its companion category, "passing time," is also on the decline during this period. I think this trend reflects the fact that children are less prone to accidents after infancy and therefore are not as often kept in confined areas, or at least under close watch by their parents, from this time forward.

Eating accounts for another 5 percent of a child's waking time during Phase VII. You can see that relatively few types of nonsocial experiences account for the bulk of the child's activities during a typical day. In fact, the seven types of experience discussed above account for about 53 percent of the child's waking hours at three years old. At two-and-a-half years of age, the same seven account for about 47 percent of that time. This difference is significant in that with each passing month experience becomes richer; more and more types of experience are engaged in by children.

Social Experience

We find that the two-year-old (onset of Phase VII) engages in very few kinds of social experience for any appreciable length of time, and the amount of time devoted to these activities is considerably smaller than that given over to nonsocial experience. The most common social experience you find in Phase VII is the child attempting to hold on to another person's attention, that is, to maintain social contact. As might be expected, mother is the person most involved, about 90 percent of the time. At about two years of age maintaining social contact accounts for about 6 percent of all waking time. The two-and-a-half-year-old is considerably less clingy, with this type of experience accounting for only 4 percent of her time.

The second most common social experience is complying with simple requests that parents make—about 3 percent of waking time.

The third most common social experience is attempting to get somebody's attention—from 2.5 to 3 percent. Bear in mind the child's skill at getting attention and/or maintaining it has increased considerably beyond previous years; therefore, it takes less time.

Two additional categories of social experience of importance are attempting to get some help from an adult—about 2 percent of waking time—and resisting suggestions by an adult or another child—between

1 and 1.5 percent of the time. All five of these social experiences combined take less daily time than active exploration and practicing of skills on small objects.

You will notice that the picture drawn of the life of a three-year-does not project a child sitting morning till night by his mother's side. Older literature on early child development was so concentrated on the importance of the mother-child relationship that people tended to assume that all a child did all day long was relate to mother. The fact of the matter is that, for the vast majority of the child's waking hours throughout his first three years of life, he will be exploring the nonsocial world and practicing motor skills. From the perspective of a full-time parent, babies spend much more time in close contact with them, but there is a substantial difference between psychological time and objective time.

THE APPARENT INTERESTS OF PHASE VII

Continuing Interests

The three dominating interests of Phase V and VI children—interest in the primary caretaker, exploration of the world, and practicing new motor skills—continue as dominating interests during the third year of life, but with some important changes. For example, in the area of social development, a child's almost total concentration of social interests on parent's behaviors—especially their reactions to the child's own acts—lessens, and during Phase VII the new and important element of true socializing with peers emerges and grows steadily. With respect to exploration of the world at large, you'll find that children in their third year have major interests on which you can capitalize. Especially noteworthy is the increasing interest in language, especially if the language is directed toward them.

Concerning the practicing of new motor skills and the mastery of the body, the child is now adept at most of the fundamental motor skills that emerge during infancy. All children over two years of age can generally handle walking, running, and climbing with ease, and immensely enjoy the two latter activities (although they are not as skillful at climbing as they will become). Children can acquire new specialized skills during the third year of life, but no dramatic changes at this point. For example, you can teach a Phase VII child to ride a small tricycle. Children continue to enjoy swing sets in the third year of life every bit as much as they did in the second. Many fine motor challenges, such as learning to use a nutcracker or a hole punch, will intrigue a Phase VII child.

EMERGING INTERESTS

Creative Activities

Toward the end of the third year children begin to put together various prerequisite skills and information they have been gathering so busily for the preceding two years; they combine these into what we call "consummatory activity." During Phase VII you'll see the first representational drawings by children, especially if they are encouraged or if there are older siblings to imitate. You'll also find the first "constructions." Playing with blocks may now include the creation of forts or towers—again, especially if encouraged or modeled. The creation of family, farm, or town scenes, facilitated by some first-rate commercial toys available, are another sign of the newfound capacity for coordinating and organizing activities. These newly emerging interests will grow quite steadily in the months to come.

Pretend Activities

Another emerging activity of particular interest and importance is a newfound capacity to enter into more and more imaginative fantasy situations (combined with improved speech skills), either alone or with parents. The meaning of the earliest pretend activities is not clear; however, a good deal of such behavior is a distinguishing characteristic of well-developed children.

Interest in Television

Yet another emerging interest of the third year is television viewing. This interest began with reflexive responses to commercials when the child was about three months of age, particularly commercials with many changes in sound levels. Progress in television viewing—that is, sustained viewing—must wait until the end of the second or the beginning of the third year, simply because television viewing depends upon mental and linguistic developments that do not sufficiently surface until then. Don't expect your two-and-a-half-year-old to watch somebody give a lecture on how to sew an apron, but he will watch the changing sounds and moving forms on cartoon shows. Also he is likely to show a good deal of interest in programs like "Sesame Street," which are specifically designed to capture and recapture the attention of a very young child.

LEARNING DEVELOPMENTS DURING PHASE VII

The four educational goals described earlier—language, curiosity, intelligence, and social development—continue as objectives throughout the child's third year of life. The three dominating interests of Phases V and VI also continue to be of fundamental importance during Phase VII. Again, the desired goal is not only to encourage those interests but to keep them in balance.

Language Development

If all has gone well, your two-year-old should understand about 300 words, which include the majority of those that you address to her in ordinary conversation. She should be speaking regularly, although she may not be saying very much as yet. Some two-year-olds use short sentences and carry on simple conversations. Others are still only using simple words or sentence fragments. Again, you need not worry too much about a two-year-old's speech, as long as her *understanding* of language is moving along well.

Development of Curiosity

In the areas of curiosity, the hope is that you have a two-year-old who can play alone well and who is genuinely interested in anything that is new. We basically want to see the same intense curiosity that the child showed during the days of sustained hand regard, at about three months old.

Social Development

The third area, social development, is considerably more complicated. We want a two-year-old child who has acquired an initial set of social skills, the deails of which will be discussed later in this chapter. We want her to be a pleasure to live with most, if not all, of the time. We want her to have left negativism behind for the most part. We want her to like herself, to have come to feel that she is valued by others. We want her to get along reasonably well with everyone in the family, not just her parents.

These social goals apply for the family with one child or for the family with several children spaced widely apart. But the picture changes in important ways if there are closely spaced children.

Older Phase VII Child of Two Closely Spaced Siblings

Let's start first with the case of two closely spaced children, the older of which is in Phase VII. We have cautioned you to expect dramatic changes in the behavior of a slightly older child when a younger sibling becomes a crawler. We described what we had found in our extensive observations of families, that is, that older children found it most difficult sharing the attention of their parents with a newly crawling child. The older Phase VI child was in a particularly difficult situation, because of the intensity of her social needs as she moved through the second half of the second year of life, and because of her intellectual and emotional immaturity during that time. Such a child moving into Phase VII is very likely to continue to put a good deal of stress on parents. In other words, unfortunately, the hard feelings from older child to younger child don't go away during this phase of life. There are, however, two principal changes that warrant special attention. The first is that the younger child is no longer a pushover. The only defense an eight- or nine-month-old has against a twenty-month-old who is behaving aggressively is to cry. Physically and mentally the younger child is no match for the Phase VI child. The cry, however, usually does the job: an older person nearby will hear the cry and will become the protector of the baby. The Phase VII child may very well have gone through many months of intermittent discomfort as a result of the existence of the baby in the home. Once the baby reaches fifteen or sixteen months of age, however, that baby becomes a different kind of foe for the Phase VII child. The younger child is entering into a genuine awareness of herself as a person, and into negativism and self-assertiveness, and she may begin to behave toward the older child in a manner similar to the older child's behavior toward her in the preceding year. In addition, younger children in such circumstances will sometimes acquire two kinds of weapons that can become potent indeed: hair pulling, and biting. Combined with the fact that the Phase VII child has had a fair amount of experience with pain, the result sometimes is domination by the younger child of the older one. At the very least the children are more evenly matched at this stage of the game.

Furthermore, a new problem surfaces for a full-time caretaker. Whereas in earlier months the parent could safely assume that any sounds of unhappiness from the children were usually caused by the older child, now that assumption is no longer always appropriate. The younger sibling may increasingly become the initiator of arguments and fights between the two. This particular situation is, first, quite normal and, second, *the most common source of stress for full-time parents.* The harsh feelings between closely spaced siblings often manifest themselves day in and day out. Imagine the difficult situations faced over the years as parent after parent has gone through this experience completely unprepared, wondering what on earth is going on and why parenting is not what it was cracked up to be. *It is for reasons like this that we advocate part-time substitute care at this stage of parenting.* We doubt that very many people, regardless of their talents, can handle the chronic stress that comes from closely spaced siblings when one is in Phase VI and the other in Phase VII.

Younger Phase VII Child of Two Closely Spaced Siblings

A second situation that warrants discussion at this point is when the Phase VII child is the younger of two closely spaced siblings. In our discussion of Phase VI (see pp. 165, 166, and 167) I described how Phase VI children often become aggressive with their slightly older siblings. That pattern usually continues as the child moves through Phase VII. In this situation the circumstances are a bit better for the parents. The older sibling, now at least four years of age and perhaps five or more, is spending much more of her time out of the home, in nursery school, in play groups, at friends' homes, and so forth, and has had a good year or two of growing interest in age-mates. These facts make life considerably easier for all concerned, especially the parents. Nevertheless, you should expect interchanges between the Phase VII child and older siblings to continue to feature aggression and disagreements at times. No one really knows how long this will continue, but it certainly isn't going to go away quickly.

Middle Phase VII Child of Three Closely Spaced Siblings

Finally, there is the situation where the Phase VII child has both a slightly older and a slightly younger sibling. With no research available on this subject we must resort to speculation in discussing this situation. Probably the most important point to understand is that the middle child has never suffered the kind of displacement that the first child did. She never had the exclusive attention of inexperienced, anxious, and excited parents during her first eighteen to twenty-four months, and therefore, moving over to make room for a younger sibling did not have quite the impact that it did on her older sibling.

The starting point in coping with these interesting and important sibling combinations is a basic understanding of social development in young children. If parents understand the fundamentals of social development, they have at least a basic beginning with respect to coping with the problems that come from close spacing. Hopefully, people who are either expecting their first child or have only one child now will be somewhat persuaded to space their children three or more years apart as a result of reading this book. If you end up with closely spaced siblings, there are procedures you can use to minimize the problems. Unfortunately, as far as we know, raising closely spaced children is, in nearly all circumstances, a considerably more difficult task than raising either single or widely spaced children.

Interest in Age-mates

Under good circumstances, as children move into Phase VII they begin to show a steadily increasing interest in true socializing with age-mates. The negativism and self-assertiveness of Phase VI is pretty much behind them; they know where they stand with respect to their parents, and now they turn their developing social interests to peers. Temper tantrums simply are not a feature in the lives of such well-adjusted children.

Unfortunately, however, quite a number of children move into Phase VII with unresolved issues in connection with their principal relationships. If a child has been dramatically overindulged during the first two years of life, that child may have developed certain persisting conflicts that will manifest themselves during the third year of life, and generally in ways that are not terribly pleasant. Many a twenty-eight-, thirty-, or thirty-two-month-old child will still be involved in a chronic tug-of-war with his parents, having learned that if he complains loudly enough he can often get his way. Such a child is also inclined to throw temper tantrums, especially during the first half of the third year. Of course, if parents have read this book and followed our advice faithfully, they won't have to put up with such difficulties and their child will sail smoothly into his or her third year.

For such a child the third year will feature the emergence of the three remaining social competencies that are well developed in the outstanding three- to six-year-old child. They are (1) being able to express emotions easily to peers, (2) being able to both lead and follow peers, and (3) being able to compete. We have already discussed the first of these competencies. Expressing emotions easily to peers reflects the same sign of social confidence that well-developing children show in their expressions of affection to parents in the preceding eighteen months or so.

Of the second, children in the three- to six-year range are comfortable only when they are allowed to direct the activities of other children—they can't play the follower role; others are comfortable when following but don't have much facility in leading; still others can't do either. The well-developed three- to six-year-old child can both lead and follow effectively and comfortably. The emergence of this social ability can take place during the third year of life.

Finally, there is the competitive behavior of well-developed preschoolers. Three-year-olds who have developed well seem to know that they're capable, and are eager to show you it and to tackle new challenges. "I can make a better one than that" is a typical Phase VII statement. You can look for this new competitiveness to surface as Phase VII develops.

We know that certain cultures in our society frown upon competitive behavior, as well as the tendency of children to express their annoyance with other people. Should you choose not to have your child exhibit such behaviors, that is, of course, your right. Such characteristics, however, have been routinely found in the everyday behavior of very well-developed three- to six-year-old children from many ethnic and socioeconomic backgrounds.

One last remark about social behavior of children in Phase VII: Phase VII children seldom do especially well in groups of more than two. Indeed, this tendency to interact with only one other age-mate will persist well into the preschool period.

The Development of Intelligence

In the area of intelligence, by Phase VII we hope that the two-year-old will have entered a new level of intellectual functioning that increasingly features the use of mental problem solving as well as trial-and-error problem solving with hands and eyes. Most intelligence shown in the first two years was of the latter kind, sensorimotor intelligence. An infant trying to get a hard-to-reach object will usually try various physical methods to reach the object, whereas the child over two years of age will very often consider alternatives in her head, choosing the one most likely to succeed and *then* acting. *It is this shift from working problems out with actions to thinking them through that takes place in late infancy. The child is now much more able to reflect upon events and situations than she was at age one, for example. She has become a thinker.*

The Phase VII child is a considerably more mature mental creature than he was in the second year of life. He knows much more than
he did previously about the world of objects and their permanent
existence even when not there to observe them. He knows much more
about the paths of motion of moving things, and about simple cause-
and-effect sequences. He knows enough about how change occurs to
anticipate the consequences in many situations. He has a fully developed short-term memory. Now the Phase VII child is a thinker, or
what Piaget has called an egocentric thinker. By *egocentric* Piaget
means he tends to see things exclusively from his own point of view.
For example, as noted earlier, it is very difficult to convince a two- or
three-year-old child who has been bumped into by an older sibling that
the bump was unintentional. The concept of an accidental occurrence
is foreign to such a child. Also, recall the incident involving the late
Phase VI child who had spilled some milk on a kitchen table as she
played with her parents. After a few moments of hard thinking, she
announced that it was her older sister who had spilled the milk, even
though her parents had been with her throughout the episode. As a
very early thinker, she was unable to take into account in her own
thinking processes anything but her own need to escape punishment.
Piaget describes other peculiar mental qualities of the Phase VII
child as well. One of particular interest has to do with the concept of
life. At this point in time anything that moves is alive. It is, therefore,
not safe to assume that a child will view a leaf being blown about the
street by the wind the way you will. Let me illustrate this point with an
anecdote involving my own family. I used an intact lobster shell to
explore my three-year-old daughter's ideas about the concept of life.
Her first view of the empty shell produced a small but real fear
reaction, until I assured her that the shell could not hurt her because
the lobster was not alive. She did not fully believe me at first, but she
was intrigued enough to make a cautious approach. Suddenly the shell
(which was on a step) slipped slightly; she abruptly jumped backwards—for her that movement meant that the object was alive. In
dealing with a two- or three-year-old child, it is important to remember
that his mind is still very immature. (For more details on the inner
workings of the very young mind I again recommended some of the
earlier works of Piaget, cited in the recommended readings section of
this book.)
A final approach to educational goals for the Phase VII child is in
terms of the dimensions of competence discussed in Chapter Six. Our
evaluation of the competent three- to six-year-old child becomes increasingly relevant to this book as the child moves through Phase VII
and approaches three years of age. During the third year of life, if
things go well, you can expect to see all of the dimensions of compe-

tence become functional. We will examine how parents can foster the development of these competencies during Phase VII in the following section.

RECOMMENDED CHILDREARING PRACTICES: PHASE VII

Coping with Sibling Rivalry

By now it should be clear to you how impressed I have become over the years with the difficulties most parents have with sibling rivalry. If you have both a Phase VII child and a newborn, you are not, as yet, in substantial trouble on this issue. If you have a Phase VII child and a baby who is nine or ten months of age, you have already very probably learned that sibling rivalry, indeed, is something both troublesome and requiring special attention. If you have a Phase VII child and a Phase VI child, you may be looking forward to this section of the book with substantially more anticipation, because the chances are very high that you have been living through a chronically stressful situation for several months. In discussing the Phase VI child, I treated the subject of coping with sibling rivalry rather briefly. At this point a more extensive treatment is clearly appropriate. The following advice works. We have used it over many years in our work with hundreds of families, and we feel comfortable passing it on to you.

The first consideration is danger to the baby. At the risk of alarming you, let me emphasize that perfectly normal Phase VII children can and have in the past inflicted serious damage on younger siblings. So be watchful. Make it as clear as possible to your older child that hurting the baby is something you will not tolerate. Furthermore, do not assume that because you have repeated this kind of statement to your Phase VII child, your job is over. Vigilance is necessary.

Next, bear in mind what underlies the older child's unhappiness about his younger sibling; understanding this is the first step toward coping effectively with the situation. It follows, therefore, that making a big fuss over the baby in the presence of the older child is going to make matters worse. Not only should parents be careful in this respect, but they should also make a special effort to inform others, especially grandparents, that such behavior should be avoided. Next, if you can reduce the pressure further on the older child by giving him an opportunity to be out of the home regularly, you will find this to be effective. Having the child out of the home might sound at first like a form of rejection, but this is not generally assumed by the older child.

The use of playgroups, nursery school, or a babysitter to take the child out of the home or on trips is a very good move. The alternative—the older child constantly pressured by the unfair competition of the younger child in the home all day long, day after day, is not the best way to go.

Perhaps the most important part of the plan, next to safety precautions, is to have one of the parents provide private time with the older child on a daily basis. A half-hour or so of such time is strongly recommended because *undivided attention is what the older child needs more than anything else.* No amount of verbal explanation about how much the child is still loved will make a substantial impact. No classes in sibling relations or books that assume an unrealistic capacity on the part of the older child for understanding and emotional control can substitute for *undivided attention.* This, of course, must be done without the younger sibling on the scene.

As the months go by, the situation will gradually ease. During the third year of life the older sibling in such circumstances is very likely to show a combination of resignation and a reduced zest for life. Do not be too disheartened by these personality modifications, as they are a natural response to the situation. If both parents participate actively in coping with these problems, the older child will make her way through them. As her interest in age-mates and activities out of the home grows, as it will steadily, the situation will become much better for all concerned.

People routinely ask what the long-term outlook is for children of such sibling rivalries. Unfortunately, there is no substantial research on the subject and, therefore, we cannot predict whether such children will ultimately become close friends or whether these early harsh feelings will persist for long periods of time.[1]

FOSTERING THE DIMENSIONS OF COMPETENCE: SOCIAL ABILITIES

Getting and holding the attention of adults: The early-developing ability of attention-getting was discussed on pages 63 and 64. The child's techniques for getting and holding adult attention become

---

[1] A small number of reports on sibling relations in later years have been published. Invariably, the information was gathered through interviews. I believe observations of actual behavior under many kinds of conditions is the only valid way to study such subjects.

increasingly sophisticated during Phase VII. It is important at this stage to be sure that the skills children use in holding your attention are socially acceptable and reasonable, as well as effective, and that the child knows when to stop. Earlier I pointed out the natural tendency of infants to concentrate on their primary caretaker at the expense of other kinds of experiences. Suffice it to say that if you will be alert to how and how much the child is trying to hold on to your attention, it will help you shape a solid ability in this particular area.

Using adults as resources after having first determined that a task is too difficult: There are two ways in which children can determine that a task is too difficult for them. The more obvious is to try it out for themselves. This is especially common in conjunction with the predominance of practical intelligence in a child less than two years of age. During the third year of life, as children increasingly develop more thinking ability, they resort to the second method of determining the difficulty of a task—trying solutions out in their minds. When a child makes no effort at actually trying to physically solve a problem before asking for your assistance, this does not necessarily mean that the child has not thought it through and concluded that he could not handle the problem. This shift in problem-solving style may lead you to the erroneous conclusion that a child is making less effort than previously before asking for your help.

In cases where a Phase VII child is seeking your assistance solely for the purpose of monopolizing your time, his motives are usually obvious. As in Phase VI, my recommendation is to show a certain amount of indulgence regarding appeals for aid, but do not encourage children to mask their true purposes or to overconcentrate on close contact to you. This problem, like many other related ones, is generally more difficult to deal with in the case of first children. Do not be surprised if you have to deal with it during the first half of Phase VII.

Expressing affection and moderate annoyance to adults: In reference to the Phase VI child, we spoke of the importance of spontaneous emotional expression. Again, my advice is to try to encourage a Phase VII child to express her feelings toward you whenever she is so inclined. By that we do not mean that you should continually ask her whether she loves you or dislikes you. But when a child spontaneously shows affection, you should (of course) welcome it and enjoy it. And correspondingly, if she registers mild displeasure at you or someone else, pause to think—is she justified in the behavior? If so, give her some leeway. (This does not mean condoning seriously hostile behavior or temper tantrums, which require understanding but very firm handling.)

It is not uncommon that parents find it difficult to accept expressions of dislike by a very young child. But you should be prepared to deal maturely with such situations if they arise by reminding yourself that the expression of negative feelings is a natural part of growing up. Be firm about setting limits, and be careful to explore possible causes for this behavior.

Leading and following peers: You should be watchful for the emergence of leading and following abilities in the third year of life. One way you can facilitate their development is by giving your child the chance to exercise simple leadership skills in interactions with you. Although we do not know to what degree skills, attitudes, and behaviors that have to do with leading and following an adult or older sibling will transfer to interactions with peers, some transfer most probably does occur.

There is, of course, proving ground for these abilities like play with peers themselves. Thus, a second way to help a child develop leading and following skills with other children is to arrange for regular experiences with age-mates in pleasant and supervised circumstances. Such experiences can be arranged in many ways—playgroups, nursery schools, and even daycare centers, from the time the child is two-and-a-half years, are examples.

During the third year of life a child's natural peer group size is two; therefore, there is no need for large numbers of other children in such a child's life. If there is another child or two living nearby with whom yours can play regularly, your child may have the opportunity for peer play at no cost to the family. The problem here is that with only one or two other playmates the opportunities for diverse kinds of group experiences are, of course, strictly limited and, unfortunately, Phase VII children can quickly form relationships with each other in which one child is dominant. As a result, the opportunity for practicing both leading and following skills is less available than it might be when several peers are involved. A good reason for experiences with several peers during Phase VII is to provide diverse social-learning opportunities. Such considerations are also relevant to decisions about the advisability of playgroups and nursery schools.

Expressing affection and mild annoyance to peers: In regard to free self-expression and peers, advice is similar to that for leading and following peers. The capacity to express your feelings, both positive and negative, to other people is probably developed in the first three years of life, partly through nuclear family experience, partly through peer experience. It is valuable and should be encouraged in both the home and nursery school.

Competing with peers: The notion of fostering a competitive spirit in children is distressing to some people. For those of you who have no strong objections to this behavior, let me urge you to encourage a reasonable spirit of competition in your child. For years a Harvard psychologist, David McClelland, has been doing research on what he calls "the achievement motive." Particularly in this country, with its orientation toward individual excellence, independence, and personal responsibility, a child who is reluctant to compete is probably at a disadvantage. Furthermore, many connotations of the word "competitive" are generally accepted as desirable. Implicit or implied in the concept of competitive behavior is some perception of when a job is well done, some understanding of a beginning and an end to a task, and some interest in how to find and use resources to do a job. Competition is occasionally, in my opinion, misinterpreted when it comes to child-rearing practices. In the best sense of the term, a competitive person is very much interested in achieving and doing things well, and in having his work compare favorably with others. It is in that healthy sense that the children we have studied have been competitive, and it is in that healthy spirit that I urge you to encourage your child in that regard. This encouragement is easily provided through attention to the child's achievements and appropriate expressions of pride, as well as the provision of assistance that might enable him to develop his skills better, produce better products, and, in general, become a more capable person.

Showing pride in personal accomplishment: Along with the growth of sophistication and awareness in the third year of life comes an increasing tendency to seek approval for activities or products successfully achieved. This tendency can be relatively well established by three years of age. Phase VII children will, from time to time, comment proudly on a new skill or on a new creation of their own. New abilities in the third year of life may include riding a tricycle, making a simple construction out of blocks, or producing a drawing or some writing that crudely resembles an older child's work. In numerous ways a child will show an interest in achievement, and in pleasure at being praised for that achievement. Of particular importance here, I think, is the reminder that you do the child no good if you praise him for things that are not really worthy of praise. This does not mean that you should set unrealistically high standards, but if a child is praised for an accomplishment considerably below his real ability level, he may begin to develop invalid standards or inappropriate levels of aspiration. Keep your praise tied realistically to the level of achievement, remembering that achievement should be generously rated in the light of the child's relatively simple level of development, even in the third year of life.

Engaging in role play or make-believe activities: In Lois Murphy's pioneering work, *Personality in Young Children*, one of the interesting qualities of behavior of her central figure, a well-developing boy, was that he frequently would come into the nursery school dressed up as one or another character, and spend a good deal of the day acting as if he were that character. The role selected was generally that of an adult. Role play is engaged in to some extent by virtually all two- to four-year-old children. However, in our study of well-developed three- to six-year-old children, their role play differed both in amount and in type from that of children not doing so well. In general, the roles selected by the former group were adult roles. These children routinely acted out such parts as doctor, lawyer, nurse, actress, truck driver, and pet store owner. In addition, these children would occasionally make believe that they were fictional heroes like Batman or Superman. Children not developing particularly well were more inclined to participate in role play that looked backwards or involved more modest aspirations. The two most common forms of such role play were acting like a baby or an animal.

In addition to role play, other types of behavior included in this dimension have to do with make-believe fantasizing, for example, baking cakes or interacting with imaginary playmates.

Role-play behavior is one of the more enjoyable areas in which childrearers have an opportunity to interact constructively with their Phase VII children. Some parents may feel that a child's grasp on reality will be loosened if she is encouraged in unreal kinds of talk and play. Our observations suggest otherwise. Most well-developed children seem to have received a good deal of encouragement from their parents to indulge in fantasy play. You probably would do well to give your Phase VII child similar encouragement.

Fostering the Dimensions of Competence: Nonsocial Abilities

Good language development: We have repeatedly noted that well-developed three- to six-year-old children speak especially clearly, use a good deal of expressive language, and are in general strikingly advanced in all language skills. By the time a child reaches her third birthday, she should be able to understand the majority of all language she will use for the rest of her life in ordinary conversation. The more you use langauge effectively with her, the better off she will be in this regard. Remember the particular description of the ways in which apparently effective childrearers respond to overtures from their children. By now you will have had many thousands of opportunities to respond to such overtures and, hopefully, have acquired a comfortable and effective style of interacting with your child. Identifying what the child is interested in at the moment is the key to good language teaching. Once you know this, you can talk to that topic and maximize your effectiveness. As noted earlier, this reactive style is the easiest way to get a very young child to attend to what you say. In contrast, chasing her across the room, trying to get her to look at a book, can be both tiring and ineffective. Neither underestimate the child's language level, nor speak at a level that is considerably beyond her capacity. You will be providing the most effective raw materials from which she can extract maximum benefits.

Of course, during the third year—as the child moves from understanding perhaps 300 words to understanding 1000, and his intellectual skills grow substantially—stories become extremely interesting to him. Dorothy Butler's *Babies Need Books* is particularly useful as a guide to the selection of materials for the Phase VII child. But, of course, every child has his own pattern of interests, and language materials that relate to those special interests are going to be the most effective. I recommend "Sesame Street" for the Phase VII child. Although it was originally designed for slowly developing three- and four-year-olds, a well-developing Phase VII child will generally enjoy "Sesame Street" enormously. I urge you not to become overly excited about modest precocities in the language area, but of course it can be very exciting for parents.

The ability to notice small details or discrepancies: Well-developed three- to six-year-old children are extremely accurate observers— quick to pick up differences and anomolies in a variety of areas.

Helping your Phase VII child to refine his observational capacities is a simple and pleasurable job. If, for example, a child comes to you and shows you something in a picture book, you have a natural opportunity to feed langauge development, heighten curiosity, and sharpen observational skills. Suppose your child has come to you with a picture of a train: rather than simply remarking "Oh, yes, that is a choo-choo," you can take another moment to say something like, "Oh, sure, that is an interesting looking train; it's got three wheels on this side and probably three on the other. Daddy's car has only two wheels on each side." The particular information provided is really not so important, as long as it is logically related to the material or situation and stretches the child's mind a bit.

A number of subjects that can serve as a basis for pointing out similarities and differences is infinite, and most of them are interesting to the Phase VII child. Let me remind you not to overextend such interchanges with your child. Keep them short and sweet unless the child wants to prolong the event. You will find that the child's interest in these kinds of topics is real but usually limited.

The ability to anticipate consequences: A child who, when someone is filling the tub, thinks ahead to the events that are likely to follow a failure to turn off the water, is a child *anticipating consequences.* Thus if another child is trying to carry more than he can handle, a child with this talent is likely to point out that the other child is going to drop or break something.

Again, it is relatively easy to help your child move into the habit of thinking ahead: just point out from time to time what is about to happen next. You can do this naturally whenever a child is hungry if you point out to her that she must wait while you prepare her meal. There may be times when the child will be more receptive to learning than when she is feeling the discomfort of hunger, but a moderate degree of hunger is good for a learning situation in the sense that the child is likely to be paying attention to what you are saying.

The ability to deal with abstractions: This is a very broad cognitive ability. A child who can count, one who can use words well and understand the names of classes of objects, one who knows letters and colors, is a child who is dealing effectively with simple abstractions. A child who can hold a conversation about things that are not physically present, or events that took place earlier, is a child who deals well with abstractions. Usually conversations between three- to six-year-old children depend very heavily for their success on the actual physical presence of a person, toy, or other object around which the conversation revolves. Although abstract abilities have definitely emerged, children in the preschool years routinely do better when dealing with the here and now.

Here is an area in which you must maintain certain limits in childrearing practices, due to the mental immaturity of the child. For example, you can demonstrate to a Phase VII child how a key works, using several keys and locks in the home. You can then talk about keys as they relate to locks in general so that an abstract conception of a key and its unlocking function may be learned to some extent. But if you raise the stakes and introduce topics such as truth, morality, or random events, you will find that you quickly exceed the capacity of the child. I recommend that you be modest in your attempts to heighten the child's capacity to deal with abstractions, since such teaching will happen naturally in your spontaneous conversations together.

The ability to put oneself in the place of another: Piaget has an interesting little test for this ability. He uses a model of a mountain range, onto which he puts doll figures at different points. He then asks the child what it is that the dolls can see from the different spots where they are standing. The child who has not yet achieved much talent in this area can only describe what he himself sees. But the child who is well developed can tell you, with a fair degree of accuracy, what it is that each doll sees from its own perspective. We have found this ability substantially developed in well-developed three- and four-year-olds, even though, as noted earlier, this is considerably younger than the average age at which Piaget pointed out the emergence of this behavior.

The ability to put oneself in another's place is a relatively difficult competency to encourage in the young child. Such behavior during the third year of life is contrary to a very powerful tendency *not* to take the perspective of another. The Phase VII child tends to see the world exclusively from the point of view of her own needs. The name for this style of thinking, as mentioned before, is *egocentrism*, a phenomenon extensively discussed and studied by Piaget.

Let me illustrate egocentrism with an example I like to cite about different parental responses to the same incident. If a two-year-old child approaches his parent wearing a bright, excited look on his face and a substantial amount of chocolate frosting on his clothes and hands, the response he will get is likely to vary with the adult involved. The parent may perceive both elements of the situation—that is, the frosting and what it may mean, plus the bright, excited look on the child's face—to an equal degree; or she may concentrate on the child's bright look, be pleased by it, and wonder why he is pleased; or she may barely

Test case: The chocolate child

notice the expression on his face because of an overriding concern for the chocolate frosting and what it signifies. Parents who focus only on the chocolate frosting are probably experiencing the situation from an egocentric point of view, in other words, with their own interests and needs uppermost in their minds. Parents who concentrate on the child's excitement are probably more oriented toward the child's perspective.

Egocentricity is not exclusively a characteristic of the young child's thinking; we all engage in it throughout our lives. Ordinarily whether or not we are egocentric, or the degree to which we are, varies as a function of the given situation and its emotional importance to us.

Given a child's tendencies at this stage, we suggest you be modest in your aspirations to influence a child's egocentrism. But whenever you get a chance to do so, point out to the child what the world looks like to someone else; you will find that the child will occasionally show some interest in such observations. Do not, however, try such teaching when she is feeling a good deal of anger or displeasure. If the Phase VII child comes to you furious because her older brother has taken back her favorite toy, this is not the moment to attempt to teach taking the perspective of another. You will naturally want to point out that the toy is one of her older brother's favorites. You probably will ask, "How would you feel if someone kept a toy of yours?" But do not be surprised if your remarks make surprisingly little impact on a Phase VII child. According another person his rights at the expense of your own is a very difficult notion at this stage.

A good person to introduce to a child on this subject of separate points of view, is yourself. It is fairly easy for most people to explain to children, even as young as twenty-four to thirty months, how they feel about something, particularly when there are concrete clues present to facilitate such explanations. If you are talking about a pair of shoes that you are having trouble squeezing your feet into, you can make an example, pointing out that although the shoes seem too small for you and hurt your feet, they would not hurt the child's feet because they are obviously not too small for her.

The ability to make interesting associations: In our observations in nursery schools and kindergartens we often watched teachers in story-telling sessions with children. Such stories sometimes dealt with exotic topics such as prehistoric monsters or fairy tales. We found especially well-developed children introducing interesting and apparently original associations and trains of thought to story sessions, often enough so that our group agreed that this is a regular distinguishing characteristic. Such creative imagination can be seen by the third birthday.

Listening to stories—whether they originate from superior television shows like "Sesame Street," or from some adult or older sibling—helps spark the imagination of a very young child. If you provide encouragement for any reasonable effort at original thinking, modest though it may be, you will be helping to stimulate the growth of a considerable talent.

The ability to carry out complicated activities:　We have characterized this as a "managerial" ability. The three-year-old who is developing very well can bring another child and a collection of materials together and introduce, organize, and carry out complicated activities like playing store or house or lion hunting.

Here again is a talent that takes a certain degree of living and mental maturity to develop. In the first three years of life, it can be helped along only modestly. For example, you can draw a child's attention to the ways in which you organize activities. Without overdoing it, you can describe some of the steps you use when baking a cake, putting together a meal, or repairing an appliance. You can encourage the child to look over his father's shoulder while a toy is being assembled, with some attempt to explain the steps in the process. Getting into the habit of talking out loud as you are doing things while the child is paying attention is probably the simplest way to be effective in this domain.

The ability to use resources effectively:　Real lions are ordinarily in short supply for children of this age, along with cages to put them in and nets in which to trap them. Taking big cardboard boxes and using them as cages is an example of using resources effectively.

Here is another area in which talking out loud can be helpful. If you do so as you decide on how to organize a task, you can teach the child the idea of multiple uses of resources. Tell him, for example, that if something needs a little force and a hammer is not available, force can be exerted by using substitute materials. Point out that using a heavy rock to pound in a stake can be as effective as a hammer, or that getting three or four people to help lift something rather than straining yourself is another good way to flexibly get jobs done.

Dual focusing:　"Dual focusing" means the ability to maintain focus on an immediate task while at the same time keeping track of what is going on around you in a busy situation. As noted earlier, the well-developed three- to six-year-old children we have studied in group situations are particularly able in this area. The average child in a group, on the other hand, may have trouble splitting attention in this way. The child, in the face of an overture by another, is likely either to yield to that overture and drop what he is doing or, at the very least, to lose his train of thought or concentration. Some children in the three- to six-year-old range can never do concentrated work in a busy situation. They just cannot focus their attention given the distractions typically present. Again, we do not know how to foster this ability.

To sum up, each of the above dimensions of competence can be used as a guide to effective childrearing practices. It is not necessary, however, to concentrate on teaching them all of the time; few people can. The families that we have watched doing a find job with their children do not put a tremendous amount of work into the process during the third year of the child's life; nor do they give up all of their other interests, pleasures, and activities at any point during the child's first years of life in order that the child acquire an excellent early education. It is not unduly time-consuming to do the job extremely well, and we would be misleading you if we suggested or implied that it was. By actual count, parents with well-developing children spent about 70 minutes a day paying undivided attention to their one-year-old children. It should be noted that first-time parents spent twice that much time, but then first-time parents are a breed apart. Even at later stages during the first three years, the amount of time spent by apparently effective parents in direct interactions with their children rarely exceeded 90 minutes. Some parents wonder about the accuracy of these statistics. They certainly *feel* like they are spending more time than that, particularly during Phase VI. But there is a substantial difference between psychological and real time. We have been consistently impressed with how many other things parents do in the course of their day at home, even in the most advantaged household.

CHILDREARING PRACTICES NOT RECOMMENDED

Overemphasis on Intellectual Achievement

Perhaps the most common child-learning problem seen during the third year of life among caring families is a tendency to be too concerned about the intellectual achievements of their children. Because of inadequate information on early education, many people have come to the conclusion that it is extremely important for their two- to three-year-olds to be in an educationally effective nursery school. *I know of no good reason why this should be so.* This does not mean that I do not recommend nursery schools. There are many reasons why nursery school might be a useful experience for a child at this age, and a help to his parents. In terms of solid intellectual growth, however, I do not believe that nursery schools are essential. A child is a complicated creature with many processes moving forward at the same time. To elevate intellectual growth to a position where it becomes the primary concern is, in my opinion, potentially harmful to a young child. In extensive observations of three- to six-year-old children, we have found many children who are intellectually quite precocious, able to converse fluently, able to do simple arithmetic, equipped with all sorts of information far in excess of what most children of their age have, and yet they are quite unhappy and uncomfortable in dealing with other children and adults, other than those of the nuclear family.

It may be that a child who is moving ahead in a balanced way will not be able to achieve a degree of precocity in any single direction that a child especially taught might. If you work very hard to produce a musical prodigy, for example, the number of hours spent in teaching, in learning, and in practice may very well produce a child with extraordinary musical skills. On the other hand, such a child may experience comparatively few interactions with other children outside of the home, may not master general motor skills of the sort that most children master at that time of life, and may have her spontaneous interest in a variety of life's activities interfered with. My message is: beware of equating brightness with good development. Intellectual superiority is too frequently obtained at the expense of progress in other areas of equal or even greater importance.

Expensive Educational Toys

Everything I have said about overvaluing the importance of nursery school experience applies equally to the question of how much families should spend on expensive educational materials for Phase VII children. No matter what you receive in the mail or what you read in the newspapers, I cannot think of a single proven educational product for the Phase VII stage that it would hurt a child to do without. Do not worry about the child next door who has every educational toy ever manufactured; he has no advantage over your child. It just is not so.

Unsupervised Play Groups

Particularly in the early stages of Phase VII, I would advise you to be very careful about play groups for your child or, for that matter, daycare programs or nursery schools. The child of three is already a small person with a fair degree of mental and emotional maturity. As we have seen, however, the child of two is still a far cry from this kind of person; he is still capable of succumbing to primitive destructive emotions. It is painful to watch two children who play together regularly form a relationship in which the submissive child becomes resigned to intimidation by the other week after week. This form of psychological pressure may not be as obvious as the occasional physical abuse that is often evident in such situations, but may be of even greater long-term significance. I do not oppose group experiences for children under thirty months, but you should know that your child can undergo experiences of a relatively painful kind if supervision is not adequate and effective.

Overindulgence

The third year of life is a time when children often show the unpleasant consequences of overindulgence. Some children become very difficult to handle during Phase VII, particularly if there is a crawling baby in the home. Yet this is a time when discipline must be firm. You do your child no service by routinely giving in to her or allowing her to engage in temper tantrums or other undesirable behaviors. You do her no service by loosening up on limit setting and on control in general. Do yourself and your child a favor—maintain a loving but very firm hold on the life of your child in her third year.

A note of caution: in our otherwise very effective model programs in Missouri, we have found the single most difficult problem for first-time parents to cope with is overindulgence. In spite of the finest educational support system I know of, first-time parents still tend to overcompensate to make sure that their children are happy and continue to love them. The result is at least a little overindulgence.

Let me reiterate a couple of tips that seem to control overindulgence well. First, a guiding principle for parents should be to teach their child that he is very special, but no more so than any other person. Second, parents should adopt an attitude of healthy selfishness. The people most likely to produce an overindulged young child are his own parents or grandparents. We suggest that parents picture a circle within which are the rights of the child and another within which are their own rights. They should examine a child's behavior to make sure that while all of the child's legitimate rights are being met, the child is not intruding upon the circle bounding the rights of others.

CHAPTER *NINE*

An Overview of Educational Developments During the First Three Years of Life

---

GENERAL REMARKS

This chapter is devoted to summing up the many aspects of early educational development that we have examined in detail in the preceding pages. It features nine charts designed to provide the reader with concise overviews of the topics discussed and to serve as simple points of reference.

The charts are divided into three groups. The first group is labeled "Prerequisite Information," by which we mean information about the growth and development of a young human during the first three years needed in order to approach the task of education sensibly. The second group, called "Educational Foundations," deals with the development of the four major educational processes that have been referred to throughout the text. The third section, labeled "The Growth of Special Abilities or Competencies," deals with the characteristics seen in well-developed three- to six-year-old children. The term *special abilities* is used because this book does not deal with *all* the abilities that develop in the first three years of life. Others are left off this list because, as far as we can tell, no special teaching or circumstances are necessary for their good development. For example, in our research we did not find that children developing poorly were usually less competent in the areas of perceptual or motor development. This statement will be perceived as controversial by people with special interests in those processes. As you probably know, there are books available that offer guidance on how to develop your child's motor abilities in the first years of life; there are other books that claim it is very important to guide a child's sensorimotor development—especially visual motor development—in the first three years of life. If you choose to follow the advice of such authors, that is, of course, up to you.

One of the key problems facing childrearers is confusion—rooted in the lack of dependable knowledge about early development and in inadequate guidance from our educational system. Follow the recommendations of this book, and we are confident that your young child will be well educated. If, however, you want him to play the violin, do push-ups, or swim at two or three years of age, you will have to look elsewhere for guidance.

These charts are organized around a scale going from birth to three years of age and subdivided into quarter-year units. The age at which you should expect the typical child to exhibit the behavior in question is indicated by the point at which a short vertical line bisects the horizontal line. The horizontal line, in turn, is meant to describe how variable is the date of onset of that behavior or process. In some instances it is also meant to indicate that the process is ongoing from the beginning of the time indicated through the end of that time, as represented by the horizontal line.

In most instances the length of time a process is undergoing development will be self-evident. In Chart A–1, on motor development, you will see that the first entry is head control—the vertical and horizontal lines indicate that on the average you can expect children to acquire head control, the ability to hold their head steady when held upright, at about three months of age. The horizontal line indicates that this ability first may be seen at any point from two to four months of age. By way of contrast, if you look ahead to Chart C–1, social abilities, in the section on the growth of social abilities, you will find that there is no vertical mark across the top line of the graph, labeled "Getting and Maintaining the Attention of Adults," that stretches horizontally all the way from birth to two years of age. This suggests that there is no particular point at which these abilities come into a child's repertoire, but that they are emerging more or less continuously from the time he is born until he is at least two years of age.

Even though the horizontal line representing attention-getting abilities ends at age two, this does not mean that children do no further learning in regard to such abilities after their second birthday. It means that the bulk of the learning process takes place during the first two years. Furthermore, the fact that Chart A–1 shows a central tendency and a range under head control does not mean that a child who acquires

A. PREREQUISITE INFORMATION 1. MOTOR DEVELOPMENT

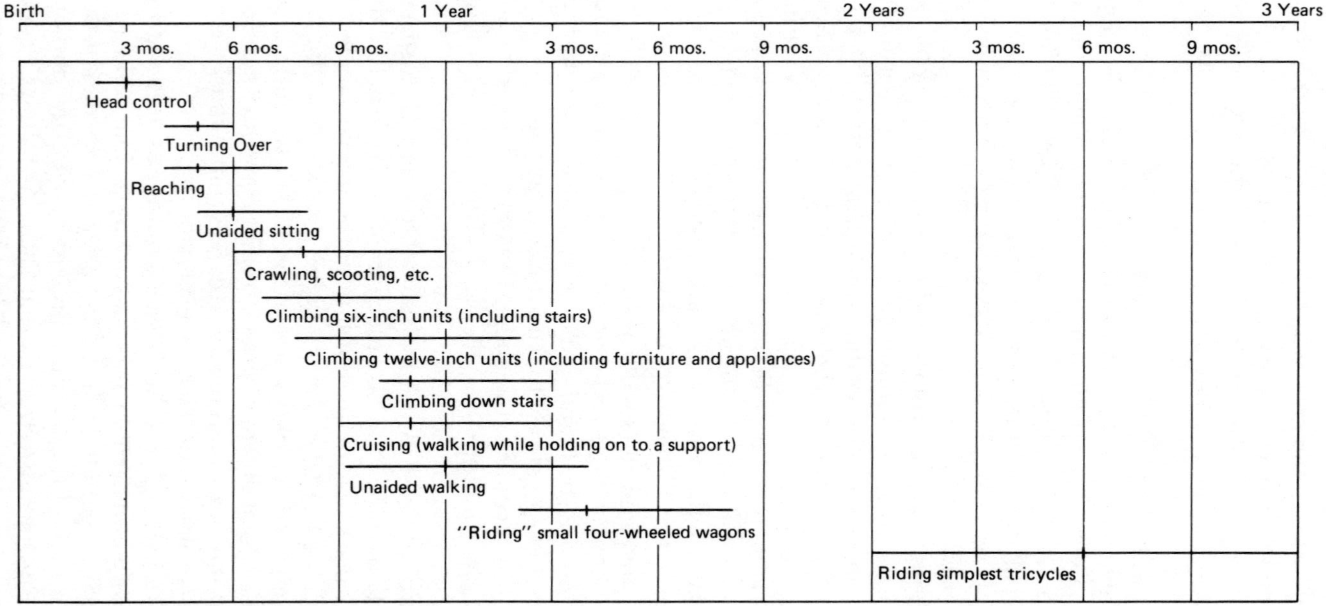

head control earlier or later is necessarily atypical. These charts are meant to describe how most children develop. Three-quarters or more of all normal children will probably fall within the ranges indicated.

PREREQUISITE INFORMATION

Chart A–1 portrays the major motor developments as they appear during the first three years of life. There are additional motor developments that are not included. These include the eye-blink to the sight of a rapidly approaching target during the first three months, and the focusing ability of the eyes that appears during the same period, give or take a week or two. Both behaviors are important, but Chart A–1 is intended to include only those motor achievements that have major learning implications. It has been suggested throughout this book that problems in motor development are not nearly as prevalent as those in language, intelligence, and social skills. Given the average predicted environment, most healthy children develop normal motor abilities. The topic thus has not received special emphasis.

In order to educate a baby, and to enjoy her to the fullest, I believe you should know what she is likely to be doing from day to day. Chart A–2 and the activities it deals with, is complicated. For more detail, I suggest you refer back to relevant sections in the text.

Chart A–3 deserves a few special remarks because the concept of shedding limitations has not as such been focused upon in the preceding text. It seems to me that a knowledge of what a child's natural limitations are as he goes from a state of total helplessness at birth to a state of rather miraculous accomplishment at age three, is important. For example, a child under three months is a crib-bound creature with modest sensory-motor capacities. Looking at mobiles is one of the few activities he can engage in during those limited periods when he is awake. In this regard it is useful to know about the role of the tonic neck reflex, which predisposes the normal child under two months of age to look to his far right or far left, rather than directly overhead. For example, if you want to design a mobile for your two-month-old baby, you had better not place it directly overhead.

Similarly, the fact that all children require some degree of control and guidance by older people in their first years of life, and that most grownups tend to make some use of language in controlling and guiding them, means that basic information about the language young children cannot cope with is a prerequisite to effective parenting.

A. PREREQUISITE INFORMATION 2. TYPICAL EXPERIENCES

Timeline: Birth — 3 mos. — 6 mos. — 9 mos. — 1 Year — 3 mos. — 6 mos. — 9 mos. — 2 Years — 3 mos. — 6 mos. — 9 mos. — 3 Years

Sleep/Sucking and gumming the fists/Brief visual interest/Arm and leg motions

Extensive visual interest (own hands and faces of others)/Batting with hands/Arm, leg, and head motions/Sucking and gumming anything handy/Socializing with anyone, intentional crying (for company)

Extensive visual interest/Hand-eye activities (batting, feeling, reaching, and grasping/Arm, leg, and torso exercises (including turning over)/Sucking and gumming anything handy/Play with own sounds/Socializing, especially with primary caretaker

Extensive visual interest/Simple manual activities with small objects/Practice in sitting up/Leg exercises/Sucking and gumming anything handy/Play with own sounds and attending to words/Socializing, especially with primary caretaker

Extensive visual interest/Practice in emerging gross motor skills, (crawling, climbing, cruising, walking)/Socializing with, and getting to know, primary caretaker/Exploring the qualities of objects, especially small portable ones/Gumming anything handy/Attending to words/Practicing simple skills, e.g., closing and opening doors and covers, filling and emptying containers, standing objects up, etc./Learning about simple causes and effects, e.g., light switches, pushing balls, jack-in-the-boxes, TV switches, etc./Coping with a slightly older sibling (reactively)

Extensive visual interest/Listening to language/Practicing simple skills, gross motor skills (running, "riding" wagons, etc.)/Exploring objects/Doing very little (idling)/Procuring objects/Getting and holding the attention of the primary caretaker/Going along with simple requests (cooperating)/Asserting himself and testing wills/Coping with a slightly older sibling (reactively and proactively)/Seeking assistance when needed/Practice in emerging gross motor/Emergence of late night sleeping problems

Extensive visual interest/Using and listening to language/Practicing motor skills, gross and fine (including tricycle riding and scribbling)/Exploring new objects/Engaging in fantasy activities (make-believe)/Creating products (simple drawings and puzzles, buildings, etc.)/Getting and holding the attention of the primary caretaker and peers/Practicing leading and following peers/Going along with simple requests/Conversing/Seeking assistance when needed

A. PREREQUISITE INFORMATION   3. SHEDDING LIMITATIONS

Birth — 3 mos. — 6 mos. — 9 mos. — 1 Year — 3 mos. — 6 mos. — 9 mos. — 2 Years — 3 mos. — 6 mos. — 9 mos. — 3 Years

Capacity to remain awake for many hours each day/First simple ability to control hands

Freedom from tonic neck reflex control (full head mobility)/Freedom from grasp reflex (fingers unclenched)/Visual convergence of the eyes (three-dimensional sight)

Head control (when torso upright)

Torso control (turning to the side)

Torso control (turning over)/Vision—mature focusing ability

Visually directed reaching

Unaided sitting

Locomobility/First language (understands a few words)/Intelligence (first use of means to achieve ends)

Vision—fully mature/Climbs very low objects (six inches)

Stands, with support/Climbs chairs and furnitire to several feet/First deliberate use of an adult for assistance

Walks alond/Understands a few dozen words and a few phrases

Basic control of the body complete/First spoken words—several dozen understood and many grammatical structures used

Freedom from negativism/First capacity for basic mental intelligence (problem solving through manipulation of ideas in advance of motor action)

229

EDUCATIONAL FOUNDATIONS

Do not be confused by the fact that the first few entries on Chart B–1 do not, strictly speaking, have to do with language per se. Since they do involve the child's earliest responses to sounds, they do indeed belong here. Note in particular the wide ranges in onset of the various language capacities. These can be observed in preceding charts as well, but language seems to be an area in which wide variability is particularly evident. Parents often become needlessly concerned by insignificant delays in the acquisition of speech. Speech, like walking, is a behavior that has a remarkably broad range of onset. The key that parents should be concerned with during the first two years of life is the growth of the *understanding* of language, rather than expression.

As noted earlier, there is very little data available in this area. I am particularly pleased to be able to provide the information included here and to, again, stress my conviction that nothing is more important for a child's educational development than a well-developed curiosity.

The only potentially confusing thing about Chart B–3 has to do with special entries about a child's development in regard to older siblings, if an older sibling is less than three years old. No information is presented as to relationships with siblings considerably older than the baby.

Chart B–4 leans very heavily on the work of Piaget. For more information on this fascinating topic, I urge you to look at the reference readings, particularly J. McVicker Hunt's *Intelligence and Experience*.

THE GROWTH OF SPECIAL ABILITIES (COMPETENCIES)

The two charts in this section point to particularly important educational abilities that can emerge during the first three years of life. As we have seen, these abilities develop over many months. Note, for example, that the long and steady process surrounding "getting and holding the attention of adults" spans two full years. A word about "expressing affection and mild annoyance when appropriate to adults and to peers:" Most of the well-developed children we studied were capable of expressing mild displeasure or annoyance, although they did not act this way very commonly. They were also able to express affection easily, and this they did much more frequently. In contrast, children who were developing relatively poorly seemed to be constricted in the expression of their emotions, both to adults and to other children.

Like the social abilities shown in the preceding charts, the

B. EDUCATIONAL FOUNDATIONS

1. LANGUAGE DEVELOPMENT*

Birth | 3 mos. | 6 mos. | 9 mos. | 1 Year | 3 mos. | 6 mos. | 9 mos. | 2 Years | 3 mos. | 6 mos. | 9 mos. | 3 Years

Startles to sharp noises

Interest in sounds/play with saliva/responds to voices

First words understood

3   12

Growth of receptive vocabulary (average number of words understood)

50   100(E)†   >300(E)†   >750(E)†   >1000(E)†

First instructions understood ("Wave bye-bye," etc.)

First words spoken

(0–5)   (10–15)   (20–25)   (200–275)   (400–450)   (800–900)

Growth of spoken vocabulary (average number of words)

1   2   3

Length of spoken sentences (average number of words)

Typical Language Achievements

At Two Years of Age

Repeats two consecutive numbers
Understands a few prepositions—*out, in, on*
Understands some common pronouns, e.g., *me, mine, you*
Uses the word *no*
Produces the sounds *p, m, n, b, w,* and *h* at the beginning of words
Uses words to make requests

At Three Years of Age

Uses pronouns *his* and *my* and prepositions *in front of, toward* and *behind*
Uses *what* and one or two other question words
Forms negative sentences
Uses present and past tense of verbs
Pronounces the letters *p, b, w, m, n, h, t, d, -ng, k,* and *g*
Repeats three numbers
Understands most adult sentences
Understands reflexives (touches herself), possessives (daddy's boy)

† (E) = Estimate

231

Birth — 3 mos. — 6 mos. — 9 mos. — 1 Year — 3 mos. — 6 mos. — 9 mos. — 2 Years — 3 mos. — 6 mos. — 9 mos. — 3 Years

Sustained hand regard/Some interest in faces/First interest in objects (batting, feeling, and gumming)

Own hand as a tool/Faces and voices/Sounds (including own with saliva)/Socializing (primitive interchanges with people)/Own feet

Effects of actions on objects (Dropping and throwing)/Small particles/Faces and voices/Sounds/Socializing

*

Exploring entire living area/Causes and effects (simple mechanisms, consequences of actions, etc.)/
The primary caretaker (all behavior, but especially reactions to subject)

Same as previous period, but with more interest in effects of motor actions (re mechanisms and objects) than simple exploration/Special emphasis on language and on interpersonal experiences

Intellectual curiosity with considerable reflection/
Continuation of themes of eight- to twenty-four-month periods with peer focus emerging

*A period of life virtually dominated by pure curiosity

B. EDUCATIONAL FOUNDATIONS   3. SOCIAL DEVELOPMENT

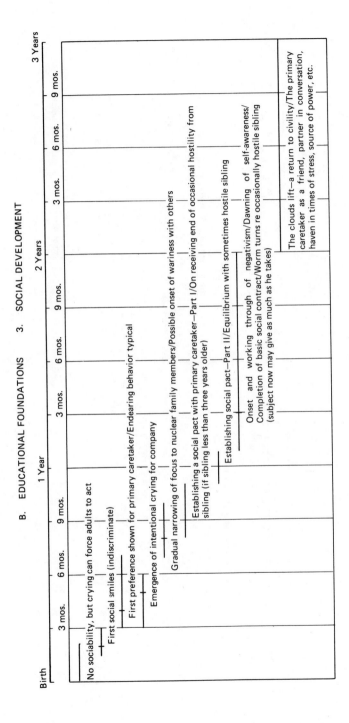

Birth | 3 mos. | 6 mos. | 9 mos. | 1 Year | 3 mos. | 6 mos. | 9 mos. | 2 Years | 3 mos. | 6 mos. | 9 mos. | 3 Years

No sociability, but crying can force adults to act

First social smiles (indiscriminate)

First preference shown for primary caretaker/Endearing behavior typical

Emergence of intentional crying for company

Gradual narrowing of focus to nuclear family members/Possible onset of wariness with others

Establishing a social pact with primary caretaker—Part I/On receiving end of occasional hostility from sibling (if sibling less than three years older)

Establishing social pact—Part II/Equilibrium with sometimes hostile sibling

Onset and working through of negativism/Dawning of self-awareness/Completion of basic social contract/Worm turns re occasionally hostile sibling (subject now may give as much as he takes)

The clouds lift—a return to civility/The primary caretaker as a friend, partner in conversation, haven in times of stress, source of power, etc.

B. EDUCATIONAL FOUNDATIONS   4. ROOTS OF INTELLIGENCE

Birth | 3 mos. | 6 mos. | 9 mos. | 1 Year | 3 mos. | 6 mos. | 9 mos. | 2 Years | 3 mos. | 6 mos. | 9 mos. | 3 Years

Exercising crude reflexes

Refining simple reflexes/Discovers hands/Beginning of object interest/Gathering information through visual exploration

Achieves reaching ability/Sharpens sensorimotor skills (vision localizing and identifying sounds)/Gathering information through visual exploration

First signs of intelligence (problem solving)—moves obstacles aside in order to grasp desired object/Shift of interest from mastering hand-eye skills to their effects on objects/Continued visual exploration/First language learning

Burst of active exploration (with locomobility)—special targets for learning: small objects and their physics, language, causes and effects, social phenomena

Growth of practical (sensorimotor) intelligence culminates in emergence of mental abilities of reflection, manipulation of ideas, etc./Dramatic language learning/Dramatic social learning, emergence of fantasy behavior, role play

Growth of capacity of mind to control impulses, emotions/Majority of basic language acquired/First creations (scribbled drawings, constructions, etc.)/Continued expansion of imaginative role play

C. THE GROWTH OF SPECIAL ABILITIES (Competencies)   1. SOCIAL ABILITIES

Birth	3 mos.	6 mos.	9 mos.	1 Year	3 mos.	6 mos.	9 mos.	2 Years	3 mos.	6 mos.	9 mos.	3 Years

Getting and holding the attention of adults (in socially acceptable ways)

Expressing affection and annoyance (when appropriate) to adults

Using adults as resources after first determining a job is too difficult to handle alone

Showing pride in personal accomplishment

Engaging in role play or make-believe activities

Leading and following peers *

Expressing affection and mild annoyance (when appropriate) to peers *

Competing with peers *

*Major development of this ability continues beyond 36 months of age.

235

C. THE GROWTH OF SPECIAL ABILITIES (Competencies)   2. NONSOCIAL ABILITIES

Birth	3 mos.	6 mos.	9 mos.	1 Year	3 mos.	6 mos.	9 mos.	2 Years	3 mos.	6 mos.	9 mos.	3 Years

The ability to notice small details or discrepancies *

Anticipating consequences *

Good language development *

Dealing with abstractions *

Making interesting associations *

Planning and carrying out complicated activities *

Using resources effectively *

Dual focusing—maintaining concentration on a near task, and simultaneously keeping track of what is going on nearby *

Putting oneself in the place of another person *

*Major development of this ability continues beyond 36 months of age.

236

abilities in Chart C–2 typically are acquired over a period of time. For example, the ability to "notice small details and discrepancies" is shown as developing throughout the entire three-year range. The moment the three-week-old child learns to discriminate between a nipple that contains milk and the adjacent parts of the human body, he has begun the long-term acquisition of the ability to notice differences. And when he is thirty months old he may catch an adult making an error in logic. I believe these two instances of noticing differences are part of the one common process.

It is interesting to note that the majority of these nonsocial abilities begin substantially to develop shortly after the child's second birthday.

TOPICS RELATED TO CHILD-REARING DURING THE FIRST THREE YEARS OF LIFE

Introduction

I have been involved in research on the development of the young child since 1957. Beginning in the late 1960s with the Harvard Preschool Project, my staff and I became involved in a type of activity that has not been very common in the careers of child-development workers: we extended our research into actually working with young families. During the course of this work we always hoped we were providing useful services, but our principal goal was nevertheless applied research for the purpose of creating the kind of knowledge about childrearing that might ultimately lead to benefits for large numbers of parents and children. At Harvard, and then at our Brookline project, and more recently in our Missouri work, we have had the pleasure of working with literally thousands of families of all kinds. These families ranged from Boston-area couples, where both parents held doctoral degrees, on through a wide variety of families from all levels of society, including young folks from rural Missouri with very limited education and very few resources.

As we look back on all these experiences we feel a strong sense of gratitude for having been offered such an opportunity. As the years have gone by, our views about early development have been refined, sometimes corrected, sometimes reinforced. We also learned a fair amount about how to prioritize issues. For example, in our work with families with two or more children, the factor that caused the most grief in a wide variety of families was having children spaced too closely in age, that is, less than three years apart. This finding was so routine that I have felt justified in spending a good deal of time in this book and elsewhere attempting to deal with it. Similarly, in work with first-time parents we have learned that *the* most difficult part of childrearing seems to be the problem of avoiding overindulging or spoiling a child. We have also been enormously impressed by the pervasiveness of the problem of undetected mild to moderate hearing losses during the first three years of life. Finally, the inflammatory topic of substitute child care for babies has, over the last five or six years, been the source of much controversy and guilt all over America and in foreign countries as well.

Our experiences, then, both extensive and intensive, are the basis for the arrangement, selection, and ordering of the topics presented in this section.

PART I: MAJOR ISSUES

How to Avoid Spoiling Your Child (or How to Help Your Child Become Delightful as Well as Talented)

Let me describe the most common way in which children can develop into unpleasant people.

Spoiled children develop in families that love their children very much. The origins of spoiling lie in the natural and vitally important tendencies of most parents to lavish attention, affection, and care on their babies in the first months of life. I have described in respect to the first four phases of life the cycle that begins with the child's distress, followed by crying and then comforting. This is a natural and necessary process. Indeed, during the first half-year of life, babies in distress must be promptly comforted. The goal of this activity is to produce a child who, at six or seven months of age, has learned through thousands of experiences to associate someone out there with the sensation of feeling better.

Because of the natural learning that takes place when experiences and the people involved in them recur over and over again, babies learn by the time they are four to five months of age to deliberately use the cry as a call for attention. From that point in development on to the age when mobility surfaces (usually at seven months of age but occasionally as early as five-and-a-half or as late as eleven), children very often find time hanging heavy on their hands. The six-month-old, for example, cannot do much more than lie on her stomach or back or sit in place in an infant or jump seat, while looking about and occasionally listening to sounds. Contrast that condition with what happens when the child is a nine- or ten-month-old crawler and actively exploring every situation she can get into. Thus it's not surprising that a six-month-old might try to use the cry in order to be picked up or at least have some older person come to entertain her. If this strategy succeeds, the usefulness of the cry becomes reinforced during this period. So far so good, no harm done.

But the situation may take a less than ideal turn a few months later when the nine- to ten-month-old child begins to create problems for his parents when he is supposed to be sleeping at night. It is extremely common for such a child to begin to wake up at anywhere from 9 P.M. on through 2 or even 3 A.M. and begin to cry. Of course, there may be times when such crying is due to illness or other physical distress, but very often it is simply the result of the fact that the child is alone, usually in a dimly lit room, is not very sleepy, and hasn't much to do.

Therefore, he brings into play the one tool that has alleviated boredom before—the cry.

It is easy to see how the tendency could have become ingrained as a result of the beneficial experiences of response to cries of distress during the preceding months. It is equally easy to see how it might be the beginning of an inconvenience to parents, and how it might even get to be quite a burden as time goes by. Not long ago I had a long-distance emergency call from a dentist in Georgia who was mildly embarrassed to describe the lengths to which he and his wife were going to stop the nighttime crying of their ten-month-old child. They had reached a point where they were taking the child on a minimum of two automobile rides, *after* midnight and *before* six in the morning, nightly. No wonder they were beginning to see the situation as an emergency. They, like others in the same boat, were beside themselves. (I should mention, parenthetically, that they had discussed this problem with their pediatrician and were told that the baby was in fine shape physically and they should simply let the baby cry it out.)

The next observable step in the process is visible when children are a little over one year of age. Now, for the first time, such children begin to skillfully use a whine to overcome resistance. We have observed many a thirteen-and fourteen-month-old child very effectively insist on getting his own way using this little strategy.

At fifteen or sixteen months of age, with negativism and self-assertiveness surfacing, another stress is placed on parents. Now they have to cope with a child who deliberately tests their authority. Many a parent will habitually make allowances for the fact that the child is just a baby and will allow unpleasant behavior, such as throwing of objects or kicking people. These allowances seem to be made partly because they love the baby, partly because they are afraid that the baby might not love them quite as much if they were firm, and partly because they just don't know how to cope with a child who repeatedly seeks out situations where he can challenge the authority of his parents. Whatever the reasons, a pattern of letting a child behave in a manner that to outsiders is clearly unacceptable becomes entrenched. Closely associated with the problem of coping with negativism is the tendency of parents at this stage of the game to allow the minor needs of the child to inconvenience them. In their zeal to make sure that the baby is always getting his needs satisfied, the parents get into a habit of chronically inconveniencing themselves.

Finally, there is the tendency of parents to not follow through when they set limits during the second half of the second year. A parent, seeing a Phase VII infant doing something objectionable, might say something firmly to end the behavior and then turn away and become reinvolved in cooking or a telephone conversation, ignoring the fact that the child is repeating the behavior. What the child learns from such experiences, when they happen often enough, is that if she pays attention to her parents for a few moments when they are angry at her, they will soon turn away and she can then continue to do whatever she wants.

The result of this very common path of development can be a two-year-old who may very well have a good mind and fine language and physical abilities but who is downright unpleasant to live with. We have even seen parents leave home for a couple of weeks to simply get away from such a child for a little while.

The problem is aggravated by the tendency of a Phase VII child in the process of the final stages of early attachment to stick close to her parents throughout the day. Such a child is very likely to move into the third year of life without having fully resolved the question of what she can and cannot do in the presence of adults. This child is likely to be the one who will routinely throw temper tantrums, especially during the first half of the third year, and is likely, too, to cause maximum grief when it comes to a closely spaced younger sibling. For obvious reasons, this problem seems to be greatest in the case of first children.

Can you avoid this outcome? The answer is an emphatic *yes*.

To begin with, you must bear in mind the differences in the evolutionary stages—the Phases—we have been discussing, for timing is important. You could, for example, guarantee avoiding a spoiled baby by neglecting him in the first months of life, but that would be extraordinarily ill advised. The baby must receive the kind of routine comforting and fun experiences that we have described earlier in the book during the first six or seven months of life. But you can start to make a difference with spoiling at about four months of age, bearing in mind the fact that it is from about four months that the child will begin to use crying intentionally to get company rather than only when he is in pain or discomfort. From that point on, parents should make a conscious effort to avoid excessive picking up and carrying of a child during the course of the day.

That is easy to say, but how specifically can you do that without sentencing your child to long periods of boredom? One tactic is to use an infant or jump seat and to move your child to different parts of the home, to occasionally prop the child up before a low window if that is at all possible, or to bring small toys for the child to examine and to play with. If none of this works well enough, we recommend the use of a well-designed walker, in spite of opposition by some specialists in the field. A walker can be the ideal solution to the problem of attention-getting crying. Babies love them. They can occupy themselves profitably in a walker for several hours a day, and the use of a walker in this manner doesn't in any way interfere with affectionate interplay between parent and child. To be sure, a five- or six-month-old in a walker is more likely to have an accident than one who simply remains in a crib or a playpen, or who is lying on a blanket on the floor. *Always supervise a baby every moment she is in a walker.* And remember, once the child is able to move about on her own, the walker should be discarded.

Even if you have followed my advice in the four- to seven-month period, you may still find your child waking up late at night once she reaches eight, nine, or ten months of age. If such behavior does emerge, respond promptly and check thoroughly to make sure there is nothing wrong with the child. If you determine there is nothing wrong with the child, give the child a hug and a kiss and say, "Sweetheart, it's time to sleep, we all need our sleep, I'll see you in the morning, nighty-nite." Then leave.

If the child continues to cry, ignore her, or, if you must (and I know this is sometimes a necessity), go back a half-hour later and repeat the same brief behavior. Do *not* remain long with the child. Do *not* provide a bottle for fear the child is going to be undernourished. Do *not* take the child into your bed. If you are resolute and consistent, you will produce a child who will routinely sleep through the night, often in a matter of no more than seven to ten days.

We have noted before that some people who work with young parents disapprove of such advice. They claim that any time a child cries it is vitally important that those cries be answered with a totally loving response. All I can say is that, in my firm judgment, that's not the wisest way to proceed.

The next step of the process involves setting limits. You will remember the parent we quoted who said of her one-year-old, "I love her enthusiasm and her curiosity, but she doesn't *have* to play in my makeup." The healthy selfishness involved in such a statement is a sound basis for starting to set limits. Right from eight or nine months on, children should know that there are some things they will not be allowed to do in their homes. Almost anything that intrudes substantially upon the rights of other people, *especially the parents*, should be forbidden. Children who have been dealt with firmly (but lovingly) between the time they start to crawl and the onset of second-year negativism are generally easier to live with throughout the balance of the negativistic period. This does not mean it will ever be a picnic, but they *are* easier to deal with. And the alternative—waiting until your child gets to be seventeen or eighteen months of age before beginning limit setting—is a mistake, for then it is very much more difficult to do. Remember also my advice that a child should be taught during this time that though they are indeed special, they are not more so than anyone else.

If you stick with this prescription and if you avoid overly stressful conditions by spacing your children three or more years apart, I am willing to guarantee that you will have, first, a delightful companion by twenty-four months and on through to thirty-six and, second, that you will not have to suffer through temper tantrums during the third year of life. How's that for a promise?

Sibling Rivalry and the Spacing of Children

There is little question that the difficulties associated with having closely spaced children under age three constitute the single most pressing concern for families with more than one young child. Among the hundreds of questions addressed to me since the original publication of *The First Three Years of Life*, the most common concern closely spaced siblings, and I am sorry to say I still believe that there is no satisfactory way to eliminate the special difficulties associated with this situation. All you can hope to do is keep the problems within reasonable limits.

The resentment that a two-year-old shows toward a younger sibling may be good evidence that that older child has formed normal and beneficial ties with his parents, but the parents must nevertheless recognize that the two closely spaced young siblings are living in a chronically difficult state. A special effort is needed to help both children get through their first few years together.

Rivalry problems usually do not begin during pregnancy or even soon after the second child is born. After all, a newborn sleeps most of the time, is very small, has a relatively soft cry, and spends most of his time stored in a crib in another room. Normally the older child will maintain her good temperament until the new baby starts to crawl, at which point the younger child will not only need more of the parents' attention but will also probably be getting into the older child's toys as well.

The older child may now try to hit or otherwise hurt the baby. She may regress, becoming more babyish herself, take to crawling if she has been walking, go back to a pacifier or bottle, revert to negativism or tantrums, return to wetting herself if she is already toilet-trained. She may show marked signs of being unhappy, appear sad, cling excessively to her parents or burst into tears for no apparent reason. In fact, the number of different ways in which children reveal their jealousy in such situations is remarkably large.

That this is a thoroughly undesirable state of affairs is obvious; but if it exists, what do you do about it? The first order of business is to understand what is happening. You cannot get anywhere if you do not know why the older child is behaving the way she is. The second is to protect the younger child from aggression. Babies have been seriously injured by their own older siblings, and you should not underestimate the danger. At the same time, you should be aware that it makes no sense to try to make the older child feel guilty about expressions of aggression toward the baby; after all, her dislike of the sibling is natural. It must simply be made clear to her that aggression of any sort is unacceptable and will not be permitted.

The second task is to make life more bearable for the older child—the happier she is, the easier the life of the new baby and of the parents will be. Many parents ask if there is a way to prepare a two-year-old for the arrival of a little sister or brother. Unfortunately, rational explanations of complicated future situations are useless when the listener is so young. Once the baby is home you can reduce the upset by avoiding any lavish praise of the younger child in the presence of the older one. Also, as soon as possible, provide out-of-home experiences for the older child. These help to relieve the pressure in the family situation. If the older child is over two-and-a-half years, a regular play group could be an excellent idea. In any event, the use of a babysitter to take the older child on trips to the park, the zoo, and the like would help. But please remember that while out-of-home experiences can help to reduce the older sibling's exposure to the jealousy-producing new situation in the family, they must *never* be used in such a way as to make the older child feel she is being shoved aside.

It is extremely important for the older child to have undivided attention (a half-hour or so) from either parent regularly, every day, to reassure the older child in the only language that she can fully understand that she is loved just as much as ever.

Do not make the mistake that many parents make by placing extra demands on the older sibling. The older child may be much more mature than the baby, but he cannot for that reason be expected to act with restraint and wisdom. He should not be asked to be extra grown up, not to be "a bother," and so on. For natural reasons parents in these situations tend to overestimate the abilities of the older sibling. Hard as it is on parents, the fact is that when there are two very young children in the home, both need special attention, and the job of the parents is going to be much more demanding than it was before.

Finally, let me restate the blunt truth of the matter: though parents can do much to alleviate the problem of closely spaced siblings, there is simply no way of making the situation as easy as dealing with a first child only or with widely spaced children. Both parents must understand and accept that fact.

Discipline

For first-time parents, only overindulgence supercedes the closely interrelated problem of discipline. Discipline problems generally arise in children in the second and third years of life and are not likely to surface until the child reaches crawling age.

Few functions of the parenting process are more important than performing the role of disciplinarian. It is, after all, in the civilizing process that parents can either produce a three-year-old who is a delight to live with or one who is a holy terror. It has been our experience that helping a child become intelligent and articulate is considerably easier than helping him to develop a healthy capacity to get along well with other people.

When and How: I do not believe that discipline is necessary for a child *under* seven months of age. People who concern themselves with making a child "mind" during that period are ill-advised. A baby that young does not act in a self-conscious way and, therefore, is not going to profit from scoldings. From seven months on, however, the child is not only more sophisticated but is beginning to move about on his own. Now occasional limits will have to be set on his behavior. This limit setting is not the kind of discipline that one would apply to an eighteen-month-old. You are not trying to teach the baby self-control; you are only imposing external control. If, however, you do not begin then with *some* sort of effective controls, the problem will become much more difficult later. In one sense, effective control is easier earlier due both to the weakness of the child's memory and to the strength of his curiosity. A child of eight or nine months who has come across something you do not want him to play with, perhaps something dangerous or fragile, has no internal controls to prevent him from approaching the object. As soon as you notice such a problem, it is an easy matter to move the child out of trouble's way—in effect, to distract him: you can bring a couple of plastic cups or a toy to the baby, draw his attention to the new items, and, at the same time, remove whatever it is that you do not want the baby to play with. His strong interest in new experiences will provoke immediate attention to the new objects, and his undeveloped memory will preclude any complaints about the removal of the item that you took away.

Some parents try to teach the baby the meaning of the word "no" at this stage of the game. I believe that this may not be wise. Certainly a baby in Phase V is old enough to assimilate the meaning of the word "no"; however, when you use that term to a baby who is reaching for an object, you are beginning to associate disapproval, from someone who means more to the child than anyone else, with his natural tendency to satisfy his curiosity and to explore the world. This is not a particularly good association to imply. If you had safety proofed your home before the child became a crawler, you could doubtless reduce the number of situations in which you would be obliged to use the term "no," but the combination of safety proofing along with the use of *distraction* is the better way to go.

Distraction as a limit-setting tactic works well for several months, but inevitably the normal baby will outgrow it. Slowly but steadily her capacity to retain an image in her mind will grow to the point where the baby will be able to remember for quite a few seconds what it was she was doing before you interrupted her. If you have managed to remove the materials that precipitated the problem, that's fine; but if the problem concerns something you cannot readily remove, simple distraction will not be enough, and you are going to have to provide a genuinely superior alternative. If you take a thirteen-month-old child into another room and provide her with four or five items to play with, this will usually solve the problem. (You may need a special toy or two kept in reserve for such occasions.) In the time it takes to play with several new items and to return to the room where the initial problem surfaced, the thirteen- to fifteen-month-old baby will forget what she was doing and will usually not cause you any additional grief.

It is important to keep two principles in mind. The first is that *there is a line where the baby's legitimate rights end and those of other people begin.* Common sense will tell you when the baby is infringing upon the rights of others. It may be doing something as blatant as taking a toy away from a visiting baby, or something somewhat more subtle, such as asking for more and more of your attention when you are concerned with an older child. You do a baby no favor by making too many allowances for the fact that he is just a baby. Some infants, by the time they are two years old, are convinced that nobody else in the world is quite as important as they. Although that might be a healthy sign that they have been dearly loved and cared for, it is obvious that if such an orientation persists, those babies will become accustomed to a self-centeredness that will in the long run be bad for all concerned. It is up to parents to draw the line and draw it clearly. They should discuss the matter explicitly and come to a common position.

The second basic principle is to *follow through consistently.* Parents must *persist* when they indicate they want a child to behave in a particular way. If parents get into the habit of following through and seeing to it that commands are obeyed, then the much more negative behavior that emerges in the middle of the second year will be easier to handle. This advice is at times difficult to follow because it requires patience and single-mindedness, and because it can be time-consuming. If you tell a fifteen-month-old not to pull on the drapes or not to climb up on the coffee table, you have to stick with that command for however long it may take to get the child to cease and desist. If you relent or allow your attention to wander, the child will only learn that if he stops doing the forbidden activity for a few moments and waits, he can go right back to it as soon as the parent turns away.

Excessive Control: As important as it is to set limits, let me emphasize again that it is equally important for the child to have enough freedom of movement to explore the world. If you find that your child is constantly getting into trouble, the problem may well not be that she needs more discipline but that the environment is wrong for her. If you have either to be with her constantly or to confine her to a playpen, both you and your youngster are in for bad times. It really is essential to redesign a home for a newly crawling baby. An occasional prohibition is not only much less work than chronic "don'ts," it is likely to be much more effective. The parent who is constantly nagging at a child is usually unhappy, and the same goes for the baby, who either fights back—setting a pattern of conflict that may persist for years—or gives up, which is even sadder. It is a matter of striking a just and sensible balance. Resolve to be firm and follow through, but do not fight about anything that is not worth a fight. And set up your home to minimize conflicts.

When Does a Child First Understand the Meaning of the Word "No"? In the first six months of life children do not understand the meaning of words whatsoever. By four months of age, you can expect your child to respond to his name, provided that he is in a good mood and not too preoccupied. (Interestingly, such behavior does not indicate that he actually *knows* his name. You can prove this by waiting a few minutes and calling him again, only this time using some other name. Use the same bright, pleased, pleasant tone, but call him "Godzilla" instead of Gordon. You will get the same response: he will pause, turn to you, and smile. Why doesn't he discriminate? Because he does not yet understand the meaning of words.)

Children begin to learn the meaning of words at about six months. Progress is slow for the balance of the first year and then accelerates at the beginning of the second. They normally acquire a basic understanding of the word and the concept of *no* somewhere between the eighth and tenth month of life. From that point on, *no* is a word you are going to be using with some frequency—which is not to say that it will always be used with perfect effectiveness, particularly if it is overused. Indeed, if you hear yourself saying *no* very frequently, stop and figure out what is causing the regular conflicts and then try to make changes that will reduce the source of trouble.

Will Strictness Make a Child Feel Less Loved?   Many parents seem to feel that love and discipline are incompatible, that the more a child is disciplined, the less he will love and feel loved. This simply is not the case. In my experience, if parents are consistent in setting limits from seven to eight months on, and if these limits reflect a fair distribution of rights between parents and children in the family, then the child will feel completely loved. When you begin with elementary limit setting, both parents and children become accustomed to basic egalitarian ground rules. A child does not feel less loved when she learns from her first experiences that she cannot always go when and where the spirit moves her. When her itinerary includes parts of the floor where you are sweeping up broken glass, or to the top of the stairs when you have forgotten to close a gate, you'll not think twice about the issue of control. You should be just as forthright when the baby is destroying an unread newspaper. Although the child may not be in any danger in the latter case, if you allow her to destroy the newspaper you are extending her rights too far into your territory. If such an analysis seems somewhat selfish, it is; but it is healthy selfishness. Bear in mind that the child who concludes during her first year that no one else is as important as she, may all too easily develop into the kind of person who really *is* less loved.

The Age of Rebellion: From age fifteen to twenty-one months true negativism emerges and disciplinary problems escalate. Yet the same basic principles of discipline that you followed when the child was younger still apply now: you stand your ground and do whatever is necessary, within reason, to see to it that the child knows when you say something, you mean it. The toddler's memory has now reached the point where distraction (unfortunately) will not work any more. By the same token, his language and intellectual capacities are so much better that you can give simple commands and instructions and expect that he will understand them reasonably well. Your child's receptive vocabulary at this time should range from a minimum of a few dozen words up to a couple of hundred, and most children can understand several dozen simple instructions. It is now that parents' earlier work on setting limits really helps. If the child has been accustomed to living with controls since he was eight or nine months of age, he is going to be comparatively easy to handle during the negative period.

From twenty-one to thirty-six months of age we expect to see a decline in the almost reflexive negativism of the preceding five months. Now the child's behavior becomes much more reasoned. This may or may not be a blessing. Two-year-old children can be delightfully reasonable and pleasant to live with when all goes well. On the other hand, they can be entering into a phase referred to as "the terrible twos." If a child moves into the third year without it having been made clear who runs the house and whether you really mean it when you forbid something, then you are in for trouble. Remember that during the third year the child's power as an individual—his intellectual ability, his forcefulness, his imagination, his capacity for devious and difficult behavior—all grow at an impressive pace. If you are still having control problems during the third year, it is time to get on top of them as quickly as possible. You may not have all that much time left.

Types of Discipline: Firmness does not mean abuse. To my mind abuse involves something more than simply physical pain. A blow that leaves a bruise is indeed abuse; but locking a two-year-old in a closet is also abuse; leaving a three-year-old alone in her room for hours is abuse; and in some cases ridicule can be abuse. Discipline should never exceed that degree of coercion necessary to stop a child from doing what she is not supposed to do.

Some children are quite pliant; they can be brought around by a scolding or by the old technique of having a special corner to stand in or a chair to sit in. Some children need to be confined until they are ready to behave. And perhaps some children may need to be physically punished.

The idea of physically punishing a child is unacceptable to many grownups, and I have encountered many strong statements against spankings of any sort. There are many who believe fervently that spanking (1) constitutes clear evidence of a failure on the part of parents to manage a child well, and (2) teaches a child herself to be aggressive and physically abusive. The research that has been done on this issue is far from conclusive. There is no evidence that children who have been spanked (*not* abused) when they are young become either aggressive older children or abusive parents. Indeed, the long-term research needed to test this thesis has never been done. Nevertheless, I can state that some two-thirds of the successful families we have observed from all levels of society have used occasional mild physical punishment with their children after they entered the second year.

Physical discipline need not, of course, involve spanking. There are other ways for adults to use physical strength to prevent unacceptable behavior, the most obvious being to hold the child firmly until he has calmed down and becomes controllable.

Explaining may not always be the perfect alternative to physical discipline. Elaborate explanations to a child under two years of age are futile. Such young children simply do not have the linguistic or intellectual capacity to cope with complicated explanations about why they are not supposed to do something. Long lectures are ineffective and frustrating for both parent and child. Explain your reasons simply and no more than twice. You can say "knives are dangerous" or "that is my newspaper," but leave it at that and then go on to enforce the rule.

If you ever do use physical punishment, keep in mind that no good lesson can be taught through pain alone. Physical contact can be effective when it is surprising and unusual but a battered child never learns control, only fear and hatred.

If you prefer never to use force at all, then I can at least offer some modest encouragement. A small fraction of the parents whom we studied did manage, through the use of distraction and gentle persuasion, to avoid physical means of discipline altogether; they nevertheless raised delightful children.

Summary: Children dealt with sensibly, firmly, and lovingly from eight to fourteen or fifteen months become used to not always having their own ways. The result is that when normal negativism and testing of wills appear shortly thereafter, they are easier to live with than a previously overindulged child. Even so, the period of Phase VI negativism is difficult. Yet, the child whose parents continue to treat him with clear and reasonable controls will usually leave negativism early and return to friendly sociability and rationality by the second birthday.

In studying children in their own homes, some happily developing well and others not so satisfyingly, we paid special attention to discipline. We found that regardless of the family income, cultural background, or educational level, firm discipline always accompanied good social development. From the moment these children began to crawl, their parents took the time to make sure that when behavior was unsafe or otherwise unacceptable, the infant received a clear and persistent message to that effect. In these homes, telling a child not to do something was ordinarily *not repeated more than once*, and the command was almost always followed up if the child resumed the behavior he was supposed to have stopped. Despite the real effort needed to follow through on such occasions, all the successful parents we studied did so. In return, as the weeks went by, such parents had an easier time than most.

The Critical Importance of Hearing Ability

Precisely because the symptoms of impaired hearing are not always obvious, parents should be especially alert to this danger. It is just about impossible for an infant to grow to her full potential if her hearing is impaired during the first years of life. The ability to acquire language depends on the ability to hear well, and children normally do their basic language learning during the early years. Retarded language development in three-year-olds is one of the most common symptoms of future educational difficulties in underachieving preschool children.

Severe hearing loss is defined as 70 or more decibels of loss. Mercifully, such losses are comparatively rare. Far more common is the mild to moderate hearing loss of from 20 to 55 decibels. It has recently become clear that anywhere from one-quarter to one-third of *all* children, regardless of family income level, suffer from repeated intermittent hearing loss during the first few years of life. This, then, is a topic of vital importance for everyone responsible for raising children.

For an older child, or for an adult, a moderate hearing loss might not be a major problem, since previous learning makes it possible for an older person to interpolate most of what he cannot actually hear. In contrast, when language is being learned for the first time, even a minor loss of hearing can be a significant obstacle to understanding and learning. Not only is intellectual development likely to be impaired by reduced language capacity, the development of social skills can also be affected. The ability to gain someone's attention, to get information from an adult, or to exercise leadership depends in large part on the capacity of the child to use and understand words. We do not socialize our children through gestures or through grunts and groans.

An extremely serious situation exists in this country with respect to the early detection and treatment of mild to moderate hearing loss in children from all levels of society. Severe losses (for example, from nerve-cell or conductive deficits) are relatively rare, but mild to moderate losses arise frequently from respiratory distress, to which infants are particularly susceptible, and from allergic reactions. Respiratory infections often lead to the middle-ear problems (otitis media) that are quite common during infancy and toddlerhood. This condition is often accompanied by the presence of fluid in the middle-ear system and by a functional hearing loss. To be sure, when the infection is cleared up, the fluid usually disappears and hearing returns to normal; but such episodes commonly occur repeatedly during the first two years of life, and, for however long a child is unable to hear normally, he is experiencing a loss no less important to learning than if it were caused by congenital nerve damage.

In very young children mild to moderate hearing losses often remain undetected for several years. If a child has a severe hearing loss (70 to 80 decibels), even as a newborn her behavior will be quite different from what people expect and, in any event, a severe handicap will usually be noticed early in the child's life during routine medical examination. This is not the case with moderate hearing loss. Although mild or moderate hearing loss is usually detectable when an older child or an adult is affected—the affected person's speech may be slurred or louder than is necessary; the person may be slow to respond or may misunderstand conversations—none of these signals is easy to detect in a child under two years of age. One does not expect a baby to speak clearly at a normal level, or to understand speech well.

I wish I could tell you that your pediatrician will always alert you to symptoms of moderate hearing loss, but that may not be so. Pediatricians have to cope with many symptoms in infants that *might* indicate a developmental difficulty. At times, perfectly normal children behave in ways that suggest there could be something significantly wrong with them; yet time after time such symptoms vanish and the child develops normally. It is because of this peculiarity of the first years of life, and because of a desire to avoid needless anxiety in parents, that medical practitioners often find themselves reassuring parents and telling them that one or another worrisome behavior is not really serious and will be outgrown. This practice infuriates people in pediatric audiology, for the consequences of inattention to suspected hearing loss during the first years of life are serious.

What to Do: First, be on guard for mild or moderate hearing loss throughout your child's first two years. In the absence of adequate professional practice you may have to take on this responsibility yourself. Follow procedures we recommend (see chart below) to be sure that this part of your child's development is going well.

Any significant symptom of hearing loss should be treated with the same urgency as a high fever. If a pediatrician were to look at your baby and found his temperature significantly above normal, he would hardly shrug the matter off and tell you that he'd see the baby again in six months. On the contrary, he would do everything he could to see that the temperature returned to normal as soon as possible. From a learning standpoint we believe that the same policy should be followed with respect to hearing losses. If you are told or suspect that a child under three years of age may be susceptible even to a temporary hearing loss as a result of, for example, an ear, throat, or bronchial infection, have the condition assessed *immediately* by a specialist in pediatric audiology.

What Can Be Done about the Early Detection of Mild to Moderate Hearing Loss?   The following checklist includes some of the signs that should alert you to a hearing problem in your baby.

Parents' Checklist for Detecting
Hearing Losses in Babies

At Age	Danger Signals
Birth to 3 months	Baby is not startled by sharp clap within three to six feet; is not soothed by mother's voice.
3 to 6 months	Baby does not search for source of sound by turning head and eyes; does not respond to mother's voice; does not imitate own noises, *oohs, ba-bas*, etc.; does not enjoy sound-making toys.
6 to 10 months	Baby does not respond to own name, telephone ringing, or to someone's voice

	when not loud; is unable to understand common words, for example, *no, bye-bye*.
10 to 15 months	Baby cannot point to or look at familiar objects or people when asked to do so; cannot imitate simple words or sounds.
15 to 18 months	Baby is unable to follow simple spoken directions; does not seem able to expand understanding of words.
Any age	Does not awaken or is not disturbed by loud sounds; does not respond when called; pays no attention to ordinary crib noises; uses gestures almost exclusively to establish needs and desires, rather than verbalizing; or watches parents' faces intently.

Steps to Take if Hearing Loss Is Detected

Step	By Whom
Pediatric assessment with particular attention to upper respiratory system.	Physician/Pediatrician
Otologic and audiologic assessment to find out what is causal picture—physical condition of ears, nose, and throat. Is hearing involved, and if so, how much does the child hear? What course of treatment and education is indicated?	Pediatric Audiologist
Attention to factors including social and economic deprivation that affect developmental language and speech.	Parents/professionals in medicine and audiology
If irreversible loss is established, refer to agencies that can assist parents with an educational program.	Professionals in medicine and audiology; well-baby clinic; hospital or university speech and hearing center or health center; Easter Seal or Crippled Children Society; Alexander Graham Bell Association for the Deaf

Source: Compiled with assistance from the Alexander Graham Bell Association for the Deaf. For additonal information from the Association, write to 3417 Avolta Place, N.W., Washington, D.C. 20007.

How to Screen for Mild to Moderate Hearing Losses: The fact that from fourteen to sixteen weeks of age infants reflexively turn toward any nearby sound gives parents an early opportunity to screen for mild to moderate losses. We strongly advise all parents to administer the following procedures every couple of weeks from four months on, especially if they may have any suspicion that their child is not hearing perfectly.

Choose a quiet place. Stand out of sight six to ten feet away from the child, who should be on her stomach on a blanket placed on the floor. When she is awake, but neither distressed nor overly involved in any particular activity, in a normal tone of voice call the child's name. The response should be a rather prompt and accurate turn toward you. (In other words, this turning should come within a few seconds.) At intervals of a few minutes repeat the same trial four or five times from different locations. By this time your child should have gotten into the spirit of the "game." You should then follow up with the more critical part of the procedure, which is to repeat each trial, this time whispering the child's name rather than using a normal voice.

The normal-hearing child should react in exactly the same way to the whisper as to normal voice tones. Should the child fail to respond predictably, repeat the test an hour or two later and then again the next day. If, after three successive attempts, the child has not routinely responded to the whisper test, it is time to act.

Take your child to your medical practitioner and voice your suspicions. If your pediatrician is merely reassuring and indicates that there is nothing to be concerned about, *I urge you not to accept such a response*. For example, if your physician argues that minor respiratory distress or allergic responses are common in infancy, not life-threatening, and therefore are best ignored, that may be true from a medical standpoint but it is *not* an adequate response from the standpoint of safeguarding learning development. You should respectfully request a second opinion from a pediatric audiologist. Any responsible physician will honor such a request. I think you will find that a pediatric audiologist will take your concern very seriously indeed.

The professional treatment of mild to moderate hearing loss consists of two major elements: medical attention, and special assistance to parents. Typical medical treatment includes the use of hearing aids— for children as young as six months. It could also include minor surgery to relieve conductive difficulties—for example, the insertion of small tubes to cope with the buildup of pressure in the middle ear.

Even when nothing can be done medically, it is essential that parents be informed about a hearing loss immediately. If they accept the reality of the impairment and are willing to take guidance from specialists, parents can help enormously to minimize the consequences of a hearing handicap for the rapidly developing child. But parents *must* face the reality of the situation. Some specialists report that parental resistance to acknowledging a child's hearing defect is common. Such a response may be understandable, but it is no less mistaken or damaging to a child's welfare for that.

There are plenty of difficulties in early human development that we cannot at present overcome, but mild or moderate hearing losses represent an altogether different situation. The knowledge and techniques exist that enable us to deal successfully with the vast majority of children in need, and the cost of detection and treatment is small. All the more reason, then, why it is imperative that we should adopt more effective national policies with respect to this issue—and soon.

The Importance of Early Detection of Developmental Difficulties

You may wonder why I have been making such an insistent point about the need to detect developmental problems as early as possible. The principal reason is that attempts to overcome such problems later, during the early school years, have proven stubbornly resistant to our best efforts. The same is true of the educational deficits such problems create. By the time a child reaches three years of age, professionals have only very limited power to make up for any previous delays in the natural evolution of learning. Unfortunately for new parents, the U.S. educational system has been very slow to accept the importance of this reality.

There are, to be sure, some exceptions: the state of Missouri has passed legislation making mandatory the availability of comprehensive educational screening for all children across the state, and we are hoping that with our assistance such screening will be sophisticated. To give you a sense of how this screening can be performed, let's look at what we do in our model programs in Missouri.

To begin with, we tell all of our families that if they participate in the program we will guarantee not only to find any significant developmental problems that may arise in their children, but to find it quickly and to tell the parents where they can go for help. We then proceed with the following schedule of screening practices:

Age	Procedures
3 weeks	Questionnaire: Family History of Hearing and Vision Problems and Information on Birth Process
4 to 5 months	The Denver Developmental Screening Test (modified), and the Ewing Hearing Test (modified)
8 through 30 months	The Harvard Preschool Project Social Competence Rating Scale (modified)
12 months	The Denver Developmental Screening Test (modified), and the Ewing Hearing Test (modified)
14 months	The Harvard Preschool Project Language Abilities Test (modified)
24 months	The Denver Developmental Screening Test (modified), the Ewing Hearing Test (modified), the Harvard Preschool Project Language Abilities Test (modified)
30 months	The Denver Developmental Screening Test (modified), the Ewing Hearing Test (modified), the Harvard Preschool Project Language Abilities Test (modified)

But what about those of you who are not involved with the Missouri program? Where do you go? What do you do?

Since about 1970, numerous local programs devoted to good learning progress in the first years of life have sprung up all over America, as well as in many other developed nations. The existence of these programs, which now number well over 10,000 in North America alone, has raised the likelihood that parents can find *some* sort of assistance in this matter, particularly if they live in urban areas. Yet the fact remains that even if you can find a parent-support or early-education program in your area, you still may very well not find personnel who are adequately trained for these tasks. In other words, the task of early detection of developmental problems may still be left largely up to you.

This being so, let me review some of the key elements in our recommended procedures for detecting developmental difficulties so that you can get a better sense of the priorities you should attach to the different facets of the problem. Any information gathered when the child is three weeks of age is *not* usually information you can or should act upon immediately. To know, for example, that the birth process was more difficult than it might have been does not usually indicate any action that a medical practitioner would not normally take. The principal value of information about a difficult delivery is not likely to be clear enough to demand immediate action and may indeed not have any long-term significance. Any influence it may have on the child's development will usually surface considerably later. If at one year of age, for example, a child starts showing one difficulty or another, a professional will want to know everything he or she can learn about the child. The reason for seeking this information is to try to build as complete a picture of the child's history as possible to help distinguish between sources of difficulty that are rooted in something the child was born with versus something that might be due to the child's learning experiences.

Denver Developmental Screening Test: At four months of age we use the Denver Developmental Screening Test to get an overall picture of how well the child is developing. The Denver Test, however, is a relatively crude device and should not be thought of as providing precise answers to any questions. Built upon earlier tests like the Gesell Developmental Schedules, it allows a pediatrician or pediatric nurse to use reasonably standard procedures in a short span of time to see if the child is grossly normal or falling behind in any important way. If we find a developmental delay on the Denver Test we can be pretty sure (in any typical family situation) that it is due to some sort of congenital problem, rather than something that parents have been doing in their childrearing activities.

Ewing Hearing Test: It is the Ewing Test, at four months, that directly screens children for mild to moderate hearing losses. (The information gathered when the baby was three weeks old is more likely to identify the child who was born with a reasonably severe hearing loss.)

Social and Language Skills Screening: Screening for the development of social competence in the age period of eight to thirty months brings us into a somewhat more sophisticated area of early childhood. Social competence, as we define it, has to do with interpersonal skills—how to get along with other people. You know, having read thus far, that we value the child who is socially skillful at least as much as the one who is bright. Research in this particular area has been very sparse, especially in comparison to studies of the growth of intelligence, language, physical skills, and so forth. Nevertheless, we have done enough research on the emergence of healthy social functioning, and have enough experience with families, to urge everyone to do what they can to monitor the growth of social skills during the first years of life. From the chart on page 235, you can see that we emphasize (1) five types of behavior during the first two years of life, and (2) three additional social skills during the third year of life. Unfortunately, it is unlikely that you will find early childhood professionals in your general area who are knowledgeable about monitoring development in these functions. And equally unfortunate, few parents will have had the benefit of observing many other children go through these developments, nor will they be as free from bias as would be desirable. Yet that is far from saying that you, the parent, can do nothing. Armed with this book you very well may be able to identify a professional who *can* do this job. And even in the absence of such a person, you can use the book as a guide on how to watch for the emergence, at the appropriate ages, of various social skills. Should you find that some skills are not surfacing well, you will want to put a bit more emphasis on them in your interactions with the child; this may well be all that is needed. Fortunately, during the first two years of life, social skills are far less likely to develop poorly (especially in the case of interested and loving families) as are the language and related skills that mild to moderate hearing losses can affect.

At one year of age we suggest a repeat of the Denver Test, to reassure you that the child is developing generally well. Also, there should be a repeat of the hearing/screening procedure, which you cannot do too often. And finally, there should be a screening for receptive language development.

Receptive language development screening, which is somewhat similar to screening for mild to moderate hearing loss, is quite important and too often neglected. There is a longstanding tendency in the field to identify early *speech* with early *language*. This is a mistake, and you should be well aware of the important differences. From the chart on the development of language abilities on page 231, you will note that the onset of speech is extraordinarily variable, with the first words sometimes coming well before the first birthday and sometimes not until the second. On the other hand, the onset and growth of receptive language (the understanding of words) is much more consistent. A fourteen-month-old child who does not speak is quite likely to be normal, but if she does not understand at least two dozen words, it is likely that she has a developmental delay of consequence.

Your situation as you try to monitor receptive language growth is somewhat similar to the problem with monitoring social skills: you may well not have easy access to sophisticated professionals in this developmental area. Once again, your best asset is yourself. If you become knowledgeable about test procedures, not only are your chances of finding a properly qualified professional much better than one who is ignorant, but you can, if you are careful, do a bit of testing on your own.

A key consideration when testing your child's receptive language capacity is to avoid the use of manual gestures. Set out in front of your seated one-year-old baby a half-dozen common objects—a cup, some keys, a bottle, a doll, a ball, etc. Don't point or indicate; avoid triggering an accidentally correct response. Ask the child to give you the ball without either looking directly at it or holding your hand out in its direction. Now you are likely to get an accurate sense of whether he understands a particular word or not. It is better having a qualified professional do such screening for you, but in any case such testing needs to be done. It is tragic for a child to reach a second birthday without proper progress in language development—and avoidable.

At ages twenty-four and thirty months we repeat a number of screening tests: the Denver Test of general development, the Ewing hearing screening, and the receptive language testing. Along with the continued procuring of information on social-skill development, these tests round out our recommendations for comprehensive, learning-focused, early detection of developmental problems.

As children approach their second birthdays, the likelihood of finding qualified professional help increases substantially. This is due to longstanding practices in early childhood work that favor examining children once they reach thirty months of age or so.

I cannot end this discussion on early detection of educational difficulties without mentioning once more the important subject of spoiling. Though none of the procedures provided in our chart is addressed to the issue of spoiling, in our work we find that it is precisely the informed, caring families—those who value their children more than just about anything else in life—who are most likely to run into problems in the areas of *both* undetected and untreated mild to moderate hearing losses *and* spoiling. In both cases, the parents' failure to spot developing troubles can doubtless be ascribed to a lack of objectivity bred of love, an unwillingness to admit that anything could be wrong with a child so cherished. It is a subtle danger, and one to which wise parents should be especially alert.

Summary: Now let me close this section with a brief recapitulation. There are two powerful facts that underline the necessity for paying close attention to early detection of educational difficulties. The first is thoroughly documented—our limited capacity to undo poor development once the child has reached three years of age. The second is the happy other side of the coin, to wit—the child who at age three is functioning well on the various goals described in this book— intellectual, linguistic, and social—is very likely to be well-launched toward excellent later development, including in school. These are the simple reasons why I have pleaded so vigorously in so many forums that the first goal of any public educational system should be to get a child to the third birthday in optimum condition. Fortunately, the chances that *your* child will do so are vastly better today than they would have been as recently as thirty years ago.

New Information on the Benefits of Breastfeeding

In my early experiences in the field of child development the question of breastfeeding versus bottle feeding was of practical concern to professionals as well as to parents. Until about twenty years ago the consensus among professionals was that there was little to choose from between the two methods. Although breastfeeding might have seemed more "natural," many took pains to point out that the climate of love associated with the process could just as easily be created by a bottle- feeding mother, provided she made an effort to create the right condi- tions. As for nutrition, there seemed to be little medical concern about bottle feeding because of an abundance of apparently suitable for- mulas.

There was, of course, some concern about the impersonal kind of bottle feeding often given infants raised in institutions. In such cases it was not uncommon for bottles to be propped up on pillows or blankets so that a staff member, who might have had eight or more infants to feed, could handle a large number of them at once. The work of numerous researchers, including Rene Spitz, on the dramatic harm that could come to children so reared, served to alert professionals to the importance of human contact during the feeding experience.

But this special situation not withstanding, during the 1950s and 1960s there was no special effort to laud the advantages of breast- over bottle-feeding. Unquestionably, professional opinion was influenced by the desire to support women who, for any number of reasons, did not choose to breastfeed.

Sometime toward the end of the 1960s a change occurred. Medi- cal studies began to provide evidence that breastfeeding really was superior to bottle feeding in a number of important ways. While specifics of the argument are beyond my area of expertise, in essence breastfed babies were found to be significantly healthier. Since then, most professionals, at least Western ones, have become increasingly firm in their advocacy of breastfeeding, and we, too, have consistently recommended breastfeeding on the basis of medical evidence.

Not long before the preparation of the revised edition of this book, I participated in an annual conference of the La Leche League. The La Leche League was started in the 1950s by seven Midwestern mothers who felt that they wanted to breastfeed but were unable to find support for that desire among their friends and professional advisors. The League, by any standards, has become enormously successful, now having well over 100,000 members and branches in over two dozen countries. Members of the League currently are consulting in developing nations in an effort to help reinforce the concept of breastfeeding.

My prior contact with the La Leche League had been very limited. I had been aware of the existence of their organization and of their passionate devotion to breastfeeding; but this very passion had led me to be somewhat reserved about their work because it could easily lead to overstatements and unsubstantiated claims. Otherwise, however, from a distance, I valued the organization's humanistic goals and its emphasis on close, caring relations between parents and children.

After my presentation at the conference I had an opportunity to meet and talk with a number of their leaders. As we talked it became clear that they were surprised that I endorsed breastfeeding solely on the grounds of its proven medical advantages (not only from the point of nutrition but also with respect to prevention of allergic reactions during infancy). Several members of the group insisted that there was much more to breastfeeding's advantages than that.

Subsequent to those meetings I was sent several research reports on differences between breastfed and bottle-fed babies that I now feel are worthy of your serious attention. It appears that now something new, and of potentially great importance, *has* surfaced on this topic.

Over the last decade in our work with families we had become particularly sensitive to the apparently widespread threat to the hearing of children under two arising from a condition known as *otitis media*, or middle-ear infections. As noted before, there seems little question that chronic episodes of such infections give rise to mild to moderate hearing losses in a goodly percentage of young children, with consequences that can be serious and longlasting. Although these consequences usually are not life threatening, they do pose many problems to the acquisition of language, higher mental abilities, and effective social skills.

One of the most important research reports sent to me came from the University of Helsinki in Finland. Its main findings were as follows: some 237 breast- or bottle-fed children were studied. Recurrent otitis media was strongly associated with early bottle feeding in contrast to prolonged breastfeeding (defined as six months or longer), which had a long-term protecting effect up to three years of age. The authors were not clear as to whether the human milk actually gave protection against infections and allergies, or whether these harmful effects were somehow associated with cow's milk.

This report—along with two more, of equally high-calibre research, reporting on the studies of Canadian and East Indian babies—made a strong case for the link between bottle feeding and the frequency of mild to moderate hearing losses. This link, found in several countries, is potentially of great importance for the development of young children everywhere.

The studies also raised an interesting point about substitute care. Substitute care not only reduces the likelihood that a child is going to have prolonged breastfeeding, but moreover, it also exposes children in group-care centers to infectious threat to a much greater degree than found in home-reared children.

Interestingly, two articles on research in New Zealand seem to indicate that breastfeeding is strongly associated with improved speech clarity and better reading ability in five- and six-year-old children. In the New Zealand studies the benefits were limited to male children; and it has been found repeatedly, throughout this century, that girls are generally more advanced with respect to early language acquisition than boys. It is possible, although at this point only speculation, that if we could reduce the frequency of mild to moderate hearing losses in boys during the first years of life, that such differences in early language acquisition might also be reduced or even eliminated.

These and several related studies have led me to modify my previous stance and to recommend to all new parents that they attempt prolonged breastfeeding if it is at all possible. It must now be said that breastfeeding is *clearly the preferred method.* Benefits are not just confined to nutrition but very probably extend to learning as well. If for any reason you do not breastfeed, then you should be especially alert for a somewhat higher likelihood of middle-ear problems, perhaps especially in the case of boys.

Substitute Child Care

Ever since the summer of 1979 when I innocently responded to a Los Angeles *Times* reporter on the subject of substitute child care, I have been in the middle of a controversy. I stated then, and I will state again now, that full-time substitute care for babies under three years of age, and especially for those only a few months of age, does *not* seem to be in the best interest of babies. Let me try to explain why I maintain what to some people seems such an ogerish view.

Traditionally in our culture women have assumed the primary responsibility for raising their children, especially during the first years of the child's life. Today that tradition is being challenged. More and more infants and toddlers are spending the majority of their waking hours in the care of someone other than a member of their immediate family.

As one who has specialized in the study of the development of children, I am disturbed by the situation. Of course, I worry most about the effects on children, but I also worry about the pressures being put on those women who do not want to join the trend. Moreover, I am saddened by the thought that many adults are missing some of life's sweetest pleasures, those that parents receive when they spend time with their own babies.

I do not pretend to be an expert in *all* aspects of family life, but I do claim to have some special knowledge of the educational needs of young children. On the basis of that consideration alone I take my stand: Simply stated, I firmly believe that most children get a better start in life when, during the majority of their waking hours of their first three years, they are cared for by their parents or other nuclear family members, not by any form of substitute care.

The Needs of Infants and Toddlers: The first three years of life are like no others. With regard to the emotional development of babies, a fundamental significance has long been accorded to the parent-infant bond, and the first two years is the time when that bond forms.

During this century many studies have been made of physically normal babies reared in institutions in which, as a rule, no single adult had primary responsibility for any individual baby. The studies have almost always revealed that the absence of a primary caretaker during a child's first few years produces serious emotional and psychological debilitation.

Although few people advocate institutional childrearing, these studies are not irrelevant on that account, for now we must go on to ask: What of lesser deviations from the norm of parental care? Several forms of part-time substitute childcare—from British nannies to Israeli *kibbutzes*—have existed long enough for us to learn something from them. Although these and related practices suggest that an adult outside of the baby's family *can* assume the primary caretaking role without any *obvious* harmful consequences, the exact consequences of different forms of such practices are *not* known. In the cases of both the British and Israeli systems, it is worth noting that the selection and training of substitute caretakers is usually done with great care, and the caliber of treatment the baby receives in most such situations appears to be good. But by way of contrast, a recent large study of salaries for child-care personnel in the United States indicated an average hourly rate of just over $4.00. In the normal course of things, this could not be considered high enough to guarantee expert care. While there are undoubtedly many intelligent, well-trained, dedicated people currently working in substitute-care situations, it is equally clear that there must be many many others, probably the majority, who do not meet that description.

We know that among other warm-blooded species whose offspring are initially helpless, the general rule is that newborns are cared for by their parents during the early stages. To me this apparent fact of nature, coupled with a predominant tendency in many human societies for babies to be reared by their parents, strongly suggests that parental care is uniquely important. Although I grant that neither animal analogies nor widespread and longstanding custom is conclusive in itself, I take them as powerful indicators, as I do the fact that progressive programs in Western countries have almost always aimed to make it possible for parents to care for their babies at home rather than be obliged to enter the workforce.

Added to these facts is what I have learned from my own research in human development. I have had the privilege of being able to compare the everyday experiences of very many children, from many kinds of families, and the evidence of my own observations is overwhelmingly that, all things being equal, a baby's parents are far more likely to meet her most important developmental needs than are *any* other people.

The special qualities of the parents' role is illustrated by one of the many inevitable achievements of all healthy infants: the first steps. Unaided walking usually first takes place when a child is about eleven months old. When the baby is being raised at home, especially if she is a first child, both parents and everybody else in the nuclear family look forward to the event. There is anticipation and perhaps even some mild anxiety. When the time comes, the impact on the family is powerful and very exciting. Parents ordinarily become absorbed in the experience to a degree that friends cannot adequately understand unless they have been through the experience themselves.

Parents' typical response to those first steps is to envelop the baby in praise and enthusiasm, and such intense experiences seem to me to be extremely important. For the parents, they reinforce the commitment to the child in the family life. For the child, they contribute to a sense of personal security and worth that is one of the building blocks of lifelong pride in achievement.

Between seven and eleven months of life most babies learn to sit up, crawl, stand up, lower themselves to the floor, climb, walk while supported, and finally walk alone. Each of these achievements, and many more, are occasions for parents to lavish attention on the baby. In this, parents have a natural advantage over other adults. Although loving childcare workers will usually enjoy and applaud a baby's achievements, they simply cannot match the enthusiasm and excitement expressed by most parents. After all, when one has seen two hundred babies take their first steps, one's reaction to the two-hundred-and-first cannot possibly contain the same enthusiasm typically shown by the baby's parents.

Another area in which parents have an advantage over substitute caretakers is in the encouragement and satisfaction of an infant's curiosity. Once a baby learns to crawl (at about eight months) she becomes capable of exploring a much expanded world. Over the next year-and-a-half a major part of her day consists of closely examining small objects and their motions, wondering at the way simple mechanisms work, studying people, and physically exploring the space around her. To get the most out of these experiences, it is best if an infant has ready access to an older person who is especially interested in her and is eager to serve as a personal consultant. No one fits that definition quite so well as a baby's parents or grandparents.

Substitute caretakers come in many styles; they can be well-trained, experienced child development specialists with master's degrees in early education (and if so, the cost of their services will be high); or they can be high school graduates with special training in child development; or they can be aunts, cousins, or even older siblings. They may care for one baby or a group of babies, in an infant's own home, in their home, in a nonprofit center, or in a commercial center. As you might expect, the quality of care a baby receives varies as widely as the caretakers, from warm and knowledgeable to indifferent and unskilled. What the impact is on babies is not yet known. The few studies that have been done on the subject have produced ostensibly reassuring results, but unfortunately the programs studied represent only a small, high-quality minority of those in operation. But even though what reports we have show no obvious harm being done to the infants in superior programs, I still would not endorse such programs, except for families with special needs, or on a part-time basis after a child reaches six months. I am not concerned *only* with avoiding obvious harm, but with encouraging the *best* development as well, and none of the few evaluations performed so far has addressed the question of what situations are actually *good* for children.

To put it bluntly, after more than twenty-five years of research on how children develop well, I would not think of putting a child of my *own* in any substitute-care program on a full-time basis during the first few years of life—especially a center-based program.

Situations Where Full-time Substitute Care for Infants Makes Sense: Having said that, I would also agree that there are two kinds of situations where substitute childcare may be a necessity.

1. When a Family Cannot Raise Its Own Children

   In certain families alcoholism, drug abuse, or some other debilitating condition afflicts parents to such a degree that childrearing is a casualty. In such families the environment is so bad that the only hope for the children is to remove them from the family and place them in foster care. Nor does the situation have to be that extreme. Unfortunately not all the parents of the approximately 3 million babies born in the United States each year are happy, intelligent, in love, or psychologically fit for parenthood. Many babies are born of mothers under eighteen years old and who already have two or three other children. In some of these cases the prospects for the new baby may be so grim that full-time substitute care, if it is of good quality, may very well make sense. There are some good government-sponsored programs geared to such circumstances.

2. When a Family Just Does Not Want the Job

   The second situation is harder to define, but is no less real for that. There are some parents who simply do not want the time-consuming, occasionally stressful job of raising a baby. This is a psychological matter, and one that I prefer not to comment on, except to say that in such situations I believe some substitute arrangement may be preferable.

Part-time Care: To the surprise of some, I am a strong advocate of substitute childcare *on a part-time basis,* for all families who would like it, from the time a child is six months of age. In our research I have met parents for whom the concept of any substitute care was unthinkable: they were having such a wonderful time with their baby that they dreaded any separation. Although I would be reluctant to *urge* such people to use substitute care, to avoid overattachment I believe the use of an occasional babysitter, at the very least, is good for the family right from the beginning. But these families are the exception. For most, part-time care from the time the child is six months is both desired and desirable.

Part-time care can free up the time of either or both parents to earn needed income. It can also give parents, especially the mother, the opportunity to pursue careers, studies, or the like. But by far the most important reason for part-time substitute care is that it gives parents a break from the continuous responsibilities of child-rearing. Psychological relief, whether through outside work or relaxation, is very important for full-time parents. For years young women have carried by themselves the continuous responsibility for the well-being of their children. To many people this might seem perfectly normal and not worthy of comment, but if you observe women with infants in their homes, as we have done, you cannot help being impressed with the stress that can be generated, particularly if there are two or more closely spaced young children in the family. One of the most popular features of our programs for young families is the opportunity for people to simply get away from their children for a few hours every week. When you combine that psychological relief with the opportunity to talk to other young parents in similar circumstances, you get some significant benefits.

Fathers and Grandparents Make Good Mothers, Too: No study anywhere has indicated that mothers are the only people capable of raising babies. We have observed many fathers and grandparents who seemed well suited to the task and were willing and even eager to share the job. I have always thought it unfair when fathers and grandparents have limited opportunities to share in the many exciting and memorable everyday events in babies' lives. Babies begin life and get to know the world only once, and they grow up very fast.

If You Have no Choice, or I Have not Convinced You: Here is my rating of types of substitute care in descending order of preference:

Individual Care in Your Own Home: A warm, intelligent, and experienced person caring for your child in your own home.

Individual Care in Someone Else's Home: A warm, intelligent, and
experienced person caring for your child in her or his own home.

Family Daycare: The same kind of person caring for no more than
two children under eighteen months and no more than three from
eighteen to thirty-six months in her or his own home.

Nonprofit Center-Based Care: A carefully selected center where the
ratio of children to staff is no more than one staff member to two
children under eighteen months or to three children from eighteen to
thirty-six months and where the total number of children is low,
preferably less than ten. There should be at least one person with
formal training in early childhood development among the supervisory
staff. Note: if you choose center-based care you are very likely to find
that your child will be subjected to infectious diseases, especially
minor respiratory distress, far more often than if she were at home most
of the time.

Profit-Oriented Center-Based Care: A very carefully selected center
that meets all of the aforementioned requirements.

Summary: If you feel you have no option but full-time substitute care
for your baby, so be it; but for those fortunate enough to have a choice,
it is, I believe, best for most of the baby's waking hours to be spent with
parents or grandparents. Such an arrangement is usually the surest
way to see to it that a baby gets a fine beginning in life. Furthermore
child-rearing, especially when it is shared, can be one of life's sweetest,
most rewarding experiences.

    For further information on this topic, please refer to the recom-
mended readings section of this book.

Variations in the Onset
of Early Behaviors

When should children first begin to crawl, talk, stand alone, or exhibit
any of the hundreds of other accomplishments we associate with normal development? Devoted parents often become anxious about the

appearance of these behaviors in their preschool-aged children, and over the last few decades, with the increased awareness of the importance of early childhood development, such concerns seem to have become even more widespread. This anxiety is reasonable and, indeed, healthy to the degree that it indicates a sense of responsibility and an awareness of the importance of orderly development during the first years of life. But much of the existing concern is also based on a lack of understanding of the essential nature of early development.

One of the most common sources of concern is whether or not a child is doing "well enough"—an almost impossible question to judge if you happen to be the parent of the child in question. It is a query that is emotionally loaded; and even if it were not, it would be difficult to answer because of the scarcity of reliable information. Almost everyone who studies young children agrees that one of the invariables of early human development is its *variability*. After all, children are not production-line products. You can expect that just about every Ford Pinto will look and perform pretty much like every other Ford Pinto. But such is not the case with a young human.

Take, for example, the age of walking. Children in various parts of the world have been reliably reported to walk as early as seven or eight months. On the other hand, a substantial percentage of perfectly normal children do not walk before they are one-and-a-half years old. Yet parents persist in wanting their children to walk early. The amount of anxiety a parent feels varies from none at all to a fairly significant quantity, depending upon the developmental rates of other children as compared to his own. The fact of the matter is that enough is known about children to conclude not only that the date at which walking comes into a child's repertoire varies widely, but that in most cases that variation means absolutely nothing in terms of the child's educational future or physical well-being. (This is not to say that you *never* need worry about when your child starts to walk. If the child is eighteen months old and not walking, you would certainly want to check out the child's physical health and make certain that you received professional guidance. But I still would not be alarmed. Only if at the age of two years she *still* did not walk, would I think there would be some reason for serious concern.)

Perhaps even more than in the case of walking, parents very often show concern about the age at which their children start talking in intelligible ways. The onset of meaningful speech—that is, using particular labels to routinely indicate one kind of object or person—can happen in normal babies anywhere from seven or eight months to the second birthday. As with the emergence of walking ability, you can expect wide variability in the onset of speech in any group of children.

Certainly, if a child of nine to ten months already has a speaking vocabulary of several words, that may be taken as a reassuring sign. If, on the other hand, after fourteen to eighteen months there is still a total absence of speech, the indications are, while not necessarily negative, no longer reassuring, and professional consultation may be advisable. But bear in mind that wide variations *are* the norm.

In fact, the growth of the *understanding* of language is much less variable and is a much more reliable indicator of developmental progress. The first understood words begin to appear shortly after the child is about eight months of age. Progress at first is generally slow, so that the one-year-old child is likely to understand fewer than a dozen words, perhaps no more than five to ten. But progress accelerates during the second year of life and even more during the third. Statistically, a fourteen-month-old child who does not *say* anything is likely to be perfectly normal and developing well; but a fourteen-month-old child who does not *understand at least two dozen words is very likely to be suffering from a developmental delay of consequence.*

People responsible for rearing children need to be well informed about the normal range in the dates of onset of certain landmark abilities and capacities. There is no reason why such information should not be common knowledge, and people who have *good* medical care for their children will, in fact, inevitably be given this kind of support by their physicians. Unfortunately, there are other physicians who lose credibility with parents by overusing an all-purpose answer to questions about the onset of children's abilities. Many parents have complained to me that their pediatricians routinely say of late onsets that the child in question is probably just a "late bloomer" and that there is no cause for concern. Up to a point, that is undoubtedly an appropriate verdict and the parent may be needlessly anxious. But beyond a certain point, and to the extent that it is used indiscriminately, such a diagnosis *may* be a substitute for a knowledgeable and useful response.

In summary, then, you should expect significant variation in the date of onset of a wide variety of abilities and other phenomena in the first three years of life. The charts in the preceding sections indicate how consistently these variations are seen in development, where you can expect wide variation, and where in relation to other processes you should look for a narrow range of onset of the behavior in question.

Play

Children's play, a subject of broad public appeal, nevertheless has received little attention from those who study the development of young children. (Two notable exceptions are the works of Brian Sutton-Smith and Dorothy and Jerome Singer, cited in the recommended reading section at the end of this book.)

When I first began to think seriously about play and babies, two thoughts struck me. Babies don't have to earn a living (that is, work), and therefore, when people talk about the behavior of babies, the word *play* is used automatically to describe most of what they do. Thus babies are thought to *play* much more often than adults. But then I began to wonder precisely what kinds of behaviors babies engage in that could be called "playful."

If playful behavior involves pleasure, lightheartedness, smiling, laughter, giggling, and so on, then babies act this way only sporadically. They spend another part of the day in various states of need or discomfort (for example, hungry or wet). And together, these two types of activity amount to less than half of their waking hours. What about the rest of the day?

When a ten-month-old is trying to push a lever on a toy to make the cover pop up, the expression on her face is likely to be quite serious. If she succeeds, probably no one will reward her for her efforts, and since what she's doing is not obviously useful anyway, we might be tempted to call her activity play. But I would suggest that the baby has every right to be serious, for what she is doing could be very important. In fact, Erik Erikson has persuasively suggested that the play of babies is actually crucial for the growth of a healthy personality. In his view, the play activities of babies give them a chance to try out experiences in circumstances that are safe. These rehearsals help to prepare the child for later challenges, much as the playful fighting of kittens and puppies helps them learn skills needed for survival when they become mature animals. Erikson also claims that simple successes in the play of babies help to establish a strong ego and sense of worth. It is hard to argue against such a position in the face of the universal interest healthy infants display in the sensorimotor achievements of infancy.

What then do we mean by children's play? The most conservative definition would be: an activity in which a child was clearly having fun while being *active*. (A baby who is laughing or giggling but otherwise doing nothing would be considered happy but not actually playing.) The problem with such a definition is that much of a baby's activity that we ordinarily call "playful" would be excluded. Practice in hand-eye skills—which occupies hundreds of hours, especially from the second month of life through the second year—is mostly a serious activity, often featuring purely sober facial expressions, even when toys are being used.

In addition to playing with toys or any other object, young children also enjoy playing simple games with adults. Although such behavior often is more correctly categorized as maintaining social contact than as a structured game, the tone is definitely playful. Similarly, large-muscle activity is often done just for fun: jumping on a bed, running, climbing a rock. And it may overlap with what I call *gain-pleasure* experiences: being tickled, being swung in the air, turning somersaults. As the child grows older, these two kinds of play usually increase. Any new environment may evoke exploratory play: thus sand, water, or any sort of modeling material, such as Playdough, can stimulate play.

What about pretending? Pretending to be something or someone else occurs only rarely during the second and third years of life—1 or 2 percent of all experience—in comparison to exploratory and mastery tasks, which together account for from about 15 to 22 percent of all waking time.

Pretending or making-believe appears to be especially common in the behavior of unusually competent three- to six-year-old children. Pretending, or role play, or make-believe include impersonations (for example, being Batman) and ascriptions of unreal qualities to situations or materials ("baking" with playdough). Such behavior first appears at about the middle of the second year and increases steadily on through the third year. In our research, children who were developing very well consistently engaged in more of such behavior than children developing poorly. Parents, therefore, should encourage such behavior, especially when it first appears shortly after the first birthday. The fact that it is great fun for everyone else is a bonus.

During the first ten months of life there are some interesting developments in the area of play. Given the opportunity, crib-bound infants six weeks to eight months old will play for hours. I have observed many instances of two- to four-month-old babies totally absorbed in vigorous hand-eye play or entranced with a small mirror placed overhead.

From eight to fifteen months of age, exploring the qualities of objects is more common than practicing simple skills with them. But between eighteen and thirty-six months there is a steady decline in time spent in exploratory behavior. During the same period, mastery experiences, especially hand-eye exercises, increase rapidly. This pattern of mastery behaviors taking the place of exploratory behaviors proceeds faster in the lives of children developing unusually well. Children destined by three years of age to look very different in terms of achievement look very much alike in terms of their primary play behavior at one year of age.

There is a clear suggestion in our research that development in the first three years of life is linked with the quality of the play of a young child. In this sense, the play of very young children seems to be an important affair, and its quality appears to depend on many factors. These include the manner in which the primary caregiver handles the baby's curiosity, the freedom allowed for exploration, the responsiveness of adults to the baby's efforts to master his body, and the establishment of a stable social relationship with the central person in his daily life.

Looking at the larger process of the development of play during the first three years of life, it seems to me that exploration and mastery tasks are examples of *learning to learn* activities, which underlie the acquisition of skills and information. These, in turn, seem to lead to a new form of play activity that surfaces toward the end of the third year of life: *constructing a product*. This activity, fairly common in three- and four-year-olds in nursery schools, may appear as early as the third birthday, but usually only in precocious children. The first products constructed are simple and few in number—a tower of two or three blocks, a scribbled drawing, a simple puzzle put together—but they are developmental landmarks, all the same.

Piaget has brilliantly sketched some of these developments for us. His work, and that of others, enables us to see the strands of development that lead from little interest in the outside world during the first month of life; through play and practice with the hands as reaching tools; on to mastery of other basic manual skills, such as grasping, releasing, and throwing; and finally to an increasing interest in the world of objects, their qualities, and paths of motion.

What role do toys play in this development? It would seem that their contribution is potentially significant, for our studies indicate that babies are involved in nonsocial experiences more than half of their waking lives. Although some of that time is spent eating, and a good deal is spent looking steadily at things or people, defending territory, or just idling, much of it—thousands of hours—is spent in interactions with physical objects, large and small. Furthermore, this involvement with objects leads to interchanges between infant and mother that generally set the stage for verbal and social learning. (For a sense of how a child spends time, see the activity charts that follow.)

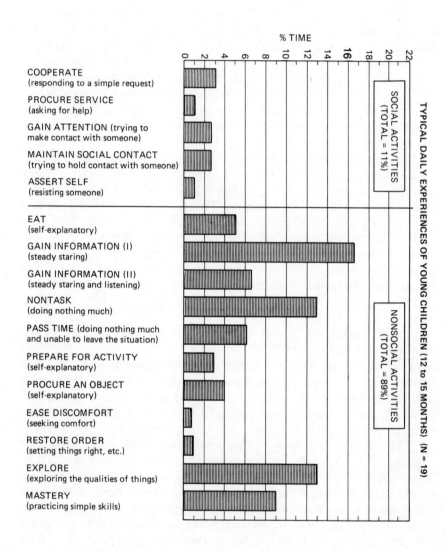

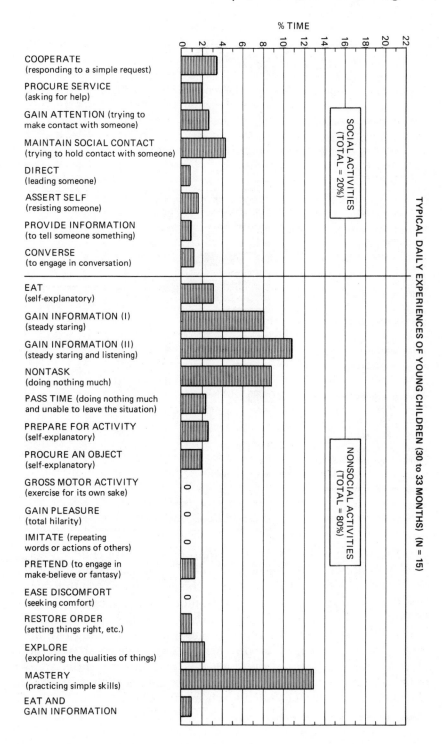

% TIME

COOPERATE
(responding to a simple request)

PROCURE SERVICE
(asking for help)

GAIN ATTENTION (trying to
make contact with someone)

MAINTAIN SOCIAL CONTACT
(trying to hold contact with someone)

DIRECT
(leading someone)

ASSERT SELF
(resisting someone)

PROVIDE INFORMATION
(to tell someone something)

CONVERSE
(to engage in conversation)

SOCIAL ACTIVITIES
(TOTAL = 20%)

EAT
(self-explanatory)

GAIN INFORMATION (I)
(steady staring)

GAIN INFORMATION (II)
(steady staring and listening)

NONTASK
(doing nothing much)

PASS TIME (doing nothing much
and unable to leave the situation)

PREPARE FOR ACTIVITY
(self-explanatory)

PROCURE AN OBJECT
(self-explanatory)

GROSS MOTOR ACTIVITY
(exercise for its own sake)

GAIN PLEASURE
(total hilarity)

IMITATE (repeating
words or actions of others)

PRETEND (to engage in
make-believe or fantasy)

EASE DISCOMFORT
(seeking comfort)

RESTORE ORDER
(setting things right, etc.)

EXPLORE
(exploring the qualities of things)

MASTERY
(practicing simple skills)

EAT AND
GAIN INFORMATION

NONSOCIAL ACTIVITIES
(TOTAL = 80%)

TYPICAL DAILY EXPERIENCES OF YOUNG CHILDREN (30 to 33 MONTHS) (N = 15)

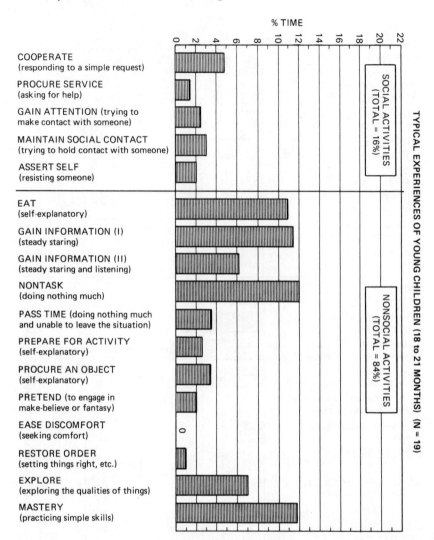

The ideal toy would be safe, appropriate to the child's level of development, fun, and even educational in the sense of stimulating the child's body and mind. Unfortunately, the challenge of creating even a good toy seems so far to have been too much for most designers in the toy business. Perhaps in the future, when we shall have developed a dependable catalog of the interests and abilities of young children, along with descriptions of the physical materials that mesh with those interests and abilities, not only will the toy industry do better, but parents and other caretakers will have more reliable help to guide the educational development of children from birth.

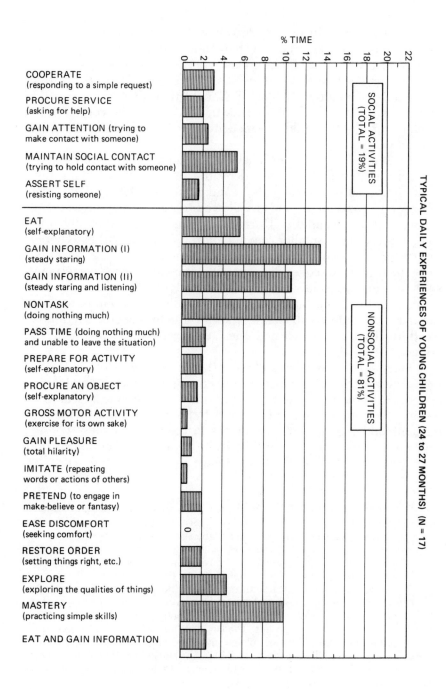

Toys

"Toys" can be specially designed to be toys, or they can be any objects children play with regardless of their intended use. Either way, toys are part of the lives of children from very early on.

During the first three years of a child's life we see four distinct stages in respect to toys. In Stage 1, from birth to about seven months, children get around little on their own, and toys can be very useful in helping to make the child's immediate surroundings interesting and instructive.

In Stage 2, from about seven to fourteen months, children are normally excited and challenged by the process of mastering their bodies, especially in moving about and climbing. They find ever-new vistas for exploration (if they are allowed to), and social development begins to proceed rapidly. During this stage, toys, especially store-bought ones, play a smaller role in children's daily activities. There is simply too much competition for their attention.

The third stage covers the rest of the second year and corresponds to Phase VI of the child's developmental pattern.[1] Social development in relation to the primary caregiver, usually the mother, tends to dominate the child's daily life. As a result, the toys of greatest interest are those useful in social activities, especially those involving the primary caregiver.

Stage 4 corresponds to Phase VII, the third year of life. In this time grows language, intelligence, imagination, memory, and interest in people. The role of toys is great in this period. In our research we routinely recorded what infants and toddlers did from moment to moment under natural circumstances in their own homes. We also kept track of their movements about the home and what objects they dealt with. At times over the years, I have also worked for or consulted

---

[1] With respect to Phase VI, I would like to make a correction. Since publication of *The First Three Years of Life* in late 1975, I have received numerous letters reporting-an apparent error in the book. In reference to the skill of opening doors, I wrote that children less than two years of age have difficulty with tasks that require unscrewing motions. Later I discouraged parents from buying for the Phase VI baby toys that must be wound up or that involve rotations of more than one revolution.

Far from needing a 360-degree turn, however, doorknobs usually require less than a quarter-turn to release their latches. Moreover, parents have informed me emphatically that some toddlers cannot only open doors but can also unscrew toothpaste caps, bolts on gates, and jar lids. The fact that this author has never personally encountered a child under two years of age who could unscrew something requiring more than one full turn is beside the point. Although I still believe that such babies are rare, I must now—with all due apologies to them and to their parents—concede that they really do exist.

with the majority of major toy manufacturers for children under three. It is from this background that I state, with no pleasure, that of the hundreds of toys commercially available, very few are worth buying. What I mean by this will, I hope, become more clear as we discuss the main categories of toys commonly given to young children.

Mobiles: For years parents have bought or received mobiles (along with rattles) as the first toys for their child. Mobiles, in fact, have legitimate uses for children. Toward the end of the first month, babies begin showing their first substantial interest in exploring their surroundings. Since their abilities are very limited, a mobile is one of the few toys that would make sense for a child. Strictly speaking, I should be using the term *stabile* rather than *mobile* (a correction suggested by Dr. Richard Held, Professor of Psychology, Massachusetts Institute of Technology). A mobile, by definition, is something that moves, and most commercially made mobiles for infants do not move much.

Babies between three and nine weeks, when on their backs, lie in that interesting posture we call the *tonic neck reflex* (TNR) position, in which the head is turned to the side, usually the right. It is rare for such an infant to spend much time looking directly overhead. Under these circumstances, anything hung directly over the center of the crib is not nearly as likely to be looked at as would something suspended above and to the far right or to the far left. Most currently available mobiles are designed to be placed where babies will hardly ever see them.

There is also the question of *what* the baby sees when she does look *up* at a mobile. The typical mobile sold today is designed to look good to downward-looking adults in a store or in a nursery. But if you look at such a mobile from the baby's point of view, you will find that by and large all that is visible are the thin bottom edges of the suspended objects.

This does not make any sense for a baby. Mobiles should be designed so that whatever the baby looks up at *faces the baby*. Moreover, it must look interesting to the baby. We know, for example, that babies especially like to look at the upper half of the front of the human face. A well-designed mobile could easily include a pattern of that sort.

One other consideration is how far away the mobile should be placed. When it comes to viewing their surroundings, babies do not do as well at three to nine weeks as they will when they are a few months older. In the three- to nine-week period, they are most comfortable looking at targets from seven to sixteen inches away. Another reason for placing mobiles at least seven or eight inches away is so babies won't be able to reach them: these first mobiles are for looking only. When the baby gets to be eight to ten weeks of age she will become interested in more than merely looking, but then her interest will shift toward her own hands and the task of learning to use them. From that point forward your baby will need something that ordinarily would not be called a mobile (or a stabile), but which would fall more properly in the category of a crib gym. In light of all these factors, you can see why I think there is plenty wrong with most of the mobiles you will find available for purchase.

Several years ago I designed some mobiles according to these principles, and we did, in fact, produce them. Unfortunately, those toys are no longer available, but the good news is that you can easily make mobiles yourself.

Here is what to do: to support the mobile, you can use a wire stand from a low-priced commercial mobile. If you do, you must bend the stand about 30 degrees so that what the baby looks at is positioned off to her right side. As an alternative you might suspend the mobile from the ceiling, using masking tape and string. Since the baby will not be pulling at the object, the support need not be very strong. The important thing is placement.

Draw a sketch of a human face on a six-inch white cardboard disc in a dark color (black is ideal). Exaggerate the features of the eyes.

Suspend the disc (by a string) so that it ends up ten to thirteen inches above the crib surface, on the baby's right. You can place another disc on the baby's left side if you wish.

If you stand back and look at what you have created, it may not look like much, but over a period of days or weeks, chances are pretty good that your baby will spend a fair amount of time looking at the faces. An added tip: some people have found that mounting such a toy over the changing table helps make diapering easier.

Whether or not you use a mobile is not likely to be of vital importance for the baby's development. It is merely a first step in a process of designing a world around the baby that is appropriate to her rapidly changing interests and abilities.

Rattles: Another perennial gift for the newborn child, the rattle, is likewise not a good toy. In the first weeks of life babies neither see well, nor can they reach for, or hold on long to, small objects. A rattle usually has to be forced into the newborn baby's clenched fist. Once there, it will be ignored by any baby under two months of age.

Once the baby gets to be old enough to reach out for objects (at five to six months), she will reach for any small object that is offered, including a rattle. But having grasped and examined it briefly, most babies simply find a rattle boring; their world is bound to contain many more interesting things for them to attend to. Not to belabor the point, but I really cannot think of any age when rattles are much good.

Crib Gyms: Once your baby starts to look steadily at his own hands, he has entered a new stage. He will no longer be content with just looking; he will want to touch as well.

This desire to touch is part of the process that will eventually lead to the reaching ability (by about five months). In the beginning, however, touching consists mostly of striking or batting objects with a fist. It is not until sometime during the third month that babies are able to use their fingers effectively for exploring. Nevertheless, from age six weeks, objects within striking distance should be provided.

There are a number of crib and bassinet toys that could serve this function. The central fact to remember is that a baby who has become a hand watcher will enjoy banging objects, and (as he gets a bit older) exploring their shapes with his fingers. For this reason, objects suspended by string are less appropriate for this stage than those that yield slightly when struck, then return to place. String-mounted objects can be frustrating to an infant just beginning to learn to reach.

Busy-box Toys: Millions of versions of the legendary busy-box, or activity-box toys, have been sold in recent years. In fact, during the last four or five years, with the increasing interest in materials for very young children, three or four copies of the original busy-box have been created by several different toy-manufacturing firms. None of them is a good toy for babies.

Busy-boxes are recommended by their designers for children six months to two years of age. Yet if you spend time watching children in their own homes, you will find that this type of toy never receives much attention at any point between six months and two years. In the second half of the first year babies might show some interest in the toy, but no more than they would show in a wrapper from a package, or an empty cigarette carton, or a piece of wool, or indeed anything that they had never seen, felt, or gummed before.

Presumably any toy, in order to be called "good," has to have more than just the momentary appeal of novelty. It has to have enough intrinsic play value so that the child will go back to it at least once in a while and for at least a few minutes each time. That is not the case with the busy-box or similar activity-box toys.

The sole power of such toys is, in my opinion, their appeal to adults—they *look* as though babies *should* like them. Admittedly, a child a little older than two may use any kind of toy, including this one, as a device for engaging the attention of an older person. There is nothing wrong with this, but it does not mean that the toy has intrinsic play value.

There are a few exceptions: two are the previously mentioned Surprise Busy Box sometimes sold as the new Disney Busy Poppin' Pals. These consist of several boxes (in a row) with tops that spring open, each cover being operated by a different mechanism. Children between ten and twenty months of age usually find this challenging and fun. The infant less than one year old can operate only a simple lever mechanism, similar to a light switch, only bigger. But by age eighteen months or so, children can usually work all of the switches. Apparent reasons for this toy's appeal include the youngster's strong interest in tasks that challenge hand-eye skills, his interest in the abrupt lifting of a compartment cover, the universal popularity of hinged objects among children of this age, and the pleasure that comes from successfully relatching the cover. Furthermore, these toys are sturdy: they can be dropped from chairs and tables repeatedly without breaking. All in all, these are good toys for children ten to twenty months old.

Why Not Better Toys?   The major reason why we don't have better toys is the same as why we don't have more fun and less stress raising our children: because we have never learned enough about the subject.

I have spent many hours talking with leading toy designers in the country. They are very able people who understand the economic factors affecting toy design very well. They know how much individual pieces and whole toys are likely to cost, and they have a good feel for whether or not that cost will get in the way of sales. They know a great deal about materials and about mass manufacturing. And they know how to appeal to toy buyers—parents and grandparents in particular. They know how to make an attractive package and how to advertise a toy. And they have made lots of money selling toys for babies over the last several years.

But they still don't understand as much as they should about the creature for whom they are designing the toys. Babies change very rapidly in the first three years, more rapidly than they do during all the remainder of their lives. You cannot, for example, make a toy for a baby who is two months of age and expect it to be appealing to a baby who is two years of age, even though, from the perspective of the toy manufacturer, it would be very nice if you could.

In my mind there is absolutely no question that we could have better commercial toys than are currently available. Particularly during the last fifteen or twenty years, much really useful information about children has been developed through research. By making more use of this information, toy companies could do a valuable public service and make money as well.

For example, babies in cribs develop a fair amount of strength by the time they are three or four months, and they can treat toys that are appealing to them quite harshly. Even laboratory-constructed toys we've used in our research have been battered into submission by normal, healthy babies. But there is no mystery about how to make strong toys, and the toy companies have the materials and techniques to make toys sturdy enough and safe enough for any infant and toddler. Why, then, have they made so few?

Toys for the child under three years of age are as important to the child's education as books are to the older child. If what I believe about the educational significance of the first years is even partly true, the production of basic toys for the first three years of life may someday have to be considered a responsibility of the school system. In the meantime, however, responsible toy manufacturers could do a lot to fill the gap.

Yet even if, as I believe, the demand by parents for better toys will eventually be met, first by private enterprise, and then more gradually by the public and private school systems, this progress will undoubtedly encounter obstacles. Educators are slow to adopt new ideas, and the toy industry is equally reluctant to concentrate on toys for babies.

For toy manufacturers, a marketing breakthrough occurred a number of years ago when the Mattel Company began to use Saturday-morning TV to advertise their toys for children. This was a very successful marketing technique, hence, other big companies followed suit, and the toy industry became big business. Since that time, the larger companies have found that to keep up with the competition they must create new toys each year. Because of the huge costs involved in nationwide TV advertising, and in molds for each new toy, the stakes are high and the risks great. A fair number of new toys do not sell. Such failures are very costly. The result is that fewer chances are taken.

Television advertising for certain children's toys can be very effective, since lots of children five years of age and older watch Saturday-morning TV. Infants, however, do not watch TV very much; even if they did, they would neither be able to go out and buy toys for themselves nor talk their parents and grandparents into doing it. Thus, if you want to use television to sell toys for babies, you have got to use the kind that reaches mothers and grandmothers rather than the children themselves. That is not Saturday-morning TV but the more expensive weekday programming, including evening prime time. This expense dampens the interest of toy manufacturers for investment in toys for children under three years of age.

Another obstacle to substantial investment in baby toys is a baby's rate of development within those first years. A "Matchbox" car, for example, can be sold to children from age five or six all the way up to teenagers. Considering that there are from 3 to 4 million children in each age-year group, you can see that an item like a Matchbox car or a Frisbee can be sold to millions of children. But it is not the same with babies. Not only is a two-month-old a different customer from a two-year-old, she is likewise a different customer from a ten-month-old. Toys for babies can be sold—at best—to only one year's worth of babies. In short, toy manufacturers know they cannot possibly make as much money with toys for babies as with toys for older children.

A further obstacle is the selling pattern of the industry. In department stores, toys for older children are bought by toy buyers for sale in toy departments. Toys for infants and children under three years are more often acquired by other buyers and sold through infants' departments. But the major toy manufacturers seem to prefer the most familiar procedures and continue selling primarily through toy departments.

The last obstacle worthy of mention is the danger of accidents and subsequent lawsuits. The younger the child, the less able he is to protect himself against hazards of all kinds, including accidents with toys. The result is that toy companies are particularly nervous about possible legal troubles involving toys for babies.

Put all these factors together and you can see why the time when we will have better toys for babies and toddlers is not likely to arrive as soon as many of us would like.

Standard Equipment: Safety should be your paramount concern when choosing materials for use with infants and toddlers. Beware of poorly made toys. Beware especially of small objects that might become lodged in a baby's mouth. Parts that can become separated from larger objects are just as dangerous as individual small items. No object with a major dimension less than one-and-a-half inches is safe for an infant or toddler.

Also be careful about paint used on toys, furniture, and even rooms for babies. Most paint in current use is safe, but some is not. All lead-based paints must be avoided. Even though such paint is not used much anymore, it is present in many older apartments and houses. Please note that even though the top layer or layers of paint may not be lead-based, undercoats may be. Lead-based paint on windowsills, for example, has been a significant source of poisonings of children less than three years of age.

Basic Toys to Have on Hand:

1. A comfortable rocking chair. For use from birth on. Cost: $60.00 or more. To help you comfort a baby in distress, and for sheer enjoyment for both adult and baby. Close body contact while being moved rhythmically is enjoyed at all ages. It is particularly soothing to infants during the first months of life.

2. Six Nuk or other major brand of modontic pacifiers. For use from birth to seven months or older. Cost: $1.50 per pacifier. To help you soothe an uncomfortable baby. Specialists in pediatric dentistry see nothing wrong with the use of a pacifier during the first years of life. Sucking, even when not followed by ingestion of fluids, is particularly soothing to infants during the first months of life.

3. One or more stabiles (a mobile that does not move). For use from three to nine weeks only. Cost in materials: $1.00. To provide something attractive for the baby to look at when she is alone. Babies begin to show interest in the outside world toward the end of the first month. A stabile can be very appealing for a few weeks. You'll probably have to make your own. See instructions in text.

4. A stainless steel mirror, minimum size five to six inches in diameter, with no sharp edges. For use from six weeks to six months, with occasional use for several additional months. Cost: about $10.00. Several types commercially available. Both you and the baby will have a great time with this item during the baby's fourth month. Mount the mirror about seven inches from his eyes.

5. A crib gym. For babies from six weeks to six months. Cost: about $10.00. Several types are commercially available. To provide opportunities for the baby to have fun exploring his nearby world while also learning to use his hands under the guidance of his eyes. Avoid the kind that has objects suspended by strings as this arrangement tends to frustrate infants. Note: a child who is sitting up is too old for a crib gym.

6. An infant seat. Make sure that it is well made and stable. For use from birth to three months. Babies over three months are often able to tip these seats over. Furthermore, they are better off on blankets or safe, flat surfaces. Cost: about $20.00. Many good ones available, and they make it easy for you to move the small infant around the house. As head control gets better, babies enjoy looking at more and more of their surroundings; and an infant seat also increases the opportunity for adults and babies to play face-to-face games.

7. The Surprise Busy Box or Disney Poppin' Pals. Manufactured by Gabriel Industries, Elmwood Park, N.J. Cost: about $10.00. For age

seven to eighteen months. Available to all toy stores and through the Sears Catalog. Helps to feed the baby's interest in operating simple gadgets and is a great toy to hold in reserve for emergency distraction. It is one of the very few commercial toys with great play value, and it is almost indestructible.

8. Busy Bath. Another Gabriel toy. There are also other good alternatives available. Cost: about $10.00. For age seven months to two years. Babies love water play. The variations are infinite. It will help during bath time. Again, this item has lots of play value and it is very sturdy. However, don't forget to duck!

9. Six books with stiff pages and ring backs. Cost: about $1.00 to $3.00 each. For age seven to fourteen months. To feed the baby's interest in hand-eye practice and his fascination with hinged objects. Do not expect much interest in stories or pictures yet. As the child enters the middle of the second year, books can be used for more conventional purposes.

10. A toy telephone. Cost: about $8.00. For age one to three years. To mesh with the emerging interest in make-believe activity. The baby will have just as much fun with the real phone.

11. Six to twelve balls, especially inflatable beachballs up to 24 inches in diameter (the bigger the better); also ping-pong balls, but only for a child over one year of age and with supervision. For use from age one year on. Cost: about $.50 to $1.00 each. *The single most popular type of toy during the second year of life.* Great for learning about the movement of objects; great for practicing throwing, chasing, picking up, and carrying; great for getting someone to play with you. The epitome of elegance in babies' toys.

12. Pots and pans, as many as you can spare. For children age six to twelve months. To feed the child's curiosity about objects and sounds. No toy list would be complete without them.

13. A stair gate. Cost: about $10.00. For seven months to two years. To allow stair climbing without anxiety or supervision, place the gate *on the third step*. Supervise the baby's first attempts and make a big fuss over her successes. Climbing *down*stairs is mastered several weeks after climbing *up*stairs.

14. A playpen. Yes, a playpen. Cost: about $25.00. For age five to fifteen months. To fill the need for a safe place to put a baby for a *few minutes;* for example, when the floor is drying or when a pot is boiling over, etc. *However, do not get into the habit of putting a child in a playpen or any other restrictive device for long periods of time.* The second syllable is much more accurate in describing this device than the first: play*pen*. Interestingly, manufacturers have recently begun to produce narrower versions (to get through doorways more readily) and simultaneously they have coined a new name, play*yards!*

15. Plastic containers with lids. Empty ice-cream containers are fine; the

more the better. For age seven to fifteen months. To feed a baby's strong interest in mastering hand-eye skills. These containers can also be used for water play. Babies in this age range are intrigued by their developing hand-eye skills. They enjoy removing and replacing lids on containers. Some frustration is likely—keep it down by providing materials that are not too difficult for the baby.

16. A large plastic container with at least a dozen small but safe objects (e.g., large thread spools, small plastic doo-dads). For age seven to fifteen months. To facilitate exploration of small objects and practice of hand-eye skills. They will examine these one at a time or, at other times, they will dump them all out at once.

17. A miniature potty, a small plastic toy with a hinged moveable seat. Cost: about $1.00. For age seven to fifteen months. To facilitate exploration of small objects and practice hand-eye skills. Finer motor skills and hinged objects go together. Another winner—although psychoanalytic theorists would unquestionably find grist for their mills here.

18. Small, *low*, four-wheeled toys to be sat upon or straddled while moved here and there. Cost: about $15.00. (There are many good models on the market.) For age seven to fifteen months. To facilitate mastery of large-muscle skills.

19. Large empty boxes. For age one to two years. Purpose: having fun.

20. Doll and doll carriage. Cost: about $25.00. For age fourteen months to three years. To feed a rapidly growing imagination. The toy's worth has been validated by time.

21. An outdoor swing. Cost: about $35.00. For age one to three. Make sure the swing is sturdy. Most children love being swung through the air.

22. About twenty story and picture books (the more the better). Cost: about $3.00 each. For age eighteen months to three years. To support the development of language, curiosity, and a healthy social life. The child's language achievement level is now suited to story telling. The strong social interest of the second year heightens the pleasure. You can start a bit earlier, but do not be surprised if the child shows very little sustained interest until eighteen or more months of age.

23. Many scribbling and drawing materials. Cost: about $3.00 for the basics. Age two on. Get *washable* crayons, markers, etc. Also, be sure that all materials are *nontoxic*. Purpose: to encourage drawing and use of writing implements. Representational drawing emerges during the third year. Do not be surprised if crayons sometimes are used on surfaces you would rather not see decorated.

24. Several simple wooden puzzles. For age two to three. Cost: about $5.00 each. To provide a simple challenge to intellectual and hand-eye skills. Keep the puzzles easy enough to sustain the child's interest. Some children get to be amazingly skillful at these, sometimes succeeding faster than adults.

25. The Fisher-Price Play Family toy, or any of the collection. Cost: about $15.00 each. For age one to three years. To encourage imagination and fantasy activities—and for fun. Imagination and mental ability are now ready for play that involves organization and themes. For these and other reasons, this toy works. All Fisher-Price toys are well made, and these are great for children of this age.

26. A large, low container for water play outdoors. Play must be supervised. Cost: about $15.00. Encourages hand-eye skills and curiosity, as well as making the child feel good. On a hot day, lolling or splashing in a few inches of regularly replenished water can be a taste of heaven. Make sure that containers for pouring are also available.

27. A slide and a *climbing toy*, with ladder and play area under the platform. Cost:$30.00 to $35.00 in most stores. Available from more expensive toy stores and order-by-mail catalogs. For age eighteen months to three years. For fun and to help with the development of large-muscle skills and mastery of the body. Interest in gymnastics is high throughout these first years. This toy is well made; too bad it costs so much.

28. A sandbox. Can be built for about $15.00. For age one year and on. For development of motor skills (digging, pouring, etc.) and fantasy play. Can (with luck) be used at the same time by children of different ages.

Toys and Education: Toys in general vary in their attractiveness as a function of the developmental level of the child. Before a baby can crawl, toys can hold his attention better than they will in the months that follow. This is because the very young infant can neither change his own location (and scenery) nor practice the various motor skills involved in crawling, climbing, walking, and so forth. From early crawling to about fourteen months, the excitement and challenges associated with the new ability to move about overwhelm the appeal of nearly all toys. From fourteen to twenty-four months, most children become intensely interested in the person with whom they spend the bulk of their waking hours. While motor activities and visual exploration continue, social needs assume the highest priority. Toys that are conducive to social interchanges, therefore, become more appealing. Storybooks and fantasy tools (for example, telephones, dolls) become dramatically more popular in the second half of the second year. Finally, during the third year, the progress made in language and intellectual skills and the child's new ease in his attachment to those who take care of him all combine to make toys much more enticing than they have been since the first months of life.

Throughout the first three years you should try to maintain a balance in the child's interests: give him not only the chance to play with toys, pots and pans, and the like, but also the opportunity to exercise and practice physical skills; and give him the opportunity to interact with other people in fantasy games, ball games, reading, and so on. There is rarely any need to push a child from one activity to another. The best clue that learning is taking place is the child's own interest in what he is doing. If he is fascinated by any activity, it probably means that it has learning value for him.

Admittedly, there are some exceptions. A child may become obsessed with his relationship with his mother or begin to sit silently in front of the television set for long periods of time. Such behavior, however, is outside the normal range and should be given special attention.

"Educational" Toys: I feel quite confident in telling you that—to do a superb job of educating a child in the first three years of life—you do not have to buy a single so-called "educational" toy. Anything that genuinely interests a child, be it nothing more elaborate than an empty ice-cream container, is educational.

Many parents wonder whether certain kinds of toys will help to lengthen a youngster's attention span. Three factors are involved: (1) the basic ability of the child to maintain focused attention on *any* single topic or target, (2) the attractiveness—or interest value—of a topic or target, and (3) individual differences among children.

As to the young child's basic ability to maintain steady attention, some professionals feel that young children are quite limited in this regard, and may not actually be ready for school even by their sixth birthday. Everyday observations tend to reinforce that view. Toddlers and preschoolers sometimes seem to move from one activity to another more rapidly than older children and adults. But why a person at any age shifts her focus depends on more than the capacity for sustained attention (at the very least, on whether she is still interested). But attention also depends on physical factors, such as fatigue or jitteriness, and on whether there are distractions present.

Phase I babies (birth to six weeks) rarely show sustained visual attention to anything. They may, of course, be pondering some subject within the mind's eye, but the burden is on someone to prove it, and that is not likely to happen. From the end of Phase I on, however, the growth of the capacity for sustained visual attention is obvious. Three-month-old babies can and do study their own hand and finger movements for as long as ten continuous minutes, and for a total of several hours a day. They do so apparently because it is very important for all humans to learn to use their own hands as tools. In other words, the basic capacity for sustained attention of impressive duration emerges very early in life: ten continuous minutes of attention is a long time at any age.

This fact points strongly to the conclusion that lack of sustained interest by a two-year-old—whether it involves a toy, a story, or a television program—is not likely to be due to an inadequate capacity for sustained attention. But as for helping to expand a child's basic attention span, whether through toys or any other medium—I am afraid we know little about *how* we could or, for that matter, about *whether* we should. The only hint we have arises from two related research findings. In one study we found a strong positive correlation between the usual length of time young children spent in steady looking (at objects and people) and their later general level of achievement. In another study we found an even stronger positive correlation between the usual length of time spent in steady looking, *while an adult talked about what was being looked at*, and later achievement. Thus, it is possible that talking to a baby about what she is attending to may help increase her ability to attend. Of course, we are not sure of this. We cannot even prove that greater attending ability of this kind is *good*. But if you suspect that it is, you are not alone: so do I.

Experience Versus Heredity: The Nature-Versus-Nurture Controversy

The relative contribution to achievement of experience versus heredity has dominated early childhood research throughout its history. From time to time this debate seems temporarily resolved (at least in a superficial sense), only to resurface a decade later just as vigorously as before.

During the late nineteenth century it was assumed that "inherited" characteristics were of the greatest importance with respect to achievement. The child's "nature" was considered to be pretty much brought into the world with him. The influence of Freud and his followers and of people in learning theory, starting with Ivan Pavlov, the Russian physiologist, rebutted this orthodoxy; and during the second and third decades of the twentieth century people became increasingly impressed with the importance of early experiences (particularly those of the first five years of life).

A kind of counterreaction began during the 1930s, with Gesell among its leaders. The result was a host of experiments designed to show that there were limits to what early learning and early teaching could achieve for the child. There were, for example, interesting studies in which identical twins were used to show the effects of the limitations of immaturity. In one case a twin was taught to roller skate earlier than he might ordinarily have learned the skill. The other twin was prevented from learning to roller skate; yet when the latter twin took up the activity at a more appropriate (later) age, he caught up quickly. Similar experiments were done in using scissors and climbing stairs. The tide in the 1930s turned away from emphasis on the power of early experiences and back toward the importance of maturation and inherited traits.

We saw a reversal yet again in the 1950s and 1960s, as the work of Piaget became more influential and as the civil-rights movement gathered power. The undying optimism that we always seem to have about the potential of children pushed again to the forefront. This resulted in more and more research and practical activity based on the notion that early experience was important. Thus the 1960s saw the establishment of such programs as Project Head Start, designed to help young children obtain a better set of early educational experiences.

Today, the controversy is far from over. We still do not have enough dependable evidence to make reliable judgments about how much achievement can be ascribed to experience and how much to innate competence. Perhaps the most succinct way to express my own judgment in this matter is this statement: What a child brings into the world may set an upper limit to the achievement level that he can attain, but it provides no guarantee whatsoever that any particular level of achievement will be reached. A child with the best possible central nervous system and physical apparatus at birth may not achieve even average levels of competence unless the experiential requirements are there. For example, the most beautifully endowed baby can be prevented from ever learning language simply by being prevented from ever hearing any. Such a child will never reach his intellectual potential, nor will he be a particularly effective social animal.

But the responsibility of those of us who rear children is not really much affected by the nature-nurture debate. It must always be to provide the best possible set of experiences that we can, particularly in the first years of life, *regardless* of the amount of inherited potential of the child.

PART II: OTHER ISSUES

Programs that Promise Precocity

The Better Baby Institute, founded by Glenn Doman and based in Philadelphia, promises parents smarter and more capable babies if they (the parents) attend a four-and-a-half-day training program. A few years back Doman and a colleague were urging parents to help their children learn to read during infancy by using their specially prepared kit. National news magazines such as *Time* and *Newsweek* have also featured Doman's work in recent years.

Professionals have been either puzzled or enraged. Does Glenn Doman know a dramatically better way to raise a baby? Are parents making a mistake if they are not closely monitoring and stimulating development from birth? Are the typical anxieties and exaggerated ambitions that some parents have for their children being exploited?

The national YMCA has been similarly upset about some programs designed to teach swimming to infants. On the other hand, many have been impressed by violin and piano skills shown by preschool students with the Suzuki method. What does it all mean?

The achievements people seek in their children range from the conventional to the extreme. Most parents want their very young children to develop free from handicaps, to be capable, well balanced, confident, and comfortable with other people. "Capable" usually means as far above average as their congenital potential will allow. Most parents' aspirations do not include preprofessional skills in such areas as tennis, ice-skating, music, and so on, nor genius levels in math. This is not to say that parents would not value such skills, but rather that they usually do not set such goals and pursue them avidly.

Some people, however, very much want very high levels of achievement for their near-infant children as soon as possible. Such achievements range from reading before three years of age, to prodigious vocabularies, to learning to swim during infancy, and to learning to play a musical instrument.

Can anyone really produce such results? The most widely accepted study of the growth of intelligence during the first three years of life is the work of Piaget, yet nothing in his work directly addresses the question of how to help a child become very bright very early. He simply was not interested in the subject. At present there are also many studies of gifted children taking place, but as yet no substantial knowledge on how to bring about giftedness exists.

One closely related study was our own Harvard Preschool Project. With a large staff and generous funds we spent thirteen years examining the histories of children who developed unusually well during the preschool years. But we are interested in *balanced* development and, in fact, deliberately excluded intellectually or artistically precocious children who were not equally capable of interacting with others or who were weak in any other major area of development. So neither we nor anyone else can provide any direct basis in research for any program that promises intellectual giftedness.

Is there nevertheless a basis in well-established practice? In Montessori preschools the teaching of reading and writing to preschoolers has been demonstrated repeatedly over the decades, in many places, by many practitioners. At the University of Kansas preschool, teaching preschoolers to tie their own shoelaces (no easy task) has also been demonstrated repeatedly. These may be examples of superior teaching methods, but they are not examples of inducing extraordinary achievement. In my view, *there is no basis in well-established practice for any program that promises intellectual giftedness.*

That is not to say that Mr. Doman or any number of other people could not have discovered some effective procedures. Rather it is to say that no such methods have received widespread examination or approval. Indeed, Mr. Doman's group has refused to allow any professional group to evaluate his procedures. Furthermore, his equally dramatic claims of success in working with brain-damaged patients have never been supported or replicated by others in the field. Therefore, we are unable to recommend his services to parents.

What about Suzuki procedures? The Suzuki method, unlike Doman's Better Baby Institute, does not claim to produce extraordinary achievement in all major facets of development. In existence in many locations with conspicuous success for many years, there is nothing secretive about the Suzuki method; the procedures are available for examination by anyone. Although some teachers of music will no doubt have objections to the Suzuki method, we see no obvious reason to be concerned. On the contrary, we should probably be more concerned about a program that required regular lengthy drills to induce learning at a fast pace and in great quantity during the early years.

What are the potential disadvantages of special-teaching programs for the very young? If the program involves several hours each day for parents and children over a long period of time, we believe that a child's spontaneous interest and pleasure in learning are likely to be jeopardized. If large portions of time are spent in any narrowly focused direction, such as tennis, ice-skating, violin, or reading, we believe that the child will probably have to pay a significant price in other developmental areas as well as in motivation to learn. If a child comes to be valued too much for what she has achieved or whether she has met certain goals dictated by a program, rather than for what she is, we feel that could be a serious negative factor in any young child's life.

During the early years children learn to relate to people in fundamental ways. That learning takes a lot of time. They learn to use their bodies, and that learning takes time. They spend much time in experiences not dictated by any adult lesson plan, but nevertheless these experiences seem to be an important part of healthy early development. They even spend a lot of time relaxing. Any program that promises precocity ultimately has to be evaluated in the light of how much it may subtract from other important, even crucial, learning times; and for this reason we urge you to be conservative in your approach to such programs.

There are, in fact, some good lower-intensity alternatives. Many of the thousands of parent-support programs that have sprung up over the last fifteen years include attention to healthy learning during the first years, but they are not really concerned with setting new records in infant achievement.

Teaching Infants to Swim: Beware!

During the past few years, as part of the dramatically increased interest in educating babies, there has been a good deal of attention paid to teaching infants to swim, or at least attempting to drown-proof them. Given my feelings about high-intensity early-achievement programs in general, you might not be surprised to learn that I was unenthusiastic about this class of programs in particular.

Actually, the topic of swimming lessons is something of a special case, made more confusing because of the conflicting safety and enjoyment factors involved. No one would disagree with the desirability of helping to avoid infant-drowning accidents, nor would anyone object to an activity that brings parents and their young children together for the kind of delightful shared experiences that programs of this nature promise.

But now a new consideration has surfaced, one that is of great importance and that must be brought to the attention of everyone concerned with infants. It is called "infant water intoxication." In a recent issue of the magazine *Discover YMCA* (May/June 1983), an article by Marjorie M. Murphy, Aquatic Director of YMCA of the United States, and Charles Fiske, editorial assistant on the magazine, registers substantial concern about infant swimming lessons and cites several instances of serious harm done to infants during the course of such lessons. In each case, harm was attributed to confirmed reports of an infant swallowing too much water, resulting in the condition known as water intoxication. Consequently, the YMCA has endorsed the policy of the Council for National Co-operation in Aquatics, as expressed in its statement that "Children under three should not be entered into organized swimming instruction classes." The CCNA has adapted 10 Guidelines that recommend safe programs for children under three years of age.

I consider this so important that I shall quote at length from the YMCA article:

Water intoxication occurs when a person swallows enough water to lower significantly the concentration of salt (sodium) in the blood. This causes the brain to swell, which in turn produces a decreased level of consciousness—progressing from lethargy to stupor to coma. Seizures may also occur.

With appropriate treatment the condition is reversible, as long as there isn't oxygen deprivation due to prolonged respiratory arrest during seizures, vomiting, or choking.

The symptoms included restlessness, weakness, nausea, muscle-twitching, convulsions, and coma. *None of the children was noticed to be in trouble when in the water*—choking or gasping. Doctors did not find water in their lungs. . . .

Adults and larger children cannot normally drink enough water to cause water intoxication. But small infants are vulnerable for two reasons: their lower body weight (and blood volume) and the natural reflex of an infant to swallow when anything enters its mouth. . . . Swimming experts agree that an infant automatically holds its breath when merged; but infants do open their mouths and swallow all the water that comes in. . . .

Doctors have identified water intoxication as a problem for years, but not until recently did they notice it could occur while swimming. The cases they saw usually resulted from improper feeding of an infant when, for whatever reason, the parents gave water or diluted formula to the child . . .

Symptoms follow the swallowing by three to eight hours, so many instructors never see them. Mild symptoms of lethargy or irritability might be thought to be normal signs that the baby is tired. . . . In such cases children had a fine time swimming—the problem came later. . . .

And the YMCA article notes: (Finally, it is not established that any of the goals of swimming lessons for infants) can be reached in a lasting way. Children with very early exposure to water have not proved to do any better in the long run than children who start later. Drownproofing is pointless until a child is old enough to know what is going on—that is, really know that if he propels himself he will go in a certain direction, that if he just floats he will stay in one place, and so on.

Any good that comes from infant swimming programs is certainly outweighed by the risks of water intoxication . . . Based on what we have seen so far there is a clear danger that water intoxication can occur during any (swimming) lesson . . . The YMCA strongly urges that programs for children under the age of three should include a parent, and that very small children should not be placed underwater or allowed to drink pool water.

I can only concur: any teaching program that includes *submersion* of the infant *definitely is not recommended.*

The YMCA guidelines for infant swimming programs are available from local YMCAs, physical education specialists, aquatic coordinators, and from YMCA of the United States. Write: the YMCA of the United States, 101 Wacker Drive, Chicago, Ill. 60606; tel.: (312) 977-0031.

The Role of the Father

In recent years several widely read books have been published on the role of the father in the development of the young child. In addition, research reports in leading journals and statements at conferences and in the popular media have focused on how important the input of the father is to the developing child. Unfortunately, many of the assertions made about this topic have been unsupported and contradictory.

The most fundamental question is whether the absence of a father makes a significant difference in the development of a very young child. Since women have traditionally had the responsibility for most of the direct child-rearing activities with infants and toddlers, it is reasonable to ask whether a father or other man is necessary in early child-rearing in order for the process to be fully successful.

If the father *is* expendable, all succeeding questions take on a different degree of importance, and the many women raising babies alone can breathe a collective sigh of relief. If on the other hand the father has a significant role to play, either directly with the child or indirectly through the mother, a whole host of other questions surface. For example, are the child-rearing styles of a father different from a mother's? How much direct input from fathers is best? How does the impact of fathering style affect mothering style and, in turn, the child's development?

Where do I stand on these questions? As is the case with full-time substitute care for infants, existing research is simply too scarce for anyone to be dogmatic. Some older research has been used to claim that prolonged father absence leads to sexual problems for both boys and girls, with boys becoming less masculine and girls less feminine. That claim has not evolved into a generally accepted principle and remains only as an interesting speculation. In our own research at the Harvard Preschool Project a few of the children developing very well were being raised without fathers at home, but the number was too small to allow for generalizations.

In my personal, extensive observations of the behavior of many young children, both in research and in raising my own, I have often shared moments of excitement and pure pleasure with babies and with other adults. One of the less emphasized aspects of traditional child-rearing has been the marked disparity between the opportunities that women have for such experiences as compared to men. Although it is fair to say that men have not had to share equally in the less pleasant aspects of child-rearing—such as diapering, discipline, everyday stress—it is also true that they have had far less opportunity to share in the day-to-day rewards.

A case can be made for the role of the father, if not with respect to the welfare of children, then to that of parents. Both for the psychic rewards and because full-time parenting of babies is for most people a very difficult job at times, we are strongly in favor of equally shared parenting. From our point of view the (difficult-to-attain) ideal of child-rearing practice would consist of: (1) equal time for both parents in raising babies, (2) along with part-time work—perhaps as much as two-thirds times—for both parents, and (3) occasional use of high-quality substitute child care.

A Look at the Subject of Bonding

The concept of "bonding" has come into the media limelight during the last decade. It is best known through the work of two physicians at Case Western Reserve University (Cleveland, Ohio): Drs. Marshall K. Klaus and John H. Kennell. They reported that when mothers were given sixteen extra hours of contact with their children immediately after birth, the relationship between those mothers and their infants seemed to become generally more beneficial for both mother and child. In the more common situation a mother of a newborn spends very little time with that infant during its first day of life. In fact, Klaus and Kennell reported that several years after birth, the mothering behavior of those who had a chance to spend extra time in close contact with their newborn babies was generally of more desirable quality than that of mothers without such special experience. The mothers in the first group tended to be more affectionate, more interested in, and less harsh with their children. Thus arose the concept of bonding, the rapid development of an intense and healthful attachment between a newborn and an older person, usually the mother, in the first hours of life.

This dramatic announcement, which seemed to offer exciting new information, immediately received great publicity. In the years that followed, quite a number of hospitals modified their practices so as to allow young mothers and their newborn babies to enjoy as much close contact as possible right from the very beginning.

Since the original reporters of the bonding phenomenon had studied women of low-income families living in the Cleveland area, an attempt at repeating their findings with middle-class mothers was performed at Stanford University. The Stanford study found that in the first month of childrearing, mothers who had the extra contact with their newborn babies were more inclined to cuddle their infants and be physically affectionate with them. They also seemed more confident as mothers. Yet by the time the first year of the child's life was over, there seemed to be no differences between the behaviors of mothers who had been given the extra contact experience and those who had not. More important, no differences were found in their children. The project concluded that factors such as the socioeconomic status of the parents and the sex of the infant were considerably more powerful in respect to childrearing styles than the amount of early contact. When another attempt at repeating the original finding was conducted at the University of Colorado Medical School Center, this time with lower-middle-class mothers, the results were similar to those of the Stanford study.

Beyond these three studies there have been few direct tests of the concept of bonding, but if only for that reason we should be all the more cautious about accepting the original claims.

When researchers are deciding whether to accept a new finding, they also look to see how it fits in with other known evidence. There is a good deal of available information that bears indirectly upon the issue of bonding. Some of this evidence concerns the general attachment process thought to operate with varying degrees of intensity during the first two years of a child's life. The balance concerns the inherent nature both of the newborn child and the mother.

In regard to the attachment process, we have evidence from many studies of children and also of other animal young strongly indicating that early experiences are important for lifelong emotional and social health, and that a good early attachment is vital for physical, emotional, and educational growth. Yet by the same token, there is also much evidence showing that during the first three to four months of life children are quite primitive. By that I mean they lack the mental equipment to understand what is going on around them or to identify any individual with any accuracy. It would appear that newborn babies will become attached to *any older human* who spends much time with them. For survival it is so important for them to become attached to an older human that from about two months on they will respond with affectionate signs to just about anybody. It is not until about the fourth month of life that babies begin to be selectively responsive to the people with whom they have been living, usually their mothers. From that point on the attachment becomes more focused, and toward the end of the second year the baby's entire day revolves around his mother or other primary caretaker.

This general picture of the process of developing attachments does not fit very well with the notion that the first few hours are especially significant, from the baby's point of view. It could, however, be a special time from the point of view of the baby's mother.

Although newborns are quite simple, undeveloped creatures from an intellectual, emotional, and social standpoint, that is, of course, not the case with respect to their parents. It is possible that mothers undergo some uniquely important experience during the first day after the birth of their children that will somehow have lasting effects on their childrearing styles and on their feelings for their babies.

What then about the original claim about the crucial importance of bonding in the first day of life? In favor of the claim we have only one study on a small group of mothers, and we have two other studies that fail to support the first one. Also casting doubt on the claim is a whole host of other evidence which points to the notion that bonding should be considered a subheading under the larger subject of attachment, a process that takes the better part of the first two years of life in most cases, and one that is so important to the survival of the species that it is not likely that its success depends heavily on a single event.

My conclusion is that the idea of bonding is merely speculation rather than established fact. But what would happen if we acted as though it were established fact? If this merely caused parents to spend more time with their babies in the first hours of the babies' lives, no harm would be done. Indeed, it would probably be quite an enjoyable experience for everyone concerned. But then any mother who was prevented from having close contact with a new baby might very well come to fear that there would be no way she could have a first-rate relationship with her child. When you consider the fact that for a variety of reasons many young mothers *are* unable to be with their babies during the first few days, the consequences of such fears would be widespread and harmful. The same would be true for adopting parents, who are almost never present during the first hours of their child's life. In the interests of all such parents, I think it is important that we treat the entire concept of bonding with reserve. It is no more than a hypothesis, and not a very well-supported one at that.

I might add here that in the twenty-seven years that I have been studying early human development I have seen any number of unusual ideas about birth and childrearing surface, most of which could not be validated. For example, some years back there was an obstetrician working in Africa who was treating his patients with a depressurization machine, a sort of inverted metal kettle within which the air pressure could be reduced. It was designed to fit over the abdomen of a woman in late pregnancy, and the lower pressure would reduce the external pressure on the abdominal walls. The woman would remain in this device for about a half-hour, and this treatment would be repeated several times during the third trimester of pregnancy. The claims of the doctor, published in legitimate journals, was that babies born after such a fetal experience were healthier, more alert, and generally better off. Further, reports claimed that when the babies were a year of age they had achieved higher developmental levels. You can imagine the impact of such a report. People everywhere wanted to know where they could find doctors who had depressurization machines. Yet the depressurization fad soon evaporated, and today you never encounter information on this particular procedure. It is not impossible that in times to come we shall hear no more about bonding, either.

In summary, the more physical contact babies have in the first months of life the better for all concerned. But, clearly, to not have sixteen extra hours of close bodily contact in the first day of life should in no way jeopardize the growth of a healthy attachment relationship between parents and children.

Playgroups for Infants and Toddlers

A "playgroup" is a group for babies too young for nursery school. Traditionally, this has meant children less than two-and-one-half years of age, although lately some nursery schools have been accepting children as young as two years. Indeed, with shifting ideas on the importance of education during the first years of life, new "educational" programs are being created for children even younger.

Most people who get involved in playgroups do so on a cooperative basis, with responsibility for the group taken by each family in turn. Children involved may range widely in age, but here I would like to confine my comments to playgroups for children between twelve and thirty months of age.

One thing we have seen repeatedly in studying children under thirty months is that it is wrong to expect them to play together civilly. They are not ready for it. Toddlers possess negligible social skills. Most of their social experience has usually been with only one or two very special caring adults. Not only do they lack social sophistication, but their age-mates are equally inexperienced. Left unsupervised, toddlers will behave more like small monkeys than small angels, using force to determine who is in charge. Moreover, children with siblings, especially those close in age, are more likely than only children to be either aggressive or wary as preschoolers.

There is absolutely no justification for letting a baby be abused by another child. If you have a child who encounters hostility from another preschooler *do not* try to teach her how to deal with aggressive peers. Instead, minimize the contact with such children. If it is your own child who is being aggressive, put a stop to the behavior and limit her contact with her peers to those times when an adult can supervise closely what is happening.

If your child attends a playgroup, you must keep in mind that the only way to prevent some children from suffering and others from indulging in cruelty is to maintain close supervision, with repeated teaching of more civilized contact. Do not *assume* that such supervision is taking place. If your child seems unhappy and complains that others are pushing her around, check out the situation; the chances are good that she is telling the truth. If so, you should remove her from the situation.

Do children get any benefits from a playgroup? One current view is that experience with age-mates promotes social development. Another is that babies can be helped intellectually by the stimulation of group activity. No one has as yet generated any evidence to support either thesis, and in my view, parents should not count on such benefits from playgroups. Ordinarily, some time during the third year of life, children begin to turn their attentions away from an intense focus on the home, parents, and siblings and toward the exciting world of peers. That new interest grows ever stronger as the child grows older, but for children under two-and-one-half years the benefits of a playgroup are problematical at best.

Do parents get any benefits from playgroups for children under thirty months? Undoubtedly. Parents can always profit from regular brief interruptions—using babysitters, for example—in the ongoing responsibilities of child-rearing, and there is nothing wrong in that. But if you do decide to use a playgroup for your twelve- to thirty-month-old child, be clear about what the hazards may be.

When There Are Two Languages in the Home

A common question put to me is what to do for a child being raised in a bilingual family. Since I am not an authority in that area, I asked some specialists who are. It turned out that although nobody has done substantial research on the effects of one or another approach to language acquisition in a bilingual home, there is almost unanimous agreement among language acquisition experts on some points. Experts say that if both languages are spoken well, then both should be used with the child from the beginning in a natural way. Furthermore, some even suggest that one parent use one language consistently and the other parent use the other language consistently. The results, they theorize, should be as follows: during the first two to three years of life the child will be a bit slower than a monolingual child of comparable ability in the acquisition of language; but by the fourth or fifth birthday the child will not only have caught up, but will be bilingual.

How Amazing Is the Newborn?

Recently a few research reports have indicated that babies less than two months of age stick out their tongues in imitation of a researcher, turn accurately to look for sounds, coordinate their looking with their parents' behaviors, and listen to and store specific thoughts and words. Does that mean that they are much more capable than we have previously thought? Before 1960 newborns were generally thought to live in what William James called a world of "buzzing booming confusion." Today some students of human development would have you believe that babies are already busy "tuning in" on their mother's thoughts and feelings a month *before* birth. Others talk of active appreciation of experience by babies as they undergo the birth process. Still others insist that infants see, hear, compare, and make decisions followed by intentional behaviors within their first weeks of life.

What can fetuses and very young infants do? What goes on in their minds between conception and their first birthday? Analyses of these subjects can (and have) filled several books on the subject. Even so, most that we would like to know remains to be learned. Such evidence as does exist comes from several sources: anatomical studies of the growth of the central nervous system; studies of problem solving by babies, older children, and animals; Piaget's studies of the growth of intelligence; and observational studies of the behavior of the human fetus and infant.

The prevailing picture of early human abilities was first modified significantly by studies of vision, especially those of Fantz, published in the early 1960s. Fantz demonstrated that babies could "discriminate" among targets during their first months of life. But whether they were comparing targets or only looking at those they could make out was not clear. Nor was it clear whether they were perceiving "faceness" or just complexity. In any event, Fantz convinced most people that babies could see better than William James thought they could, especially after they were two months old.

Two months seems to be a turning point in regard to the development of vision. At about that time visual convergence and tracking become functional and focusing ability becomes adequate for looking at nearby details. At about the same time children begin to study their hands. For the first time they move their gaze back and forth over the features of targets while looking at them. But although this behavior is impressive, it could hardly be called sophisticated.

As for hearing, although it is true that the newborn *can* orient to sound given highly restricted conditions, do not expect much behavior of this kind before the fourth month. Unless held in the prone position and exposed to a particular kind of sound, infants during the first weeks of life routinely do not do more than blink, startle, or pause in their activities in response to sound.

For most people who study human development, Piaget's analyses of intellectual development remain the most accurate. The picture he created from his continuous observations of his own three children has been supported by many studies over several decades. Although it is true that tongue protrusion in the first month of life, now confirmed, contradicts his views, it is clearly offset by hundreds of studies that support his general picture of intellectual development. And anyway, imitative behaviors with the tongue in the first weeks of life are not followed by a continuous growth in imitation behaviors but, rather, die out by the time the infant is two to three months of age.

Imitation does begin again shortly thereafter, but it is what Piaget called "quasi-imitation." For example, the baby can be induced to continue playing with her own saliva if the parent tries to duplicate that sound. Imitation of what others are doing resurfaces in the third quarter of the first year and from then on increases in quantity and type, especially during the second and third years of life.

In Piaget's view, babies start pretty much from scratch at birth. They do not think or process specific experiences in the aware, conscious style of older children or adults. They have no inborn memories or appreciation of the world around them. They make no decisions and perform no intentional acts for several months. The first intentional problem-solving appears at about six or seven months when a baby moves an obstacle aside in order to procure another desirable object.[2] It is not until eight or nine months that babies develop the first short-lived memory capacity. By eighteen to twenty-four months they begin to solve problems by thinking about them.

This picture of the developing mental capacities of the infant is far

---

[2] Some recent studies suggest that intentional behavior may start a bit earlier than six or seven months in the case of the baby's deliberate use of the cry for attention. That begins during the fifth month.

more consistent with a great deal of evidence that exists than any other that is claimed for the fetus and the young infant. Claims of the amazingly capable newborn may be seductive, but to accept such claims without due regard for legitimate and substantial evidence to the contrary makes little sense.

Indeed, uncritical acceptance of such claims could have harmful consequences for new or expectant parents. For example, the film, *The Amazing Newborn,* which shows neonates engaging in imitative behavior such as tongue protrusion and a few other atypical activities, has a brief disclaimer at the end informing viewers that they should not expect to elicit such behavior from their own babies at home. We cannot imagine new parents *not* attempting to repeat various demonstrations shown in the film and *not* being disappointed when their baby does not respond.

Any strictures I have made on exaggerated claims on behalf of the newborn go double for claims on behalf of the unborn. That the fetus is capable of perceiving his mother's thoughts and feelings *in utero* and that these perceptions will have significant, long-term effects on the child's mental and emotional health after birth, are not only unproven assertions, but not even likely. And the same potential for needless worry over disappointed expectations exists here as for the "amazing" infant claims.

Adopt a conservative stance with regard to claims about "amazing" mental and emotional capacities in newborns and fetuses, and about prematurely incorporating *any* revolutionary new ideas into your child-rearing styles.

Toilet Training: When and How

Toilet training is another childrearing issue about which there is a surplus of opinion and a shortage of evidence. According to Freud and a large number of psychoanalytically oriented professionals who succeeded him, toilet training can be a source of enduring emotional problems and personality traits. In the opinion of many people (including this author), Freud was a genius whose views on the causes of emotional illness and the motives that guide human lives have unquestionably advanced our knowledge. On the other hand, I do not believe his theories about infantile sexuality have ever been substantiated in any but minor ways.

Freud believed that toddlers are at the stage in psychosexual development when primary gratification is through the pleasurable sensations experienced in the anal region; disturbance of, or conflict involving, the periodic rewards through anal stimulation thus is likely to cause lasting damage to the growing psyche. Parents who communicate feelings of shame and guilt while toilet training can, said Freud, easily cause serious and lasting emotional damage. Moreover, toilet training attempted at age twelve to twenty-four months confronts the normal willfulness of a child of this age. A child tends to resist the adult and, according to Freudian theory, the result for the child might be lifelong internal conflicts concerning the anal function.

Naturally, psychologists influenced by Freud's thinking are more than slightly concerned with the issue of toilet training. In the 1950s and 1960s Erik Erikson continued in the Freudian tradition to emphasize the significance of toilet training.

Nevertheless, such theoretical analyses have not been supported by research. Given what we know today, there is still no justification for elaborate treatises on toilet training. It is simply one of a large number of necessary chores that are required of all parents.

In the studies we have done, the majority of children developing well were not toilet trained before their second birthday. That may have meant an abundance of diapers to change and clean or purchase, but there was, on balance, less stress for everyone when training began after the child was two. It is easier to deal with diapers than with endless accidents involving clothing, linens, furniture, and so on.

Around age two most children spontaneously show an interest in learning to use the toilet. A potty on the floor that the child can use himself encourages this interest. If there is an older sibling in the home, the desire to imitate may be stimulus enough, and the child may virtually train himself. Much praise from the parents for every success helps. Scolding for accidents, unless really deliberate, never does, and parents should bear in mind that for many children it is impossible always to stay dry at night until they are somewhat older than two.

There is a book that sets forth a method for toilet training your child in one day. The authors recommend conditioning techniques developed in work with retarded children. There is nothing wrong with the procedures, but they are so elaborate that it would be a day I myself would rather skip, either as trainer or trainee.

I don't really think there is any need for extraordinary measures in toilet training. The main thing is that it should not be upsetting to parent or to child. If it is, wait a few weeks, and try again.

A Guide to Various Professionals and Services

There are many different kinds of professionals who work in the area of early childhood education, but I shall restrict my comments to those who work with children under three years of age.

Parent Educators: I believe that in the next few decades we will see a tremendous change in professional treatment of young children. The first people you might think of in regard to early educational develop-ment would be professional educators, but up until the last decade a professional concerned with the first years of a child's life did not exist. I am happy to report that times have changed. As major efforts like Project Headstart matured, there was an accompanying growth in the public's interest in learning during the first years of life. Since the early 1970s, many programs that have focused on learning during the first three years have come into existence throughout the developed world.

Unfortunately, parents may still find it difficult to locate a well-trained and qualified parent-educator in their local area. The number of institutions that train such personnel is small, and there has been no governmental support for the practice. But at least your chances of finding such a professional are considerably better today than at any time before 1970.

Perhaps one of the greatest needs of all is for professional educators who can teach parents how to educate their own children. You cannot, however, have extensive numbers of people trained ade-quately to educate parents without institutional support, at least not until jobs in the field pay better than they do now. For a time, during the early 1970s, we seemed to be moving fairly steadily toward such institutional support, but more recently interest in that movement among federal administrators and major philanthropical organizations has declined strikingly. A bright exception to the trend is Missouri's earlier-mentioned New Parents as Teachers Project. Also, in many parts of the country the Junior League has vigorously endorsed and sponsored more than sixty parent-education programs that focus on learning during the first years.

I remain convinced that the field will continue to grow and that, ultimately, institutional support will be available as a matter of routine governmental responsibility. In the meantime, we have well over 10,000 programs that do focus on learning in the first years (mostly sponsored by grassroots organizations), and we have a very substantial number of professionals in early education who are devoting them-selves to the subject. As inadequate as the current situation is for meeting the needs of all new parents, it is light years ahead of any time before in history. I am not discouraged.

The Physician: Probably the most common kind of parent educator is the physician. Pediatricians, nowadays, are not as worried about rickets and malnutrition and other infant diseases as they were thirty or forty years ago. Instead, most of their time seems to be spent in coping with the management problems of young mothers. After all, until very recently, and in many instances even today, the pediatrician was the only professional with whom new parents had routine contact. Unfortunately, except for brief exposure to the subject of child development during medical school training, and whatever they may have gleaned from childrens' parents, most physicians have not been adequately trained for this particular task. That picture seems to be changing, and there are signs of a move within pediatrics to improve training in early education. For the time being, however, it probably would be wise for you to consider pediatricians, physicians, or nurses as best qualified to provide help with the child's medical needs, narrowly defined, rather than to look to such sources for information on language acquisition, personality growth, and discipline.

Also note that pediatricians vary extensively in their approaches to educational issues. Some, for example, may have a strong psychiatric orientation and may offer psychological guidance about the emotional well-being of the baby. Will this guidance be entirely appropriate? Very possibly. But you can see that in such cases the proper roles of educational and medical professionals might become somewhat blurred. When in doubt, try to solicit a variety of guidance on a subject rather than depending upon a single source.

Social Workers and Related Professionals: There are also people in social work who pride themselves on providing professional assistance in the area of child-rearing. Since social workers become intimately involved in the problems of a large number of families, they are often asked by young parents to give advice. Public health nurses, visiting nurses, homemakers, and Child Study Association people—a volunteer group that advises parents, all from time to time offer guidance, yet none of their professions provides high-caliber training in parent education. And even if someone in one professional capacity or another were to claim to have had exposure to all the information that was available about early educational development of children, if that exposure took place more than fifteen years ago the chances are high that he would not still have a substantial background in this topic.

The Developmental Daycare Professional: A new kind of professional has been surfacing in recent years as the result of the growth of daycare. Although daycare was not primarily intended for children under three years of age, increasingly such young children are being entered in daycare.

Daycare was conceived primarily to serve the purposes of parents rather than children. Until fairly recently, as long as a child was safe and reasonably happy, the daycare experience was considered adequate. In the last ten to fifteen years, with the growing interest in early learning development, such requirements have no longer always been considered adequate, and the result has been what is called "developmental" daycare. The definition of developmental daycare not only includes, but has as its highest priority, the educational development of the child. So far so good, but though there are increasing numbers of talented professionals in developmental daycare, the caliber of training most have received still suffers from the general immaturity of the field. If you are lucky enough to get into a developmental daycare operation attached to a university or a government facility, your child will probably receive much better care than in most unaffiliated daycare situations.

Child Psychiatrists: Child psychiatrists do not often work with children under three. Occasionally you will find a program for the early treatment of actual or potential emotional handicaps, but these are areas where science has little to offer parents beyond a sympathetic shoulder to lean on and some general support or advice. A two-year-old child with a significant behavior disturbance is a difficult case for *any* professional. If you have a child with a behavior disturbance that could be significant, you should of course consult and work with your physician or other health professional; but you must not expect the same type of "cure" that you might expect in, say, the areas of orthopedics or infectious disease. If you find a psychiatrist who seems to you too overconfident of positive results, you have reason enough to beware.

A few years ago a fine book was published that I have been recommending to people ever since. Called *A Parent's Guide to Child Therapy*, by Richard Bush, it offers a well-written commonsense approach to the subject of behavior disorders and emotional difficulties in early childhood. The book provides guidance for parents facing a child with possible emotional difficulty who are unhappy with the help they are getting from a physician and have nowhere to turn. It gives a full picture of the various kinds of behaviors that worry parents and sorts out those that have significance from those that do not. It also indicates the different kinds of professionals that one can use in dealing with different sorts of problems. All in all, this book is a very valuable contribution to the literature.

In 1977 an organization known as the National Center for Clinical Infant Programs was established to improve and support professional initiatives in infant health, mental health, and development. This multidisciplinary group with headquarters in Washington, D.C. was started by a wonderful physician named Reginald Lourie; today it sponsors a good deal of the best research and training on the subject of the very young child and mental health. It is from organizations such as this that we can expect to see the growth of a very substantial resource for parents as the years go by.

Then, too, do not overlook the counsel you might get from someone who has raised three or four, or more, children and has, along with a good memory, a great deal of warmth and common sense. You may well find that such a veteran parent will be better able to help you deal with your concerns about the first years of life than most professionals.

A Guide to Information about Children

Where can you go to get the best information about children?

First of all, you can both make use of the materials found in this book and of the advice of reliable friends who have already faced some of the problems that now confront you. In addition, you can resort to a huge number of books, both technical and nontechnical, droves of magazine articles, many government publications from the U.S. Printing Office, an occasional TV program, and films and videotapes that can be rented. You can also seek advice from various professionals, of the sort mentioned in the previous section. Don't put all your eggs in one basket, however. Consult more than one source, and try to get the best materials available; never depend solely on any one of them. The more information you can get, the better.

Books: There are three kinds of books that first-time parents should have. One kind of book should deal with the physical well-being of the child. This book should be written by a qualified physician or group of physicians. The classic of the field is, of course, Dr. Spock's *The Common Sense Book of Baby and Child Care.* But there are other equally valid treatments, such as *The Child Health Encyclopaedia,* authored by the Boston Children's Medical Center and R. I. Feinbloom. Please note that we recommend these books principally for their practical knowledge on the physical well-being of the child; they excel on topics such as nutrition, disease, and growth of the body. But if a subject like discipline is included, as it often is, I would suggest that you need not take the book's advice too seriously. The same would apply to any topics that have less to do with medicine than with learning or education.

The second kind of very useful book is the kind that my colleague, T. Berry Brazelton, specializes in. During his long, distinguished career as a practicing pediatrician, Dr. Brazelton became especially sensitive to the classical anxieties that plague intelligent young parents. In books such as *Infants and Mothers* and *Toddlers and Parents* he does a fine job in pointing out typical sources of anxieties and providing suggestions on how to cope with them. Another sort of book in this second category also provides support on parenting young children, but from the point of view of parents themselves. An excellent example, *The Mother's Book* by Friedland and Kort, contains several dozen candid personal accounts by mothers on the emotional aspects of motherhood. Some of the topics are pregnancy, post partum changes, breast- or bottle-feeding, and redefining relationships. It is a beautiful piece of writing.

The third category of book is about behavior and learning, a book that tells you what babies are like during the first years, how they learn, obstacles to the best learning, and things that you can do to help. Behavior and learning are, of course, what this book is about.

Although these are the basic kinds of books most needed by young parents, there are many other books that you might find interesting, informative, or valuable. For example, Konrad Lorenz's *King Solomon's Ring* has an absolutely marvelous description of behaviors of other animal species, many of which help cast light on the behavior of human babies. Parents who want to pursue the fascinating subject of the development of intelligence in children further should look into the research and writings of Piaget, and the best single introduction to that work can be found in the book *Intelligence and Experience* by my old friend of many years. Of Piaget's own writings, the most important is *The Origins of Intelligence in Children*, but I would first recommend either Hunt's book or Maryanne Spencer Pulaski's, *Your Child's Mind and How It Grows*, since Piaget is not easy reading.

For more specifics on these and other potentially interesting books, please see the section on recommended readings.

Films and Videotapes: You can rent good films and videotapes on the development of the young child from rental libraries all around the country. Yeshiva University, Boston University, Penn. State University, all have film libraries, and there are others who will send you materials for private or group showings at very moderate rates. You can get specific information on such materials by writing to us at the Center for Parent Education, 55 Chapel Street, Newton, Mass. 02160. We offer literature that contains reviews of most such available materials. From the Center you can also obtain our TV series, "The First Three Years," on videotape or film.

Magazines: For years magazines have specialized in the subject of parenting, and for good reason, since there is no more interested, motivated, and open-minded student of early childhood than a first-time parent.

Magazines for new parents are of decidedly uneven quality, the most consistently solid material we have read appearing in the magazine *American Baby.* But you must never assume that just because something appears in print, it is likely to be true. In our Missouri Project Resource Centers we have a large sign on the wall that reads: "Caution. Just because it is in print and here, you must not believe it is true. If it worries you or conflicts with what you have been learning in our program, please talk to us about it." Enough said.

Government Pamphlets: The U.S. Government Printing Office has produced a series of brief pamphlets on raising young children. *Infant Care,* the best known of these, is available for about $1.00. Along with the Bible and Dr. Spock's books, it is one of the best-selling publications in this country. Still, though such pamphlets are adequate beginners' texts, you will have to look elsewhere for many important details.

Since early education is basically a responsibility of government, the federal Department of Education or your local school system *ought* provide the childrearing information that you need. I predict that sooner or later they will.

Professional Testing of Young Children

The testing of young children for educational progress during the first years of life is of absolutely fundamental importance. To be able to spot something going wrong as soon as possible is essential if we are to give each child the best possible chance of making the most of whatever they bring into the world. Unfortunately, this is yet another area that has been adversely affected by the scarcity of useful research. For example, I have emphasized repeatedly the role of curiosity in early learning development. Yet to this day we have next to no scientific knowledge about its day-to-day development. Nevertheless, we do have enough information and experiences to make this promise: With a proper program of screening we can spot anything important that is going wrong in most of the major areas of development.

The Importance of Gesell's Work: Dr. Arnold Gesell did pioneering work on the general development of young children back in the 1930s. From his research, done with the children of 109 middle-class families in New Haven, Connecticut, he was able to describe the general shape of early development. On the basis of that early research Gesell produced a test that could be used by any pediatrician to screen children for gross normality. His test, in widespread use ever since, has proven to be extremely valuable in research studies and private practice all over the world.

Shortly after Gesell's test came into general use, new and supposedly improved tests of a similar nature began to be produced; we now have a fair number of them. They include the Bayley Test of Infant Development, the Cattell Test, and the Denver Developmental Test. Significantly, all of these tests depend largely on the work of Gesell, with each of them using items that very much resemble those of the original Gesell schedules.

If these later tests have any advantages over Gesell's original test, they lie solely in the realm of technical improvements. For example, the Griffiths Scale from England (created by Ruth Griffiths) is technically much better than the Gesell Test, but its items very closely resemble those of Gesell. The last fifteen to twenty years have seen some progress in early-assessment and general-developmental testing, but much more basic work still needs to be done.

The Necessity of Varying Evaluation Systems: A consideration to be kept in mind in early testing is that at about thirty months, a child changes in important ways from one kind of testee to another. The child over thirty months is assumed to have enough language skill so that language can be used in instructing him during the testing process. The child under thirty months, on the other hand, is unreliable in language skills and is, therefore, generally tested as if he had little or no language. In this respect, testing of a very young child more closely resembles evaluation of the abilities of simpler animal species, while testing of children over thirty months of age more closely resembles the kind of testing you may remember from your own school days.

Testing of infants has traditionally employed both the mother's reports of what a child can do and the use of machinery—such as the electroencephalograph, which produces records of brain activity that can be examined for signs of abnormal development—or optical instruments, such as the retinoscope or the opthalmoscope, to check vision. Mothers' reports are also essential, even though it has been repeatedly found that their reports of the capabilities of their children, particularly in the realm of learning achievement, are seldom as reliable as those generated by less partial observers. But mothers, nevertheless, have important information about their children that no one else could possibly have.

The Problem of False Positives: A problem that complicates the testing of young children is that of false positives. Put simply, a *false positive* is a symptom or a behavior that suggests there is something wrong with the baby but that eventually proves not to have been meaningful. This is so common that pediatricians and other child development testers have adopted a very conservative attitude toward the significance of occasional symptoms during the child's first year.

The problem of false positives puts the professional into a dilemma. If she conscientiously reports every anomaly or unusual element of behavior to the baby's parents, she can cause the parents much needless anxiety. Yet if she ignores such signs, she runs the risk of paying insufficient attention to the earliest point at which a real problem begins to develop. Parents should, therefore, be patient and understanding with their physician or a psychological or educational tester when it comes to the evaluation of behavior during the first two years of life.

General Development Tests: By far the most common procedure that could be called educational testing is the testing of general development. The Gesell Schedules are widely used for that purpose, in spite of their age, as are some of the newer tests. In our own work, for example, we routinely use the Bayley Scales to test all of our children under two years of age. Such scales generally produce at least two and sometimes as many as four scores. From the Bayley the tester calculates a mental and a physical score. The Gesell generates four subscores and a fifth overall score called the "development quotient," or DQ, so called to distinguish it from the "intelligence quotient," or IQ. For many years professionals have acknowledged that children under two years of age do not show the same forms of intellectual capacity that older children and adults do. Nevertheless, the Bayley Scale does have a mental index, though what kind of mentality it measures is unclear.

The Gesell Schedules enable a tester to gauge a child's overall DQ. The tester also calculates a motor score, a personal-social score, a language score, and an adaptive score. The testing on these general developmental tests, particularly for the child under two years, is predominantly a matter of eliciting performance by the baby through the use of attractive materials or by asking the mother to report on the child's behavior at home. The examiner may present the baby with one-inch red wooden cubes; the examiner then moves aside and watches the baby's behavior with these cubes. The behavior can range from ignoring the cubes to building towers with them.

On the basis of typical behaviors of the children in this original sample, Gesell created a framework within which the behavior of other children might be placed and compared. Other items on such tests involve eliciting reflexive behaviors. For example, you can determine how much head control a baby has by placing him on his stomach and waiting a while; he will generally produce the behavior in which you are interested, head rearing. Often in the thirty minutes an examiner sees the baby, he will not hear many of the words that a baby of eighteen months might occasionally use at home. Even if he hears them he might not recognize them. This is where the mother's knowledge of her child's vocabulary comes into play.

These developmental tests are widely used, and some people use them to test children right up through entry into kindergarten. Generally speaking, scores on these tests with children under one year of age do not have any predictive value, with one important exception: if a child repeatedly scores very low you probably have something to worry about. By "very low" we mean somewhere below 85 on tests where the average score is 100. To score a little below average is not usually significant. Consider two one-year-old children, one who scores 95 on one of these general tests and another who scores 115; at *three* years of age, the low-scorer is no more likely to score under 100 on an intelligence test than is the high-scorer.

Testing the Foundations of Intelligence: Let us turn now to the testing of the four educational foundations of the first years of life as described earlier in this book.

Testing Language Development: In a crude sense, the general developmental scales, particularly the Gesell type, can be used to generate information about a child's language development. There is, indeed, a language subscale within the Gesell, but such tests are neither powerful nor very reliable.

The Harvard Preschool Project developed a very good scale for assessing language development starting when a child is around seven months and extending to his third birthday. It assesses the development of receptive language, *not speech*. It depends very heavily on what the child *does* in response to situations and verbal instructions. This scale, though experimental, is very useful, and we use it in monitoring language acquisition in our Missouri Project. We have found children who, at fourteen months, scored fine on the Denver Developmental Test but, in fact, were significantly delayed with respect to early language development.

Recently there has appeared a second language scale that we feel comfortable recommending. It is called the Reynell Developmental Language Scale, created in Great Britain out of a project working with developmentally delayed children. Although its normative data refer only to children growing up in England, that information sufficiently appropriate for use in the United States and Canada, and indeed the scale is gradually coming into broader use here. Technically more sophisticated than the Harvard Preschool Project Test, for more precise examinations it is to be preferred.

Both screening and testing (which provides more precise information than screening) are invariably fairly difficult procedures with children less than thirty months old. In addition to the fact that such children have fragile language skills during the period from fourteen to twenty-four months, the typical child's reluctance to interact with unfamiliar people will interfere with any procedure of this kind. Interestingly, it is easier to test a child either of three years or one year than it is to test a child of twenty months. Clearly then, in trying to interpret the meaning of the screening or testing procedure for children under two, one has to be cautious. Repeated indications that a child knows something can usually be depended on, but if a child fails on some item on a test it is often not from inability but rather that he is simply not cooperating.

Testing Social Development: Social development is assessed, in the same generally crude manner, by general developmental tests. It is also assessable using experimental instruments that our Preschool Project has produced. We have, as this book has indicated, identified eight qualities of interaction with people that can properly be called social skills and that seem to have substantial importance in terms of normal social development. The Preschool Project instruments do a fair job of judging how well a child is proceeding in these areas. Nevertheless, they are still crude, unfinished instruments that leave much to be desired.

Unfortunately, even to this day there are no other choices of consequence. There are several other procedures that are labeled tests of social ability or status, but none of them focuses on such interpersonal skills as effectiveness in getting someone's attention, ability to use another as a resource, and so forth. This lack of procedures is directly linked to the absence of fundamental research in this vital area of human development. Until now intelligence, language, and perception have been much more popular than social development as topics for research in infancy. Given time, the situation will improve, but for now we have much to do in this area.

Testing Curiosity: We draw nearly a total blank when it comes to testing curiosity. Difficult though it may be to believe, there has been no basic research in this area. We have no standardized instruments for assessment, nor do we even have any well-developed experimental instruments.

Measuring the Development of Intelligence: The development of intelligence is crudely tested by certain portions of the general developmental tests. The Bayley Mental Index is related in some sense to the growth of intelligence, as are the Language and Adaptive Scales of the Gesell. How they are related is not precisely known. The Bayley Mental Scale begins to relate well to later, more established tests of intelligence once the child reaches her second birthday, and very high or very low scores on the Bayley Mental Scale from age two on generally indicate underlying stable patterns of development. These extremes, however, only help us to identify the true intellectual status of a relatively small portion of two- to three-year-old children.

For the first two years of life the most sophisticated treatment of developing intelligence has to be based on the work of Piaget. There are now a few tests available that have been drawn directly from his basic research. Although these tests are nowhere as technically well developed as some of the older developmental tests, they are the most promising with respect to monitoring intellectual growth in the first two years. These "tests of Sensorimotor Intelligence," like the tests for general development in the first two years of life, only identify whether a child is progressing normally or is falling behind. In a population that consists of children free from pathology, growing up in average families, you rarely will find delays on tests of sensorimotor intelligence in the first two years.

The situation changes once children reach two-and-a-half years of age. For a long time about the only test that could be used for such children was the Stanford-Binet, not the powerful instrument with a thirty-month-old that it is with older children. More recently a more appropriate test was produced by the late Dorothea McCarthy—the McCarthy Scales—and early in the 1980s another new test appeared that may be better still, the Kaufman Assessment Battery for Children. We are, therefore, currently able to do a much better job in assessing intelligence in the age range of thirty to thirty-six months than ever before.

Testing Other Fundamental Types of Development: Moving from learning achievement, we now turn to other types of development tests that are sometimes given during the first three years of life.

Assessing Neurological Damage: The central nervous system is the physical site of all learning achievement and much else beside. Traditionally its condition is the province of the physician. At birth and soon after, most babies are examined closely to determine if there is any significant damage to the central nervous system, since severe damage is generally detectable early on. Yet it is also the case that many children who appear to be seriously damaged in the first days of life often later prove to be normal.

For quite some time poeple have been working on ways to test for borderline, yet prognostically significant, neurological damage. Not much progress seems to have been made. In some of our research, when the children were about two weeks old, we used a neurological examination developed by the European pediatric neurologist Heinz Prechtl, but a fair number of leading physicians in this country do not accept his views. These very early neurological examinations consist primarily of eliciting reflex behaviors in the baby, for example fanning the toes after stimulation of the soles of the feet (Babinski reflex) and eliciting the head-righting reflex, a sucking or pupillary reflex, and so on. Such tests overlap with the general developmental tests whose motor scale items are often identical.

Assessing Vision and Hearing: Vision and hearing are such important prerequisite capacities underlying learning development that they should be treated repeatedly during the first year of life. In fact, they are only tested adequately in rare cases, though that situation appears to be changing.

There has long been a disagreement between ophthalmologists and optometrists about visual function in early development. The ophthalmologist is a physician who specializes in diseases of the eyes; whereas the optometrist is not a physician, his role being to measure eye function. The territories of these professionals overlap, and instead of cooperating they tend to quarrel.

All physicians who have responsibility for health care do some sort of visual examination of children beginning shortly after birth. These examinations are generally cursory. (Although some highly trained and outstanding pediatricians do considerably more than the average, some even going so far as to check visual abilities in three-, four-, and five-month-old babies—for example, looking to see if their eyes focus well on nearby objects, whether they track moving objects well, etc.) But the first time the *majority* of children get sophisticated visual assessment is when they enter school. This is much too late.

Ophthalmologists, who do more sophisticated examinations of the eyes, are nevertheless more inclined to focus on the state of health of the eyes than they are on the important visual functions such as focusing. Indeed, the opthalmologist characteristically uses drugs to put the eyes into a state where the focusing mechanism is not working.

To be sure, a small minority of leading optometrists may do considerably more, even in the first months of life, in that they also check the function of the eyes in their natural undrugged state, attempting to measure the infant's capacities in such areas as three-dimensional vision, visual convergence, and tracking in one or another major direction. But as I say, they are the minority.

There is, however, some good news. The frequency of deficits in vision during the first few years of life is remarkably low, probably less than 1 percent of all children. In addition, many of the defects that do occur tend to be so obvious that almost any cursory examination will detect them.

As bad as it is to have children with undetected but significant visual deficits, it may even be worse developmentally for a child to have an undetected hearing deficit. Hearing usually is crudely tested at birth and at regular pediatric examinations, but the typical test does not amount to much more than determining whether a child is quite deaf. Obviously this is not enough; children can respond to fairly loud noises and still have very substantial deficits in discriminative power. It is now clearly within our capacity to do sophisticated hearing screening from the time a child is about fourteen months of age. Since language development begins at about six or seven months and moves forward substantially in the next year or two, it seems obvious that any child who has a correctable hearing deficit should be assisted before he gets to be six or seven months of age.

Although this is not now being done routinely in this country, I predict that it will be in another decade or two. For example, two institutions have in recent years created new instruments like the acousticotoscope that make the assessment of early hearing function, at least on a screening basis, simple enough for most any organization to do. Because of the development of better instruments and because of the rapidly growing awareness of the importance and the prevalence of mild to moderate hearing losses in the first two years, I am confident that we will eventually see this problem properly tended to. In the meantime, I urge you to make sure that this particular part of your child's functioning is looked after properly. For more information see the section on the importance of early detection of hearing losses.

What Happens after Thirty-six Months of Age?

Sometimes when I present my views about the importance of the first three years of life I notice sad looks coming over the faces of parents. These sad expressions are usually followed by the several questions: "Is it all over after three? Is there nothing further I can do about my child's development? Is there no way I can compensate for the inevitable mistakes that I probably made?"

Answering these questions is rather difficult for me because to some extent I really *do* believe it is too late after age three. But the qualifications I place on this statement are important. Of course, children continue to develop after age three. Indeed, I am inclined to believe psychologists like Erik Erikson who hold that human beings continue to develop in important ways until they die.

Based on almost three decades of studying human development, however, I do believe the degree of flexibility that humans have, their capacity for fundamental change in lifestyles, their intellectual abilities, all decline steadily with age. This has been the theme of any number of studies of child development, and I do not know of anyone who has studied human development in any serious way over the years who disagrees with it. What is at issue is the *degree of flexibility* that remains at various stages of life and our capacities as individuals and as a society to make optimum use of that flexibility.

In this respect, Hollywood may have misled us. During the golden years of Hollywood, when so many of us spent so much time at the movies, a thematic staple was sudden and dramatic conversion. On the screen, before our very eyes, we would see adult human beings being converted from nasty, vicious, small-minded people to abruptly enlightened, brand-new, wonderful human beings, all thanks to a single dramatic event. Often the principals were teenage boys and girls who seemed to be on the wrong track but who, as a result of meeting up with somebody like Spencer Tracy or Edmund Gwenn, suddenly "found the way."

When a movie like "The Bad Seed" was made in which a young child was portrayed as completely evil from the earliest days of her life, regardless of experience, audiences throughout the country were shocked. Such a point of view is inconsistent with American principles such as "hope springs eternal; there's always room for change; we can always aspire to the best; it is never too late."

The truth is less consoling. My feeling is that once a child reaches two years of age, his primary social orientation has been established and from then on it becomes increasingly difficult to alter it significantly. For example, if a child has been taught that the world revolves exclusively around him, that if he simply insists on having his way he will always find resistance crumbling, he will be predisposed to operated in a self-centered fashion in his subsequent interpersonal relationships. This does not mean that a three-year-old spoiled child cannot be changed; what it does mean is that it probably will not be easy to do and that it will become progressively less easy—and at some point probably impossible—as the child grows older. Nowhere in child-development research have we demonstrated a strong capacity to alter early personality patterns or early social attitudes.

Of course, despite this lack of demonstrated ability to make fundamental personality changes after the early years, we have all got to keep trying. It seems to me that each person responsible for influencing the growth and development of young humans has no choice but to continue to do the best he can, at *all* times, to induce the most beneficial course of development for every child in his or her care. Indeed, I believe, though I cannot prove, that there *is* capacity for change, even including dramatic improvement, after the child is three years of age. But the burden of evidence, along with common prudence, compels us to put most of our faith in the *prevention* of difficulties, rather than in the hope of being able to remedy them later on.

In our research on the first six years of life we found that children doing remarkably well at three years of age would be much more likely to exhibit the major elements of competence that distinguish the outstanding six-year-old. What we found between the ages of three and six years was a process of refinement of abilities already in place, rather than the emergence of new abilities. Thus the description in this book of the special attributes of the well-developed three-year-old applies just as well to the six-year-old, the differences being only of degree.

Another aspect of the three- to six-year-old range that deserves reemphasis is the growth of interest in peer activities during this period. True social interest in peers seems to begin at about two years of age and apparently continues to grow steadily, so that by the time children enter adolescence you frequently find that what peers think about a child may be considerably more important than what parents think. This seems to be a developmental fact that accompanies the shifting of interest away from the nuclear family, a long-term process wherein a human being goes from total dependency to as much independence as any of us ever achieve.

Piaget claims that one particularly important plateau is reached somewhere between six and eight years of age, as children leave egocentric modes of thought and move toward what he calls "socialized thought." As a child comes to value her peers she becomes very much interested in being understood when she speaks to them. By seven or eight years of age this need to be understood causes her to start thinking about how to frame her ideas so that another person can deal with them. In contrast, the three-year-old does not go through such preparatory steps, assuming that because her parents seem to be able to read her mind, anybody she speaks to will be able to understand her.

In Piaget's system a later plateau occurs in early adolescence, when children achieve adult styles of thought and become mature, reasoning individuals. Interestingly, it was Rousseau who advised several centuries ago that the best we could do about early education was to guard *against* it until children reach the age of early adolescence and their "reason matured." Some modern educational theorists believe he was probably correct.

Nursery Schools

A nursery school generally enrolls children between the ages of two-and-a-half and five years of age. Programs ordinarily operate five days a week, for three to four hours daily during the usual school year. Nursery programs vary in what they promise, but most offer enjoyable, challenging group experiences with modest claims for educational benefits. The majority of schools focus more on creating a good transitional social experience between the home and the elementary school than on training for academic readiness.

But what about nursery schools that promise lasting educational gains to those many parents who believe that a successful academic career requires a good nursery school experience? Certainly a well-run nursery school can provide many interesting experiences for a young child. The equipment, routines, and the other children and teachers can be fascinating and great fun. In addition, much learning can indeed take place. Children can be taught to read and write before they enter elementary school. Most can even be taught to tie their own shoelaces. And, of course, they also learn a good deal about the people with whom they interact.

But do these experiences create long-term effects? Does a child who goes to a first-rate nursery school do better in later school programs than one who does not? The answer is *no*. No nursery school curriculum yet devised has been shown to convey any lasting educational advantage to children, not even superiority in social adjustment.

Is there, then, no reason to use nursery schools? Once again, there should be no shame associated with a parent's desire to take an occasional break from raising children. As a means of giving parents, especially women, time for themselves, nursery schools are important.

My wife and I sent all four of our children to nursery school. We did so not because we thought it would help them to excel later, but because we sometimes felt we were drowning in children. We had access to well-run local schools that were staffed by loving and knowledgeable people, and we were confident that the children would enjoy themselves and be exposed to interesting people, materials, and activities. And so they were.

1984–1990 Update

For the most part, information about the education of babies wasn't of serious interest to many people before the late 1960s. Even parents and grandparents who have always been excited by the host of new developments of the first years of life were not particularly oriented toward the long-term educational significance of what they observed. We all just loved our babies.

However, over the last twenty years or so all that has changed. Although we still love our babies, most people, especially those who are updated and informed, are now quite aware that babies are not just playing and growing but are learning a lot as well. Furthermore, most people have become convinced that such early experiences influence later learning in important ways.

Parents and grandparents aren't the only people who've acquired new ideas about this subject in the last twenty years. Research workers, book and magazine editors, radio and television producers, toy manufacturers, and school and political personnel are among the newly interested parties.

Some societal concerns surface and quickly disappear. Interest in learning during the first years of life, however, shows no sign of abating. With so many parties involved, new information and trends continue to appear. In order for a book on the subject to remain accurate and timely, new writing is periodically necessary. That does not mean that all the information in previous editions becomes obsolete. After all, babies still face the same developmental challenges: to achieve mastery over their bodies, to explore the world, to learn to communicate, and, most important, to commit to and receive commitment from at least one older person.

In the preface to each edition, I promise readers that they will find the best information available on early learning in the pages that follow. These next pages then, contain what appear to me to be the most interesting developments of the last five years.

TOYS

Each year as part of the routine professional activity of the nonprofit Center for Parent Education, which I direct, I examine commercial toys (new and old) available for infants and toddlers, a practice I've been engaged in for the last eleven years. In addition, since the late 1960s I have been a consultant for most of the major U.S. toy companies.

Between 1984 and 1987 my review articles usually started out pretty much the same way. I marveled at how many new toys were being offered and how many new companies had begun to manufacture toys for children in the first years of life. Each of those years I found it hard to believe there could be so dramatic an increase the following year. Last year things quieted down. True, there was an increase, but not as great as in the preceding years.

One of the consistent characteristics of the toy industry has been a strong monkey-see, monkey-do mentality that continues to this day. Perhaps the best example is the line of toys that evolved from the original Busy Box. Fisher-Price was the first major imitator of the original Kohner Brothers Busy Box. They renamed the product an "Activity Box" and ever since company after company has come out with their own versions of the Busy Box or "Activity" toys. In another recent instance a new company, Panosh Place, began to offer fabric rather than plastic toys for babies. They also incorporated velcro as the principal fastening device rather than cement or glue. The next year three of the older companies in the industry came out with a line of "soft" toys.

Another consistent industry characteristic is the use of whatever is currently popular in the world of entertainment as a marketing tool. As their popularity waxes and wanes, we see toys with Disney, "Sesame Street," Smurf characters, and so on. What we don't see are substantial increases in the basic value of toys.

As far as I can tell, the only genuine value of a toy is the enjoyment the child gets when he plays with it. The basic indicator of enjoyment is when the baby chooses to play with a particular toy over others. Certain kinds of toys have been consistently valuable in this basic sense. Most any bath toy is going to be played with by most children after the seventh month. The best of them feature water wheels and squirters, not merely floating objects. Also, our research over many years has confirmed that a large, lightweight plastic beach ball is enjoyed by most children in their second year. Indeed, such large, lightweight balls are enjoyed more during the second year of life than *any other* commercial toy! Decorating it with Disney characters doesn't have any impact on whether or not a baby will play with a toy. Of course, it may very well have an impact on the parents or grand-parents who shop for that child.

What, then, is really new in the toy industry in the last five years? The answer is, not much. If you've got a fair amount of money to spend, you can now get voice-activated mobiles. This is new and also more likely to attract a baby's attention than other toys. The reason is simple. Babies make noises fairly soon after they are born. If his noises move an object that is within view, the motion of the object will attract the child's attention. That may not seem like much, but very few toys for children less than ten weeks of age are actually noticed by such young infants. From three months on, an infant will begin to notice a link between the movement of the object and his own sounds. Does this then represent an important step for the toy industry? I don't think so. It's clever. It's appropriate to the child's level of development and she will attend to it at times. However, I don't think it is anything more than that. There is no reason to think that it will improve the child's development; no research has been conducted to support such claims. There is no reason to think it will be especially intriguing. A properly designed and positioned mobile, a crib gym that facilitates hand-eye activities, a mirror, or the aforementioned bath toys or beach ball all provide more effective stimuli.

It's been a disappointment to me that we've not seen any progress in the improvement of the crib gym. For the baby between two and five-and-one-half months of age a crib gym is a highly recommendable toy. Unfortunately there aren't any on the market that are really well designed. We advise parents in our training program to get one of the better, commonly available ones (which we identify for them—like Fisher-Price and AMBI for example) and then follow our directions to modify them to make them more beneficial for the child. We also want the parents to follow *our* directions rather than those of the manufac-turer. Let me explain.

The first requirement for any toy should be safety. Most crib gyms are safe, but should be removed from the crib as soon as the baby shows any signs of being able to pull himself up to a sitting position. That ability can emerge at any time from four-and-a-half to seven months of age and most commonly occurs between five-and-a-half and six-and-a-half months. Next, the crib gym should feature brightly colored objects suspended conveniently for the child to view and touch with his hands. If these objects can be brought to the mouth for gumming, this is even better. Finally, and all currently available de-vices fail this requirement, the objects the child will try to grasp and handle should not easily elude the child's primitive approaches. The worst of the crib gyms use string to suspend objects. Others allow the objects to rotate on a suspension bar, once again making them more difficult to deal with. A semirigid object that yields a bit to a baby's hand pressure, then returns to its original position is the most desirable. We instruct our parents to use masking or drafting tape to make the objects as unyielding as possible. There is enough flexibility in the support system (the straps that attach to the crib rails) so that the hanging objects will remain adequately flexible.

One device that I have become increasingly impressed with is the automatic swing for the very young infant. In the past, I have routinely suggested that parents wait until the baby is at least three months of age before using swings. The reason for that suggestion was that during the first three months, neck and back muscles are generally so weak that babies are most comfortable when lying down. When their upper bodies are raised, their heads droop one way or the other and their torsos tend to curl up. They are certainly not ready to sit up. Unfortunately, chronic discomfort, primarily from various digestive difficulties, during the first two to three months makes life difficult for all concerned. I now tell people that once the baby gets to be four or five weeks old they might consider using a swing to relieve discomfort, provided that they use towels, blankets, or an accessory sold now with such devices to prop the baby's head and back. Mind you, this suggestion is really one to help parents deal with the stress of having their baby crying inconsolably during the first two to three months of their lives. This stress is normal, very common, and very hard to live with. The automatic swing used with support may not be ideal for the purpose, but it is certainly more convenient than the automobile ride that many parents feel forced to use during those early months.

Another comparatively new concept worthy of note is the portable gym for children from two to five-and-a-half months of age. Crib gyms are hard to utilize unless they are mounted on cribs. Playpens, bassinettes, strollers, and carriages are not really designed to handle a crib gym, yet few toys are as intriguing to children at this age.

What to do? Now there are at least two kinds of portable gyms available. Both have four angled legs, each about two feet in length. There is a cross bar at the top from which plastic objects are suspended for the baby to look at, strike, grope for, explore tactually, and so on. Neither model suspends these objects in the proper semirigid manner. Nevertheless, when a baby is cranky and at some distance from the crib, these devices can provide a developmentally appropriate kind of activity that calms the baby at times or seems to keep expressions of discomfort at bay.

A *warning.* One of these devices has already been recalled because of relatively small objects that could separate from the larger toy and cause gagging if they were to get to the baby's mouth. Then too, if you can do something about making the objects the baby grasps for less likely to move away as the child approaches them you'll improve the toy markedly.

BOOKS AND MAGAZINES

New books on how to raise babies just keep coming. Milestone books are very, very scarce. We have seen the passing of an era in that Dr. Spock has finally decided to turn the reins over to a younger man, Dr. Michael Rothenberg. He will continue to produce new versions of Dr. Spock's books for the foreseeable future. Dr. Spock's books have been a gold mine for his publisher and an inspiration for the industry. However, as the field has evolved, Dr. Spock has acquired competition. Lots of competition. Editions of his book traditionally have covered basic medical topics and also (to some extent) what I call educational issues, most notably discipline. During the 1960s when there were few other books available, Dr. Spock had the field to himself. There was simply no one else to turn to. Now, however, the competition is fierce. There are first-rate medical texts available. For example, The Children's Hospital in Boston has published a very popular competing volume (see Recommended Readings, p. 364). In addition, there are large numbers of books available on subjects such as discipline, language, intelligence, social and personality development, and the like.

Other types of books have surfaced within the last ten years. In the previous edition of this book, I recommended the *Mother's Book: Shared Experiences*, edited by Friedland and Kort, a collection of essays by mothers in widely varying circumstances. Since then, they have created the *Father's Book*, another solid contribution to the richness of the parenting experience. There have been several other equally delightful books written by nonprofessionals about fathering. Of course, this theme reflects societal changes since the emergence of feminism in the early 1970s. There seems to be no question about the serious interest many young fathers now show in the child-raising process.

Child-care controversies have remained intense. As you might therefore expect, we continue to see new books published on that topic as well (see Recommended Readings). There have been a number of useful books published during the last few years on problems of safety, particularly those designed to help young parents modify their homes for crawling and climbing infants and toddlers.

Another kind of book that continues to be published comes from the very large publishing firm and reflects their awareness of a very widespread need. Both Time-Life Books and Better Homes and Gardens have come out with new books, or new editions of earlier ones, on child rearing. None of their books is either groundbreaking or especially impressive in content, but the remarkable marketing ability of such organizations is a guarantee that many tens of thousands of such books will be sold.

Dr. T. Berry Brazelton's books have been around for many years and continue to increase in number. In the past I have praised them for their insight and compassion. However, in reviewing one of his new books, *What Every Baby Knows*, I had the unpleasant task of reporting that in my judgment it was a very poor product. My major concern was that instead of focusing on the identification of the normal sources of stress in child rearing and helping parents deal with them, in this new book Dr. Brazelton mostly concentrates on his ideas about the thoughts and feelings of infants and toddlers, an area where I believe he is consistently off the mark. Having been on the receiving end of critical comments, as most of us in the public view have been, I'm sure that Dr. Brazelton and many of his associates are not at all happy with such remarks from me. Frankly, however, I feel anybody who aspires to provide help to parents, no matter what his prestige or standing, has to be judged by every major product he produces. If I were to move from where my strength lies, I would frankly expect to be pummeled by critics. Sadly, a fair number of authors in this subject area (child rearing) seem to me to overreach themselves routinely.

In the past I have frequently complimented the people involved with *American Baby Magazine*. Because of the unusual ability of their long-term editor, Judy Nolte, I think their publication has, overall, been consistently superior to those of their competition. That does not mean that I think that each and every article that appears in their monthly magazine is first rate. The quality is inevitably uneven but, in my judgement, it is higher on the average than that of most other magazines of its kind. Recently the family-owned American Baby organization was purchased by a much larger corporation, the Cahners Company. Along with this change in corporate structure has come expansion. American Baby, in a remarkable partnership with the American Academy of Pediatrics, is now publishing a magazine called *Healthy Kids* and has several other ventures focusing on the first years of life. As yet, I have not seen enough of their new products to be able to make any judgments, but I am optimistic they will be of good quality.

Another major new player in providing magazines and related materials to parents is Whittle Communications of Nashville, Tennessee. They publish a magazine called *The Parenting Advisor*. They also produce large glossy posters each month along with supplemental pamphlets. Their products are more variable in quality than those of American Baby. They represent an enormous financial investment. They are expensively made, widely advertised and distributed, and many new parents are exposed to them. The reader is advised to resist the tendency to assume that expensive publications contain first-rate information. A skeptical attitude is most advisable. Seeking a second and a third opinion is really strongly advised.

NEW RESEARCH

Research on the educational development of infants and toddlers continues to be of much more interest to psychologists than it was prior to the mid-1960s. Over the last twenty years studies of many aspects of the early development of children have been reported in substantial numbers month after month. These studies, however, are not usually designed directly to help parents and others raising babies. There have been a few notable exceptions. The Missouri New Parents as Teachers pilot project (1982–1985) has opened the door for dramatic changes in educational practices. Evidence of its success is that Missouri law now requires that *every* school district offer *free* parent education and support to *all* families with children between birth and their third birthdays. Though the program is not funded sufficiently to serve all families, it does reach a substantial percentage and that percentage has been increasing. In Missouri, families apply at their local elementary schools. In other states, they are invited to join (but only in small numbers to date). In addition, at least thirty other states, most notably Texas, have also initiated their own versions.

These events represent a very rare phenomenon. The results of university-based research performed by the Harvard Preschool Project, combined with those of outstanding work, such as that of Jean Piaget of Switzerland, led to applied research in the public school system in Brookline, Massachusetts, and at four sites in Missouri. The pilot studies in Missouri led, in turn, to statewide expansion and subsequently to adoption by many other states (twenty-five to date).

If only they were maintaining the high level of quality of the pilot projects, what a wonderful evolution this would be! Unfortunately, they are not. Most of the post-pilot work has been seriously underfunded and weak. In response to demands for statewide expansion, the Missouri legislature voted to make the New Parents Program available across the state. Interestingly, they voted for expansion more than a year before they had the results of the pilot study! Because they were offering the program to 543 school districts rather than four, the legislature reduced their financial support dramatically. They also did not provide funds for staff training. For these and several other important reasons, this wonderful initiative is not being pursued effectively: Families receive input much less frequently (often only five times each year as compared to more than twenty during the pilot program), the staff teaching the parents has received four and a half days of preservice training versus nineteen days in the earlier work, and so on. There have not been other substantial applied-research studies relevant to the needs of most young families for help in raising their children.

There is, however, one interesting related study. One of the more publicized early learning programs of the 1960s and 1970s focused on families with low income and education levels. The Levenstein Verbal Interaction Project (VIP) was implemented recently on the island of Bermuda with some 125 families. This program focused on the third year of life. It featured social workers who brought one toy each week to the home and demonstrated how parents might use toys to provide useful educational experiences to their children. The toys were typical of those available in stores. The program was simple and inexpensive. The first VIP programs seemed to produce substantial gains in school-related abilities. A closer look unfortunately suggested that the good results were due to the special qualities of the volunteer families rather than the VIP program. The results of the Bermuda study sadly supported this conclusion. When families were assigned at random to either the VIP program or other services, no benefits of the VIP program were found. This problem of "self-selected samples" is common and difficult to avoid.

The effects of extensive substitute care during infancy have been an important concern since the trend first surfaced during the early 1970s. About two years ago, Jay Belsky, a developmental psychologist from Penn State University, summarized the results of several recent studies on the subject. He concluded that when extensive substitute care begins during the child's first year of life, serious negative consequences develop in the child's subsequent social and emotional life. His report received widespread attention, especially since he is a respected and experienced professional. Several angry rebuttals were issued by equally qualified research workers. No clear winner of the debate has been declared.

In my view, the research that Belsky argues from isn't overwhelmingly convincing in either quantity or quality. Nevertheless, I too remain convinced that extensive use of substitute care, especially group care, is definitely not in a baby's best interest during the first two and a half years of life. I believe it will be at least five to ten years (if not more) before enough information on the topic will be available to make judgments that rest on a substantial amount of high-quality, directly relevant work.

A valuable addition to our collection of tools to assess early receptive language development has recently come to my attention. It is called the Early Language Milestone Scale (ELM) developed by James Coplan, M.D., of the Upstate Medical Center at Syracuse University in New York, in 1982. Continuing research indicates that the ELM is indeed a dependable screening device. The fact that receptive language development can be used earlier than tests of intelligence to identify delayed development (that is, at fourteen versus twenty-four months) makes Dr. Coplan's work quite valuable.

These few comments may seem to you to represent a rather slim harvest of useful research results. I believe a major reason for this low yield has been the lack of genuine interest on the part of the federal government. After all, the enormous amount of research on early development which began in the late 1960s was clearly related to the initiation of the Head Start project. Nothing like that vigorous initiative on behalf of young children has come from Washington for some time.

GOVERNMENT AND FOUNDATION ACTIVITY

It is very unlikely that the huge increase in research on the first three years of life would have been performed if the federal government and many of our largest private foundations had not poured unprecedented amounts of money into this subject area between 1965 and 1975. It is equally unlikely that "Sesame Street," the Harvard Preschool Project, or the Missouri New Parents as Teachers Program would have been created, or indeed that this book would have been written. But what have they done for us lately? The answer is very little.

Since the mid-1970s, both the government and the large foundations have, for the most part, turned away from this subject area. The federal government has returned to its earlier practice of funding a modest amount of mostly esoteric (nonpractical) research through universities as well as a modest number of service programs for handicapped babies. A few of the large foundations have continued to provide important support, most conspicuously perhaps the Bush Foundation's support for training programs, but overall, interest in early childhood has waned dramatically.

Journals that specialize in reports of psychological and related research have regularly published an impressive number of infancy and toddler-focused reports, but only a small number are both well done and of practical value. Progress therefore has been slowed considerably. Three reports come to mind: the Coplan work on the ELM for screening for early language development, the VIP parent education project on Bermuda, and, of course, the report on the success of the Missouri New Parents education project (MPAT) by its evaluators. Of course, there have been others, but not many that I would judge to be of comparable value.

The simple fact is that research on learning and development during the first years of life is no longer a major priority for either the federal government or the country's major private foundations such as Ford, Carnegie, or Robert Wood Johnson. On the other hand, thousands of smaller foundations continue to fund service programs that offer assistance to parents raising young children in many parts of this country. They aren't, however, supporting significant amounts of research on the subject.

Topics of Especially Current Interest

THE SUPERBABY PHENOMENON

Most parents take special pleasure and pride in their baby's achievements. Even the ordinary developmental landmarks such as sitting up and, of course, taking the first steps are sources of enormous pleasure. The appearance of "Sesame Street" in the late 1960s, followed by an explosion of books and magazine articles on the subject of early learning, was in turn followed by the "superbaby phenomenon." Some parents and some entrepreneurs began to work very hard to accelerate the learning process, often in many directions at once. The most visible professional in the field was Glenn Doman of Philadelphia. He initiated the Better Baby Institute in 1978. In four and one half *days*, parents were shown how to teach their babies to read, identify painters and composers, do simple gymnastics, and so on. If you enrolled in his ongoing program, the baby *and you* could enter into Suzuki musical training for the violin and/or the piano.

And Doman was not alone. A concurrent explosion in the toy industry found many a company promising development gains or at least "enhancement." (According to my dictionary, enhancement means gains.) Then came infant gymnastics programs, promising, among other things, improved confidence, self-image, and learning to learn skills.

I have always urged caution about belief in such activities and claims. In our research on excellent development, children during infancy (the first eighteen months of life) chose most of their own activities, except for those such as feeding, bathing, and so on. Furthermore, they were accepted for what they were. In superbaby situations, adults dictate how and when learning takes place. They inevitably keep an eye on whether their baby is progressing adequately toward prescribed goals. While no research has been done on any of these programs to indicate harmful or beneficial results, I can't in good conscience recommend any of them. Infant exercise programs, however, are highly recommendable as long as they are used strictly for enjoyment and sociability.

During the last five or six years interest in superbaby activities has waned. While the Better Baby Institute still operates and has people touring the country on recruiting missions, publicity has all but disappeared. The toy companies, and infant exercise programs have gradually changed their message, though not in all cases. My guess is there will be continued interest, but unless and until someone makes a new, sensational claim, things will be quiet in this subject area for some time to come.

SUBSTITUTE CARE

No subject concerned with infants has been as inflammatory as the issue of substitute care. Unlike the superbaby phenomenon, or ideas about bonding or natural childbirth, this issue is every bit as vibrant today as it was when it surfaced more than ten years ago. It is now commonplace for parents, especially middle-class parents, to place their infants into full-time substitute care six to eight weeks after their baby is born. This dramatic, even radical, change in child rearing is now firmly established. I mourn this development. I am totally convinced that babies reared this way, especially those in group care, will suffer for it. I am equally convinced that their parents will miss some of the very best moments that life can offer.

As mentioned earlier, studies of the effects on babies of the extensive use of substitute care during infancy are being done. However, to do a thorough job of exploring this issue would cost a large amount of money. To explore the emotional consequences, considered by most of us to be the first priority, would require significant improvement in the quality and quantity of assessment techniques. Assessing social and emotional health is extremely difficult to do well. Without effective measurement, all research on causes and effects is suspect. Furthermore, studying long-term effects is problematic, time-consuming, and expensive, and the Republican administrations of the last decade have shown little inclination to appropriate the millions of dollars that would be necessary to pursue this subject seriously. Nevertheless, a modest amount of research has been done and the results have been reported. In 1978 Belsky reported on the state of our knowledge at that time. Although he could not support many of his conclusions, he did note that there were some indications that high quality care might not be harmful to middle-class children. More recently, however, he has concluded that new research strongly indicates that entering a child into full-time substitute care during the first year leads to substantial trouble. These babies develop substantial emotional difficulties, according to his reading of the literature. Advocates of substitute care angrily dispute his findings.

I continue to receive requests for television, radio, magazine, and newspaper interviews on this subject. I *always* dislike the prospect. I *always* accept each invitation, not because I'm combative nor because I enjoy evoking guilt in parents, but simply as a matter of conscience. Until the day that such practices make sense for my own family I will continue to recommend they be avoided.

THE ROLE OF THE FATHER

The rise of feminism during the 1970s spawned the substitute-care issue. It also brought fathers into the world of early child-rearing. Indeed we have even seen the "Mr. Mom" phenomenon arrive: Mothers return to work within months after birth and fathers become full-time stay-at-home parents. I don't know of any statistics on the practice, but in our model program, and as I travel the country, it seems to me that greater involvement by fathers has become a well-established trend, which I applaud. I have yet to meet the father who has invested time in early parenting, whether it be 10, 20, or 100 percent, who has regretted it.

CRYING FOR COMPANY

Nicely developing three-year-olds are very skilled at getting attention in socially acceptable ways. This useful behavior, unlike the seven other especially well-developed social behaviors of the talented three-year-old, is in the baby's repertoire at birth. The cry is an innate, unlearned response to discomfort. It obviously has a vital survival function.

From birth on, the baby's cries most of the time lead to the appearance of an adult and reduced discomfort. By the middle of the fourth month of life, the face and voice of whoever has been regularly comforting the infant elicit smiling sooner and sustain it longer than anyone else's.

At about the same time, along with this natural outcome of many repeated experiences, you will notice that the mere appearance of the regular nurturing person will often stop the baby's crying. This is a clear indication of important early learning.

The third step of this early development of the cry occurs toward the end of the fifth month. When you hear the baby cry and you approach her (from out of sight) something new begins to occur. Now, you'll sometimes find that the baby has been watching for you and using the cry to summon you. When she catches sight of you, her behavior will indicate that she has used that cry *intentionally*. She may quickly cry less or even stop completely and smile. A bit later, the smile may be accompanied by arms and hands extended in your direction: a request to be picked up.

This deliberate use of the cry appears to be the first form of problem-solving behavior in children. In Piaget's system of the growth of intelligence, he cites that during the seventh month an infant will push an obstacle aside to reach for another one. He lists this action as the first intentional behavior, but crying for company seems to fit the requirements and will usually appear at least one month earlier.

HOW TOUGH IT IS TO KNOW

The public needs and wants to know now answers to questions that will guide their child-rearing practices. Unfortunately, some of the information they seek does not lend itself to simple, clear answers. If a writer were to ask a qualified expert over the telephone how to design a new automobile, or perhaps less ambitiously, how to cope with the demands on the front end or on the tires of a new car, the expert would in all probability say something like "That's a strange kind of question to ask me. In order for me to answer it in any responsible way, I'd have to get into subject matter that you, as a lay person, simply wouldn't understand, so you can either have a very superficial answer or you can drop the subject, because it would take quite a bit of preparation before you would ever be in a position to understand the complexities of the situation, and you certainly wouldn't have a ghost of a chance of communicating what you have learned to the public." While the comparison may at first blush seem farfetched, I don't believe it is all that far off the mark.

People who write books concerning early childhood development come in all sorts of shapes and sizes. There are physicians, lay people, academic psychologists, and so on. One particularly relevant type of writer is one who writes for a living and has little or no professional training in education or psychology, but is of above-average intelligence and seeks to explore the newest and the best information in order to prepare his book or other product for the public. This kind of writer is not typical and represents only a small percentage of all those writing in the field. The television research person is of the same category. Over the years I have dealt with perhaps two dozen such people. They are invariably very smart and studious and usually operate with large budgets. Their task is complicated by the fact that in a half-hour or even a full-hour program, they have to teach about or explain issues ordinarily dealt with in a graduate school over a period of a year or more.

I submit that their task is well nigh impossible. People from the media (television, magazines, and newspapers), people who write books, politicians, and indeed the majority of practitioners in related fields having to do with young children, all face the same task, and more often than not, in my judgment, end up failing at it. The problem to which I refer is: coming up with the most accurate and reliable judgment about what to do in respect to real problems such as child care during the first years of a child's life, special teaching to help a child get a head start in life (à la Glenn Doman), and so on.

Recently, I read a review of a new book written by people working at Harvard with support from the Carnegie Corporation, one of the major foundations that tries to deal with the needs of children. The book includes analyses of various facets of the problem, along with suggested remedies. One remedy is intervention for educationally disadvantaged preschoolers. So far, so good. I quote, "The long-term effects of Project Head Start and other preschool programs are now *exceptionally well documented*. . . . Assessment of the longitudinal impact of the experimental Perry Preschool Project (a small two-year program for three-year-olds) initiated in 1962 in Ypsilanti, Michigan, and partially supported over the years by the Corporation, revealed that at age nineteen those who were enrolled in the program were found to be twice as likely as a randomly assigned control group to be employed, attending college or receiving training . . ." I don't know how many times since the first evaluations of Head Start in 1968 that I have heard observers and interpreters point to the success of Head Start and then cite the Perry Preschool Project as proof of that success. In order to do that, the project would have to be *typical* of Head Start activities across the country, yet there is no way on earth that it can be considered typical. In all probability, the Perry Preschool Project was superior to 95 or more percent of the existing Head Start centers (for instance, the teachers were very carefully selected, trained, and supervised; the budget was far more generous than nearly all other Head Start centers; and so on). For the other 95 percent, there is no substantial evidence of success parallel to the Perry Preschool Project.

Another example comes from the world of books. Take, for instance, the Johnson & Johnson product *From Baby to Toddler*, by John J. Fisher (New York: Perigee Books, 1988), a follow-up to two earlier successful Johnson & Johnson ventures written by one of the original authors. It is a considerably better than average book, and the writer is obviously very capable. Yet, I found reason, in several places, to note in the margin "uncritical thinking." What happens is that authors, in searching for the newest and best research results, find something that appeals to them and then use it. It is possible, of course, that there is some activity between the discovery of the report and its use in the book, but I am inclined to doubt that there is much. What kind of activity could there be? Well, one could examine the quality of the research, the reputation of the researcher, and the relationship of that research result to existing information on the same subject. That kind of inquiry is what any well-trained child-development professional would be expected to perform. That critical evaluation is precisely what is not within the realm of capability of people outside the field, no matter how clever they are. This particular book is not as oriented toward new research findings as some. Several books we have looked at during the last ten years have cited dozens of research findings, and usually the same criticisms apply. Indeed, in our parent training programs, we advocate putting a sign on the wall to remind everyone: "Simply because it's in print does not mean that it's true!"

What determines truth? One of the standard requirements in most scientific fields is replication. Most of the problems I see in books that shoot from the hip in terms of "new findings" is singularity. When something is reported by one research team—something different, exciting, dramatic—it should pique one's interest, but should not be immediately believed. If the same sort of finding is reported by three, four, five, or ten independent research teams, *then* the likelihood of validity is increased dramatically.

There are other indicators in determining the validity of a claim, such as the reputation of the person making the claim. One note of caution: Some of the most visible and prominent authors make claims on the basis of grossly inadequate evidence or possess shaky research qualifications even though their public visibility is substantial. Knowing the difference is difficult, unless you operate within the field as a professional.

Another indicator of relevance is whether the claim is consistent with existing information in the field. Of course, if it is a subject about which comparatively little is known, it is much easier for the unsupportable dramatic claim to prevail, sometimes for an extended period of time. For instance, interest in the behavior of babies during the first months of life blossomed in the early 1960s. Reports of remarkable benefits of close physical contact during the first days of life swept the medical community. Later studies did not support the earlier claims, but it was years before such replications were performed to test those claims. Today, no one in the research community insists that there is a "superglue" type bonding effect of close physical contact during those first days. As a result, large numbers of adoptive parents have breathed a sigh of relief.

Research on the effects of early childhood education programs is a complex and confusing affair. Very few people who write for television are aware of something called "regression toward the mean." Indeed, many trained professionals are hazy on this concept. Yet some of our most influential judgments in early childhood education are subject to the impact of this common phenomenon. What it can do, put simply, is lead people to think that a program has wonderful results, when indeed it has none.

One major project on which an expenditure of billions of dollars has been based apparently suffered critically from this phenomenon. Let me explain.

In order to receive money to perform research, the director of this project sought out state funding for research on mental retardation. The principal requirement for procurement of the funds was that the subjects have IQs of less than 85 on a standard measure, the average score of which would be 100. The director tested a large number of children from a low-income population. From previous work, the expectation from this group as a whole would have readings in the low 90s. Naturally, the scores of any sizeable population would form a bell-shaped curve, with some small fraction of the population testing perhaps as low as 75 or less, and an equally small fraction testing as high as 115 or more. What the director did was to identify a subgroup of children whose scores were slightly below 85. He then applied for state funds. He subsequently ran an enrichment program and found that after the program, these children tested at considerably higher levels; indeed, slightly above 100. The program was judged a smashing success and has gone on to make an important difference in policy in the years since.

On the surface, everything looks fine, until you explore the issue of regression toward the mean. It is a thoroughly established fact that, under these circumstances, that same group of children with which the project worked, if retested at any time after the initial test, would probably have scored considerably higher than the low 80s. Their test scores would tend to drift upward toward the mean for the total population of low-income family children. This standard finding is a consequence of our limited capacity to be precise in intelligence testing. Initial results of early enrichment programs are pretty much guaranteed to be "favorable" and, in any event, are inflated by this particular factor. There are, of course, procedures to counteract this factor, involving repeated testing of the groups, among other things. To the best of my knowledge, these were not used in this case.

This is one of a number of subtle aspects of educational research to which only someone well trained would be sensitive.

The concept of self-selected sample is another such aspect. If you are looking for a substantial number of families to participate in an educational enrichment study, the easiest way to gather a sample is to ask for volunteers by posters, word of mouth, radio programs, newspaper advertisements, bulletin boards, and so on. People in any community will hear about your efforts and sign up for your program. The problem with this procedure is that any good test scores the children show cannot be fully attributed to the effectiveness of your program. Families who volunteer for these kinds of programs are generally those who are most knowledgeable; most aware of what's going on in the community; most interested in children and education. They are therefore not representative of the entire population. This is known as a "self-selected sample."

This particular problem caused all sorts of grief in connection with Phyllis Levenstein's Verbal Interaction Project (VIP) when it was first reported. The initial success led to dramatic and rapid expansion of the program in several sites across the country, and no doubt influenced a good number of professionals in early childhood education. A few years later, the project was obliged by its funders to assign families, in a *randomized fashion*, to the VIP and to comparison circumstances. When randomized assignment to conditions was achieved, the differences among the groups of children as a result of the various conditions turned out to be nil. Indeed, the Levenstein program is one of the rare instances when a highly visible project was revisited and a significant flaw was identified and reported. Ordinarily, this simply doesn't get done, for the same reason replications are rarely made: Not many people in the business are anxious to pay for such replications. In other scientific fields this might be considered scandalous. In early childhood education it is the norm.

One more example. Recently, I consulted for one of the Fortune 500 companies interested in toys for infants and toddlers. They were spending millions of dollars to explore this venture. They had assigned some very able people to explore this direction. A substantial effort was made to "research" the field of early childhood development. Actually, their research amounted to a rather complete self-taught introduction to early childhood development, that is, it tried to identify relevant research reports, organize them and milk them for what was of practical relevance to the toy industry. In my judgment, this was an admirable but totally unsuccessful venture. They also sought out expert advice in a peculiar way. They went to people teaching courses in the relevant areas at the local university and asked these people to be their guides, recruiting two or three people this way. However, the people they recruited explored only narrow segments of the subject areas and, in general, did a woefully inadequate job. This company was faced with pretty much the same task as the television network news reporter and the gifted lay writer; a task that, after thirty-one years in and around such efforts, I am convinced is hopeless.

What, then, can people rely upon? I can see only one answer. If they are seriously looking for successful results, they are obliged to depend upon authorities. But they'd better be quite exhaustive in their efforts to identify those few who really know what they are talking about and are aware of what is and what is not known. Frankly, I think the best effort I have seen in that direction so far is represented by the Children's Television Workshop, the group that created "Sesame Street" and a variety of other educational programming materials. In my judgment, they have been successful (and, incidentally, only within surprising limits) because of the caliber of their management group, which consists of Joan Ganz Cooney, Lloyd Morrisett, and Gerald Lesser. Morrisett and Lesser were academics and Cooney was the television person.

What does all this mean to you? For one thing, it is intended to give you a sense of what I have learned about operations in a rather wide variety of important areas having to do with early childhood. What I have just described is relevant to the modern childcare scene, early intervention programs, education for parenthood programs, toys, governmental policy, books, and magazines—in other words, this analysis is applicable to just about anything associated with infants and toddlers. Second, it points to a thought I have had in my mind for many years, and that is the importance, in the training of leaders in early childhood education, of high quality exposure to problems in that branch of philosophy known as *epistemology*. Epistemology has to do with the quality of knowledge, and its study helps people evaluate the validity of proposed information. That, along with familiarity with the particular kind of educational or psychological research is, in my judgment, absolutely indispensable for first-rate practice in this field. Without it, there is no way to be sensitive to the effects of self-selected samples, regression toward the mean, dishonesty in research, inadequate replication, inconsistency of evidence, and inadequate weight of the evidence.

A HOT POTATO THAT SOONER OR LATER WILL HAVE TO BE CONSIDERED

In a recent issue of *Empathic Parenting*, Dr. Elliot Barker's journal of The Canadian Society of the Prevention of Cruelty to Children, an article worthy of attention is reprinted from *The Toronto Globe and Mail* of October 2, 1987. The title is "Time to License Would-be Parents?" The author is Marvin Glass. In the article, Professor Glass suggests that it *is* time. He is rebutted by Dr. Morton S. Rapp, a psychiatrist at The University of Toronto. I don't believe their debate settles the issue one way or the other, but I do believe that within the next thirty to forty years we may very well see licensing of this sort. If it is indeed true that what parents do with their very young children has lasting powerful effects, then it seems that licensing may not be such a far-fetched notion.

AN UNUSUAL ORGANIZATION

In August, 1989, the fourth International Congress on Pre- and Peri-natal Psychology was held at the University of Massachusetts at Amherst. The Association was founded in Toronto, Canada, in 1982 by Dr. Thomas R. Verny, author of *The Secret Life of the Unborn Child*. From its descriptive brochure the association appears to be doing rather well. Dr. Verny has written of what he believes to be the dramatically important learning that takes place while the fetus is in the womb and during the perinatal period. What I have read of this theory, especially in Dr. Verny's book, has failed to convince me that this group is onto anything of practical importance, but who knows—I've been wrong before.

THE THREE TOUGHEST PARTS OF THE JOB

For parents with only one child, there are two especially difficult chores: avoiding overindulgence and disciplining the child. For those with two closely spaced children (less than three years apart) sibling rivalry becomes a third, very difficult challenge. These conclusions have emerged from my twenty years of work with families. Helping a child acquire excellent language skills appears to be rather easy. The same can be said for helping with the development of intelligence. Of course, heredity plays a role. Some children will never achieve the levels of ability others will even though they appear to be just as normal at birth. Providing assistance to a child to help him achieve mastery over his body and develop good eye–hand coordination doesn't seem to be necessary. Nor is any special parental input needed for vision or hearing skills to develop. Almost any way you rear a child (excluding, of course, abuse and neglect) will result in good development in those areas. They are either self-taught or maturationally based.

Avoiding overindulgence is another story. Most loving parents usually have trouble in this area, especially with their first children. A description of the problem and how to deal with it has been treated in this book (see page 242). These words are only meant to report that avoiding overindulgence remains at or near the top of the list of especially difficult aspects of parenting.

The same is true of the other two topics. Discipline and coping with sibling rivalry remain as problematic as ever. All three, moreover, seem to be complicated by another recent societal trend, delaying parenthood until women are in their thirties or even older. When you are thirty-six years old at the birth of your first child, it seems as if the tendency to overindulge and/or be in conflict concerning discipline is greater than when you are a younger parent. When you are thirty-six and have a one-year-old (whom you love dearly), the urge is sometimes strong to have a second child quickly (remember the biological clock). Unfortunately, no matter how you feel about the biological clock, two-year-olds don't like one-year-old siblings. Many young couples have asked anxiously about how they can manage very close spacing, clearly hoping that I will say that I don't really mean what I say about the extent of the hazards. The sad fact is that regardless of their needs or my empathy, the rules stay the same. For understandable reasons, slightly older children become jealous and unhappy about the new baby and as a result there is a serious price everyone—older baby, younger baby, and both parents—has to pay. There is only one area where parent education can help and then only to reduce the cost, not eliminate it. By not overindulging the older child, you make it easier on all concerned. A child who becomes accustomed early to having to wait (on occasion) for what she wants; who, at times, is turned down when she asks for things; and who is taught from the beginning to respect the rights of her parents, will have less difficulty adapting to a younger sibling than one who has been overindulged.

NEW PARENTS AS TEACHERS

My Central Focus

I left an engineering career and became a psychologist more than thirty years ago because I wanted to help more people become decent and capable. I wanted to improve the world. I still do. My subsequent career in psychology and education allowed me to pursue the study of human development continuously over those years. Determination was a factor in my longevity. An awful lot of good luck was, perhaps, even more important. I had the good luck to be born in the United States. I had the good luck to be born to a family that lived in the Boston area. I had the good fortune to be working in the Boston area when interest in early learning mushroomed during the 1960s. *If any one* of these factors had not been in place, my work could not have been done.

In the late 1960s I had been directing the Harvard Preschool Project for a few years when the opportunity arose to test parent education in the public schools. Robert Sperber, superintendent of the Brookline, Massachusetts, school system asked if I would help do something with them aimed at learning in the preschool years. I agreed and within a year we had established The Brookline Early Education Project (BEEP).

BEEP's goal was to test the question: Should the public schools help guide a child's learning from birth rather than from the kindergarten age? It was a large, expensive project funded by the Carnegie Corporation, the R. W. Johnson Foundation, and the federal government at more than a million dollars a year, for more than ten years. The staff was multidisciplinary and numbered more than fifty people.

After helping plan the project and procure the money for it I was faced with a problem. I could not continue both the work at the university and with BEEP. I had to choose. I chose to stay with the university. We hired a director for BEEP, and I became the senior consultant.

The project was a failure. It didn't recruit the right kinds of families. It was inundated with affluent, well-educated people who were quick to see its potential benefits. The guidance it offered parents wasn't sufficient nor did it continuously evaluate itself. Early on, when I found that my advice wasn't being followed, I quit.

Though BEEP was a very expensive failure, it received a lot of publicity (any sizeable education experiment associated with Harvard would) and hundreds of people came to visit. One was of particular importance, the newly appointed director of elementary education in

Missouri, Mrs. Mildred Winter. Mrs. Winter liked what she saw at BEEP. In particular, she liked two aspects of the program: The ideas to be taught to parents were based on the Preschool Project's studies of successful families, and the program was offered to all families, not just the poor. She returned to Missouri, teamed up with a remarkable woman named Jane Paine from the Danforth Foundation, and proceeded to spend the next twelve years trying to convince people that BEEP would look good in Missouri.

Mrs. Paine was and remains one of the most impressive educators I have ever met. Highly respected, she worked hard to build support across the state in political, medical, business, and community spheres. She succeeded brilliantly. In the education world Mrs. Winter convinced the state commissioner of education, Dr. Arthur Mallory, of the potential value of the work. Once Dr. Mallory was convinced, he proceeded to lobby hard and effectively for the program. It also helped that the governor, Christopher Bond, and his wife, were expecting their first child (the governor was in his early 40s at the time).

We called the project New Parents as Teachers (NPAT). It was my second chance. Two of my associates and I provided nineteen days of preservice training to the staffs of four proposed sites during late 1981. We began to recruit and serve 380 families in January of 1982. Parents were treated as teachers. They were given the best information we could find about the learning process during the first three years of life. They were taught what babies were learning as they developed rapidly, what tended to get in the way, and what seemed to be effective teaching tactics. *The first edition of this book was the principal source of information.* That book, written in 1974, was a more mature and accurate source of information than was available for the BEEP project in 1970.

The program featured group get-togethers and home visits. We averaged nineteen contacts each year with each family from just before the birth of the child until his third birthday. (For more details on NPAT, see *Educating The Infant and Toddler*, Lexington Books, 1987).

In June of 1984, fifteen months *before* the results were known, the Missouri legislature, flush with enthusiasm and extensive publicity about the program, passed a law mandating the program statewide as part of the education system. This law was and remains the first of its kind. I had mixed emotions. It was potentially a wonderful development, *but* we had no proof that the program was helping children develop into better educated three-year-olds than they would have become anyway.

Throughout 1984, as talk of expansion began, I urged caution and special attention to quality control. Of the nine staff members I trained, perhaps five could become trainers of new staff (with some help from my associates and me). That small team might be able to start another twenty to twenty-five new sites in late 1985. In 1986 we might be able to expand to sixty or eighty additional sites, and so on. Unfortunately, the state department personnel weren't listening. They were planning to start all 539 new sites in 1985! I was dismayed. What to do? I argued for more than a year. I got nowhere. Once again, I quit.

A sample seventy-five children were evaluated by an independent agency as they turned three years old in 1985. Compared with seventy-five nonproject children on measures of language, intelligence, and social behavior, the measures of language and intelligence were quite powerful, while the measures of social competence were weak. There were and are *no* strong measures of social competence in three-year-olds. The project children looked great socially, better in the minds of the testers than the comparison group. In language and intelligence, however, they were clearly superior by a wide margin. In fact they were at the 75th percentile nationally on one measure and at the 85th percentile on the other! *These results were and are sensational and unique.* What an opportunity for public and private education! How gratifying to all of us involved! That's the good news. Unfortunately, there is also bad news.

Since 1985 the state has been making a mess of the program and, worse than that, exporting the mess to twenty-six other states! The successful pilot program cost about $800 per year per family. The state allocated $165 and hoped that some communities would add more, although that was not likely. The state requires five contacts per year with each family, versus our nineteen. The staffs are overworked and usually poorly paid. Turnover is high. The pilot-program staff received nineteen days of preservice training plus two days of in-service training every six weeks for the next three years, 95 percent of which was directly from me. For the statewide programs and for out-of-state people, Missouri offers thirty hours of preservice and, at most, one to two days per year of in-service. The quality of that training is very good, but the quantity is obviously nowhere near adequate. In the pilot programs we worked only with first-time parents, the easiest to work with. The state offers the program to everyone with one or more children less than three years old. There's more, but surely you can see why I'm deeply disappointed. I'm afraid that in a few years, evaluations will show little or no benefits, and the movement toward universal help for new parents will be set back ten to twenty years. I have recently begun a model program in the Boston area in order to demonstrate what the pilot projects were like as well as to train people.

Where, then, do we stand? *The ideas in this book were the sole basis* for the NPAT curriculum. They are therefore *the only ideas* on raising infants and toddlers that apply to most families and have actually been shown to be effective. To be fair, few authors ever see their ideas tested. On the other hand, it should be comforting to the reader to know that there has been solid confirmation of the general validity of this book. That is not to say that the entire contents of this book have proven to be valid: There are bound to be errors. There is still a long way to go before we reach anything resembling a complete science of early human development.

How does the NPAT experience affect you? Interestingly, at this time very few parents have access to excellent training and support such as that offered in the NPAT pilot programs. There are perhaps a very few places in Missouri where high quality has been maintained. If you live in or near Newton, Massachusetts, where I direct the Center for Parent Education, you might call us and see if we have openings. Perhaps I'll try another book showing you how to build your own program. In the meantime, all I can do is wish you and your children well.

Concluding Remarks

The original edition of *The First Three Years of Life* concluded with a few final comments. First, as I observed, it seemed to me then that no job was more important than raising a child in the first three years. Likewise, no job, indeed no other type of experience in life, could offer deeper satisfactions. Finally, I said that our research, and that of many others, seemed to show that most parents had the resources to do a fine job, provided that those personal resources could be supplemented with information and support. I still feel the same way.

Back in the early 1970s there seemed to be a new consciousness of the importance of early experience. Parents, child development specialists, medical professionals, administrators of programs for children, and even legislators, seemed to share a new enthusiasm for measures that would promote a more healthful and stimulating life for young children and their parents. I began to feel that important changes would soon take place, that more and more people would begin to treat the raising of a baby as the vitally important activity it is, and that public school systems would soon begin to assume some responsibility for guiding educational development in the first years of life by providing training and other services to new parents.

Well, it has been over a decade since that hopeful time, and it is clear that I was too optimistic. The excitement of the early 1970s has not yet led to dramatic improvements for families with young children. For the most part, our educational system still operates as if no important learning takes place until a child's sixth birthday is reached.

One particularly frustrating aspect of the current situation is that the federal Department of Education is headed by a man who has been an unusually strong advocate of just these programs. Yet during the last several years the federal government has not only failed to expand its support of such programs, it has actually *cut back* on what little it had previously sponsored.

Nevertheless, there are many tangible signs of a continuing and, indeed, growing commitment to the importance of early learning on the part of many individuals and organizations—that is, professionals, foundations, government agencies at the state level, publishing companies, toy companies, and, most of all, by parents.

Parent-education programs numbering in the tens of thousands have sprung up throughout the developed world. In the United States, they have been sponsored by schools, community colleges, churches, mental health centers, hospitals, and grassroots organizations such as, especially, Junior League groups. These programs, along with what seems to be a more informed generation of new parents, are now our strongest indicators of progress.

There are, however, other factors that complicate the picture. Difficult economic circumstances, along with the growth of the feminist movement, have resulted in a sharp increase in the number of mothers working out of the home. Unfortunately, this powerful and understandable trend conflicts directly with the message of this book. What do you do when the needs of the parents do not coincide sufficiently with the needs of children? Are there ways to reconcile the conflicting needs? I believe there are, and in the recommended readings section of this book I have cited new books that provide guidance to modern young parents as they try to reconcile the apparently conflicting needs of mothers, fathers, and babies.

I have been embroiled in controversy about substitute care ever since 1979, when I remarked to a newspaper reporter that I felt the trend toward transferring primary responsibility for raising a child from the family to others was probably not in the best interests of most children. Controversy notwithstanding, I remain totally convinced that, to get off to the best start in life, what new humans need is a great deal of waking time (first two to three years) with older people who are deeply in love with them. Although this ideal circumstance certainly does not always prevail in families, it is much more often found there than in any substitute care arrangement.

Where do we stand in terms of knowledge and techniques for dealing well with the first years of childhood? First of all we are, in general, much better informed than at any other time in history, thanks largely to the research of the last twenty years. Second, that improved knowledge base is enabling parents to increase the pleasure of raising children and to reduce the inevitable stress of the process. Third, I believe many babies *are* getting off to a much better start in life than they would have without this understanding.

I believe the prospects for universally available programs—such as the Missouri New Parents as Teachers Program—to prepare and assist new parents in childrearing remain good, though not as good perhaps as they appeared to me in 1973. But perhaps my strongest hope for better programs for families with babies arises from the abiding faith in human nature, in that it is a consistent desire of all normal adults to want the best for their children. Raising children well is best accomplished when parents are well prepared and assisted in this most cherished function.

Recommended Readings

INTRODUCTION

This section introduces what I believe to be the most useful books currently available on the development of young children. Obviously the list is not complete since there are undoubtedly writings of excellence that I do not know about. On the other hand, many popular books are missing from the list because I cannot endorse them.

As noted earlier, only a small fraction of the many books available contain detailed, reliable facts about the rapid development of the first years of life, mainly because until recently comparatively few people have sought and discovered such information. Gesell and Piaget are among that exclusive group who have made major contributions.

Though detailed information about infants and toddlers has been scarce, reliable ideas about how to rear a child have been even scarcer. Notice that I say *reliable* ideas. There has been no shortage of opinions and writings on the topic.

CHILD DEVELOPMENT

Stone, J., and J. Church. *Childhood and Adolescence: A Psychology of the Growing Person*. New York: Random House, 1964.

This particular book remains the most readable introductory textbook in college child-development courses. The very practical and knowledgeable authors present a humanistic view of early child development. Other texts may be more informative from a technical standpoint, but no other text gives a better general appraisal of development of the young child.

U.S. Department of Health, Education, and Welfare. *Infant Care*. Government Printing Office, Superintendent of Documents, Washington, D.C. Children's Bureau Publication, reprinted and updated regularly.

Infant Care has, for the better part of this century, been distributed widely to families in this country, and is the single most popular document that the Government Printing Office has ever made available to the public. The fee for the pamphlet has always been nominal (about $1.00), and within its pages you will find a distillation of the conventional wisdom of each decade as it concerns the management of the infant. Historical analyses of the contents and ideas of *Infant Care* have shown that its recommendations to parents have shifted with whatever ideas were prevalent in child development research at any point in time. In fact, the directions to parents on some topics in *Infant Care* have taken a 180-degree turn in the space of only a few years. This vacillation on fundamental issues in child-rearing reflects the immaturity of the knowledge base in the field.

White, Burton L., B. Kaban, J. Attanucci. *The Origins of Human Competence.* Lexington, Mass.: D.C. Heath, 1979.

The concept of competence includes intelligence but is considerably broader. Competence refers to all the significant abilities that a child uses in coping with his environment including language, perceptual and motor abilities, and social skills.

This volume is the final report of our long-term research on well-developing children in the first years of life. Though written for the scientific community, much of it is comparatively nontechnical. Parents especially interested in the research bases for my recommendations might find it worthwhile.

Stone, J. L., H. T. Smith, and L. B. Murphy. *The Competent Infant—Research and Commentary.* New York: Basic Books, Inc., 1973.

This encyclopedic work is a compilation of most of the major approaches to the study of the young infant. It contains selected readings that, when put together, provide the reader with a rather complete, fairly technical introduction to modern research on the very young baby.

Erikson, E. *Childhood and Society.* New York: W. W. Norton & Co., 1950.

Erikson has, in the last two decades or so, had enormous influence on the thinking in fields having to do with the motivation and personality of the young child. Erikson is a psychoanalyst, teacher, writer, artist, and, by anyone's definition, a virtuoso. If for no other reason, you should read this book for the author's beautiful writing style. Beyond a gift for words, however, he weaves fascinating theories of the relationships among early child-rearing practices and the growth of personality and character in the young child. Erikson, heavily influenced by Freud, went considerably beyond Freud's early orientation to include many other factors, giving due respect to the complexity of the human personality. A rich book, a classic, and well worth reading.

Murphy, Lois. *Personality in Young Children.* Vol. II. New York: Basic Books, Inc., 1956.

Lois Murphy, working with four colleagues from related disciplines, studied the growth of personality in a group of nursery school children at Sarah Lawrence College some thirty years ago. This entire book is devoted to the ups and downs of a single, relatively well-adapted child from the age of two-and-a-half years until he is five-and-a-half. The scene is usually his nursery school class, and the result is a rich documentation of normal personality development.

Chess, S., A. Thomas, and H. Birch. *Your Child Is a Person.* New York: Viking Press, 1965, 1972. New York: Penguin Books, 1976.

This book concerns the temperamental qualities of the young child with a special emphasis on individual differences and characteristics that the child brings with her into the world. It tries to make the case that many of the problems of raising children are due to the inherited characteristics particular children bring with them into the world. Although I am by no means totally unsympathetic to their position, I believe the case is somewhat overstated. Nevertheless, this trio of writers had done high-quality research on the early development of personality in young children, and the book is, therefore, well worth reading.

Piaget, J. *The Origins of Intelligence in Children.* 2nd ed. New York: International Universities Press, 1952. (May also be available in paper.)

Without question Piaget has been head and shoulders above the rest of the field with respect to new knowledge about how the intelligence of man develops. His writings are classics.

The Origins of Intelligence, dealing with the first two years of life, is extremely difficult reading. I would advise that you read interpretations of this book by J. McVicker Hunt (see page 360). The extremely courageous, however, may find Piaget's own version a worthwhile challenge.

Hunt, J. McVicker. *Intelligence and Experience*. New York: Ronald Press Co., 1961.

Referred to earlier, a portion of this book is devoted to a translation into understandable terms of Piaget's original work. Other chapters relate Piaget's work to other studies of the same processes. A book well worth reading, you may have to borrow *Intelligence and Experience* from a library, as it is now out of print.

Pulaski, M. Spencer. *Your Baby's Mind and How It Grows: Piaget's Theory for Parents*. New York: Harper & Row, 1978.

The work of Piaget unquestionably contains the most valid and useful introduction to the mind of a baby. Until very recently very few professionals had access to understandable treatments of his work. Pulaski has done a great service by making these brilliant and fascinating ideas available to parents.

Singer, D., and T. Revenson. *Piaget Primer: How a Child Thinks*. New York: Plume Books, New American Library, 1978.

I don't know how this book escaped my notice until now. I have known of the work of Dorothy G. Singer and her husband, Jerome, for more than twenty years. They are preeminent in the field of children's play. We have routinely recommended a book by MaryJane Spencer Pulaski as a good way for lay people to begin to understand Piaget's unique work on the growth of intelligence. Clearly this book (if you can still find it anywhere) is another valuable addition to our inventory for this important purpose. I have often pointed out that if it were not for Piaget's work we would still be largely, if not nearly totally, uninformed about how the mind of a baby works. I still believe that is true. It is therefore quite important to be able to make use of his findings, a need which cannot practically be met simply by reading his original writings. They are far too obscure and difficult to cope with. The examples that Singer and Revenson use to illustrate Piaget's ideas are just wonderful. I strongly recommend this book.

Stallibrass, A. *The Self-Respecting Child*. New York: Pelican Books, 1977.

Stallibrass has had extensive experience with playgroups for two- to five-year-old children in England. She is also an avid student of the child development literature, especially the works of Piaget and Robert White and others dealing with the subject of play. She makes a powerful case for the importance of play during the first two years of life. She emphasizes the numerous physical activities that occupy so much of the time of infants and toddlers, particularly as they relate to mental and social development. In her view the best conditions for the growth of self-respect allow two-to-five-year-olds many opportunities to choose their own activities while learning to interact with other children. This is a notable book.

PLAY AND TOYS

Sutton-Smith, B. *How to Play with Your Children.* New York: Hawthorne Press, 1974.

Singer, D., and J. Singer. *Partners In Play.* New York: Harper & Row, 1977.

Sutton-Smith and the Singers are, in my judgment, three of America's foremost analysts of the play of young children. For those with special interest in this topic you probably cannot find more valid or thoughtfully presented work.

Butler, D. *Babies Need Books: How to Share the Joy of Reading with Your Child.* New York: Penguin Books, 1982.

This is one of the finest books about the very young child that I have encountered. The author is described as a mother, a grandmother, a teacher, and children's book seller. Her position, magnificently presented in this paperback, is that books are more than just desirable and useful, they are mandatory for the very young child, starting with the first months of life. This extraordinarily written book is by an author not only knowledgeable and intelligent but also extremely passionate about the subject. Her grasp of the nature of the very young child—especially as related to the child's interest in sounds, words, themes, and stories, all placed within the parent-child relationship—is remarkable.

Kaban, B. *Choosing Toys for Children.* New York: Schocken Books, 1979.

This lavishly illustrated book on toys for children is written by a friend and long-term collaborator of mine. Mrs. Kaban has a great deal of direct experience with the uses of play materials for young children, and she is an unusually capable author. The book, therefore, certainly will be useful to parents of young children.

Burtt, K., and K. Kalkstem. *Smart Toys for Babies*. New York: Harper Books, 1981.

This is a pleasant and useful book. The authors borrow extensively from *The First Three Years of Life*, and they are at their best when they stick to the subject at hand—how to make interesting and appropriate toys at home. They do not do as well when they write about the educational implications of the toys, sometimes extrapolating inappropriately from the knowledge base. Although the authors cover most main points in regard to toys for children from birth to two, there are a few noteworthy omissions, such as the value of water play in the first year. Nevertheless, this book does contain a great deal of useful information and many good ideas.

SPECIAL ASSISTANCE FOR PARENTS

Dreskin, W., and W. Dreskin. *The Day Care Decision: What's Best for You and Your Child*. New York: M. Evans & Co., 1983.

The Dreskins bring to this important topic the perspective of people who have not only been professionally involved in early childhood education for some time but also have participated in the recent evolution leading to the popularity of substitute care. They modified their nursery school to also become a provider of substitute care, but after almost two years of such experience they were so uncomfortable that they felt they could not continue to offer that kind of service. Furthermore, they became highly motivated to write about the issues involved. The result is this book.

Loman, K. *Of Cradles and Careers: A Guide to Reshaping Your Job to Include a Child in Your Life*. Franklin Park, Ill.: La Leche League, International, 1984.

This book is a serious attempt to encourage women to "have it all," but in a realistic way. The book documents the possibility of continuing a career *and* retaining primary responsibility for one's own children, including successfully breastfeeding. There are extensive and convincing case studies of women who have managed to succeed in this impressive achievement along with discussions of concepts such as flex time, the reduced work week, shared jobs, self-employment, the role of the father, decision making, selecting child care, and so forth. The book is very well organized and written, and the appendix contains an excellent and extensive listing of resources.

Cahill, M. A. *The Heart Has Its Own Reasons.* Franklin Park, Ill.: La Leche League, International, 1983.

This is another constructive contribution to the continuing furor over substitute care for infants and toddlers. Every bit as excellent in its coverage, fairness, and warmth as the Loman book, it is highly recommended.

Brazelton, T. B. *Infants and Mothers.* New York: Delacorte Press, 1969.

Dr. Brazelton is a pediatrician who, over a long career, has concentrated on helping parents deal with the normal anxieties involved in raising babies. The popularity of his writings is ample proof of his success in this sensitive area.

Chase, R. A., and R. R. Reuben. *The First Wondrous Year.* New York: Collier Books, 1979.

This revised work from the Johnson & Johnson Company impressed me. I believe it is particularly strong in dealing with the area of emotional needs of parents from the prenatal period through the baby's first birthday. It has other virtues as well, including its generally excellent treatment of physical development and wonderful illustrations. The reader, however, should be aware of its limitations in the area of learning development. Readers are told to expect only loving behavior between siblings and, in general, told what they would *like* to hear although developmental evidence may be lacking.

Bush, R. *A Parent's Guide to Child Therapy.* New York: Delacorte Press, 1980.

For many years we have been concerned with and frustrated by the problems surrounding emotional difficulties of young children. Until recently we have been unable to suggest to parents, with any degree of confidence, what to do should their very young children begin to show such signs. This book by Dr. Bush is, in our opinion, an extraordinary breakthrough. He provides a remarkably rational and comprehensive introduction to the whole subject of child therapy. Witness, for example, the practical title of Part I: "When, Where, and

How to Get Help," a promise which Bush goes on to amply fulfill. The book is written in a realistic yet reassuring tone. The author reveals a remarkable degree of common sense and a capacity for dealing with subjects in a concise and accurate way.

Friedland, R., and C. Kort (eds). *The Mothers' Book: Shared Experiences*. Boston, Mass.: Houghton-Mifflin, 1981.

This is a superb, well-edited collection of interviews with and essays by sixty-four mothers in which they frankly discuss their feelings about various aspects of motherhood. The range of topics is broad, covering both popular issues—for example, breastfeeding, staying at home, etc.—and unusual topics—such as having triplets, dealing with the Oedipal Triangle, and so forth. The concerns shared also cover a wide range from everyday hassles to political commitments. The views expressed are equally varied and well balanced.

Lapinski, S., and M. D. Hinds. *In a Family Way*. Boston: Little, Brown & Co., 1982.

This book is subtitled "A Husband's and Wife's Diary of Pregnancy, Birth, and the First Year of Parenthood." You might ask what is so special about this sort of book. The answer is that if you are about to have your first child, reading this book will be extraordinarily entertaining. Lapinski and Hinds write beautifully, feel deeply, and have a tremendous capacity for love. Give yourself a treat.

PHYSICAL HEALTH

Spock, B. *Baby and Child Care*. Rev. ed. New York: Pocketbooks, 1976.

Dr. Spock's views on the matter of raising a young child continue to be well worth the consideration of parents. Nevertheless, it is my opinion that Dr. Spock's book is stronger in terms of the child's medical well-being than in terms of the learning process.

The Boston Children's Medical Center, and R. I. Feinbloom. *Child Health Encyclopaedia*. New York: Delacorte Press, 1975.

As an educational psychologist I am not qualified to comment extensively on books on physical health. Nevertheless, I believe it is quite safe for me to recommend this work that comes from one of the leading pediatric centers in the country and has the endorsement of the Consumer's Union.

Metzger, M., and C. Whittaker. *The Childproofing Checklist.* New York: Doubleday, 1988.

Stewart, A. *Childproofing Your Home.* Reading, Mass.: Addison-Wesley Publishing Co., 1984.

Infants and toddlers are vulnerable to accidents. Accidental poisonings and falls peak in the period shortly after the onset of crawling and on through to the second birthday. Infants and toddlers love to explore, and this is very important if they are to learn and be their best during the first years of life. The result is that parents *must* safety-proof their homes. Among the several good books available on the topic, we recommend *The Childproofing Checklist* and *Childproofing Your Home.* Very brief and inexpensive, they take you room-by-room through your home's child-safety needs in clear, concise ways. Definitely worthwhile investments.

NURSERY SCHOOL

Swift, J. W. "Effects of Early Group Experience: The Nursery School and Day Nursery," in *Child Development Research,* M. L. Hoffman and L. W. Hoffman (eds.). New York: Russell Sage Foundation, 1964.

There is a great controversy over the pros and cons of nursery school experience for children from age thirty months to five years. As far as I can see, there is no important educational reason to send an average or above-average child to any nursery school. Many persons will argue that point. For some rare, solid, unbiased information on the topic, read this review chapter by Swift. It is the only one I know of that has attempted to track down the research on the various effects of nursery school education of the young child. Though it is now some two decades old, it is still the most recent and authoritative treatment of the subject.

GIFTEDNESS

Shore, B., F. Gagneau, S. T. Lariveaue, and R. E. Tremblay (eds.). *Face-to-Face with Giftedness.* New York: Trillium Press, 1983.

For those with special interest in the topic of giftedness, this paperback volume should be of special interest. It contains selected presentations from the Fourth World Conference on Gifted and Talented Children, convened in Montreal, Canada, in 1981. There are well over 2000 members of the World Council for Gifted and Talented Children and more than 1000 attend the periodic world conferences. This collection of papers will provide the reader with insight into the diverse approaches to the fascinating topic of giftedness. The authors, from many countries around the world, present the most authoritative and modern research on the topic.

Alvino, J. and the Editors of *The Gifted Child Monthly. A Parents Guide to Raising a Gifted Toddler*. Boston: Little, Brown and Company, 1989.

We have, on several occasions, recommended *The Gifted Child Monthly* newsletter, edited by Mr. Alvino, as a first-rate product. Indeed, when questions about giftedness have surfaced over the years, *The Gifted Child Monthly* and the International Organization on the Gifted and Talented have been our two principal sources of information. They have consistently shown good sense with respect to issues involving this interesting topic. Now Mr. Alvino has put together a large number of reports previously published in the newsletter into a fascinating and extensive book on the subject. This is no mere treatise on how to raise a bright child but a work of considerably more inclusive scope.

I feel reasonably comfortable recommending this book. A principal reason is that, like the book by Zimbardo and Radl on the shy child,[1] there simply is no better book on issues of giftedness. Bear in mind that more than half of the book is oriented toward children over three, but in this case I don't think that should deter anyone from buying it. What the reader should understand is that, like many in the field, it is uneven. Our advice is that you should not believe everything you read. If you find a section of the book that looks interesting, by all means consider it a starting point. Any recommendations, whether they be in respect to bilingual education or emotional nurturance or any of the other important subjects dealt with on this subject should be taken with a large grain of salt and followed up with explorations of second, third, and fourth opinions before implementation is considered.

IMPORTANT RELATED READINGS

Montessori, M. *The Absorbent Mind*. New York: Holt, Rinehart, and Winston, 1967.

---

[1] Philip G. Zimbardo and Shirley L. Radl, *The Shy Child* (New York: McGraw-Hill, 1981).

Although Marie Montessori did not provide the last word on all topics in early education, she did have an interesting and original view of the growth and development of the young child. Indeed, many of her observations, so remarkably to the point, were only discovered by the general research community almost a century later. This well-written book is worth your time.

Ulich, R. *Three Thousand Years of Educational Wisdom.* Cambridge, Mass.: Harvard University Press, 1961.

Robert Ulich has been one of the great thinkers in modern Western education. Here, in this beautiful book, he has collected original historical writings on the subject of education. Though many do not talk specifically to topics in early education, some do: pay particular attention to the writings of Plato, Pestalozzi, Froebel, Comenius, and others who do refer to learning development in the young child. This fine book should be in the library of everyone who reads and thinks at all about the human condition.

Lorenz, K. *King Solomon's Ring.* New York: Thomas Y. Crowell, 1952.

I have always believed firmly that the study of other animal creatures helps us to understand our own condition. This book, by the founder of the science known as ethology, is absolutely delightful. Lorenz will introduce you to the fascinating study of growth and development in the young of other animal species. It would not surprise me at all if, from reading this book, you become interested in pursuing the topic of ethology.

Fraiberg, S. *The Magic Years.* New York: Scribner's, 1959.

Although Dr. Fraiberg first published this book in 1959, it maintains its magic and delight for contemporary readers. It describes the young child from birth to six years of age, dealing largely with psychoanalytic concerns buttressed by Fraiberg's clinical experience. The author's fresh, creative style overcomes most shackles one might associate with the psychoanalytic tradition. The sections dealing with sex identity—on being a boy and not a girl—however, do challenge the contemporary reader to rethink sexual assumptions. This is an excellent book for parents and professionals. It can enlighten and sensitize adults to the very special perspective of the young child.

Index